THE SCOTIABANK STORY

JOSEPH SCHULL
AND
J. DOUGLAS GIBSON

THE SCOTIABANK STORY

A HISTORY OF THE BANK OF NOVA SCOTIA

1832-1982

MACMILLAN OF CANADA
A DIVISION OF
GAGE PUBLISHING LIMITED
TORONTO, CANADA

COPYRIGHT
© 1982 The Bank of Nova Scotia
ALL RIGHTS RESERVED
The use of any part of this publication reproduced, transmitted in any form or by any means, electronic, mechanical, photocopying, recording, or otherwise, or stored in a retrieval system, without the prior consent of the publisher is an infringement of copyright law.

Canadian Cataloguing in Publication Data

Schull, Joseph, 1910-1980.
   The Scotiabank story

Includes index.
ISBN 0-7715-9609-X

1. Bank of Nova Scotia – History.   I. Gibson, J. Douglas (James Douglas), date   II. Title.

HG2708.N68S28   332.1′2′0971   C82-094836-5

The motifs used to mark chapter ends throughout this book are taken from architectural details of The Bank of Nova Scotia's Head Office, Halifax, Nova Scotia, and General Office, Toronto, Ontario. Those at the end of Chapters 2 and 7 were designed by Fred Winkler. All others are by architect John M. Lyle.

Macmillan of Canada
A Division of
Gage Publishing Limited

Reprinted 1983

DESIGNED BY FRANK NEWFELD

PRINTED AND BOUND IN CANADA

THE SCOTIABANK STORY

Table of Contents

FOREWORD BY C. E. Ritchie/vii

PREFACE BY J. Douglas Gibson/viii

List of people interviewed in the course of the book/xii

1. The Struggle for Incorporation, 1831-1832/1
2. A Bank To Be Reckoned With, 1832-1837/18
3. Surmounting Early Challenges, 1837-1875/35
4. Enter the Legendary Thomas Fyshe, 1876-1882/51
5. Further Expansion—West, South, and Northeast, 1882-1897/62
6. The Move to Toronto, 1897-1909/79
7. The Amalgamations, 1910-1923/103
8. Consolidation and Then...The Great Depression, 1924-1939/137
9. The Second World War, 1939-1945/172
10. Filling Out a National Bank, 1945-1960/185
11. More Growth and the Management Revolution, 1960-1965/225
12. A Full-fledged International Bank, 1966-1971/252
13. The Changing Face of Banking, 1971-1981/278
14. Just Around the Corner, Right Around the World, 1971-1981/305
15. A Story of Adaptability and Strength/335

The Bank of Nova Scotia – A History in Charts/351
Statements of Assets and Liabilities of The Bank of Nova Scotia/365
Directors of The Bank of Nova Scotia/400
Executive Officers of The Bank of Nova Scotia/410
INDEX/413

THE SCOTIABANK STORY

Foreword

1982 marks the one hundred and fiftieth anniversary of The Bank of Nova Scotia. It seems fitting that when such milestones are reached, we take the opportunity to review our history as an organization and as a part of the larger history of Nova Scotia, the Maritimes, Canada, and ultimately, the world financial community.

Summing up a century and a half of varied events and personalities is no easy task in any circumstances. In this case the difficulty was compounded because the unfortunate death of Joseph Schull, who had so enthusiastically begun this project, meant that someone else had to pick up the pieces in the middle and complete the history. We were very fortunate that, at our request, a distinguished former Scotiabanker agreed to do just that. J. Douglas Gibson, who had served the Bank for many years in several capacities, including that of Deputy Chairman of the Board, undertook the huge task of recounting the story of the Bank as he knew it and of tracing its developments in the years both prior to and since his own employment here. He was ably assisted in this task by his wife, Elizabeth, also a former Scotiabanker. I am sure there were days when the Gibsons wished they had turned down the job, but I am grateful that they accepted the challenge, and I sincerely hope that, with their work behind them, they will now share our pleasure in a job well done.

Obviously, a history such as this cannot mention all the people who have contributed to the success of Scotiabank, but this book is dedicated to all those who have gone before – to the men of vision and integrity who in the year 1832 founded this Bank in the city of Halifax, Nova Scotia, and to those who throughout the years have guided its destiny, served it faithfully, and nurtured its growth westward to the Pacific, northward to the frontier outposts, and south to the islands of the Caribbean – and to all those who are part of the Bank today as it continues its growth around the world.

C.E. RITCHIE

THE SCOTIABANK STORY

Preface

As the Chairman has indicated in his Foreword, the writing of this book encountered unusual difficulties. The original professional author, the well-known Joseph Schull, succumbed to a fatal illness in May 1980, at which time the book was less than half finished.

It was not until October 1980 that I undertook to complete the project at the Chairman's suggestion. Though not a professional author, I had been editor of The Bank of Nova Scotia *Monthly Review* for some years before the Second World War, and had done a good deal of writing during my career as an economist and as a senior officer of the Bank, which I left in 1965 to take up a business and consulting career. I had the advantage of knowing a good deal about The Bank of Nova Scotia and about banking procedures and practices as they were fifteen years ago. I had also known many Scotiabankers of the last fifty years. But I was to find that I needed a fresh education to understand and describe the remarkable changes in banking which had occurred in the last fifteen years.

In carrying forward the story which had been begun by Joseph Schull, I could adopt much the same method of approach. However, since I have a different background and a different style, a certain alteration in the tone of the book was unavoidable. Thus, a gradual shift from Schull's writing style to that of myself becomes evident in Chapters Eight and Nine.

The approach used by both Schull and myself is the recounting of the events and developments in the Bank's history through the actions and views of the leading participants in the environment of the time. And when it comes to the last thirty-five years, the story is told to a substantial degree in the words of a variety of Scotiabankers, not all of them senior. Many of these comments were made in the course of taped interviews and hence no source for them is given in the text.

Up to the Second World War and perhaps as far as 1960, the book may properly be described as "history." The more recent years are not presented in as much depth as might be desired. The problem is that there is not enough background information to assess the quality of the people concerned and their decisions without being influenced by the fact that many of these people are still working in the Bank, or were employed in the Bank so recently that their "aura" is still evident. Thus, as the present is approached, the book of necessity becomes more a chronicle of the events and the thinking of the times and less an adequate assessment of people and decisions.

My banking re-education was conducted by a distinguished group of Scotiabankers: C. E. Ritchie (Chairman), J. A. G. Bell (Deputy Chairman), W. S. McDonald and P. C. Godsoe (the Vice-Chairmen), R. L. Brooks (General Manager, Finance and Administration), G. E. Hare (General Manager, Operations), F. L. Rogers (Economic Adviser), and Geoffrey Holt (Economist, London, England). I express my thanks to all of them for their help and patience and, at the same time, absolve them of blame for any evidence that my old-fashioned thinking may have crept into the book here and there.

The entire manuscript was reviewed by Ritchie, Bell, McDonald, and Rogers, and, in addition, by Mrs. Candace Craddock (Executive Assistant to the Chairman), Perrin Lewis (Assistant Economic Adviser), Mrs. Drue R. Batten (Economist) and R. M. MacIntosh (formerly Executive Vice-President of the Bank and now President of the Canadian Bankers' Association). As well, W. H. Milne (the Secretary of the Bank) and Brooks read and commented on the later chapters. Again, I thank them for their time, interest, and perceptive comments.

My greatest help came from my wife, Elizabeth, who was an economist in the Bank in the early 1950s. She was my research assistant, co-ordinating the work of the various Departments of the Bank which produced the required factual material and unearthing some of the facts herself. Also, she acted as general editor and, in particular, was responsible for incorporating a sense of continuity to the style of the book as a whole, which, as has been noted, was written by two very different authors.

It is simply not practical to thank all the others who helped to see this book through to its publication. In all, fifty-six members of the present staff, one of whom has since died, twenty-five pensioners, three of whom have also died, and twelve other people were interviewed by Schull and myself. In addition, ten pensioners responded by letter to my questions. Their names are all listed in the following pages.

Of the people I interviewed, a few should be singled out for special mention: Ritchie, who gave me many good ideas and who was frank and interesting about the Bank's past and future; Bell, who expressed his views, particularly about credit, clearly and succinctly; McDonald, to whom I owe much, but whom I do not hold responsible for my crash course on international banking; Rogers, for his patient editing of some of my oversimplifications of economic phenomena; R. E. Peel, for his interesting reflections about F. W. Nicks and H. L. Enman; Brooks, for helping to fill in the great gaps in my background and knowledge of banking organization during the past fifteen years; the late Alex Shaw, for his constructive views on the supervision of bank credit, on education, and on organization; and J. W. Chisholm, for the substantial time he devoted to bringing me up to date on credit organization and development.

W. P. Meinig and J. F. Crean were more than helpful on the complicated subject of computers. In addition, Meinig was illuminating about his job as head of one of the three Canadian Divisions, as were also his colleagues, C. F. Gill and R. J. Kavanagh. On the subject of the regions I received much assistance and many useful impressions from R. L. Mason and E. D. MacNevin. André Bisson has a special story to tell, which he does with great care and earnestness, while R. G. Taylor with his "seventeen banks and fourteen currencies" has a unique perspective on his area of responsibility. Others who were helpful on the International side were Godsoe in Toronto, C. A. Barnes and R. Marsman in London, and E. D. Hunter in New York. In addition, good background material and some interesting anecdotes were gleaned from the enthusiastic H. G. McGinn in Toronto. A. B. McKie, with his special competency in the labyrinthine world of taxation, and Milne, with his understanding and friendly interest in a multitude of Scotiabankers, also provided much general background information. J. F. O'Donnell explained a variety of new developments, like Scotia Business Plan and video cash-management. Last, but of great significance for the future, I heard in clear and well-considered terms about women in banks from Louise Cannon and Candace Craddock.

Schull obtained interesting interviews from such pensioners as Harry Randall and the late T. A. Boyles, while I received a great deal of help from W. S. Bond and F. J. Finlay, both of whom had a long and varied experience in the Bank and who were able to fill in a number of important gaps. I also called on G. J. Touchie, H. H. Bartlett, and D. L. Lindsay in Florida, and they all took the time to provide some pertinent comments. G. K. MacDonell recalled the development of methods and systems in a comprehensive memorandum; H. M. Kinsman shared his knowledge of the beginnings of Scotia Plan; and R. M. Taylor wrote about staff training. In addition, another group of pensioners wrote down their reflections on the development of the regional offices, particularly in connection with profit planning and deposit development; they included C. I. Archibald, H. W. Caldwell, J. M. Hayman, A. McPhedran, and D. A. Y. Merrick. And A. H. Crockett, who has just retired, added life to the record with his enthusiastic recollections of people over the whole period since the Second World War.

Some of the Bank's Directors, past and present, were interviewed, including W. C. Harris, Donald McInnes, and the Honourable John B. Aird, the last-named having some very interesting reflections from the perspective of his new position as Lieutenant-Governor of Ontario. Malcolm Richardson and Charles Burns talked about their respective fathers in a human and engaging way, and Edward Crawford and his

Preface

mother, the late Mrs. E. S. Crawford, described life in Cuba long before the revolution.

Many Departments of the Bank were, of course, called on for assistance in the making of this book, but particular mention should be made of the contributions by Mrs. Jane E. Nokes (Archivist) and the staff of the Archives, Mrs. Beverley J. Kent (Librarian) and the staff of the Library, L. J. Chudy and Ms. Judith Humphrey (Director and Senior Writer, respectively, Public and Corporate Affairs), and R. R. Holmes (General Manager, Investments). Also, Ms. Margaret Fisher (Administrator) and D. F. Woodman (Analyst), both of the Economics Department, provided the basic statistical material in the text and prepared the charts.

My wife and I would like to acknowledge all the help we received from Mrs. Betty Hearn, pensioner and founder of the Bank's Library and Archives. Both directly, through her comments on parts of the manuscript, and indirectly, through her earlier writing on the Bank's history (in particular, two *Monthly Review*s which have been used freely), she made an important contribution to this book. We are also indebted to Dr. Phyllis Blakeley, Provincial Archivist of Nova Scotia, for her timely and authoritative assistance in verifying historical references in the earlier chapters. It should be added that we have also drawn freely on both the first history of the Bank, which appeared in 1900, and the second history, which was published on the occasion of the Bank's centenary in 1932 and was written by the late Kenneth R. Wilson. Finally, we thank Candace Craddock, who was most helpful in carrying out many tasks (including the selection of the illustrations) and coping with the day-to-day problems of producing this history.

J. DOUGLAS GIBSON
Toronto, March 9, 1982

List of Persons
Who Were Interviewed by the Authors
or Who Answered Questions

Hon. John B. Aird, *Lieutenant-Governor of Ontario, former Director,* BNS; *Toronto*

C. I. Archibald, BNS, *(retired), former regional head (most recently of Quebec Region); Bridgenorth, Ont.*

C. A. Barnes, BNS, *Assistant General Manager, Treasury & Special Loans Dept.; London, England*

H. H. Bartlett, BNS, *(retired), former Manager; Charlottetown*

A.J. Bates, BNS, *Administrator, Scotiabank Service Recognition Program; Toronto*

J. A. Gordon Bell, BNS, *Deputy Chairman, President and Chief Operating Officer; Toronto*

André Bisson, BNS, *Vice-President & General Manager, Quebec Region; Montreal*

Dr. Phyllis R. Blakeley, *Provincial Archivist of Nova Scotia; Halifax*

W. S. Bond, BNS, *(retired), former head of Administration; Toronto*

(Mrs.) Louise M. Boyd, BNS, *Assistant Secretary of the Bank; Toronto*

T. A. Boyles, BNS, *(deceased), former Chairman of the Board; Toronto*

R. N. Brandman, BNS, *Assistant General Manager, Treasury & Special Loans Dept.; London, England*

F. D. I. Bray, BNS, *(retired), former Secretary of the Pension Fund; Toronto*

R. L. Brooks, BNS, *General Manager, Finance & Administration; Toronto*

R. M. Brown, BNS, *General Manager, Canadian Commercial Banking; Toronto*

J. S. Burchell, BNS, *(retired), former Secretary of the Bank; Stroud, Ont.*

Charles F. W. Burns *(son of the late H. D. Burns); Toronto*

H. W. Caldwell, BNS, *(retired), former regional head (most recently of New Brunswick & Prince Edward Island Region); Surrey, B.C.*

(Ms.) L. Louise Cannon, BNS, *General Manager, Canadian Commercial Banking; Toronto*

Floyd S. Chalmers, *Honorary Chairman, Maclean Hunter Ltd. (served briefly in the Bank in his youth); Toronto*

G. E. Chamberlain, BNS, *Director, Agricultural Services; Toronto*

J. W. Chisholm, BNS, *Assistant General Manager, Loan Administration; Toronto*

R. Cooke, BNS, *Vice-President & General Manager, Latin American Region; Toronto*

List of People Interviewed

D. F. Cooper, BNS, *Manager, International Treasury; Toronto*

(Mrs.) Candace U. Craddock, BNS, *Executive Assistant to the Chairman; Toronto*

Edward H. Crawford *and the late* Mrs. E. S. Crawford
(family of the late E. S. Crawford); Toronto

J. F. Crean, BNS, *Vice-President & General Manager,
Toronto Suburban Region; Toronto*

Arthur H. Crockett, BNS, *(retired), former President
and Deputy Chairman; Toronto*

P. S. Dodd, BNS, *General Manager, International Loan Administration;
Toronto*

P. A. Enman, BNS, *(retired), former Assistant General Manager, Commercial Credit;
Toronto*

H. L. Fawcett, BNS, *Assistant General Manager,
International Loan Administration; Toronto*

F. J. Finlay, BNS, *(retired), former Secretary of the Bank; Ottawa*

Harry Freestone, BNS, *(retired), former Manager, Berkeley Square, London,
England; Willowdale, Ont.*

C. S. Frost, BNS, *(retired), Honorary Director & former President;
Toronto*

R. G. Gage, BNS, *General Manager, Canadian Commercial Banking; Toronto*

J. Douglas Gibson, BNS, *(retired), former Deputy Chairman; Toronto*

A. C. Giles, BNS, *Supervisor, Staff Training & Development; Toronto*

C. F. Gill, BNS, *Senior Vice-President & General Manager,
Eastern Canada Division; Toronto*

F. M. Goddard, BNS, *General Manager, International Corporate Credit;
Toronto*

Peter C. Godsoe, BNS, *Vice-Chairman; Toronto*

G. E. Hare, BNS, *General Manager, Operations; Toronto*

W. C. Harris, *Honorary Director*, BNS; *Toronto*

J. M. Hayman, BNS, *(retired), former regional head
(of New Brunswick & Prince Edward Island Region); Rothesay, N.B.*

T. A. Healy, BNS, *General Manager, Treasury Division; Toronto*

(Mrs.) Betty A. M. Hearn, BNS, *(retired), economic historian and former
Librarian & Archivist; Hampton, N.S.*

K. Helstern, BNS, *(retired), former Agent; New York*

George C. Hitchman, BNS, *(retired), former Deputy Chairman; Toronto*

R. R. Holmes, BNS, *General Manager, Investments; Toronto*

Geoffrey Holt, BNS, *Economist; London, England*

(Mrs.) Ruth M. Holt *(granddaughter of the late S. J. Moore); Toronto*

Basil Howard, BNS, *(retired), formerly in charge of Securities Dept.;
Montreal*

E. D. Hunter, BNS, *Assistant General Manager & Senior Agent; New York*

F. W. Irvine, BNS, *(retired), former Assistant Manager (in Cuba); Don Mills, Ont.*

J. D. Johnston, BNS, *(retired), former Assistant Supervisor, Personnel; Toronto*

R. J. Kavanagh, BNS, *Senior Vice-President & General Manager, Western Canada Division; Toronto*

E. E. Keith, BNS, *Assistant General Manager & Chief Trader, Gold, Treasury Division; Toronto*

H. M. Kinsman, BNS, *(retired), former Supervisor, Consumer Credit; Toronto*

W. B. Lawson, BNS, *General Manager, Consumer Credit; Toronto*

Perrin Lewis, BNS, *Assistant Economic Advisor; Toronto*

D. L. Lindsay, BNS, *(retired), former regional head (most recently of Pacific Region); Willowdale, Ont.*

M. N. Logan, BNS, *General Manager, Personal Banking; Toronto*

W. J. Lomax, BNS, *General Manager, Personnel Policy & Planning; Toronto*

G. K. MacDonell, BNS, *(retired), former head of Methods; Thunder Bay, Ont.*

D. R. MacFarlane, BNS, *Chief Inspector; Toronto*

I. M. MacGregor, BNS, *General Manager, Canadian Commercial Banking; Toronto*

R. M. MacIntosh, *President, Canadian Bankers' Association, former Executive Vice-President,* BNS; *Toronto*

A. C. MacLellan, BNS, *Assistant General Manager, Mortgages; Toronto*

E. D. MacNevin, BNS, *Vice-President & General Manager, Toronto Central Region; Toronto*

R. Marsman, BNS, *(retired), former regional head (of United Kingdom, Europe, Middle East & Africa Region); London, England*

R. L. Mason, BNS, *Vice-President & General Manager, British Columbia & Yukon Region; Vancouver*

W. Scott McDonald, BNS, *Vice-Chairman; Toronto*

H. G. McGinn, BNS, *Supervisor, North American International Region; Toronto*

Donald McInnes, *Honorary Director,* BNS; *Halifax*

A. B. McKie, BNS, *Director, Taxation; Toronto*

A. McPhedran, BNS, *(retired), former regional head (of Alberta Region); Calgary*

W. P. Meinig, BNS, *Senior Vice-President & General Manager, Ontario Division; Toronto*

W. J. Menear, BNS, *Assistant General Manager & Manager, Toronto Branch; Toronto*

List of People Interviewed

D. A. Y. Merrick, BNS, *(retired), former regional head (most recently of British Columbia Region); North Vancouver, B.C.*

W. H. Milne, BNS, *Secretary of the Bank; Toronto*

J. K. Mitchell, BNS, *Comptroller and Chief Accountant; Toronto*

(Miss) Betty Nicks *(sister of the late F. W. Nicks); Winnipeg*

J. F. O'Donnell, BNS, *General Manager, Commercial Banking Services; Toronto*

J. A. M. Overholt, BNS, *Special Representative; London, England*

R. E. Parrish, BNS, *(retired); London, England*

R. E. Peel, BNS, *General Manager, Executive Administration; Toronto*

W. P. Penney, BNS, *Vice-President & General Manager, Canadian Commercial Banking; Toronto*

Harry Randall, BNS, *(retired), former head of International Department; Toronto*

E. Ranft, BNS, *Vice-President & General Manager, Manitoba & Northwestern Ontario Region; Winnipeg*

A. R. Rendell, BNS, *(retired), formerly in Chief Accountant's Dept.; Toronto*

Malcolm Richardson *(son of the late H. A. Richardson); Toronto*

Cedric E. Ritchie, BNS, *Chairman of the Board & Chief Executive Officer; Toronto*

F. L. Rogers, BNS, *Economic Advisor; Toronto*

C. R. Ross, BNS, *(retired), formerly in General Office; Toronto*

Donald Ross, *(deceased, son of the late W. D. Ross): Toronto*

L. A. Shaw, BNS, *(deceased), former Senior Vice-President, Canadian Commercial Banking; Toronto*

J. A. Sommerville, BNS, *General Manager, Real Estate; Toronto*

(Mrs.) J. Stewart *(daughter of the late Sir William Stavert); Toronto*

C. E. Tanner, BNS, *(deceased), former Manager (in Cuba); Toronto*

A. E. Taylor, BNS, *General Manager, Personnel, Canada; Toronto*

R. G. Taylor, BNS, *Vice-President & General Manager, Caribbean Region; Toronto*

R. M. Taylor, BNS, *(retired), former Executive Assistant to the Chairman; Amherst, N.S.*

G. J. Touchie, BNS, *(retired), former Chief General Manager; Toronto*

H. R. Wong, BNS, *Assistant General Manager & Chief Trader, Foreign Exchange, Treasury Division; Toronto*

L. R. Woolsey, BNS, *General Manager, Marketing; Toronto*

J. A. Young, BNS, *(deceased), former head of Staff Department; Toronto*

H. R. Younker, BNS, *General Manager, Executive Administration; Toronto*

View of Halifax from Dartmouth Cove, 1832.
Lithograph by L. Haghe.

1

The Struggle for Incorporation 1831–1832

HALIFAX IN THE 1830s

At the beginning of the 1830s, Halifax, the capital of the British Colony of Nova Scotia, was an eighty-year-old seaport and naval base that was adjusting itself to peace. It had been founded by Governor Edward Cornwallis in 1749 as a replacement for Louisbourg, the fortress lost to the French the year before. The Citadel of Halifax looked out over narrow streets and long lines of wharves to the fine harbour and to the magnificent anchorage of Bedford Basin. With its fifteen thousand civilians and two thousand soldiers, it had been during successive wars a strategic centre for imperial fleets, a garrison for imperial troops, and a home of profitable enterprise for local privateers. Money for ships and supplies and for sailors' and soldiers' pay had poured into the town and had circulated through the shops and taverns. Often the merchants who owned the shops, or their sons and younger friends, had sailed out from the port as privateers under royal letters of marque. Licensed by the Governor to take prizes and seize booty, they had competed with the Royal Navy in the disruption of enemy commerce and had succeeded in bringing home more loot than even the navy.

Halifax had grown accustomed to the sight of captured vessels entering the harbour and of lawfully captured merchandise being offered for sale on the wharves. Even better remembered than the casks of brandy and the bales of silks and spices were the iron-strapped boxes of gold and silver "specie": doubloons, quarter-doubloons, pieces-of-eight, reals, pistareens, dollars, dinars, and sovereigns.

With the arrival of peace in 1815, this feverish activity died down and the town experienced a slump which lasted for about a decade. Then the wealth reposing in strong-rooms began to find new outlets. In the intervals between the various wars, the colonists had turned to lumbering, fishing, and shipbuilding, and above all to the development of seaborne trade. The earliest among them were settlers who had come with Cornwallis, while New Englanders had joined the British to build a base for their fortunes during the Seven Years War of 1756–63. Others had come as Loyalists after the American Revolution, and still others, mainly of Scottish and Irish origin, had arrived during the Napoleonic Wars and the War of 1812.

Almost all of the Haligonians were British, almost all Protestant, and they regarded Great Britain, and in particular London, as their spiritual and commercial home. They also had close trade connections with Boston and New York, but very few ties with the Canadas at their back. Within the triangular framework of British mercantile policy, they and their opposite numbers in the "sugar islands" of the Caribbean were suppliers of raw materials and distributors of British manufactured goods. They were also pivotal to the exchange of goods in nearer waters. Their schooners sailed up to Newfoundland and down the New England coast. They shipped their timber, barrel staves, white pine masts, and fish east to Europe and south to the West Indies. Their brigs returned home across the Atlantic with manufactured goods and up from the Caribbean with molasses, sugar, rum, and tobacco.

INCREASED ACTIVITY IN THE PROVINCE

Indeed, the 1820s saw a general quickening of activity throughout the province of Nova Scotia, with Halifax serving as the hub. Grain, apples, meat, potatoes, hides, and livestock were shipped from the old Acadian farmlands of the rich Annapolis Valley. Around the bays and inlets of the shoreline, part-time farmers and fishermen became lumbermen and builders and owners of ships. A merchant named Abraham Cunard, and his promising son Samuel, had a whaling ship in the Arctic and another in the South Pacific. In 1826, the Halifax brig *Trusty* arrived home with her cargo from Calcutta and Madras after a trip which lasted a year. Meanwhile, along the older shipping routes to London, Boston, New York, and the islands of the Caribbean, there was an expanding flow of goods financed by an increasingly complex interchange of specie and bills of exchange.

THE DEVELOPMENT OF HALIFAX

The connections with Boston and New York and the influence and affluence of London all contributed to the development of Halifax. Green lawns surrounded a stately Government House and society entertained in fine houses. Schools flourished, and seats of higher learning were established: Dalhousie College at Halifax itself and King's College at Windsor, 25 miles away. There were High Anglicans and Low Anglicans holding services under competing steeples; and Presbyterians, Methodists, Baptists, Catholics, and Congregationalists all worshipped in their own churches. Yet the old seaport still had one hundred and eighty taverns for fifteen thousand people and rum was

Dalhousie College, Halifax, circa 1887.

By 1832 the erection of government buildings, churches, and schools (including Dalhousie) had begun to change the character of Halifax from that of a rough seaport.

cheaper than milk. Rum kegs stood open in grocery stores with dippers hanging from their rims for the convenience of customers.

Opposite Halifax was Dartmouth, a heavily forested suburb, with the main link across the harbour being a "team boat." This strange contraption consisted of two hulls joined by a platform on which eight or nine horses circled an enormous windlass that turned a paddle wheel. On good days, with the help of a large square sail, the crossing of nearly one mile took only twenty minutes. From the towns of New Brunswick, as well as of Nova Scotia – Saint John, Fredericton, Amherst, Truro, Yarmouth, Annapolis; Windsor – mail came by stage-coach when the condition of the roads permitted, usually once a week.

Because communication between Halifax and Boston and New York was by water, Boston and New York were actually easier to reach than many of the towns of New Brunswick and Nova Scotia. And the arrival of mail from England was a great event each month. It came in Royal Navy brigs, the voyages usually taking from forty to fifty days, depending on the weather. The mail sacks were tossed to the wharf, then shouldered by sailors who marched briskly up to the post office with an officer keeping pace. There, the expectant recipients queued while the postmaster sorted the letters and passed them out through the wicket. They were usually business or official letters or mail for the well-to-do, since the postage rates between England and Nova Scotia were prohibitive for the ordinary citizen.

Though still a remote colonial capital and port in 1832, Halifax was third in size in British North America, after Quebec and Montreal, and it was enlarging its trade and renewing itself as a city. "At no time since its first settlement," said the *Acadian Recorder* on July 6, 1831, "did the province present an aspect of so much promise...every wharf from the Lumber yard to the Dockyard, has, within two or three years, been repaired, extended, or otherwise improved."[1] There were new stores and warehouses, many in brick or stone, property values were rising, and a hundred new houses were to be built in the coming year.

However, the town still had no sewers, much of it remained filthy, and it was plagued by epidemics. The "bloody flux," the "putrid fever," and the "putrid sore throat" were as much feared as the ever-present consumption. The waves of destitute immigrants from British slums brought with them the threat of cholera. In 1834, when a shipload of Chelsea pensioners arrived in Halifax harbour with a request for their landing, the Governor reacted sharply. He promptly sent them back, thus outraging British authority but diverting such future favours to Quebec and Montreal.

THE GOVERNMENT OF NOVA SCOTIA

The Governor, together with his appointed "Council of Twelve," in effect ruled the province of Nova Scotia. Below the Council was an elected House of Assembly, which had limited jurisdiction and which held its meetings in the renowned Province House, "the most splendid edifice in North America."[2] An appointed body of magistrates were responsible for the administration of the town of Halifax. There was no doubt, however, about where the centre of economic power lay. Money from past wars, from lumbering, fishing, farming, and from all the avenues of trade, had accumulated in the hands of the town's merchants and businessmen. It had created opportunities, opened larger vistas, and reached out onto the sea. It had sent sons to be educated in England and brought them back as gentlemen with a taste for English ways. It had built schools and churches and fine houses and estates.

Now there were larger stores and offices, more clerks and counting houses, and more substantial buildings than there had been in earlier days. Coffee houses had sprung up, and, like their counterparts in Georgian England, served as merchants' rendezvous. There was a newspaper reading room on Hollis Street which was something of a colonial Lloyd's. Commercial colleagues gathered here to read the latest papers from London, Boston, and New York and to discuss the day's shipping reports. On the waterfront was the long stone warehouse built by Enos Collins, the greatest of the merchant princes and a former privateer. "You will observe, sir," Collins was heard to say in his later years, "there were many things happened we don't care to talk about."[3]

THE DEFECTIVE STATE OF THE CURRENCY

There was, however, one pressing matter to be talked about in a town whose trade was expanding – the defective state of the currency. Specie was the ultimate means of settlement of accounts, but the mere mechanics of storage and transfer were a cumbersome business. It had to be kept in a chest in a strong-room where a clerk slept at night, and, needless to say, shipping it was fraught with danger. Furthermore, the nature of the specie itself presented a problem. It consisted of a bewildering array of gold and silver coins from different countries, and the value of each individual coin could be determined only by weight, such had been the extent of clipping and "sweating." Finally, and most important, there was the chronic scarcity of cash typical of a young and expanding colony. Heavy import needs tended to drain off specie as soon as it was earned.

Bills of exchange, or drafts, were used to some extent by businessmen as a means of payment in place of specie, but their acceptance was limited because of the variation in the credit-worthiness of the issuers. And treasury notes of the province of Nova Scotia did circulate as money, but even these were not universally acceptable. For its further development, trade required a flow of convenient money, and also a source of commercial credit – both entirely reliable.

A PRIVATE BANK IS FOUNDED

In 1825, five years after the founding of the first bank in the Atlantic area – the Bank of New Brunswick in Saint John – a bank was established in Halifax, but it was a *private* corporation, the Halifax Banking Company. Its founders were eight citizens of wealth and standing; Enos Collins was the prime mover and Hezekiah Cogswell, the province's most prominent lawyer, was the president. Housed in part of Collins's warehouse, it was known as "Collins's Bank" or "Cogswell's Bank." Cogswell and Collins were described by a contemporary in the following unflattering terms: they "are not men the less desirous of making money because they happen to be very rich – they are both as fond of a guinea as Jacob."[4] And the same correspondent's brother referred to Cogswell as "a man who looks at a penny on both sides & more than once before he spends it," whose chief pleasure "is to see the sum total of his credit side growing daily larger as it does," and who is "worth now at least £60,000 – and still collects his fifteen penny weekly rent from his half starved tenants in the Town."[5]

THE EFFORTS TO ESTABLISH A PUBLIC BANK

The founders of the Halifax Banking Company had settled for less than their original plan: that of establishing a *public* bank. In fact, their project was the fourth such venture put forward since 1801. Each proposal, including that of the Collins-Cogswell group, had been conditional on the granting of a monopoly and each had failed to gain the necessary legislative approval for that very reason. The members of the House of Assembly, particularly those from the rural areas, could not stomach the thought of a single commercial group in Halifax controlling money and credit for the entire province.

Yet, not only the Halifax merchants but also the inhabitants of the colony generally were irritated by the shortcomings of specie and the makeshifts that passed as paper money. For instance, one citizen had the following experience in the 1820s. Armed with a twenty-shilling provincial note, he set off to buy vegetables at a local market but several suspicious farmers refused to accept the note. Eventually, he found a taker and procured the carrots, turnips, squash, and two cabbages which he required. But in order to accomplish his mission, he had to change his twenty-shilling note into "eight paper notes, one silver piece and 84 coppers – in all 93 separate things before I could get vegetables for my family's dinner."[6]

THE GOAL: A JOINT-STOCK CORPORATION

The goal of all the various groups that had petitioned the House of Assembly over the years for permission to establish a public bank had been a joint-stock corporation similar to those already in operation in

Scotland and, on this continent, in several places in the United States. Owned by shareholders and authorized by government, it would be a body under the law, responsible for its obligations but master of its own resources. It would be authorized to accept deposits, to trade in specie, to discount commercial paper, and to make loans against stipulated classes of security. Above all, as its most essential service and its most important source of profit, it would issue its own notes. By issuing them to borrowers who would pay interest on their loans or discounts, the bank would have a free loan itself in the amount of its total outstanding notes.

Such an institution had already been established in Saint John, New Brunswick, in 1820 in the form of the Bank of New Brunswick. This bank was a public corporation; it was required to report on its activities annually to the government, and its obligations were the liability of its shareholders. Because fluctuations in land values had brought home the fact that mortgage loans were unduly risky, such lending was forbidden – a provision which was to become a constant feature of banking legislation in British North America. Subscribers for shares of stock in the bank were required to pay up their subscriptions within one year and a half, and the new bank's note issue was limited to twice the paid-up capital. In 1824, the Bank of New Brunswick was followed by the little Charlotte County Bank, with its home in nearby St. Andrews.

Nova Scotia Penny Token, 1832

THE PRIVATE BANK: FINANCIAL SUCCESS AND POLITICAL POWER

In March 1825, although banks had by now been established not only in the neighbouring province of New Brunswick but also in the Canadas, the Nova Scotia House of Assembly rejected the Collins-Cogswell project because the sponsors had wanted a ten-year monopoly. However, Enos Collins and Hezekiah Cogswell and their six associates being determined men of means simply took off on another tack, and formed a private partnership: the Halifax Banking Company, which opened its doors for business on September 3, 1825.

The eight partners who had subscribed the £50,000 capital for the new bank were jointly and severally responsible for its obligations and they divided its profits. They accepted deposits, made loans, discounted merchants' notes and bills of exchange, and bought and sold specie. In addition, they issued their own bank notes, which were backed by their own credit and were readily accepted by most Halifax merchants because of the partners' highly regarded business standing. Trade in the colony picked up in response to the flow of this new money, and the earnings of the Halifax Banking Company were evidently very satisfactory, although they were not divulged.

The financial success of this private bank was apparent to the Halifax business community. However, the political clout of the owners of the bank rankled; five of the eight partners were members of the twelve-man Governor's Council. This concentration of authority, together with other grievances, drew the criticism of the youthful Joseph Howe, who was becoming prominent in Halifax as publisher of *The Novascotian*. In the House of Assembly, restless under the Council, a reform movement was simmering and new ideas were being mooted, particularly that of "Responsible Government." There would be debate for years on that concept, but there was another subject of immediate concern: the conviction that the Halifax Banking Company had grown too big for its boots.

It was widely felt that the private bank controlled credit not only for its own benefit but also for that of its friends. Specie flowed into the bank's vaults at the bank's price. But it was a rare man who received gold at the wicket when he presented the bank's notes for redemption. The notes were "payable in gold, or silver, or Province paper" and noteholders often construed this to mean that they were entitled to receive whatever they wished. However, they usually found instead that they had to be satisfied with whatever the bank chose to give them. The wand of the eight partners, in the words of Joseph Howe, was creating "one currency for the rich and another for the poor."[7]

A RIVAL GROUP IS FORMED

The men most galled by the power of the Halifax Banking Company were a rival group of prominent citizens outside the charmed circle of partners of the private bank and the Council of Twelve. James Boyle Uniacke, William Blowers Bliss, and Alexander Stewart were formidable figures in the House of Assembly. The Uniackes had come from Ireland by way of the United States and had been lawyers and judges and important in provincial politics for many years. J.B. Uniacke would, in 1848, preside with Joseph Howe over the first responsible government in British North America. W.B. Bliss, aged thirty-six, was the second son of the first Chief Justice of New Brunswick. A suave, affable lawyer, he had been educated in England and would in the course of the next two years leave politics and be appointed to the Nova Scotia Supreme Court. His elder brother, Lewis, was a well-established merchant in Halifax, with extensive connections in both New Brunswick and Nova Scotia, and his younger brother, Henry, was a lawyer living in London, where he acted as commercial agent for New Brunswick and Nova Scotia. Alexander Stewart was also a lawyer; he had established a reputation for himself as an excellent debater and a leading reformer.

Two additional members of the group were James W. Johnston and his brother-in-law, Mather Byles Almon. Johnston, a prominent Tory, would in the future become head of his party, then premier of the province, and finally, lieutenant-governor. Almon was thirty-five years old, a man of Puritan stock who had joined the Church of England. Although in his later years he did become a member of the reconstructed Upper House, business rather than politics was Almon's major

The Struggle for Incorporation, 1831-1832 9

The Hon. William Lawson –
The First President of
The Bank of Nova Scotia,
1832-1837

interest; he was engaged in wholesale trade and in shipping and forwarding, and dealt with agents in New York and London. He had long been involved with coal and this interest had intensified five years earlier when he had become the Halifax agent for the London-based General Mining Association. This company had obtained from the Duke of York (in exchange for paying his debts) a sixty-year lease on all unworked coal mines in the province of Nova Scotia. Almon's widespread enterprises depended on an adequate flow of money and credit, and he resented the power of the Halifax Banking Company. And so did many others: merchants and traders, friends and rivals.

William Lawson, with his Lawson's wharf, his Lawson sugar refinery, and his seat in the House of Assembly, which he had held for twenty-five years, was an obvious link between the businessmen and the politicians who were now drawing together. He was a man of sixty, an outspoken reformer, and well-known as a man of action. His grandfather had arrived in Halifax from New England a year after Cornwallis. His father, John Lawson, had been associated with Cogswell in the cod fishery, and with Collins in the disposal of privateers' cargoes; he had also made the Lawson house-flag familiar in the West Indies. In the early 1820s William had taken over the family business along with his brother, Robert.

By the autumn of 1831, as the Halifax Banking Company closed its books on its sixth successful year, William Lawson was taking matters in hand. He was to be seen talking to the elderly Andrew Belcher, son of the first Chief Justice of Nova Scotia, who now lived in London but who still came to Halifax on business from time to time. Observers attached some significance to these conversations because Andrew Belcher had planned to be a ninth partner in the Halifax Banking Company but had withdrawn his subscription before the bank was formed. The law office of Alexander Murison, a vocal critic of the bank, was often a place of meeting between Lawson's friends in the legislature and his friends in business. Something was in the wind.

"A PUBLIC BANK AT HALIFAX IS GREATLY DESIRED"

On December 31, 1831, with William Lawson presiding in the chair and Joseph Howe, the young journalist, sitting in the audience and scribbling notes on his hat, "a very numerous, respectable and highly influential meeting" was held at the Merchants Exchange Coffee House "to take into consideration the propriety of establishing a Public Bank."[8] And on January 31, 1832, one hundred and eighty-four citizens (including Howe, who was to become a customer of the new institution) signed a petition to the House of Assembly arguing that "the establishment of a Public Bank at Halifax is greatly and generally desired."[9] The petitioners affirmed that "the circulating medium of business will be thereby increased, – the industrious and enterprizing supplied on the fairest terms with the necessary means of profitable employment, and the labor, industry and resources of the Country encouraged and brought forward into more beneficial operation...."[10] And they could not resist issuing a challenge to the Halifax Banking Company:

> Your Honourable House will not fail to observe how much its [the Halifax Banking Company's] advantages will be extended by the establishment of one on the more enlarged and liberal principle of opening it to general subscription and allowing the public at large to partake in its interests and share in its emoluments.[11]

SUBSCRIPTION LIST OPENED FOR THE BANK OF NOVA SCOTIA

The next day, a subscription list was opened at Alexander Murison's counting house, and Mather B. Almon, Lewis Bliss, James W. Johnston, John Brown (a merchant), and Murison himself were appointed provisional treasurers. William Lawson, with his reputation as a man of action, was understandably the first person to sign the list, subscribing £1,000; "it being proposed," the preamble read:

> to establish a public Bank in the Town of Halifax with a capital at its

The Struggle for Incorporation, 1831–1832   11

Sketch of the Merchants Exchange Coffee House, Halifax, 1832.

This gathering place for Halifax businessmen
was the scene of early discussions about
the need for a "public bank" in Nova Scotia.

commencement of £100,000* to be divided into 2,000 shares of £50 each, and to apply to the Legislature at its present session for an act to incorporate the subscribers thereto by the name of "The President, Directors and Company of the Bank of Nova Scotia."[12]

By the end of the first day, over £34,000 had been subscribed. And on Monday, February 6, when Lawson read in the House of Assembly the petition that would precede the introduction of a bill of incorporation, he had behind him strong popular support and also a subscription list which now totalled £43,000 and which included the signatures of prominent people, not only from Halifax but also from Saint John, Amherst, Annapolis, Windsor, Liverpool, and Antigonish, together with those of Henry Bliss in London and Rupert Cochran in New York (the latter two for £1,000 each).

Cochran was Almon's broker in New York; a former Haligonian who had been helped by Almon to establish himself, he had been pessimistic about the new Bank's prospects. "I pay particular attention to what you say respecting the establishment of a public Bank at Halifax which I have no doubt will prove a useful and profitable establishment from the names I see connected with its formation," he had written to Almon in January of 1832. "But," he added, "I should suppose this would be very doubtful from the powerful representation which the present Institution has in your Upper House."[13]

THE INTRODUCTION OF THE BILL

In his speech in the House of Assembly, Lawson made the important point that a monopoly was not being requested; "the charter this bill asks for is not exclusive – if they are required a dozen more may be given."[14] He then stepped aside for his colleague, Alexander Stewart, who assumed the task of piloting the bill through the legislature and who announced that he had withdrawn his name from the subscription list, where it had been down to the extent of £1,000, because he wished to avoid all appearance of interest biasing his judgment.

Similar in most provisions to the charter of the Bank of New Brunswick, the bill authorized The President, Directors, and Company of the Bank of Nova Scotia to conduct the business of banking in all its branches. The note issue could be up to three times the paid-up capital. As in the case of the Halifax Banking Company, the notes were to be redeemable on demand in gold, silver, or provincial treasury notes. Of the authorized capital of £100,000, 5 per cent was to be paid within fifteen days of the passing of the bill and 50 per cent by June 1, 1832. It was further proposed that the new Bank be allowed to open for

---

* "Halifax currency" (that is, not sterling); since 1 pound Halifax currency was equal to 4 dollars, the Bank's authorized capital was to be the equivalent of $400,000.

business as soon as it had £35,000 in hand. This proved to be a tactical error and the opponents of the bill took immediate advantage of it.

DEBATE ABOUT THE BILL

To Jotham Blanchard, a member of the House of Assembly and a friend of the Halifax Banking Company, the proponents of the new Bank had exposed themselves as a group of speculators by suggesting that the Bank could open with only £35,000 paid in; he doubted whether the Bank would be in existence three months from its commencement. William Bliss defended the bill and refuted the charge. The required £50,000 of paid-up capital stock would be easily raised by June, he said; but in the meantime, as payments on subscriptions came in, capital funds would be lying idle. Blanchard then moved to his main attack. Why a public bank made up of many subscribers, some of whom might withdraw, some of little means, some of them not yet known? How would its resources compare with those of the private bank and the wealth of the eight partners? For instance, what could dissipate Martin G. Black's store and property to the winds? What could destroy Hezekiah Cogswell's fortune? He felt bound to suppose that the capital of the new Bank would be drawn out in one week after its commencement and that the Bank would soon come to a stand for want of means.[15]

This diatribe did not much impress the House but it did serve as a springboard for further discussion of the bill. John Young, well known as a writer on farm affairs under the name of Agricola, raised the question of the obligations of shareholders. What were these obligations, and where did the public stand in the event of failure? Who would pay for it, and how much? If a shareholder was responsible only to the extent of his actual investment, what about the note-issue privilege which doubled or trebled the investment? Should he be responsible to that extent, or perhaps even to the full extent of his means? Scottish banks, said Young, had adopted the latter practice, which had been followed by certain American banks. He cited a clause in the recent charter of a bank in New York State: "the holders of stock at the time of mismanagement shall make good any loss..." – chilling words for prospective bank investors! But Young had not finished the sentence. "Read on," said Stewart, and the all-important limitation followed: "provided that no one shall pay more than the amount of stock held by him at the time."[16]

There was laughter in the House but William Bliss sensed the emergence of an issue. He would be prepared, he said, to add a clause similar to the one just cited: shareholders should be liable to loss occasioned by the mismanagement of directors to the amount of stock held by shareholders at the time. With that, the question arose as to what the proposed amendment would mean: would the shareholder lose only his investment, twice the amount of his investment, or three times the amount of his investment, since the note issue was to be three times the paid-up capital? The problem was solved by the Speaker, who was also the Attorney-General. The clause, he felt, should be interpreted to mean that if "by mismanagement of directors a loss of 20 percent were occasioned, then every stockholder would be called on to pay in 20 percent over and above [the paid-up capital] to make the deficiency good."[17] The bill passed, as amended, by twenty-six votes to ten.

THE BILL AMENDED BY THE COUNCIL OF TWELVE

Above the House of Assembly, however, waited the Council of Twelve, with its five hostile bankers. The bill was sent to the chamber, the doors closed ominously, and a long silence ensued. At Alex Murison's, where £60,000 had been subscribed by the end of February, only £600 more was added through all of March. Uniacke expressed his bleak opinion: the man in the moon would approve the bill before His Majesty's Council. And William Bliss's brother, Lewis, wrote to their brother Henry in London, "Cogswell would as soon part with his place in Council and his eyes and character to boot, as let us have the public Bank in a way desired if he can prevent it – I have, therefore, but little hope of our getting such a bill as the public generally will accept and use."[18]

The pessimism of Uniacke and Lewis Bliss was well-founded. The bill came back to the House "amended" to shreds. The initial capital of the Bank was to be £50,000 with no modification. The first instalment required of subscribers was to be doubled to ten percent. The directors were not to buy more shares than they already held, or sell the shares they owned, or hold shares in any other bank. The Bank's notes were to be redeemable only in specie, not in provincial paper. The question of the responsibility of shareholders was even more ambiguous than before; the amendment was interpreted (reputedly by Cogswell) to mean that a stockholder would be liable for the amount of the stock he held plus twice that, making triple liability. Lastly, there was a brand-new provision that the Bank's operations could be suspended at any time, for reasons not specified, by the proclamation of the Lieutenant-Governor or Commander-in-Chief of the province.

The Council's arbitrary action infuriated the House and, in Alexander Stewart's opinion, hastened its own demise. John Young wholly concurred. He thought the time was near at hand when the doors of that chamber would be thrown open by the force of righteous public opinion.[19] Surprisingly, however, they were opened by the Council itself to admit a skilled emissary, William Bliss, who was a good Tory and who had maintained his composure in the House. He went to his Tory friends on the Council as mediator, reinforced in his mission by the clamour rising in the town. He returned to inform his colleagues in the Assembly that he had encouraged the Council to have second thoughts.

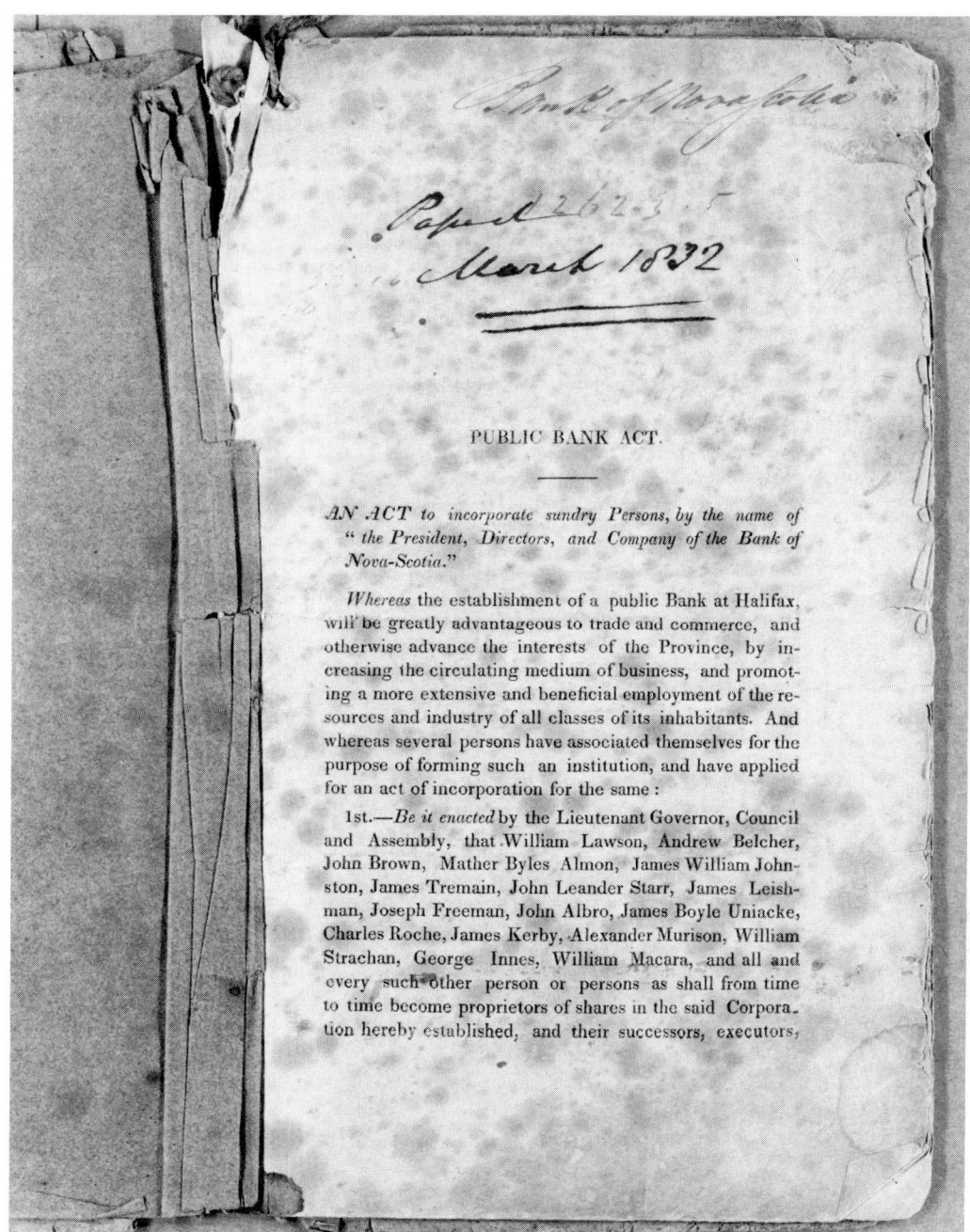

First Page of The Bank of Nova Scotia Act of Incorporation,
Royal Assent, March 30, 1832

The Council reconsidered its earlier position and sent a newly amended bill to the Assembly, which now examined it in detail. Most of the amendments which had been designed to cripple the Bank had been dropped. However, four important amendments survived: the Bank's initial subscribed capital was to be £50,000; the first call on subscribers was to be 10 per cent of that amount; the Bank would have to redeem its bank notes exclusively in specie: and the liability of shareholders would be the amount of the stock held plus equally as much again, that is, double liability.

"THE PRESIDENT, DIRECTORS AND COMPANY OF THE BANK OF NOVA SCOTIA" INCORPORATED

On March 30, 1832, with both Houses in agreement, royal assent was given to the bill incorporating "The President, Directors and Company of the Bank of Nova Scotia."* This Act calling for the double liability of shareholders was the first instance in British North America of such a provision being included. This requirement became a continuing feature of Canadian banking legislation until 1934, when a central bank was established and the note-issuing privilege of the chartered banks was gradually rescinded. And incidentally but importantly, in striking a blow at entrenched commercial power, the passage of the Act which incorporated The Bank of Nova Scotia lessened the control of the ruling clique and advanced the cause of reform in Nova Scotia.[20]

---

* This long title was the official name of the Bank until 1874, when the discovery was made that it had been listed erroneously in the 1871 Bank Act (of Canada) as simply "The Bank of Nova Scotia" and the decision was made to change the name of the Bank rather than amend the whole Bank Act.

NOTES

1. Quoted in G.F. Butler, "The Early Organisation and Influence of Halifax Merchants," *Collections*, Nova Scotia Historical Society, Halifax, 1942, Vol.25, p.15.
2. John M'Gregor, *British America*, Edinburgh and London, 1832, Vol.II, p.77.
3. George E.E. Nichols, "Notes on Nova Scotian Privateers," *Collections*, Nova Scotia Historical Society, Halifax, 1908, Vol.XIII, p.127.
4. Public Archives of Nova Scotia (hereafter referred to as PANS), MG1, Vol.1596, No.33, Bliss Papers, Lewis Bliss to Henry Bliss, dated Halifax, Mar. 18, 1832.
5. PANS, MG1, Vol.1599, No.23, Bliss Papers, William Blowers Bliss to Henry Bliss, dated Halifax, Nov. 27, 1832.
6. Thomas Raddall, *Halifax, Warden of the North* (Toronto: McClelland & Stewart, 1948), pp.174-75.
7. Joseph A. Chisholm, ed., *The Speeches and Public Letters of Joseph Howe* (Halifax: Chronicle Publishing Co., 1909), Vol.I, p.122.
8. *The Novascotian*, Jan. 4, 1832, p.6, col.2-4; p.7, col.4; also quoted in *The Bank of Nova Scotia One Hundredth Anniversary, 1832-1932*, Toronto, 1932, p.17.
9. PANS, RG5, Series P, Vol.121, 1832 petition for incorporation of the Public Bank.
10. *Ibid*.
11. *Ibid*.
12. Quoted in *History of The Bank of Nova Scotia, 1832-1900*, Toronto, 1900, p.13.
13. PANS, MG1, Vol.51, No.2112, Almon Papers, Rupert Cochran to M.B. Almon, dated New York, Jan. 25, 1832.
14. Quoted in Betty Hearn, "The Struggle for a Banking Charter in Nova Scotia, 1801-1832," a letter to *The Canadian Banker*, Vol.69, No.2, Summer, 1962, p.88.
15. *History of The Bank of Nova Scotia, 1832-1900*, pp.22-23.
16. *Ibid*., pp.24-25.
17. *Ibid*., p.25.
18. PANS, MG1, Vol.1596, No.33, Bliss Papers, Lewis Bliss to Henry Bliss, dated Halifax, Mar. 18, 1832.
19. *History of The Bank of Nova Scotia, 1832-1900*, p.26.
20. *The Novascotian*, Jan. 4, 1832, p.6, col.2-4; p.7, col.1; Apr. 26, p.132, col.1; May 17, p.159, col.1.

2

A Bank To Be Reckoned With
1832-1837

THE FIRST SHAREHOLDERS' MEETING

Following the passage of the bill incorporating The President, Directors and Company of the Bank of Nova Scotia, the flow of subscriptions resumed, and by early May of 1832, the total reached the stipulated £50,000. Also, instalment payments on these subscriptions now exceeded the mandatory 10 per cent of the subscribed capital. The shareholders were therefore in a position to choose the Board of Directors.[1]

On the evening of May 10, forty-nine subscribers who had paid their instalments met at the Merchants Exchange Coffee House. An additional thirty-one subscribers were represented by proxies. Ballots were handed out and the long procedure for the election of the prescribed thirteen members of the Board got under way. Each shareholder wrote on a signed ballot the names of those whom he (or the persons for whom he was proxy) wished to elect and the number of ballots to which he was entitled. "The ballots were then collected in a hat," the official minutes read, "and were drawn therefrom."[2] In all, 22 names were proposed and when the results were announced, the popular Alex Murison was discovered to have led the poll, surprisingly ahead of William Lawson by two votes. By that time the hour was late, only ten persons remained in the room, and the proceedings had become rather casual. Murison stuffed the ballots into his waistcoat pocket, turned with a broad smile to thank the shareholders, and on finding how slim an audience remained, "he then begged leave to thank the shades of the absent shareholders."[3]

THE FIRST DIRECTORS' MEETING

The next day, at a meeting in his office, Murison and the other twelve directors elected William Lawson as the first President of The Bank of Nova Scotia. Seven of the new Board were Halifax merchants: Mather

B. Almon, John Brown, Lewis Bliss, William F. Black, James Leishman, William Murdoch, and James Donaldson. Stephen N. Binney, a nephew of the collector of customs, was also on the Board. Finally, the legal profession was represented by Murison, William B. Bliss (Lewis Bliss's brother, who had played such an important part in the political struggle to incorporate the Bank), James W. Johnston, and James B. Uniacke.

None of the members of the first Board of Directors of The Bank of Nova Scotia had had practical banking experience, though they were, of course, familiar with bills of exchange and various credit instruments. There was no time to lose in organizing their new Bank, since they planned to open in July. Early in January, Almon had written to his broker in New York, Rupert Cochran, asking for technical help; and Cochran, a shareholder himself, had responded by forwarding a book which had recently been published in New York, *Goddard on Banking*.[4] It is no wonder that Cochran did not give the full name of this book in his covering letter, since its title page reads, "A General History of the Most Prominent Banks in Europe; Particularly the Banks of England and France; the Rise and Progress of The Bank of North America; a Full History of the Late and Present Bank of the United States: to which is added A Statistical and Comparative View of the Moneyed Institutions of New York, and Twenty-Four Other Principal Cities of the United States." Also included in the volume is "A. Hamilton's Report to Congress on Currency."[5] In addition, Cochran sent along the charter of the Bank of New York, "but it is not an easy matter to get at the particular management of Institutions of this nature," he wrote to Almon. "I think I shall be able however to get some account of the direction and management of one or two of our most respectable banks."[6]

SUPPLIES FOR THE BANK

The procurement of supplies and equipment for the new Bank was an urgent matter and since these were obtainable on this continent only in New York, the question of selecting an agent there arose. Almon's preference was obvious, the other Directors concurred, and on May 16 a letter went off to Cochran offering him the appointment. Cochran accepted with much pleasure and a number of commissions with detailed instructions quickly followed. On May 19, Lewis Bliss, Binney, and Uniacke, the committee formed to deal with these matters, wrote to Cochran asking him to arrange for the purchase of bank notes in denominations of £1.10, £2, £2.10, £5, and £10. They were to be, according to their letter, "well engraven on good paper, and from Stereotype plates. We should like them to be of a superior kind to those generally in circulation in the United States and as difficult of imitation as possible."[7] A week later came the order for vault doors, to be built of wrought iron "of the best kind, such as are most approved and in use at

New York."[8] The members of the committee journeyed to New York themselves to approve the design of the notes and the construction of the vault doors, to procure the scales and weights needed for handling specie, and to arrange for the first printing of deposit slips and cheque books.

HIRING THE STAFF

Meanwhile, the matter of hiring staff was the responsibility of other members of the Board. All-important was the appointment of the Bank's Cashier – the title of the operating head of a bank at that time. The man chosen was James Forman, who was then thirty-seven years old, well known in Halifax, and from a family as long-established as that of any of the Directors.[9] Forman, Grassie and Company, the firm founded by his father, was a large wholesale wine company. And James Forman, senior, had been one of a group which was formed in 1801 with the aim of founding a public bank and which was said to have raised £50,000 for this unrealized project in a single day. Like Enos Collins, John Lawson, and many other prominent Haligonians, he had been involved in the disposal of cargoes taken by privateers.

James Forman, junior, was more the cultivated gentleman and less the active merchant than his father. A close friend of Almon's, he lived elegantly in the old family home and took an active part in church affairs and in such cultural pursuits as the North British Society, the Nova Scotia Literary and Scientific Society, the Halifax Mechanics' Institute, the Provincial Building Society, the Horticultural Association, and the International Show Society. Although Forman was one of the 184 citizens who signed the petition for the incorporation of The Bank of Nova Scotia, he did not apply for shares of the stock.

In June, having been duly elected Cashier at a salary of £300 per year, Forman was sent off to Saint John to visit the Bank of New Brunswick. William Lawson had asked the president of that institution to permit Forman to "attend at the Bank, for a few days during the Hours of business" and to "solicit information upon the mode of conducting business in the Bank of New Brunswick."[10]

The rest of The Bank of Nova Scotia's staff was now engaged: two tellers, Alexander Paul and Benjamin Carlile, and a messenger, James Maxwell, all elected by ballot. The tellers each received £125 per annum and the messenger £50, out of which he paid rental for "lodgings and the garret" above the Bank's premises. Bonds with two sureties were required of the employees and each man in the Bank, from president down to messenger, was bound by a formal oath. "I do solemnly swear," the President and Directors intoned in the presence of a Supreme Court judge:

> that I will faithfully and to the best of my ability perform the duties now assigned, or which may hereafter be assigned to me as [President or Director] of the Bank of Nova Scotia, and that I will not

A Bank To Be Reckoned With, 1832–1837

James Forman served as the Bank's first Cashier, 1832-1870.

impart any knowledge of the concerns of the said Bank which I may have officially obtained unless required in a Court of Justice or by the Act of Incorporation of the said Bank or by any of the Bye laws thereof.[11]

The oath taken by the employees and administered by the full Board was similar, the latter part of it differing somewhat:

that I will not impart, except to the Directors, any knowledge of the concerns of the said Bank... and that I will without delay communicate to the Directors every information I may obtain of any circumstances affecting the interests of the Bank.[12]

FINDING A "SUITABLE BUILDING"

Meanwhile, another committee of the Board was searching for banking chambers, and to that end inserted the following advertisement in the Halifax newspapers of May 18: "WANTED – A suitable building for the Bank of Nova Scotia. Any person having one in a central part of the town, which can be let for that purpose, will make immediate application to William Lawson, Esquire."[13] And on May 31, the two "Western Rooms" in the Dalhousie College building were rented by the Board at the rate of £50 per annum.

Less than a month later, the Board decided that they would require additional space and they were in fact writing to apply for it when the blow fell. Lawson received a note signed by Hezekiah Cogswell in his capacity as president of the Board of Health; it will be recalled that Cogswell was also the president of the Halifax Banking Company. His Excellency, the Lieutenant-Governor, the note stated, had transferred the Dalhousie College building to the control of the Board of Health for use as a cholera hospital. (Quebec, Montreal, and New York were all hit by cholera epidemics in 1832, but Halifax was in fact spared until 1834.) Lawson promptly complained that The Bank of Nova Scotia could not operate in connection with a hospital "for the reception of so contagious and malignant a disease...it is impossible for the Directors to proceed in expensive preparations for their establishment; and still more severe will be the loss and delay and their own regret if they must at this moment forego all their arrangements and submit to be abruptly turned out of possession in search of another situation without notice and without regard to their feelings or their rights."[14] But the protest was to no avail; the Dalhousie College building's "peculiar fitness" for use as a cholera hospital had been approved, and the fledgling Bank had no choice but to look for other quarters.[15]

A search was immediately undertaken and an alternative building was soon found. On July 7, all the Directors toured John Romans's stone house at the corner of Granville and Duke streets, and, finding it satisfactory, leased it for four years. The Bank's headquarters were to remain at this location for five years – until its own building was erected

The Bank of Nova Scotia opened
for business in John Romans's building
in Halifax on August 29, 1832.

on Hollis Street in 1837. The terms were higher than those of Dalhousie College and the location was less attractive, but there was no more time to spare. Throughout the rest of July, as John Romans's building echoed with the clang of carpenters' hammers, the Directors pushed ahead with their organizational tasks. Meeting in Murison's law office two or three times a week, they reminded some of their tardy colleagues at one point that the time set for assembly was "two o'clock *precisely*."[16] The forced change of location had cost them additional expense and valuable time.

SPECIE AND BANK NOTES

However, the helpful and efficient New York agent, Rupert Cochran, was making good progress with his task of obtaining supplies of cash for the Bank. He had been instructed in late June to buy $40,000 worth of patriot doubloons in the New York market, and these arrived by schooner in mid-July.[17] "Patriot doubloons" were gold coins struck by Spain's former colonies; having a value of approximately $16 each, they were frequently divided into halves, quarters, and eighths. They were to be the most important form of specie held by the Bank; in addition, old Spanish doubloons, Spanish and American dollars, British sovereigns and shillings, and lesser varieties of gold and silver coinage backed the Bank's notes. On July 26, in another shipment from Cochran, came the first bank notes themselves, all to be signed by the President and the Cashier – no small task when one realizes that by 1840 the Bank had over 100,000 notes of varying denominations in circulation.

READY FOR BUSINESS

The Bank of Nova Scotia was now almost ready to start operating. On August 1, the following announcement appeared in the *Nova Scotia Royal Gazette*:

BANK OF NOVA SCOTIA

> As required by the Act of Incorporation, Notice is hereby given, that the sum of Fifty Thousand Pounds has been actually paid in on account of the subscriptions to the stock of the Bank of Nova Scotia, and that the Bank will be opened for business as soon as the necessary arrangements are completed.
>
> By order of the President and Directors,
> James Forman, Cashier[18]

Three days later, on the bulletin board of the Merchants Exchange Coffee House, another announcement was made:

> The Bank of Nova Scotia will commence discounting to a limited extent during the ensuing week. The Building now in preparation

for this establishment and their other arrangements not being yet completed, the Bank cannot for the present either receive deposits or open accounts with any person. Notes for discount must be left with the Cashier on Monday and Thursday before one o'clock. The Bank will be open for general business in a few days.[19]

The Directors were anxious to start business even in a limited way before the premises for the new Bank were ready. In addition to gold and silver, a substantial amount of provincial paper and Halifax Banking Company notes had been received in payment for the capital instalments. Since only specie could be used by the Bank in redeeming its bank notes, the Directors decided to "discount to the extent of the Province paper on hand in order to dispose of the same."[20]

THE HALIFAX BANKING COMPANY NOTE CONTROVERSY

But the disposal of the other paper – the notes of the Halifax Banking Company – was another matter. The Directors of The Bank of Nova Scotia decided to present to the Halifax Banking Company their total holdings of the latter's bank notes, in the amount of £23,000, with the request that they be redeemed, preferably in specie. Thus on August 8, the Cashier of the new Bank, which had not yet opened its doors to the public, appeared at the wicket of the private bank at the height of the morning's business, with the notes in a wooden box, and asked that they be redeemed. The teller was very taken aback by the size of the demand. Could Mr. Forman return, perhaps, in half an hour?

To that Forman agreed, rather incredibly leaving the box with the teller. He returned as requested and was ushered into the president's private office, where Cogswell pounced on him. Did this minion, speaking for an upstart bank, imagine that such a sum was on hand for instant redemption? This "hoarding" of a rival's notes was an "unhandsome" beginning; and in any case a verbal request was not sufficient. Forman must have a written order, signed by Mr. Lawson, that the President of The Bank of Nova Scotia had sent its Cashier to demand payment of £23,000 of Halifax Banking Company notes.

It was nearly noon when Forman returned a third time, but he had no written order. The Bank of Nova Scotia had smelled a rat; almost half of its paid-up capital was reposing in the wooden box, and there was a real question as to whether this portion was technically in the form prescribed by law. The new Bank was therefore anxious to avoid a court battle with the old established bank. Thus, Forman merely repeated his original request that the notes be redeemed. That would not be possible, replied Cogswell, without an official order; and why was that not forthcoming – was the Bank afraid of the courts? Forman recovered his box of bank notes and retired for reinforcements.

The appearance of the reinforcements in the afternoon was enough to cause a stir among the town's business community. Two of The Bank of Nova Scotia's Directors, Donaldson and Murdoch, accompanied Forman, and Maxwell, the messenger, carried the box. The teller politely asked the party to wait. Mr. Cogswell was out; a messenger would be sent to find him. Mr. Cogswell was engaged, the messenger reported when he returned; the Halifax Banking Company's board of directors would discuss the matter in the morning. But Donaldson and Murdoch dispatched the messenger again to inform Mr. Cogswell that they wished to see him this afternoon. Cogswell then appeared and ushered his unwelcome callers into his office. The gentlemen seemed in a hurry, he remarked; had they brought a demand in writing? They had not, Murdoch replied; a former (and disgruntled) customer of the Halifax Banking Company, he had decided on a different approach. Rather than asking for payment of the large sum of £23,000, he took a parcel of £500 worth of notes from the box, and asked that they be redeemed. Cogswell wavered; would Mr. Murdoch accept provincial paper as payment? He would, Murdoch replied, and the president showed the group out; the teller could pay them that. When the notes were redeemed, however, a second parcel was produced; and it was apparent that Murdoch intended to repeat the process until the entire amount was paid. At that point, with "some indistinct observation," Cogswell informed his visitors that the bank was closed for the day.

Promptly next morning, Forman turned up again. Word of the refused redemption was common talk in the town, signs of a run were developing in front of the two tellers' wickets at the Halifax Banking Company, and there was a commotion behind the closed door of the president's office. The bank's partners were assessing their position. Uniacke and Johnston from The Bank of Nova Scotia had now appeared in support of their Cashier. As grim as the two preceding Directors, who were important businessmen, these two were lawyers and prominent politicians. A decision was not long in coming; £12,000 in specie was made available, and the gentlemen were asked to accept the balance in provincial paper. The gentlemen in question agreed to that proposal.[21]

THE FIRST DIRECTORS' MEETING IN THE BANK'S OWN BUILDING

Having won the first round of what was to be a long-drawn-out battle with their rival institution, the Directors of The Bank of Nova Scotia met for the first time in John Romans's building on August 10. The first item on the agenda was a resolution of thanks to Murison for the use of his law office. The second was the drafting of a letter from William Lawson to Hezekiah Cogswell. "Influenced by the utmost *sincerity* and *good feeling*," the letter stated that,

> The Bank of Nova Scotia is by its Act of Incorporation a Specie Bank alone, and a severe penalty is imposed in case it should fail to

redeem its paper with specie. The Halifax Banking Company on the other hand professes to be under no such obligation, and acting upon this principle has of late declined altogether to redeem its notes in specie. This to say nothing more is so entirely inconsistent with the course which must be followed by the Bank of Nova Scotia under the express terms of the Law, that unless some distinct *pledge* is given that the practice will no longer be continued, nor the right itself claimed by the Halifax Banking Company, it will be impossible that its notes can be received at this establishment....[22]

This letter was the beginning of a stream of correspondence which passed back and forth between the two banks and which must have taken up a good deal of time on the part of the presidents and boards of both institutions.[23]

AUGUST 29, 1832: THE OPENING OF THE BANK

However, now was the time for a brief respite from the war of words, for it was August 29, the day on which The Bank of Nova Scotia opened its doors for general business. But, the public was respectfully informed by a notice posted in the Merchants Exchange Coffee House:

> the Act of Incorporation having made it imperative on the Bank to redeem its obligations in Gold or Silver alone, it is thereby necessarily compelled to decline receiving payments or deposits in any Notes which are not equally redeemable in specie on demand.[24]

THE BANK-NOTE CONTROVERSY HEATS UP

Not surprisingly, the Halifax Banking Company refused to honour The Bank of Nova Scotia's notes. Also, each bank declined whenever possible to deal in provincial paper and each hoarded specie. As a result, commercial loans were restricted, the prices of imported gold and silver rose sharply, and provincial notes circulated at an increasing discount.

Cogswell and Lawson each blamed the other for the resulting strangulation of trade, and the damaging battle between the two presidents continued over the course of the next few months. On February 21, 1833, Lawson defended his Bank's position in a speech in the House of Assembly. Yes, he had curtailed credit because of a lack of specie, and why had he done that? Because he could not redeem his bank notes – as the other bank could – in notes of the provincial treasury. "I was one of the first persons who introduced that [provincial treasury] paper into the country. I have always advocated and supported it and am prepared to do so now," Lawson said. And he continued,

> That gentleman [S.W. Deblois] has alluded to the formation of the Bank of Nova Scotia, but does not that hon. gentleman know that

one of the chief causes which called that institution into existence, was to counterbalance the immense power which a few affluent individuals possessed, by owning the only Bank in the country, and by its means exercising a complete control over the business and currency of the community. Does he not know that time after time, whenever it suited their whim or pleasure, they stopped discounting altogether, embarrassed trade, and threw the town into confusion.[25]

PEACE – BUT AT A PRICE

The controversy ended in an expensive victory for The Bank of Nova Scotia. On April 20, 1833, legislation was passed permitting the Bank to redeem its notes in provincial treasury notes, thus placing it on an equal footing with its old rival. Under another provision of this new legislation, however, both banks suffered a sizeable loss of revenue. Provincial paper was now to be substituted for bank notes in small transactions; the province took over from the two banks the issuance of notes in denominations of less than £5. The Bank of Nova Scotia thus had to retire its issues of £1.10, £2, and £2.10 and accept the resulting reduction in profit.

So ended the currency war between the Halifax Banking Company and The Bank of Nova Scotia. By 1834, the two banks made their peace and, though still suspicious of each other, they evolved the beginnings of a clearing system for the exchange of cheques and notes. A slump in economic conditions in the province had made co-operation essential; the general level of business activity had been depressed by two years of crop failures, a decline in cod prices, and the outbreak of cholera in Halifax.

SLOW PROGRESS AT FIRST FOR THE NEW BANK

In spite of the unfavourable economic climate, the new Bank managed to make headway, though progress was, understandably enough, slow and uneven at first. The first balance sheet, as at February 28, 1833, showed total assets of £86,000; assets increased to £136,000 during the first year of operation but there was a decline in the following year. By January 31, 1836, the lost ground was regained, and further progress was made in 1836 and 1837, with the result that total assets on January 31, 1838, stood at £166,000 – nearly double the inaugural figure. A second call on the shareholders raised the Bank's paid-up capital from £50,000 to £62,500 in 1835.

THE FIRST DIVIDEND

The Bank's first dividend of 3 per cent of paid-up capital for the half-year ending July 31, 1833 – in the amount of £1,500 – was paid on September 11, 1833. The dividend rate was increased to 4 per cent (also on a semi-annual basis) in 1837 and again to 4½ per cent in 1838. Since the first payment in 1833, The Bank of Nova Scotia has never missed paying a dividend to its shareholders.

PROBLEMS IN THE UNITED STATES

The Bank's early development took place against a background of confusion in the United States banking world. In 1791, Alexander Hamilton had established the first Bank of the United States as the depository of the principal specie reserves of the country. But in the eyes of the supporters of states' rights, this bank, and the second Bank of the United States, which replaced the first one, represented an unacceptable concentration of financial power in a federal institution. An act renewing the bank's charter was passed by Congress in 1832 but was vetoed by President Andrew Jackson and the bank was closed. Government deposits in the defunct bank were then distributed among state banks, most of which operated under charters granted by the individual states, but some of which were not subject to any form of control. For four years, down a long road of mismanagement and speculation, the United States had been heading for a crash.

Reverberations from these financial upheavals in the United States were felt in Halifax by The Bank of Nova Scotia. On February 25, 1836, Almon received a disturbing letter from the Bank's agent in New York. Ever since the opening of the Bank, Cochran had been carrying out, on a commission basis, its New York transactions – mainly covering merchants' bills of exchange and buying and selling specie. But now Cochran found his own business to be in difficulty. His debtors were delinquent, his creditors becoming insistent, and he would require £6,000 to see him through. But with Cochran in straitened circumstances, Almon's business was suffering too and he could not supply the funds. A second letter from Cochran in May sounded a more desperate note: "Money is continuing terribly scarce, and I shall be called upon for some very round Sums within the next month." Neither in New York nor Halifax were the round sums available and in June, Cochran was bankrupt.[26] In February 1837, Prime, Ward and King, another firm in New York, replaced Cochran as the Bank's agent in that city.

ADDITIONAL FOREIGN AGENCIES

Meanwhile, however, the Bank's developing foreign exchange business had led to the search for agents in London and Boston in addition to New York. Acting on instructions from Lawson, Henry Bliss, who lived in London, began negotiations with Baring Brothers in that city in 1834 and at the end of the year, Lawson wrote to Thomas Ward, the Barings' agent in Boston, "being referred to you... to know upon what terms

Messrs. Baring Brothers & Co. will open an account...."[27] In 1835, with the account open in London on terms arranged by Ward, there was still a lack of enthusiasm on Barings' part. "Your last letter," said Lawson, writing in response to Barings' letter in May, "came to me by way of New York, which I beg to suggest is a rather circuitous and expensive route – The Board will be glad to hear from you regularly by Packet from Falmouth which comes direct to Halifax or by any of the Liverpool Vessels."[28] The connection lasted only until 1836 but Barings courteously introduced Lewis Bliss, when he was on a visit to London, to Williams, Deacon and Company, Bankers, where a credit of £10,000 was arranged; this firm was The Bank of Nova Scotia's London agent for many years.

In contrast to the difficulties encountered in London, the Bank's agency arrangement in Boston was concluded with ease. On November 22, 1836, Lawson sent off a letter by way of the brig *Acadian* to Dana, Fenno and Henshaw of that city: "Mr. Almon has handed to the Board of Directors your letter of 10th Septr. addressed to him, stating the terms upon which you would open an account with the Bank, and to which he informs the Board that on their part he had given his assent....I now beg to confirm the arrangement made by Mr. Almon."[29]

THE GENERAL MINING ASSOCIATION ACCOUNT

An early example of The Bank of Nova Scotia's success in securing new business and then keeping it under adverse circumstances was the account of the London-based General Mining Association, for which, it will be recalled, Almon acted as the Halifax agent. The company ran a large-scale coal-mining complex, operating mines, wharves, coke ovens, horse-drawn railways, and some of the first steam pumps in Canada at Pictou and Sydney. Over 50,000 tons of coal were produced annually and a thousand men were employed – a very sizeable and impressive enterprise indeed. In 1834, the company was being run by a Richard Smith, who apparently had an abrasive personality. Therefore, in that same year he was replaced as resident agent and manager by Samuel Cunard, one of the eight partners of the Halifax Banking Company.

To any banker, the next step would seem inevitable: the loss of the account by The Bank of Nova Scotia to its old rival. However, the inevitable did not happen. On July 20, 1834, an incredulous Lawson wrote to Henry Bliss in London, "Mr. Cunard, as Agent of the General Mining Assn. continues to transact the Company's business at the Bank of Nova Scotia."[30] Not only that, but in 1836, Cunard dealt a body blow to the Halifax Banking Company; he withdrew from the partnership, taking not only his own account but also that of another partner, thereby reducing the bank's capital by £20,000.

A NEW COMPETITOR: THE BANK OF BRITISH NORTH AMERICA

But both banks soon had to face additional competition. During 1836 rumours circulated that the Bank of British North America, which had recently been founded in London for the purpose of conducting a banking business in the North American colonies, proposed to include Halifax among the number of centres in which it planned to operate. Early in 1837 the rumours were confirmed when it became known that a local committee had been set up to prepare the way for this branch, a committee which included two friends of The Bank of Nova Scotia, Samuel Cunard and Alexander Stewart. And when the new bank opened for business in September,* it was under the management of another friend – and Director – of the Nova Scotia's, Stephen Binney.

A NEW BUILDING FOR THE BANK OF NOVA SCOTIA

Shortly before this development, the Directors of The Bank of Nova Scotia decided that the time had now come for the Bank to build its own home. John Romans's building had its limitations as the headquarters of a bank; "I have also to acquaint you," James Forman had written to the landlord on December 29, 1835, "that there is a leak in the roof of the House and that the privy is in such a bad state that the contents of it find their way into the cellar."[31] In August 1836, land was acquired on Hollis Street, at the corner of George, and plans were drawn up for a granite building. Through 1837 the walls rose block by block and April of 1838 saw the completion of the new Bank building near Province House Square.

Twenty years later, the building was renovated and enlarged and a portico and eight columns were added, making the edifice "the most attractive ornament of Hollis Street," in the opinion of the *Daily Acadian Recorder*.[32] Another periodical considered the remodelled building "to surpass any other hitherto erected in Nova Scotia, except the Province Building." The banking room, lighted from the dome and "finished with fluted pilasters, enriched capitals, and entablature in Grecian Corinthian style," was "probably the handsomest...in North America."[33]

LAWSON RETIRES

But William Lawson would not be entering the Bank's new home as President. His business in the West Indies was experiencing a decline and was, therefore, demanding more of his attention. Also, he had encountered a setback in his political fortunes; he had taken on the job of Town and County Treasurer, a very unpopular position because the

---

* Branches of the Bank of British North America had already been opened in Montreal, Quebec, Toronto, and St. John's; this bank was taken over by the Bank of Montreal in 1918. Also, the Halifax Banking Company was taken over by the Canadian Bank of Commerce in 1903.

In 1837 the Bank erected its own building at 188 Hollis Street, Halifax.

CREDIT: PUBLIC ARCHIVES OF NOVA SCOTIA

incumbent was appointed by the Council of Twelve. Lawson's old friend, Joseph Howe, was opposed to all authority that stemmed from the Council of Twelve. In November of 1836, with a provincial election in the offing, Howe ran against Lawson for the nomination as a candidate in Lawson's own county of Halifax, where redistribution had reduced the number of seats from four to two.

Howe won the nomination and went on to win the election. But there were compensations. "Mr. Lawson," said Howe, speaking later in the House of Assembly, "though wealthy and fairly entitled to the notice of the Government, never got into the Council, and why? Because he was too plain-spoken and would not bend to the views of that body. He lost his seat here merely because he had accepted an obnoxious office; but during the long period that he served the country in this House, he had no prospect of becoming a councillor, but now perhaps he stands a better chance."[34]

That "chance" became a reality in 1838, when Lawson was appointed to the new Legislative Council—a reformed Upper House, created largely through Howe's efforts; he was to serve for eight years, to within two years of his death. But before embarking on this final chapter of his political career, Lawson severed his connection with The Bank of Nova Scotia. On March 1, 1837, he presided as usual over the annual meeting of the Bank, and on March 2 at a Directors' meeting he was re-elected as President. On March 9, however, the Directors' minute book recorded that "William Lawson, Esqe, having resigned his situation as President of the Bank of Nova Scotia, M.B. Almon, Esqe, was elected to that office."[35]

Joseph Howe (1804-1873).

A young journalist when The Bank of Nova Scotia was formed in 1832, Joseph Howe was a champion of legislative reform and signed the petition calling for the establishment of a public bank in Halifax.

NOTES

1. *Nova Scotia Royal Gazette*, May 2, 1832, p.4, col.1; May 16, p.3, col.3; Aug. 1, p.3, col.5.
2. Quoted in *The Bank of Nova Scotia One Hundredth Anniversary, 1832-1932*, p.34.
3. *The Novascotian*, May 17, 1832, p.159, col.1; also quoted in *The Bank of Nova Scotia One Hundredth Anniversary, 1832-1932*, p.35.
4. PANS, MG1, Vol.51, No.2113, Almon Papers, Cochran to Almon, dated New York, Jan. 26, 1832.
5. Thomas H. Goddard, *Goddard on Banking* (New York: H. C. Sleight, 1831).
6. PANS, *op. cit.*; also quoted in The Bank of Nova Scotia *Monthly Review*, Aug.-Sept. 1951.
7. The Bank of Nova Scotia Archives, Toronto, Lewis Bliss, Binney, and Uniacke to Cochran, dated Halifax, May 19, 1832; also quoted in BNS *Monthly Review*, Aug.-Sept. 1951.
8. *Ibid.*, May 26, 1832.
9. Phyllis R. Blakeley and Diane M. Barker, "James Forman," *Dictionary of Canadian Biography*, X (Toronto: University of Toronto Press, 1972), pp.292-93.
10. BNS Archives, Lawson to President of Bank of New Brunswick, dated Halifax, June 1, 1832.
11. BNS Directors' Minute Book, May 11, 1832. (The oath was not administered to the President and Directors until May 18.)
12. *Ibid*.
13. *History of The Bank of Nova Scotia, 1832-1900*, p.43.
14. BNS Archives, Lawson to Charles W. Wallace, Acting Trustee, Dalhousie College, dated Halifax, July 5, 1832.
15. *Ibid.*, Wallace to Lawson, dated Halifax, July 6, 1832.
16. BNS Directors' Minute Book, June 20, 1832.
17. PANS, MG1, Vol.51, No.2140, Almon Papers, Cochran to Almon, dated New York, Aug. 5, 1832.
18. *Nova Scotia Royal Gazette*, Halifax, N.S., Aug. 1, 1832, p.3, col.5; also quoted in *History of The Bank of Nova Scotia, 1832-1900*, p.44.
19. BNS Directors' Minute Book, Aug. 4, 1832.
20. *Ibid*.
21. BNS Archives, Transcripts of Correspondence between William Lawson and H. H. Cogswell, dated Halifax, Aug. 11, to Oct. 3, 1832.
22. *Ibid.*, Lawson to Cogswell, dated Halifax, Aug. 11, 1832.
23. See Victor Ross, *A History of the Canadian Bank of Commerce* (Toronto: Oxford University Press, 1920), Volume I, pp.73-81, for a detailed description of this correspondence.
24. BNS Directors' Minute Book, Aug. 28, 1832.
25. *The Novascotian*, Feb. 28, 1833, p.66, col.4.
26. PANS, MG1, Vol.60, Nos.2710, 2716, 2720, Almon Papers, Cochran to Almon, dated New York, Feb. 25, May 10, June 2, 1836.
27. BNS Archives, Lawson to Thomas Ward, dated Halifax, Dec. 16, 1834.
28. *Ibid.*, Lawson to Messrs. Baring Brothers & Co., dated Halifax, May 18, 1835.
29. *Ibid.*, Lawson to Dana, Fenno and Henshaw, dated Halifax, Nov. 22, 1836.
30. *Ibid.*, Lawson to Henry Bliss, dated Halifax, July 28, 1834.
31. *Ibid.*, James Forman to John Romans, dated Halifax, Dec. 29, 1835.
32. *Daily Acadian Recorder*, Halifax, N.S., June 13, 1857.
33. *The Novascotian*, Dec. 7, 1857, p.1, cols.4-5.
34. Joseph A. Chisholm, ed., *The Speeches and Public Letters of Joseph Howe* (Halifax: Chronicle Publishing Co., 1909), Vol. I. p.126.
35. BNS Directors' Minute Book, Mar. 2, Mar. 9, 1837.

3

Surmounting Early Challenges 1837-1875

THE FINANCIAL CRISIS OF 1837

"Before this letter can reach you," the new President of The Bank of Nova Scotia wrote to a correspondent in London on May 20, 1837, "the accounts from the United States will have made you acquainted with difficulties in which that Country is now placed – it may be truly said that the Commercial Community is prostrate, all confidence is at an end and unless assistance is to be derived from England, it is impossible to imagine the extent of the ruin that must ensue."[1]

With the closing of the Bank of the United States and the subsequent collapse of many state banks, the speculative rush to the American west had ground to a halt. More importantly for Nova Scotia, panic had seized the American industrial east. Factories had closed down in New England, thousands of unemployed had filled the cities, and the volume of shipping on the eastern seaboard – so vital to Halifax and the other Nova Scotian ports – had suffered a disastrous decline. Gold and silver coins came to be the only money in which people had confidence, and therefore were zealously hoarded by everyone. Specie prices rose not only on the New York market but also in London. In Halifax, the three banks – The Bank of Nova Scotia, the Halifax Banking Company, and the Bank of British North America – were all forced to suspend the redemption of their notes in specie for two to three months in mid-1837, following the earlier example of banks in the United States, the Canadas, and New Brunswick.

PRESIDENT MATHER B. ALMON

Such were the inauspicious circumstances in which Mather B. Almon began his thirty-three-year term of office as the second President of The Bank of Nova Scotia – the longest tenure by far of any of the Bank's

The Hon. Mather B. Almon, President of the Bank, 1837-1870

Presidents.[2] Not only did he have to cope with the financial crisis of 1837, but he also had to face increasing competition from the newly established Bank of British North America.

Almon was a successful businessman, and he played an active part in the religious and educational life of the community as well; he was a one-time governor of Dalhousie College and twice of King's College. He was strongly opposed to Confederation; along with Johnston and Uniacke, he was a member of the delegation from the Maritime provinces which appeared before Lord Durham in Quebec in 1838, following the rebellions in the Canadas. Charles Buller, Durham's secretary, was much impressed by the Maritimers:

Generally men of plain manners [he wrote afterward], they exhibited also a great deal of plain good sense and fairness. Opposed in provincial politics they could discuss even their own points of difference with candour and moderation. The deputation from Nova Scotia in particular pleased us highly. Some of its leading members were persons not only of striking ability, but of a degree of general Information and polish of manners which are even less commonly met with in colonial society.[3]

AN AGENT IN SAINT JOHN

In February of 1837, just before Almon was elected President, A.W. Whipple, a leading merchant in Saint John, New Brunswick, had been appointed agent of the Bank there. He bought and sold foreign exchange and specie on commission, along the lines already established in New York and Boston. And following the practice of Scottish banks at that time, he also "pushed" the notes of The Bank of Nova Scotia, retiring the notes of the other banks and shipping them to Halifax for redemption along with the gold and silver coins. The opening of the Saint John agency represented the Bank's first such venture in what was to become the Dominion of Canada, but it should be noted that the business conducted there was of a specialized nature and was not that of a general banking operation – the agency did not make loans or discount commercial paper.

FIVE LOCAL AGENCIES

In spite of the unfavourable economic climate prevailing in 1837, the Bank took another bold step late that year. In December, Almon wrote to James D. Fraser and Harry King in Windsor, Nova Scotia, appointing their firm as the first agency of the Bank in the province of Nova Scotia. At first, this "local" agency does not appear to have carried out general banking functions, but by the time four other agencies were established in 1839 – in Pictou, Yarmouth, Annapolis, and Liverpool – all seemed to be providing a complete banking service, including lending to the public. They were the forerunners of the branches of today. But the agent's status was very different from that of the present-day branch manager. The agent was not a paid employee of the Bank; he was engaged in his own business in addition to the Bank's and was paid a fixed sum for his services and those of his clerks and for the use of his office, together with commissions on the business done on behalf of the Bank. Furthermore – and this would certainly strike terror in the heart of any present-day manager – the agent's personal guarantee was required on bills purchased by him, and bad loans were his personal responsibility! "As regards your liabilities they are detailed in your bond, repeated in your letter, in a word it is a guarantee for all your doings," Almon wrote to the Windsor agents;"...we are aware," he concluded, "that in this Country Banking is yet in its infancy."[4]

In 1843, the Windsor agents did suffer a loss resulting from their guarantee of some bills of exchange purchased from an "absconding debtor." The Board of Directors of the Bank insisted that there would be "no exception to the established rule namely that of requiring the individual guarantee of Messrs. Fraser and H. King."[5] However, the Board conceded that the Windsor agents had been rather underpaid as compared with other agents and granted them "four hundred pounds as an additional remuneration for their past services"[6] – which must have helped them in their loss to the absconding debtor.

BANKING IN THE 1830s

The lending business of the local agencies, like that of the main office in Halifax, was the most important part of their operations. Loans took two forms. First was the still familiar one of loans against notes "with two good and sufficient names." The other was the "cash credit" – a type of overdraft, secured by bonds upon the customer and his "two sureties." However, as early as 1840, the Directors of The Bank of Nova Scotia decided that the cash credit was not a suitable form of loan, "... many of which [cash credits] from not having been granted to mercantile men do not operate, and rest a dead weight on the resources of the Bank." Furthermore, "In two instances the gentlemen had overdrawn their accounts by which the rules of the Institution are infringed, an amount being loaned to a single name only." Therefore, the Board ruled that the cash credit system be terminated "with all convenient speed..., the indulgence thus granted withdrawn, and the subject till then to be kept in the continued remembrance of the Directors."[7] The Bank's first history, published in 1900, comments that "The system called for much vigilance, as sureties disappeared through death, bankruptcy and other causes."[8]

James Primrose, Agent, Pictou, N.S., 1839-1872

The correspondence between the Bank's Head Office and its agents, which has been preserved in the Bank's Archives, gives a clear picture of the nature of banking at this time. Thus, the general instructions to James Primrose, the agent at Pictou, included a warning note about lending policy in the light of the competitive situation in that locality (where the Bank of British North America had had an office since mid-1838): "...the accommodation afforded by each Bank contending against the other may lead to general Unsoundness, the too easy facility for obtaining money will tempt the most prudent men to embark in hazardous speculation." Moreover, loans were to be "monies frequently received and paid; dead loans are avoided by all well-regulated Banks." Finally, Primrose was asked to make "the sole interest of this Bank...your polar star" and "in all other matters involving much responsibility" to "refer first to this Board for advice."[9]

However, the existing state of communications made reference to the Board for advice a problem for Primrose and the other agents of the Bank. In his letters to Head Office, Primrose often complained that he was put at a disadvantage with his competitors, particularly in operations dealing with bills of exchange for which he had to obtain approval in Halifax. Similarly, transport difficulties and expensive postage impeded shipments of bank notes and specie, and opportunities to send them by private hands were continuously sought. "You will have an oppy [opportunity] soon by the Lawyers coming up to court to send me some Agency notes,"[10] wrote Primrose on one occasion. And again, "Gather all the sterling money you can for me & I will make some person going down with a sled call for it as soon as sleighing is good."[11]

Along with transportation difficulties and exorbitant postal rates, another constant problem of the time was the shortage of small coins and bills needed for change. It will be recalled that the banks had been prohibited in 1833 from issuing notes in denominations of under £5. As Primrose noted, "Change is so scarce, I find you have never sent enough of it for which you have suffered more severely than you are aware."[12] As well, the variety of coins in circulation posed a further difficulty: "The Bag of small change by O Bryan I do not know what to make of. . . . what value do you count each of the small pieces? Those on which the pillars are legible pass for $3^{1}/_{2}$ d/y [pence, Halifax currency] here and the smooth ones for 3 d [pence], but there is not enough of them even if all [are counted as] $3^{1}/_{2}$ d/ys to make the amot [amount]."[13]

BANKER'S LOT "NOT A HAPPY ONE"

If the lot of the Bank of Nova Scotia agent in the 1830s was, like that of the policeman in *The Pirates of Penzance*, "not a happy one," consider the position of the Bank's paid employees in the Halifax office. On January 4, 1838, Henry Mundell, the receiving teller, was singled out for a reprimand in the Board's minutes:

> Whereas it having come repeatedly to the notice of the Board of Directors that certain positions of duty which are appropriated to Mr. Mundell, the Receiving Teller are inefficiently performed,
>
> "Resolved unanimously That the President be requested to communicate to Mr. Mundell that unless a more strict attention be paid by him to his duties by longer attendance at the Bank, and likewise a greater degree of accuracy be evinced in the Books under his charge, the Board will be under the necessity of taking this subject into their more serious consideration. . .[in] the opinion of the Directors. . .the Bank hours from 10 to 3 o'Clock are considered as applying to the accommodation of the Public only. . . ."[14]

And on September 4, 1840, Benjamin Carlile, one of the first tellers hired by the Bank, was requested to attend in the "parlour," where a Directors' statement was read to him. It expressed "regret and marked disapprobation" of his recent rudeness to a customer and his defence on the ground that he had not been properly introduced was dismissed as "a reason so frivolous that the Board deem it unnecessary [of] their further consideration."[15] Furthermore, the Directors stated that

> ...the tellers of the Bank, with whom in fact the Public have most to do, should at all times practise the utmost courtesy of manner and, as it frequently occurs that they are called to communicate decisions of the Board not altogether pleasing to the parties interested,... should be more than ordinarily careful to do so in a manner to conciliate the customers of the Bank.[16]

Before leaving the subject of day-to-day banking in the 1830s, it is worthwhile noting that the first reference to the Bank's allowing interest on cash deposits appears in 1837. The rate was to be 3 per cent if the money was left on deposit for three months. Fifteen days' notice of withdrawal was required and interest was to cease from the date of such notice. In point of fact, payment of interest had become a competitive necessity because the newly opened Halifax branch of the Bank of British North America had introduced the practice.

The opening of no fewer than four agencies in one year, and at a time of continuing economic problems, not surprisingly taxed the resources of The Bank of Nova Scotia. Accordingly, in 1839 it was resolved that the unpaid capital in the amount of £37,500 should be called in. And at the end of the same year it was decided that a further increase in capital stock was required. Thus, £25,000 of stock was sold early in 1840 and another £15,000 in 1841, bringing the total paid-up capital to £140,000 – at which level it remained for 30 years.

SLOW GROWTH: 1840-1870

The truth is that the overall growth of the Bank throughout the whole period from 1840 to 1870 was slow. Total assets increased in a hesitant fashion, and the dividend rate, after averaging nearly 9 per cent per annum in the first ten years of the Bank's existence, was lowered to around 6 per cent. Three agencies – in Windsor, Liverpool, and Annapolis – were closed in the early 1850s, leaving only the agencies at Pictou and Yarmouth. Later, however, in 1867, a new agency was opened at North Sydney Mines to serve the General Mining Association's operation there.

The Bank was faced in this period with the competition of not only its old rival, the Halifax Banking Company, and its younger rival, the Bank of British North America, but also a number of new banks, which opened in various localities in Nova Scotia: the Union Bank of Halifax (1856), the People's Bank of Halifax (1864), the Commercial Bank of Windsor (1865), the Exchange Bank of Yarmouth (1867), and the Merchants Bank of Halifax (1869).[17] And soon after Confederation in

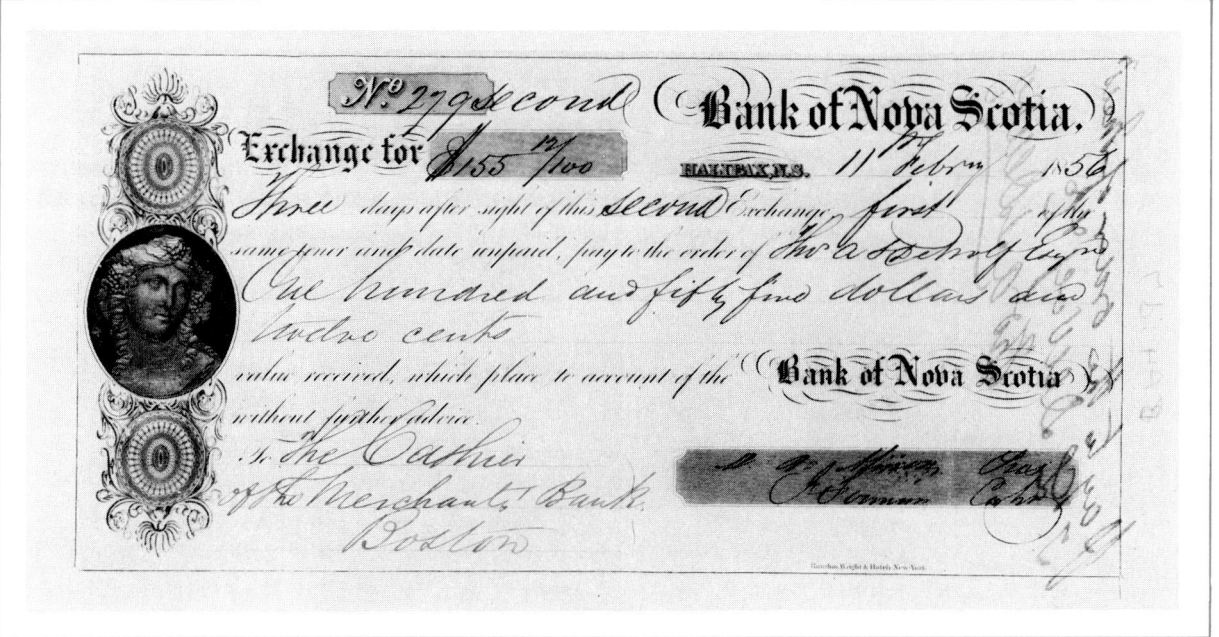

BNS Second of Exchange
Feb. 11. 1856 –
To the Cashier of the
Merchants' Bank, Boston,
signed by M.B. Almon,
President, and
J. Forman, Cashier.

1867, the Bank of Montreal began establishing branches in the Maritimes, including one in Halifax. However, The Bank of Nova Scotia did maintain its position as the leading bank in the province of Nova Scotia and was second only to the Bank of New Brunswick in the entire Maritime area.

Furthermore, the Bank had to cope in its early years with the uncertainty occasioned by the fact that its original charter covered only ten years. And then it had to carry on for the next three years on the unsatisfactory basis of annual extensions because of political problems encountered in securing a longer renewal. In 1845, however, the charter was extended for ten years and important amendments were granted.

The above reasons for the slow progress of the Bank seemed understandable enough until 1870, when the dramatic disclosure was made that James Forman, the Cashier, had been systematically stealing funds from the Bank since 1844 and had been altering the Bank's books in order to avoid detection. But before recounting that unfortunate episode, it is of interest to tell an earlier and happier story.

THE CUNARD CONNECTION

Samuel Cunard was without doubt the Bank's most important customer in the 1840s and the relationship is commemorated by the impressive mural of Cunard's steamship *Britannia* over the main door of the banking room of the Bank's Head Office in Halifax.

As resident director and manager of the General Mining Association, Cunard controlled a very important account, an account which The Bank of Nova Scotia kept in spite of the fact that Cunard had been a local sponsor of the Bank of British North America, as has already been noted. But his interests were not confined to the coal mines at Pictou. His timber tracts in New Brunswick were an enormous operation, run by his brother Joseph, with Samuel providing the supplies for the camps. Tea brought from Canton in East India Company ships was stored in Samuel Cunard's warehouses in Halifax, where it was sold at auction for distribution in the Atlantic provinces. He owned farmlands in Prince Edward Island. He was one of the largest shipbuilders and shipowners in Nova Scotia, and he was one of the first to foresee the coming revolution in the shipping industry. By the beginning of the 1830s, even as larger sailing ships were setting out from the province, Cunard had turned to steam.[18]

In 1831, the Cunard brothers had been stockholders in the Quebec and Halifax Steam Navigation Company, which had built the *Royal William*, a wooden steamship, intended for passenger and freight service between Lower Canada and the Maritimes. However, there was not enough traffic to make such a service profitable, and furthermore, the ship was feared as a potential cholera carrier during the epidemic of 1832. The big paddlewheeler, which was equipped with sails to assist her engines, was a financial disaster and she was disposed of at a bankruptcy sale at Sorel. She was then sent to England to be resold. (She was eventually bought by the Spanish government, who used her as a man-of-war.) The S.S. *Royal William* made history in 1833 by steaming her entire way across the North Atlantic, the first ship to do so, although she also relied on her sails especially while salt was removed from her boilers, one at a time. She made the trip from Pictou, Nova Scotia, to Gravesend in England in twenty-five days, about half the time of the average sailing packet.[19]

TRANSATLANTIC STEAMSHIPS

Subsequently, in 1838, a British paddle-steamer, the *Sirius*, crossed the Atlantic under continuous steam power and the British Admiralty was struck by the possibility of a regular transatlantic steamship service. Accordingly, late the same year, the Admiralty called for tenders on a line of steamships to carry mail between British ports and New York, by way of Halifax and Boston. With no British firms prepared to guarantee winter service, Cunard travelled to England, found some Scottish backers, and signed a contract on March 18, 1839. The British and North American Royal Mail Steam Packet Company, with a capital of £270,000 of which Cunard had subscribed £67,500, was to carry the Atlantic mail.

For Halifax and the entire eastern seaboard it was electrifying news; the Old World would now be weeks closer to the New World, and the time-frame in which every business operated would be speeded up. In May of 1840, the *Unicorn* arrived in Halifax, fourteen days out of Liverpool. The Haligonians went wild; flags waved, guns were fired in salute, and thousands of people crowded the wharves. Two months later, the *Britannia* arrived with Cunard himself on board, inaugurating the regular run. Cunard was also warmly welcomed in Boston, where he received 1,800 invitations to dinner!

Within two years, however, Cunard's name was being mentioned in another tone, particularly in board rooms. His love affair with steam had more than strained his resources. Payment of his £67,500 subscription towards the capital of the new steamship company was slow. So were his regular remittances to the East India Company for tea. He was short of funds because his Prince Edward Island farms were losing money; his brother, Joseph, was mismanaging the timber business; and worst of all, the costly new steamers carrying the Royal Mail were not showing a profit as soon as he had hoped. By September 1841, Cunard and his son, Edward, who managed his father's affairs in Halifax, were both up to their necks in debt. One of Samuel's creditors was a firm of bankers in Liverpool, England, who were owed a mere £2,000 but who swore out a writ of attachment. Cunard had friends, however, who saw that it was not served. One evening, as one of his steamers slipped her London moorings, the Halifax entrepreneur was rowed out under cover of night to join her well clear of the dock. He arrived home with debts of some £130,000 demanding urgent attention.

By mid-March 1842, he had mortgaged his wharves and warehouses in Halifax and had sold some of his land on Prince Edward Island. He still had ships, timber stocks, timber reserves, and other assets much exceeding his debts in value but they would take time to realize. Because he had fled from his British creditors, he was not in a position to go for assistance to the Bank of British North America, with its head office in London. He had withdrawn from the Halifax Banking Company partnership six years before, and since then had not been on good terms with the private bank. And so, through the good offices of his brother-in-law, John Duffus, who was a dry goods merchant and a customer of The Bank of Nova Scotia, he approached the Nova Scotia for a substantial loan. On April 5, a special meeting of the Directors of The Bank of Nova Scotia was called "for the consideration of the proposition made to the Bank by Messrs. S. Cunard & Co., the embarrassed state of whose affairs has on several previous days received the attentions of the Board."[20]

LOAN TO CUNARD

Cunard had asked for a loan of £45,000 which, together with hoped-for extensions of some of his debts, would tide him over, he calculated. The requested loan was approximately one-third of the entire paid-up capital of the Bank, more than double the Bank's authorized limit for advances, and was opposed by Lewis Bliss. The other Directors decided to write to Stephen Binney, the Halifax manager of the Bank of British North America, "expressive of the willingness of the Bank of Nova Scotia to meet that bank on equal terms in rendering the requisite assistance."[21] Binney suggested an alternative course of action. If The Bank of Nova Scotia would advance the full £45,000, its notes would be accepted by the Bank of British North America and held from circulation for a certain period to be agreed upon. It was an ingenious idea, since the notes, while they lay idle in the vault of the other bank, would serve as a reciprocal loan. Discussions between the two banks about the details of the proposal, and interviews with Cunard, in which more personal security was sought, extended over two anxious days. Then, at a meeting on April 11, the Directors of The Bank of Nova Scotia voted to suspend the bylaw limiting advances to £20,000. After the dissenting Bliss walked out of the meeting, "it was moved and seconded that the proposal of Messrs. Cunard having reference to an acceptance on behalf of this Bank of the terms offered by the Bank of B[ritish] N[orth] America be acceded to...Mr. Samuel and Mr. Edward Cunard waited on the Board and were informed of its decision."[22]

The man not used to waiting on boards received the requested loan of £45,000 (which had been endorsed by Duffus) but everything he owned was pledged, down to his last piece of silver plate and his last stick of furniture. Four Bank of Nova Scotia Directors, together with Duffus, were appointed custodians of all Cunard's property and, in effect, became keepers of his person since he was not allowed to leave Nova Scotia without their knowledge and consent. Nor could he set foot in England while the writ of attachment hung over his head. In June 1842, Almon set off for England to arrange settlement of this writ while Cunard remained at home. With the timely assistance of The Bank of Nova Scotia, Cunard had managed to save himself from bankruptcy and to retain control of the steamship line, later so well known as the Cunard Line.

THE EMBARRASSING FORMAN DEFALCATION

The Bank was a small institution in the 1840s when the bold – and successful – decision was made to back Samuel Cunard. Twenty-five years later, in 1870, it was still small and the character of its organization had changed very little. Though the number of Directors had been reduced from thirteen to nine, their share qualification lowered from twenty shares to ten, and though they were now paid fees, the Bank continued to be run in much the same way as it had always been. The President attended the Bank every day together with one Director for the week, the Directors taking their duty in alphabetical order. The Directors met on Tuesdays and Fridays of each week, "for the purpose of deciding on the applications made for discount."[23] Almon, now in his seventies, was still the President, a position he had held for thirty-three years. And though Donaldson was the only other remaining Director of the original group, there was still a Uniacke on the Board: Andrew M. Uniacke had replaced his older brother, James Boyle Uniacke, in 1856. John Doull, once a clerk for Donaldson, was now the proprietor of his own business and sat beside his former employer. William Cunard, Samuel's younger son, had been a Director for a few years in the 1860s but had since resigned. The remaining Directors were much like their predecessors – merchants, lawyers, and shipowners – men of substance who had large private interests and who valued their association with The Bank of Nova Scotia.

In the hierarchy of the Bank, slightly below the Directors and much above the clerks, was the Cashier, James Forman,[24] who had now been the chief operating officer for thirty-eight years. The Directors had grown accustomed to relying on him to carry out their decisions; they respected his social position and his skill with columns of figures. He prepared the necessary reports and statements and kept the books.

Not only did Forman keep the books, but he took them home with him at night! The Directors did not question this very unorthodox practice; nor did they question "the lax methods of the President who held joint custody of the cash with Mr. Forman,...it was an easy matter for the latter to help himself; indeed it is stated that Mr. Forman was frequently allowed the use of the President's keys."[25] Thus, over a period of twenty-five years, Forman was able to help himself to the truly staggering sum of $315,000* of the Bank's cash, covering his tracks by cooking the Bank's books.[26] It was subsequently revealed that "the cashier could make alterations, as many as he liked and he could make any alterations he liked."[27] As well, "the falsifications on the books were endless, but so skillfully done as to defy detection."[28]

James Donaldson, President, 1870-1871

ALTERATION IN THE BOOKS DETECTED

One alteration in the books was finally noticed in March 1870 by a junior clerk who "looked upon it as an error for over a month; did not communicate it to any director; two months after, there was enough to satisfy me there was a false entry,"[29] and he reported it to James C. Mackintosh, the accountant. (Mackintosh was the first officer of the Bank to have that title; in 1857, he had been promoted from the position of senior clerk and his salary had been raised from £100 per annum to £125.) Mackintosh had been entertaining suspicions about Forman for some time since he knew that his account was overdrawn and he "had been endeavoring for two or three years to check Mr. Forman's balances – a very difficult matter, as all the important books

---

* As of January 1, 1860, in accordance with an Act passed the previous spring by the Nova Scotia legislature, the Bank's accounts were converted to dollars and cents from the pounds, shillings, and pence of Halifax currency, at the rate of 1£ = $4.00.

were written exclusively by the latter."³⁰ Mackintosh informed Almon of the discrepancy and on July 28, 1870, the Directors' minute book recorded that "At a meeting of the whole Board this morning the President informed them that the Cashier, Mr. James Forman, had been guilty of making many fraudulent entries in the books of the Bank, by which he had abstracted a large amount of its funds."³¹

On the previous evening the keys, books, and cash in Forman's custody had all been taken from him and locked in the inner vault. After the special Board meeting, a committee of Directors proceeded to count the cash in the outer vault and the gold, silver, bank notes, and securities in the inner vault.

On August 2, John S. Maclean, a Halifax merchant and shipowner who had recently joined the Board, reported to J.W. Carmichael, the Bank's agent in New Glasgow, that "there is a serious defalcation in Mr. Forman's accounts. He has overdrawn a very large sum and is unable to meet it and there may be something wrong with his accounts which we cannot get at yet. The Directors are quite confident that the Depositors and holders of deposit receipts *are perfectly safe*, there can be no doubt of that, and you will please assure any enquirers of this fact. The President has between twenty-five and thirty thousand dollars at his credit and the other directors large sums. So they have full confidence in its stability. I merely write you this to put you on your guard in case you are asked about it."³²

The next day, Forman assigned to the Bank his estate of "Thorndean," together with "all the household furniture, plate, horses, carriages, harness, stock, cattle, farming implements, goods, chattels and effects of every description."³³ Six days later, a special shareholders' meeting was called, and so many came that it had to be moved from the board room of the Bank to the much larger quarters of Province House. Almon, in poor health and nearly blind, was in the chair. The defaulter, a year older than the President, was reported to be prostrate at home. A motion was made for his arrest, but it was withdrawn, as "his medical attendant who is also a shareholder stated that he is now so seriously ill that his life might be endangered by such a course."³⁴ Forman did, in fact, die a few months later in London, where he had fled.

At the shareholders' meeting, a joint committee of Directors and shareholders was appointed to sort out the Bank's books. The Directors must have been stung by some of the press comments on the Forman affair; for example, "Mr. Forman's operations were not so cunningly conducted that they could not be easily discovered. It was well known that he was engaged in heavy speculations, and that his expenditures were far too great for one of his means. Yet the suspicions of those drowsy Directors were not aroused.... No careless clerk, no foolish storeman could have committed blunders less excusable than those of the Directors of The Bank of Nova Scotia...it is high time that they should either resign their positions or be ejected from them."³⁵

Untangling the maze of the Bank's falsified accounts turned out to

John Doull,
President,
1871-1872 and 1889-1899

be an impossible task for a committee. Thus, after spending several fruitless weeks in the attempt, it recommended "that a banker of long experience and known ability, having no previous connection with the Bank should be engaged, so that an independent report might be presented to the Shareholders, and necessary changes made in the Bank's methods."[36] Acting on this suggestion, the Directors appointed W.C. Menzies, of the Bank of British North America, to the position of Cashier, on October 31, 1870.

The new Cashier reported to the March 1871 annual shareholders' meeting that the Forman defalcation amounted to approximately $315,000, as has already been noted. To put this figure in perspective, it was nearly half the shareholders' total equity in 1870, and more than 15 per cent of the Bank's total assets. After deducting recoveries made from Forman's forfeited properties and the amount due from his bondsmen, the net loss to the Bank wiped out the $80,000 reserve fund, absorbed its earnings for the first half of 1870, and impaired the capital stock by $27,672. However – and this was a remarkable declaration of confidence in the Bank's future – a dividend of $22,400 was paid. At a special meeting of shareholders in October 1871, 10 per cent or $56,000 was written off the capital account and set aside as a contingent fund, the capital stock was reduced from $560,000 to $490,000, and each individual share from $200 to $175.

ALMON RESIGNS

Meanwhile, Almon had resigned as President in September 1870. "Having in consequence of a severe inflammation lost the sight of my eye, I am unequal to the task of signing the new issue of notes contemplated by the Bank, and for this reason I am compelled to resign to the Board of Directors the office I now hold as President of the Bank."[37] James Donaldson, the only remaining Director of the original group, succeeded Almon, but merely to sign the notes and, having done his duty by signing 11,304 sheets containing 45,216 notes – "sufficient for the needs of the Bank" – he retired in favour of his former clerk, John Doull. But within another year, as the business of his wholesale dry goods firm expanded, Doull found the Bank's demands upon his time too great and he was in turn replaced by Andrew M. Uniacke, who held the position for two years (until 1874). At the annual meeting in March 1871, three shareholders who had been members of the joint committee of Directors and shareholders established to investigate the after-effects of Forman's defalcation were elected to the Board of Directors.

Thus, the Bank entered the 1870s with a new, efficient Cashier and with a more broadly based Board of Directors. As a consequence of the Forman affair, however, there was an apparent – and understandable – hesitancy on the part of the individual Board members to assume the demanding position of President for an appreciable length of time.

Andrew M. Uniacke, President, 1872-1874

MENZIES, THE NEW CASHIER

The first task for William C. Menzies, who took over as Cashier in 1870, was to sort out the fraudulent entries in the Bank's books made by the previous Cashier. That task completed, he stayed on until 1876.

The Bank was particularly fortunate in its new Cashier; W.C. Menzies was one of a procession of well-trained Scottish bankers who had been recruited by the Bank of British North America for service in the New World and who were subsequently hired by American and Canadian banks, where they had distinguished careers. Unfortunately, Menzies was plagued by ill health and was able to continue in office for only five years.* However, in that very short period of time, he was able to steer the Bank back on course; as early as March 1872, he reported to the annual meeting that "both as respects its finances and credit [the Bank] may now be said to have recovered from the effects of the loss by its late Cashier."[38] This was a truly formidable accomplishment.

Furthermore, even though the economy of the Maritimes was in the throes of a difficult period of adjustment, Menzies embarked on an expansion program for the Bank, opening agencies in Kentville in 1870 and in Amherst in 1871. In the five short years of his tenure of office, the Bank's total assets grew from $2 million to $3½ million. And not only was the reduction in shareholders' equity occasioned by the Forman defalcation quickly restored, but also substantial additions to capital stock and reserves were made, with the result that shareholders' equity nearly doubled in the period, to almost $1.2 million in 1875, as compared with $640,000 before the Forman affair.

In response to his mandate to "make necessary changes to the Bank's methods," Menzies laid down the first rules and regulations for the Bank's operation (although they were not formally codified until 1885), and he inaugurated the procedure for sending circulars of instruction and information to the agencies. Finally, and perhaps most significantly of all from the point of view of the Bank's future progress, he hired a former colleague at the Bank of British North America, Thomas Fyshe, who entered the service of The Bank of Nova Scotia as agent in Saint John, New Brunswick, in 1875. Eleven months later, following Menzies' death, Fyshe was appointed Cashier.

---

* In the Bank's Archives, there is an interesting letter written in the 1940s by Menzies' son, Dr. W.F. Menzies, who, having seen the picture of his father in *The Bank of Nova Scotia One Hundredth Anniversary, 1832-1932* (Toronto, 1932, p. 54), points out that the elder Menzies was suffering from consumption. "I think my father has the plainest physiognomy in the book, very typically tuberculous," Dr. Menzies commented.

NOTES

1. BNS Archives, Almon to T.B. Ford, dated Halifax, May 20, 1837.
2. K.G. Pyke, "Mather Byles Almon," *Dictionary of Canadian Biography*, X (Toronto: University of Toronto Press, 1972), pp.6-8.
3. Sir C.P. Lucas, ed., *Lord Durham's Report on the Affairs of British North America* (London: Oxford University Press, 1912), Vol.III, Part III, Sketch by Charles Buller, p.362.
4. BNS Archives, Almon to James D. Fraser and Harry King, dated Halifax, Dec. 8, 1837.
5. *Ibid.*, President's Private Minute Book, Feb. 24, 1843.
6. *Ibid.*
7. *Ibid.*, Sept. 4, 1840.
8. *History of The Bank of Nova Scotia, 1832-1900*, p.48.
9. BNS Archives, Almon to James Primrose, dated Halifax, Feb. 20, 1839; also quoted in BNS *Monthly Review*, Aug.-Sept. 1951.
10. *Ibid.*, Primrose to James Forman, dated Pictou, June 9, 1842.
11. *Ibid.*, Jan. 10, 1840.
12. Quoted in BNS *Monthly Review*, Aug.-Sept. 1951.
13. BNS Archives, Primrose to Forman, dated Pictou, Oct. 31, 1839.
14. *Ibid.*, President's Private Minute Book, Jan. 4, 1838.
15. *Ibid.*, Sept. 4, 1840.
16. *Ibid.*
17. *History of The Bank of Nova Scotia, 1832-1900*, p.49.
18. Phyllis R. Blakeley, "Sir Samuel Cunard," *Dictionary of Canadian Biography*, IX (Toronto: University of Toronto Press, 1976), pp.172-86.
19. William Wood, "The Record-Making *Royal William*," in *Canadian Geographical Journal*, Vol.7, No.2, Aug. 1933, pp.58-63.
20. BNS Archives, President's Private Minute Book, Apr. 5, 1842.
21. *Ibid.*
22. *Ibid.*
23. Quoted in BNS *Monthly Review*, Aug.-Sept. 1951.
24. Phyllis R. Blakeley and Diane M. Barker, "James Forman," *Dictionary of Canadian Biography*, X (Toronto: University of Toronto Press, 1972), pp.292-93.
25. *History of The Bank of Nova Scotia, 1832-1900*, p.50.
26. *Ibid.*
27. "The Bank of Nova Scotia vs. James Forman et al," February 4, 1873, p.144, in *Decisions of the Supreme Court of Nova Scotia, 1872-1875*, edited by John M. Geldart, Jr., and James M. Oxley, Vol.III, Halifax, N.S., 1883, pp.141-61.
28. *Ibid.*
29. *Ibid.*
30. *History of The Bank of Nova Scotia, 1832-1900*, p.50.
31. *Ibid.*
32. BNS Archives, J.S. Maclean to J.W. Carmichael, dated Halifax, Aug. 2, 1870.
33. *Daily Acadian Recorder*, Halifax, N.S., Aug. 22, 1870, p.2, cols.3 and 7.
34. *Morning Chronicle*, Halifax, N.S., Aug. 10, 1870, p.2, col.2.
35. *Ibid.*, Aug. 16, 1870, p.2, col.1 editorial.
36. *History of The Bank of Nova Scotia, 1832-1900*, p.50.
37. BNS Archives, President's Private Minute Book, Sept. 19, 1870 (recording Almon's letter dated Sept. 17, 1870).
38. *History of The Bank of Nova Scotia, 1832-1900*, p.52.

Thomas Fyshe,
Cashier, 1876-1897

4

Enter the Legendary Thomas Fyshe 1876-1882

THE NEW CASHIER'S BACKGROUND

Thomas Fyshe was thirty-one years old in 1876 when he became Cashier of The Bank of Nova Scotia – a position he was to hold for twenty-one years. Born and brought up on a farm in Scotland, he had acquired his education at a grammar school which, he said later, "was probably the poorest school in Scotland."[1] Leaving it at fifteen, he worked briefly for a sugar merchant and then for the Bank of Scotland, spending three years in Leith and one year in Glasgow. In 1864, he entered the Bank of Birmingham, and recalled, "I was then barely 19 years of age, and left dear old Scotland forever."[2]

He was not impressed with English banking; methods were "rough and ready compared to Scotland – nothing like the same perfect system and organization – much hugger-mugger and confusion." Also, "I found the supercilious English too much for me – almost unendurable." After three years in Birmingham he resigned and, with a view to seeing more of the world, he applied to some foreign banks in London without success. However, his luck changed, for "one day walking along Bishopsgate Street I saw on the opposite side the sign of the Bank of British North America at which I stopped and looked, and reflected that next to India I would rather go to the United States than anywhere else being a natural republican, and that Canada was at any rate next door.... in a short fortnight I was on my way to New York, where I arrived on Christmas Day 1867."[3]

In New York, he met Menzies and some other congenial Scots and in the succeeding two years he was posted to Montreal and Toronto. Back in New York in 1872, "I did what I suppose was the most foolish thing in my life. I resigned and went into stockbroking and exchange broking with a man who was not too much good....In about a year... I was then thrown on my beam ends."[4] Next he went into business for himself as a curbstone broker in sterling and earned more than he ever had in his life. Thus, he was unreceptive at first when Menzies wrote from Halifax in 1875 offering him the post of Bank of Nova Scotia agent in Saint John.

"...I promptly declined his offer, while thanking him for it. For some days after my refusal of his offer business with me was very dull. I got a fit of the blues and during that time I reflected that I had got out of the business I was brought up to and was now engaged in a business that meant more of a competition with legs than with brains, and that wasn't my strong point....I wrote to Menzies and told him that if he had not disposed of the St. John appointment I would take it."[5] Two years later, Fyshe returned to New York to be married to Avis Leonowens, the daughter of the original Anna of *Anna and the King of Siam*. Anna Leonowens lived with the Fyshes until her death in 1914. Stories of her active life enliven the Fyshe letter books in the Archives of The Bank of Nova Scotia and these same letter books indicate the mutual admiration and respect that Fyshe and his famous mother-in-law had for each other.

"ONE OF THE OUTSTANDING BANKERS IN CANADIAN HISTORY"

Thomas Fyshe, like Mrs. Leonowens, was very able and had a strong personality. As the history of the Bank which was published on the occasion of its centenary put it, "The Bank had now at its helm a man who by sheer ability and force of character ranks as one of the outstanding bankers in Canadian history."[6] And it went on, "Forceful and determined he nevertheless had a caustic tongue which inspired the awe of every member of his staff."[7] One of his staff, David R. Forgan, described him as "a Scotchman of cranky disposition, but great ability."[8] And one of the Bank's agents whose health was very poor was said to have invariably had a little drink before opening an envelope bearing the head office mark. One such envelope contained the following letter signed by Fyshe: "The Pictou Agent has sent me yr [your] letter of 19th Inst[ant] with re[ference] to a prop[osal] to erect a tombstone over the grave of the late Francis Collins at the expense of his creditors. This is probably the most extraordinary prop[osition] that was ever submitted to a body of crs [creditors] & I am amazed to find you the means of conveying it...Collins' Es[tate] still owes us $6,267. When this is pd [paid] in full we shall be willing not only to share in the subc [subscription] for a tombstone but we shall cheerfully pay for the whole of it. If that is not liberality I shall be glad to know what more can be expected of crs [creditors.]"[9]

In addition to his competence and wit, Fyshe possessed two other almost contradictory qualities which made him eminently suited for the challenges of the Bank at this time: an enterprising spirit, together with a great caution engendered by an almost fatalistic conviction that good times would inevitably be followed by bad. As he once expressed it, "if we don't make hay while the sun shines, we shall have small chance of a harvest,"[10] and "BAD TIMES, GOOD TIMES, BULLY TIMES,

COLLAPSE" was the warning statement he wrote on the inside cover of the Account Book of the President and Directors.[11] In 1883, he noted that, "Now, I must devote a little consideration to the Salaries question, and try to get them raised to a proper height...for the evil days come and the years draw nigh when the Directors will have no pleasure in anything of the kind...."[12]

Indeed Fyshe's personnel policies had quite a modern ring. Not only did he emphasize the importance of adequate pay, but he also laid great stress on the training of the Bank's younger staff and their promotion up the ranks (as an alternative to the recruiting of experienced bankers from outside) for the new positions which were opening up in the Bank. These new positions were a result of the expansion program which had been initiated by Menzies and which was developed further by Fyshe. Later on, Fyshe showed his innovative approach to the problem of keeping trained staff by introducing an Officers Mutual Guarantee and Savings Fund in 1886 and an Officers Pension Fund in 1888. The provision of pensions is, of course, standard procedure now, but was rare in those times.

DIFFICULT PERIOD OF ADJUSTMENT IN THE MARITIMES

The growth of the Bank in the late seventies is quite remarkable in the light of the turbulent economic conditions then prevailing in the Maritimes. At the same time that the region was coping with the stresses and strains of the new national economy created by Confederation in 1867, it was being forced to adjust to a world where wooden ships and sail had finally given way to the iron steamship and the railroad. The rapid decline of shipbuilding and its many subsidiary industries and the ousting from ocean-carrying trades of the wooden ships owned and operated by Maritimers were serious blows to the whole area and particularly to the ports.

In addition to the decline in shipping and shipbuilding, the period was one of difficulty for the important industries of lumbering and fishing. There were frequent severe depressions in the world's timber markets. And the rise of the beet-sugar industry in Europe resulted in low prices for cane sugar and hence reduced purchasing power in the West Indies – the very important market for cod. Finally, the completion of the Intercolonial Railway to the central provinces in 1876 meant an increase in competition for smaller Maritime industries in their home market.

On the other hand, the larger economic unit brought about by Confederation, together with the 1879 "National Policy" of increased protective tariffs, gave rise to new opportunities in the Maritimes. The demands of railways and steamships, combined with tariff protection, stimulated coal mining and the iron and steel industries. New manufacturing was attracted to railway centres, and new sugar refineries and cotton mills were established. New and larger lumber mills were built as sawn lumber replaced the old square timber. Fish canning and the fresh fish trade were becoming important, as were such specialized farming activities as the growing of apples and potatoes for export.

THE FORGAN BROTHERS JOIN THE BANK

Helping Fyshe to take advantage of the new opportunities opening up for The Bank of Nova Scotia during this period of fundamental economic change was another Scot whom Fyshe hired in 1876: James R. Forgan. Forgan had actually arrived in Halifax ahead of Fyshe, having come there by the now familiar route of the Bank of British North America. He left the bank to join the Canadian branch of the R.G. Dun & Co. mercantile agency, because the bank had not allowed him to marry on his salary of $800 per year. When Fyshe arrived in Halifax, Forgan was a married man and an employee of the credit agency at $1,000 a year.

Like Fyshe, however, Forgan had "a strong desire to return to my former calling."[13] He returned to his former calling as a result of an unusual incident. On August 1, 1876, while Fyshe, who was at that time not only Cashier of the Bank but also manager of its Halifax main office,* was out of town visiting one of the Bank's agencies, Barnum's "New and Greatest Show on Earth" came to Halifax. It was the first visit of this world-famous circus and when the street parade passed the office of the Bank, the staff went outside to get a better view, locking the door behind them. But while the steam calliope was whistling the latest hits of the day and Roman chariots and caged cars of wild beasts were rumbling past, a door from the basement into the deserted banking room opened. When the teller returned to his cage, some twenty thousand dollars had been stolen![14]

Fyshe returned the next day and fired the accountant who had been left in charge of the office, and both tellers. He then approached Forgan – whom he had known in New York – with an offer to join The Bank of Nova Scotia as accountant. Forgan became Fyshe's right-hand man and in 1880 was appointed the Bank's first inspector. The year before that appointment, David R. Forgan, James's younger brother in Scotland, had made an application to the Bank for employment, an application which was supported by a strong letter of recommendation from his superior at the Clydesdale Bank in St. Andrews. Fyshe instructed James Forgan to send for his brother at once and a cable was dispatched. "That cable was Scotch, for it wasted neither words nor money. It consisted of the one word '*come*,'"[15] David Forgan recalled many years later. Young David did come and he entered the Bank "at the correspondence desk" in 1879.[16] Thus, there were now two Forgans on the staff of the Bank.

James B. Forgan,
First Inspector
of the Bank,
1880-1884

CREDIT: MINNESOTA HISTORICAL SOCIETY

* It was not until 1888 that the local Halifax operations of the Bank were separated from those of the Head Office, and a separate Halifax office with its own manager was inaugurated.

THE FAILURE OF THE BANK OF LIVERPOOL

One of the most difficult problems with which Fyshe and James Forgan had to deal in these years was the failure in 1879 of the Bank of Liverpool, a small local bank which had been incorporated only eight years earlier with a paid-up capital of $100,000 – the minimum required at that time. The timing of the founding of this small bank was most unfortunate; Liverpool's prosperity had been built on lumbering, shipping, and shipbuilding, all of which were already in decline. In addition, the new bank was ill-served by its founders; it was milked by its large shareholders and mismanaged by its directors. The two principal creditors of the bank – the Government of Canada and The Bank of Nova Scotia – watched with concern as the Bank of Liverpool tottered from a shaky start to a situation of near-disaster. For some time, The Bank of Nova Scotia attempted to help the struggling bank by continuing to discount its bills, honour its foreign drafts, and support its note circulation.

By 1876, when Fyshe was appointed Cashier of The Bank of Nova Scotia, the debt of the Bank of Liverpool had risen to some $117,000 – $17,000 more than the paid-up capital. In response to this deterioration in the Bank of Liverpool's position, The Bank of Nova Scotia had already intervened directly in its affairs: the President, J.S. Maclean, who himself was an investor in the Bank of Liverpool, had imposed a change of management. John A. Leslie, another Scottish-trained banker who had once been James Forgan's superior at the Royal Bank of Scotland in St. Andrews, had been hired with the purpose of either instituting drastic reform or, if that was not possible, arranging for a gradual liquidation.

It was soon evident, however, that reform was beyond Leslie's power and that the Bank of Liverpool's directors were desperately attempting to stave off liquidation in view of their double liability. The bank's statements were suspect, large loans were renewed again and again, and bills discounted by The Bank of Nova Scotia in Halifax returned nothing from Liverpool when they were sent back for collection. Politics had entered the picture because prominent Liverpool citizens, many of whom owned shares in the Bank of Liverpool, were proclaiming the need to maintain the bank as the backbone of the community. However, by December of 1878, when the debt of the Bank of Liverpool had reached nearly $150,000, both Maclean and Fyshe had had enough.

A few days after Christmas, but hardly in the Christmas spirit, James Forgan appeared in the office of the Bank of Liverpool. He did not come without warning; his arrival had been preceded by a barrage of letters from The Bank of Nova Scotia. "I have consulted with Mr. Fyshe," Maclean had written in September. "You had better seriously consider the *best* way to wind up the whole business of the Liverpool Bank."[17] "I am getting very anxious," had come word a little later, and again, "Mr. Fyshe and I are much worried about it. . . . I have been thinking it would

John S. Maclean,
President, 1874-1889

be well to send Forgan down immediately...."[18] On December 24, a decision had been reached: "Forgan goes to consult with you about the bank and our interest in it.... You will require to submit your discounts to Forgan which you desire passed here – he will have to countersign any drafts you may make."[19]

Forgan had been Leslie's protégé in Scotland, and now, still a young man (he was in his late twenties), here he was an inspector of The Bank of Nova Scotia in control of the Bank of Liverpool's credit. His instructions were to examine the books and to prepare his own statement. He was to refuse to countersign drafts and was to take back with him to

Halifax the discounted bills of exchange, the uncollected notes, and all other securities of The Bank of Nova Scotia. "Mr. Leslie," not surprisingly, "...exhibited great annoyance at my visit, and was very independent and reserved."[20] The bank's directors backed up their Mr. Leslie. "...the president informed me," said Forgan, "that the Bank of Liverpool was an independent institution, and would not necessarily stop business in case The Bank of Nova Scotia closed its account."[21] And so Forgan returned to Halifax empty-handed.

Three weeks later, however, Maclean and Fyshe went to a Bank of Liverpool directors' meeting and obtained possession of Bank of Nova Scotia securities under threat of legal action. Furthermore, since the other principal creditor was the Government of Canada, with whom The Bank of Nova Scotia had already consulted, liquidation would now be imposed rather than suggested. If the assets of the Bank of Liverpool should prove to be insufficient, there would be a call on shareholders not only for any outstanding subscriptions but also for payments under the double liability clause.

By July 14, 1879, the process of liquidating the Bank of Liverpool was under way. The bank's door still remained open for business however, with the sign saying "Bank of Liverpool" still hanging over it. But The Bank of Nova Scotia was providing the necessary funds – an arrangement arrived at as the best method of collecting debts and realizing the Bank of Liverpool's assets. There was no intention, however, of relieving the directors of their responsibility.

On November 11, Sydenham Howe, an auditor of the Government of Canada and a son of Joseph Howe, was sent by the Government to Liverpool. There he met Forgan, sent by The Bank of Nova Scotia, and they summoned the directors. The next day, the assets of the Bank of Liverpool were assigned to The Bank of Nova Scotia.

Forgan was now in charge and he dealt with Leslie in his own way. He bolted a door which gave Leslie access from his living quarters upstairs to the manager's office on the ground floor, and thus he shut him off from the ledgers and the vault. With his privacy now assured, he immersed himself in the bank's books for three weeks. He emerged with a report that resulted in swift action. Leslie was called to Halifax, where he walked out of the office of the Cashier of The Bank of Nova Scotia as a man without a job. He had, he confessed, expected the worst when Sydenham Howe arrived and he had therefore taken the precaution of drawing his salary in advance.

Ahead of Fyshe, though he did not yet know it, were forty separate lawsuits and twelve years of litigation. Throughout those long years, Fyshe doggedly pursued the "Liverpool boodlers,"[22] who took advantage of loopholes in the Bank Act and used their political power; among the shareholders were senators, members of Parliament, and important ecclesiastics, who made every effort to avoid honouring their double liability obligation. In Fyshe's eyes, they were men who "button up their pockets and regardless of all considerations of honour, honesty, or even law, their own private character or the public good, fight for years against the payment of their debts and the people they have wronged."[23] Finally, by 1891 the tenacious Fyshe had achieved his objective and all the "Liverpool boodlers" were compelled to pay up.

THE BANK ENTERS PRINCE EDWARD ISLAND

Meanwhile, on February 15, 1882, at the annual meeting of The Bank of Nova Scotia it was resolved that an application be made to the Parliament of Canada for permission to increase the Bank's authorized capital from $1 million to $2 million,* "It having appeared to the Directors that several of the smaller Banks in the Lower [Maritime] Provinces may desire to become amalgamated with larger institutions, to their mutual benefit as well as that of the community at large...."[24] Seven months later, the Directors approved the absorption by the Bank of the Union Bank of Prince Edward Island.

The Union Bank of Prince Edward Island was one of the three banks which had been established on the Island and all three banks were experiencing difficulty in the 1870s. Just when the situation appeared to be improving, the largest and oldest of the three was forced into liquidation by the discovery that its cashier had absconded with nearly $400,000, twice the amount of the paid-up capital. Runs commenced on both the other banks and, although still solvent, the Union Bank of Prince Edward Island decided to seek amalgamation with a larger and stronger bank. The Bank of Nova Scotia was agreeable and the formal indenture of union was signed in 1883, with the Bank acquiring not only the Charlottetown business but also that at Summerside and Montague, where there were established agencies.

Thus, The Bank of Nova Scotia acquired good representation on Prince Edward Island. It also benefited in two indirect ways from the difficulties experienced by the other two banks. It took over the fine head office building in Charlottetown of the bank that failed. And it obtained the services of a young agent of the other remaining bank when the latter was forced to close its only agency; this young agent was H.C. McLeod, who was destined to succeed Fyshe as Cashier of The Bank of Nova Scotia fifteen years later.

---

* Since banking was one of the areas of responsibility assigned to the new Government of Canada under the terms of Confederation in 1867, The Bank of Nova Scotia was now subject to federal, rather than provincial, regulation. The first Canadian Bank Act - "that masterpiece," in the words of A.R.M. Lower[25] - was passed by the Canadian Parliament in 1871. The new Act did not differ appreciably from earlier legislation but it laid down in detail the rules of operation for the nineteen chartered banks then existing and established the requirements for the incorporation of new ones. Most significant was the limitation of bank charters to a period of ten years - the origin of the decennial review of the Bank Act.

The Bank of Nova Scotia began business in
Prince Edward Island in 1882. This building
was erected in Charlottetown in 1921.

EXPANSION IN THE OTHER MARITIME PROVINCES

Coincident with The Bank of Nova Scotia's extension into Prince Edward Island was its active expansion program in New Brunswick; no fewer than nine branches* were opened in that province in the early 1880s. Meanwhile, in Nova Scotia, two branches which had been closed in the 1850s had now been revived, and another new branch opened. Thus, at the end of 1883, when the takeover of the Union Bank of Prince Edward Island had been effected, The Bank of Nova Scotia had 23 branches throughout the Maritime provinces, an increase of 15 branches in as many years.

This was an outstanding achievement, accomplished as it was against the background of unfavourable economic conditions already referred to. At the same time that The Bank of Nova Scotia was expanding, two other Maritime banks failed and several others made little headway, succumbing in the next decade. The Nova Scotia, because it had developed wider connections and a more diversified business than the small local institutions, was better able to adapt to the financing of the new industries which came into being in this period. And it was eminently successful in its operation of a branch system – a system which, with rapidly improving transport and communication, was becoming best suited to Canadian conditions.

"A GOOD EXHIBIT"

The year 1882 marked The Bank of Nova Scotia's fiftieth anniversary. At the end of that year, the Bank's total assets were almost $6 million, as compared with a little over $2 million in 1870; paid-up capital, at $1 million, was nearly half a million larger; and there was $400,000 in the reserve fund. The Toronto *Monetary Times*, now commenting for the first time on the affairs of The Bank of Nova Scotia in far-off Halifax, declared its 1882 profits of $155,000, of which $75,000 was placed in the reserve fund, to be a "good exhibit."[26] Fyshe himself remarked in March of 1883, "I don't know whether we are better or worse than our neighbours. I only know that I have done my level best for the institution during the last seven years, and that it is in a very different position now from what it was when I took hold of it."[27]

---

* Though the Bank's offices outside Halifax were still referred to as "agencies" with "agents" in charge, they were more like present day "branches" run by "managers," since the staff was now directly paid by the Bank. The official change in nomenclature did not occur until 1898.

NOTES

1. BNS Archives, Thomas Fyshe to H.A. Flemming, dated Montreal, Nov. 18, 1907.
2. *Ibid.*
3. *Ibid.*
4. *Ibid.*
5. *Ibid.*
6. *The Bank of Nova Scotia One Hundredth Anniversary, 1832-1932*, p.55.
7. *Ibid.*
8. David R. Forgan, *Sketches and Speeches*, Chicago, 1925, privately printed, p.64.
9. BNS Archives, Fyshe to Agent, Saint John [June 1884].
10. *Ibid.*, Fyshe to George McLeod, dated Halifax, Jan. 10, 1888; also quoted in BNS *Monthly Review*, Aug.-Sept. 1952.
11. *Ibid.*, Account Book of President and Directors of The Bank of Nova Scotia, 1865-1896.
12. *Ibid.*, Fyshe to J.M. Robinson, Agent, Saint John, dated Halifax, Jan. 8, 1883; also quoted in BNS *Monthly Review*, Aug.-Sept. 1952.
13. James B. Forgan, *Recollections of a Busy Life* (New York: The Bankers Publishing Co., 1924), p.71.
14. Phyllis R. Blakeley, *Glimpses of Halifax, 1867-1900*, Halifax, N.S., 1949: Pub. No.9 of Public Archives of Nova Scotia, pp.147-49.
15. David R. Forgan, *op. cit.*, p.58.
16. *Ibid.*, p.59.
17. Public Archives of Canada (hereafter referred to as PAC), RG 19, Vol.3069, file 4242, J.S. Maclean to John A. Leslie, dated Halifax, Sept. 25, 1878.
18. *Ibid.*, Dec. 21, 1878.
19. *Ibid.*, Dec. 24, 1878.
20. PAC, RG 19, Vol.3059, file 4241A, affidavit of James R. Forgan, Supreme Court of Nova Scotia, Nov. 5, 1884, p.30.
21. *Ibid.*
22. PAC, RG 19, Vol.3060, file 4243, Fyshe to J.M. Courtney, Deputy Minister of Finance, dated Halifax, March 30, 1887.
23. *Ibid.*
24. BNS Archives, Report of BNS Annual Meeting, Feb. 15, 1882.
25. Arthur R.M. Lower, *Colony to Nation* (Toronto: Longmans, Green and Co., 1946), p.341.
26. Quoted in BNS *Monthly Review*, Aug.-Sept. 1952.
27. BNS Archives, Fyshe to Robert Steven, dated Halifax, Mar. 17, 1883; also quoted in BNS *Monthly Review*, Aug.-Sept. 1952.

5

Further Expansion – West, South, and Northeast 1882 – 1897

THE WINNIPEG EXPERIMENT

The year 1882 marked not only the Bank's fiftieth anniversary but also its first venture outside the Maritime provinces. In March of that year, E.H. Taylor, then the accountant in the Halifax office, was sent by the Board of Directors to Winnipeg to investigate the possibility of opening a branch in that boom town. On April 4, he wired Head Office excitedly, "Would strongly recommend opening immediately."[1] This the Bank did; Taylor was appointed acting manager and young David Forgan, who was now in charge of the general ledgers in Halifax, was sent out to be acting accountant. Having parcelled up a shipment of ledgers and banking forms and taking with him a leather bag filled with bank notes, Forgan followed Taylor's route: he went to Toronto via the Intercolonial Railway, from there to Chicago, thence to Minneapolis, and finally, north to Winnipeg.

The Pembina branch of the St. Paul, Minneapolis and Manitoba Railway had been completed only three years earlier and this new line, together with the newer prairie section of the Canadian Pacific Railway which was now well west of Winnipeg, had broken the relative isolation of the young province of Manitoba. Men and capital to develop the land and to provide the needed goods and services poured into the newly opened region. Soon, speculation in farmlands, townsites, and Winnipeg lots took hold. As a contemporary described it, "The excitement during the fall of 1881 amongst real-estate owners was intense. Thousands of dollars were made in a few minutes. Vast fortunes secured in a day."[2] And the *Monetary Times* made the wry comment, "Every day brings its new city, three feet square or more on paper – each claiming all kinds of super-excellent advantages, not to be found in London or Paris, Naples or Rome, New York or Chicago, or anywhere else in this habitable earth."[3]

By 1882, there were already four banks on Winnipeg's Main Street: the Merchants Bank of Canada, the Bank of Montreal, the Ontario

MAIN STREET, FROM DUNDEE BLOCK, LOOKING NORTH.

Bank, and the Imperial Bank. The cashier of the Merchants Bank later gave the following graphic description of banking in Winnipeg during the land boom:

> Swarms of Eastern people came to Winnipeg with money, deposited it in the bank, and bought all [the land] they could lay their hands on, paying down money for the first instalment and giving mortgages for the balance....
>
> Deposits increased *tenfold*. The amount of transactions passing through the office was incredible. The counter was thronged from morning to night by such crowds as are found at the doors of an Opera House when some celebrated prima donna is performing. A stranger would have supposed that some heavy run was taking place; but it was just the opposite. Most of these people wanted to deposit money, or to put in drafts for collection on distant points, transferring money to Winnipeg.[4]

The Bank of Nova Scotia entered this scene of banking frenzy immediately after the arrival in Winnipeg of David Forgan and his all-important bag of bank notes. Like his Merchants Bank colleague, he too reminisced years later about his experiences:

In its first venture outside the Maritime provinces, The Bank of Nova Scotia opened in Winnipeg in 1882 at the height of the land boom there. It closed its office in Dundee Block in 1885.
CREDIT: PROVINCIAL ARCHIVES OF MANITOBA

I took with me $40,000 in cash, and was seven days on the way, stopping a night at Chicago and two nights at Minneapolis. The cash was in a leather bag, and as I never parted with it for a moment day or night it became a great deal of a burden during that long journey. By reason of missing connections at Minneapolis I had to stay there over Sunday, and was two days later in reaching Winnipeg than I should have been. I resented the burden of carrying the cash, and so I forebore to telegraph the General Manager from Minneapolis. I thought I would give him a taste of the anxiety about that $40,000 which he had laid upon me, and I did, for when I reached Winnipeg, the Manager, who had preceded me, showed me several telegrams from the General Manager inquiring if I had arrived "with the remittance."

We had difficulty in securing an office in Winnipeg, but as soon as I arrived with the money we started business. For a few days, while a corner of an office was being prepared for us, I paid checks out of the leather bag attached to my person. After a while, we secured a fair office, but the security of the safe being doubtful, it became my duty to sleep in front of it on a shake-down and armed with a revolver. Our books from Head Office were expected daily, but owing to floods they did not arrive for six weeks, during which period I kept the records of the Bank on large sheets of manila wrapping paper. When the books came I had to copy the six weeks' work into them besides keeping up the daily records. This kept me at work every night until midnight for a while, and then I would prepare my bed in front of the safe and sleep until seven A.M., when I had to get out to make room for the scrubwoman. This was rather strenuous work, but I did not object. It was tinged with adventure and romance to my mind. Was I not a tenderfoot in the great Northwest, roughing it like a man...?[5]

Although The Bank of Nova Scotia's Winnipeg experiment was "tinged with adventure and romance," it did not turn out to be a profitable operation. The timing could hardly have been worse; the land boom lasted for a mere six months after the Bank opened for business. As well, Taylor was not a happy choice as manager; "a fine fellow – but not very shrewd,"[6] was David Forgan's opinion, expressed forty years later. Taylor made the mistake of getting caught up in the boom psychology and his business judgment was not sound. In his reminiscences, David Forgan tells a revealing story about Taylor's showing him "fourteen demijohns of liquor standing in an imposing row" – a present from a liquor dealer who "made a disgraceful failure within a few months," Forgan comments. And Forgan goes on, "these liquors cost the Bank exactly one thousand dollars a demijohn, or fourteen thousand dollars."[7]

Fyshe probably did not know the details of that bad loan, but he did chide Taylor on another aspect of his lending policies. "I cannot say I am very much impressed with the kind of paper which appears on your first discount list. A glance at it will show its prompt payment depends on the maintenance of increasing prices for land.... The moment they stop increasing these notes will be paid with difficulty."[8] Fyshe's fears were well-founded; when land values collapsed towards the end of the year, the Winnipeg branch of The Bank of Nova Scotia suffered substantial losses. "They tell me you have turned quite grey. I hope it is not through worry,"[9] he wrote to Taylor in January 1883. And in February, he sent David Forgan's older brother, James, out on an inspection trip.

Inspector Forgan's report to Head Office was not encouraging: "The business looks worse the farther I get into it. How such an accumulation of worthless parties could be taken on as customers is yet a mystery. Mr. Taylor seems to realize the mess matters are in.... He seems to have been carried away with the boom.... Some of his real honest decent men have a strange resemblance in my opinion to sharpers, and his good business men to bungling blockheads. His intentions have certainly been of the best and his energy in what he thought the Bank's interest of no ordinary quality. His judgment has however been bad and his energies misdirected."[10]

James Forgan stayed on in Winnipeg to direct the painful exercise of curtailing credit and realizing security. In the process, he noted that the Bank had acquired some "assets of rather a promiscuous nature here," including 147 spring beds and the furniture of a defunct hotel.[11] But he was able to state in April that "we have been wonderfully successful. In three months the loans have been cut down by...2/5ths of the whole.... If I am not mistaken we are now as unfettered and as well prepared to attend to new legitimate transactions as any of our contemporaries."[12]

However, new legitimate business was hard to come by, even though Fyshe hired Robert Steven, another former colleague from the Bank of British North America, to take over the troubled Winnipeg branch, and demoted the hapless Taylor to assistant manager. Fyshe's discouragement at the lack of progress in Winnipeg is very evident in his letters to Steven. Early in 1884 he wrote, "...I am not very well pleased with the appearance of your Liability Return.... I cannot help thinking Taylor has given the business a complexion which seems as difficult to get rid of as the Ethiopian found it to change his. I believe you listen too much to Taylor and are influenced by him unconsciously.... Now I want you to make it a point *never* to ask Taylor his opinion about anything and *never* to listen to it if you should hear it accidentally. And for God's sake try and get the old business into smaller dimensions."[13] And again, "Furthermore, it is quite evident that any accommodation paper whatever discounted in Winnipeg is intended to be carried till doomsday, which generally means till the failure of all the parties."[14]

In November 1884, H. C. McLeod, who was by now the Bank's agent at Amherst, Nova Scotia, was sent to Winnipeg to be the new manager of the branch, with a view to winding it up. James Forgan was also dispatched to Winnipeg again, this time to assist McLeod in his assignment. "Should either Mr. Steven or Mr. Taylor decline to resign you are authorized to dismiss them," Forgan was instructed.[15] Thus, McLeod and Forgan had a free hand in the task of terminating the Bank's unhappy first operation in Winnipeg, which they accomplished in 1885. The Winnipeg experiment had dragged on for three years and had been the source of substantial losses rather than the hoped-for profits. It would be another fourteen years until the Bank opened in Winnipeg again – in 1899 – that time to stay!

THE MOST DIFFICULT YEARS – THE EARLY 1880s

Unfortunately, the Bank's problems in Winnipeg in the early 1880s occurred during a period of general economic depression in Canada. A rash of business failures caused serious losses on loans for Canadian banks generally; they found it hard to employ their funds, competition among them became extreme, and money rates fell.

Banking in the Maritimes was especially difficult. The situation in Prince Edward Island which led to the absorption of the Union Bank of Prince Edward Island by The Bank of Nova Scotia in 1883 has already been recounted. In Nova Scotia, the Pictou Bank, which had been founded by a group of shipowners and merchants in 1874 and which had enjoyed several years of moderately healthy growth, was struggling to stay solvent. "Now its turn to go through the Mill has come,"[16] Fyshe commented in 1884. In 1886 the Pictou Bank transferred its agencies at Amherst, Stellarton, and New Glasgow to The Bank of Nova Scotia. And in 1887, it went into voluntary liquidation, "under the strong protecting arm of The Bank of Nova Scotia," in the words of the New Glasgow newspaper.[17] The same year, 1887, saw the failure of the Maritime Bank in New Brunswick. And two banks, one of them the historic Bank of New Brunswick, sharply reduced their capital stock. The *Monetary Times* commented, "two well-managed and enterprising institutions [reduced] their capital because they cannot employ it profitably in the locality and have not the machinery to employ it at a distance."[18]

The Bank of Nova Scotia was not immune to the trials and worries of this period. After the "good exhibit" of 1882, it was to have two of its worst years. Heavy losses were sustained in business failures in both 1883 and 1884. Early in 1884, Fyshe wrote to one of the Directors, "1883 is at last closed up in the Bank's books or nearly so. I never longed so much for the close of any year as for last.... We have written off our probable losses and will still have something to add to our Rest – But of course we have had to make use of our Contingent Reserve Fund.... The people, I am afraid, will think we have been cooking our books."[19]

However, the worst was yet to come, as Fyshe realized. In another letter in early 1884, he commented, "Failures are increasing rapidly,

H.C. McLeod,
General Manager, 1897-1910.
Considered to be one
of the Bank's best men,
McLeod was sent in 1884
to Winnipeg to wind up
what had proved to be
a costly experiment.

Further Expansion, 1882-1897

and they are now always disastrous.... The lumber trade is thoroughly flattened out. The tanning is not much better. Shipping or shipowning is almost worse than either. Marine insurance has become so unprofitable that... a dozen companies or associations... have had to wind up.... You know what Cotton is. We have three Companies in Nova Scotia and as many in New Brunswick struggling for a bare living.... The Dry Goods trade is in a bad way – both wholesale and retail and the West India business is again in the Hospital getting coopered up by the Ottawa Doctors.... Verily the National Policy is a great success!"[20] In July of the same year, he was of the opinion that "this is going to be the worst year for the Bank in its whole history."[21] And he was right (with the important exception of 1871, when the Bank's reserve was wiped out and its capital reduced as a consequence of the Forman defalcation). The Bank's 1884 statement showed a net loss of $46,000, and $130,000 was written off the published reserve. But the regular dividend was paid as usual. "We have had a terrible year's business," Fyshe commented. "It is to be hoped we may never see another such."[22]

The statement for 1885 did show considerable improvement. At the annual meeting in early 1886, the shareholders were presented with "a very plain" statement, but "much better than last year's." They were also advised of another development. "During the year we have had a very large amount of idle money which we were much puzzled to know what to do with; and knowing that other Canadian Banks have found profitable employment for their surplus funds in the United States... we determined after due consideration to send two of our best men... to Minneapolis."[23]

A SUCCESSFUL VENTURE INTO MINNEAPOLIS

"Two of our best men" were H. C. McLeod and James Forgan. In the autumn of 1885 they were sent to Minneapolis to investigate the possibility of the Bank's embarking on a lending and foreign exchange business in that thriving town in the American Midwest. Minneapolis was the leading flour-milling city in the United States and its wheat trade was second only to New York's. Its strong ties with Winnipeg, dating back to the bygone days of the Red River carts, were now strengthened by the new railroad. Also, and perhaps most important from the point of view of The Bank of Nova Scotia, it appeared to be under-banked.[24] According to a statement by the Minneapolis Chamber of Commerce in 1884, "with the large grain and manufacturing business carried on in Minneapolis, a much larger banking business could be profitably employed.... Most of our larger millers and manufacturers are forced to seek accommodation from eastern bankers during the busy season."[25]

McLeod and Forgan reported enthusiastically on the opportunities available in Minneapolis and accordingly, an announcement appeared in the *Minneapolis Tribune* on October 20, advising that The Bank of

Nova Scotia was now open for business on "premises lately occupied by Jobbers Association" and was ready to make loans, buy and sell exchange, and make collections "in all parts of Canada on the most favourable terms."[26]

Forgan, indeed, was so enthusiastic about the Bank's prospects in Minneapolis that he proposed that he and McLeod switch jobs.[27] In due course, this rather unusual arrangement was made, with McLeod returning to Head Office as inspector and Forgan remaining in Minneapolis as agent. Thus it was that, two years later, Forgan was in a position to be lured away from The Bank of Nova Scotia by the Northwestern National Bank of Minneapolis, which offered him the position of cashier at double his current salary;[28] he subsequently became president and then chairman of the First National Bank of Chicago. And he was also able to get a job in Minneapolis for his younger brother David, who had become discouraged by his slow promotion in The Bank of Nova Scotia.[29] David Forgan later succeeded his brother as cashier of the Northwestern National Bank of Minneapolis and then went on to be president of the National City Bank of Chicago.

When James Forgan resigned from The Bank of Nova Scotia in 1887, McLeod returned to Minneapolis as the Bank's agent. The two agents in succession, aided by Daniel Waters, who had been sent out to Minneapolis as assistant agent, built up a very active business, which was concentrated in foreign exchange dealings and in seasonal wheat and flour loans. It was not a general banking business such as had been carried on in Winnipeg and, significantly, loans were to be made only to "the best houses on good collateral security."[30] For seven years, the Bank was successful in using the expertise that had been developed in its ill-fated Winnipeg venture and in employing surplus funds in a profitable way in Minneapolis.

But, in 1892, when the Bank decided to open an agency in Chicago in anticipation of the Chicago Columbian Exposition of 1893, it was decided to close the Minneapolis agency. Minneapolis was no longer as attractive a location as it had been earlier. Between 1885 and 1892, twelve banks had been started and *Bankers' Magazine* commented in 1893, "The city is well supplied with banks."[31] Furthermore, as a consequence of a number of mergers, the Minneapolis milling industry was now dominated by a small number of large firms which generated much of their own capital and which looked to eastern rather than local banks for their short-term credit requirements. Finally, the Bank was concerned about its tax position in the state of Minnesota. The Bank had had an informal arrangement with the state authorities whereby taxes were imposed on the basis of only the capital assets employed in Minneapolis. It was feared that this arrangement might soon be terminated and, indeed, that taxes on total capital – which, of course, would be prohibitive – might be imposed retroactively.[32]

Occupying premises in the Loan & Trust Building
(at left, with spire), the Bank ran a highly
successful office in Minneapolis from 1885.
CREDIT: MINNESOTA HISTORICAL SOCIETY

THE MOVE TO CHICAGO

Thus, in September 1892 McLeod moved from Minneapolis to Chicago, where he leased space for the new agency of The Bank of Nova Scotia in the recently completed twelve-storey Northwestern Guaranty Loan Company building, the first skyscraper to be erected between Lake Michigan and the Pacific coast. The prospect of a profitable foreign exchange business during the impending Exposition was the immediate consideration in the Bank's decision to enter Chicago. A more fundamental reason was Chicago's recent rapid growth – it was now the undisputed hub of the American Midwest. And its importance as a banking centre was enhanced in 1892 when it was designated a central reserve city. The Bank's move to Chicago was a success, as is evident from an oblique complimentary remark made by Fyshe in one of his famous circulars to Maritime branch managers in June of 1893: "The Bank's loans in the lower provinces have increased nearly $400,000 since the 15th of May. All this money has had to be brought from Chicago where it might have been earning 10% or more."[33]

OPENING IN MONTREAL

When The Bank of Nova Scotia opened its agency in Minneapolis in 1885, it had no representation in Canada outside the Maritime provinces. As early as 1883, Fyshe had been considering opening in Montreal: "If we had an Agency of our own there we might utilize to the utmost all temporary floating balances, besides being in a better position to bid for Deposits when money gets tighter down here...."[34] However, no action was taken until August 10, 1887, when Fyshe read in the *Halifax Morning Herald* that "our friends, the 'Merchants' [Bank of Halifax],* have stolen a march on us and are about to open an Agency in Montreal."[35] Thereupon, a site for an office for The Bank of Nova Scotia was promptly chosen and in February 1888 Thomas V. MacDonald, "the best accountant we ever had," was sent to Montreal to open the branch. (Incidentally, it was MacDonald who had originated the idea of setting up a clearing house for the banks in Halifax in 1887 – the first such clearing house in Canada).

"What you say of the progress the City is making chimes in with my own ideas. I cannot see anything but a great future for Montreal,"[36] Fyshe wrote to MacDonald soon after his arrival. In July he visited the office and was satisfied with what he found. "I spent four days in Montreal and was very much pleased to see the business increasing there. It is not very much but it is improving and I am inclined to think that the improvement will continue."[37]

---

* Later (in 1901) The Royal Bank of Canada; its Head Office was moved from Halifax to Montreal in 1907.

Montreal, circa 1930.

When the Montreal office opened in 1888, it was the Bank's only Canadian office outside the Maritimes, the Winnipeg office having been closed three years earlier.

SOUTH TO THE CARIBBEAN

Two years after moving into Montreal, The Bank of Nova Scotia took a bolder plunge: in the summer of 1889 it opened a branch in Kingston, Jamaica. This was the first branch to be established by any Canadian bank in the West Indies. Indeed, it was the first time a Canadian bank had ventured outside the United States or the United Kingdom in its foreign operations. And the opening in Jamaica signalled a very important development in the Bank's history: it was its first step into active participation in the banking business in the islands of the Caribbean Sea.

Over a long period of time, The Bank of Nova Scotia had formed many close business connections in Jamaica, based on the substantial trade between the West Indies and Halifax. Fyshe's decision to open a branch of the Bank in Kingston in 1889 was prompted by a letter he received in March of that year from a former colleague in the Bank of British North America in New York. The letter contained a glowing account of a trip to Jamaica and Fyshe replied, "We have been repeatedly urged to open a Branch in Jamaica but we have always resisted – principally because we had enough to attend to nearer home, but also because we had the impression the Island was unprogressive....your letter, however, has started me on a course of inquiry....I shall... probably...go out myself."[38]

Fyshe did in fact "go out" the following month and found that his "impression the Island was unprogressive" was out of date. Economic conditions in Jamaica had improved in recent years as a result of several factors. The colonial government had instituted a number of political and social reforms. There had been advances in agriculture, particularly the introduction of irrigation. And exports had been facilitated by the improvement in shipping service. The output of the island's traditional products, sugar, rum, and coffee, had greatly improved and a new crop, bananas, was now being grown for the United States market.

"I have recommended that we open in Kingston, and the Board have agreed to it,"[39] Fyshe wrote on his return from his trip to Jamaica. And on June 13, William E. Stavert was transferred from Moncton to Kingston as the first manager. Stavert, later Sir William Stavert, did a good job of building up the Bank's business in Jamaica during the six years that he was there. Subsequently, he left The Bank of Nova Scotia and joined the Bank of New Brunswick and after that the Bank of Montreal, in both of which institutions he held senior posts. He was knighted for his service in the British Ministry of Information during the First World War.

NORTHEAST TO NEWFOUNDLAND

But Stavert had another assignment with The Bank of Nova Scotia before he resigned: in 1895 he was transferred from Kingston, Jamaica, to St. John's, Newfoundland, where the Bank had recently – and unexpectedly – opened its doors.

On December 10, 1894, remembered afterwards as "Black Monday," the two local banks which served Newfoundland failed within an hour of each other. The two banks had been unable to withstand the pressure of a chain of bankruptcies which had occurred because of a severe depression in the all-important fishing industry.

Understandably enough, panic seized the colony; the bank notes in circulation were worthless and there were no banking facilities. Three Canadian banks – the Bank of Montreal and the Merchants Bank of Halifax, in addition to The Bank of Nova Scotia – promptly sent officers to St. John's to help cope with the crisis, and also to look after their own interests. The first to arrive was Daniel Waters, who was now The Bank of Nova Scotia's Inspector, accompanied by J.A. McLeod (a distant young cousin of H.C. McLeod's), at that time assistant agent in Chicago. J.A. McLeod was to become the Bank's General Manager in 1923 and its President in 1934. Waters and McLeod opened a temporary branch of the Bank in St. John's on December 21, ahead of both the other two Canadian banks.

Thus, The Bank of Nova Scotia gained its first foothold in Newfoundland. By the time Stavert arrived a few months later to replace Waters, the office in St. John's was a permanent branch, and the Bank had extended its operations in Newfoundland by opening a branch in Harbour Grace as well.

Further Expansion, 1882-1897 73

FYSHE RESIGNS

The entry into Newfoundland was the last expansive push by The Bank of Nova Scotia under the Fyshe regime. In June of 1897, Fyshe, who was then only 52 years old, tendered his resignation as Cashier in order to accept an offer by the Merchants Bank of Canada* to be its associate general manager and, subsequently, its general manager. His second banking career lasted for nine years, this time in Montreal. After he finally retired from banking, he served on a Royal Commission on the Civil Service of Canada.

The minutes of the Board of The Bank of Nova Scotia on the occasion of Fyshe's resignation referred to the "most cordial and agreeable" relations which had existed between the Board and the Cashier. "Whenever we have differed...in the majority of instances we have been glad to defer to your judgment," the Directors stated.[40] The President of the Bank was now John Doull, who had succeeded J. S. Maclean on the latter's death in 1889. Doull, it will be recalled, had been President for a short span of only one year, seventeen years previously, when he had resigned because of the pressure of his own wholesale dry goods business. His second term of office as President lasted much longer – 10 years – from 1889 to 1899.

Fyshe's colleagues in the Bank paid him an apt tribute: "This long period embracing many of the best years of your life has been marked by occasions of great financial depression and consequent disaster to Banking Institutions but we cannot forget that adhering unfalteringly to the course of conservative management you have advocated, this Bank has been unaffected by the vicissitudes of the hour, and its progress in strength and stability has been steady and continuous."[41]

Notwithstanding the severe setback suffered in 1883-84, the Bank's overall progress during Fyshe's twenty-one-year tenure was certainly outstanding, though perhaps not "steady and continuous." Between 1876 and 1897, total shareholders' equity (capital stock and reserve) rose from $1.2 million to $3.1 million and total assets grew from $3.5 million to $15.1 million. In 1876, the Bank was represented by only nine branches, of which only the branch in Saint John, New Brunswick, was outside Nova Scotia. At the beginning of 1897, there were thirty branches: 13 in Nova Scotia, 9 in New Brunswick, 2 in each of Prince Edward Island and Newfoundland, and 4 outside the Atlantic provinces.

There is no question that Fyshe did adhere to a "course of conservative management" in his very meticulous direction of the day-to-day operations of the Bank, particularly in regard to credit: "The main condition of success in banking is not large profits but small losses,"[42] he said. Nevertheless, at the same time he pursued a policy of vigorous expansion which transformed the Bank from a relatively small Nova

* A Montreal-based bank which was taken over by the Bank of Montreal in 1922.

Staff of New Glasgow Branch in Nova Scotia, 1897.

The absence of desks behind the counter at the turn of the century left room for a bicycle, but staff worked standing or perched on high stools with no knee room at the counter. At back left is the stand-up ledger desk, and between that desk and the bicycle can be seen a letter press used for making copies in the days before typed carbons and photocopiers were in use.

Further Expansion, 1882-1897

Scotia enterprise to a sizeable institution, well represented throughout the Maritimes and also in such far-flung foreign points as Chicago and Kingston, Jamaica. And he pursued his expansionist policy during a period when economic conditions were unpropitious, to say the least, and failures of other banks were all too common an occurrence, particularly in the Maritimes.

In later life, he wondered about the outlook for continued banking growth. In 1905, in an article entitled "The Growth of Corporations," he wrote,

> Banking has been built up, or rather has grown up naturally out of two conditions, namely, industrial individualism and the credit system. We see that individualism rapidly is being replaced by what we have called collectivism in the shape of corporations; and when these are properly organized they will have little to do with credit. Given a legitimate business, well organized, and even to-day there is nothing easier than to raise the necessary capital to run it. Why then should it be necessary to borrow at all?[43]

Fyshe's successor, H. C. McLeod, later talked about his former chief's "incomparable rhetoric" and some "Fyshe stories" have already been told here. Not surprisingly, there are many other examples of Fyshe's wit in the Bank's Archives. However, the recipient of a communication signed "Your Obedient Servant, Thos. Fyshe, Cashier" might well be excused for failing to see the humour in such remarks as "We cannot afford to have an office chock full of dunderheads, as yours seems to be"[44] or "such loans as you have been making...will have no more chance of being authorized than there would be of a loan to a convict"[45] or "But it is useless to talk about colours to a blind man."[46] And the following message to an officer in Kingston, Jamaica, is certainly a model of brevity and comprehensiveness: "Business is quiet. Money abundant. Exchange hardly moving. Weather magnificent. Your dog is dead – poisoned."[47]

Though his humour could be biting, Fyshe had a very human side, which was evident in his frequently expressed concern for the welfare of the Bank's employees. "The Bank's officers are the Bank," he stated on one occasion.[48] And "apart from the interests of the Bank I cannot divest myself of my interest in you,"[49] he wrote to one officer, and to another he wrote, "If my criticism of your management has been harsh and unjust I shall greatly regret it."[50]

Writing about his former chief many years later, James Forgan attributed "a large part of such success as I may have since achieved as a banker to the experience gained under his discipline and tutelage....his heart was always in the right place."[51] And Forgan recounted the following illuminating story about a drive he and Fyshe had taken in Minneapolis:

> As we crossed the bridge over the Mississippi River, we saw some boys running back and forth over the logs in a boom. Suddenly, a

log at the edge of the boom on which a boy stood rolled over....We saw him disappear and then rise again in the strong current which carried him down with it....[Fyshe] jumped out of the buggy, ran down the bank and plunged into the river without removing his coat, his hat or the cigar in his mouth....a strong swimmer, he soon reached the boy whom he seized and succeeded in bringing to the shore. A number of people who had gathered on the bank of the river surrounded him to express their appreciation of his heroic action, but he pushed through them, jumped into the buggy and asked me to drive him to the hotel for a change of clothes.[52]

H. C. MCLEOD SUCCEEDS FYSHE

As has already been mentioned, Fyshe was succeeded in 1897 by H.C. McLeod, who was at the time the Bank's agent in Chicago. It is also worth noting that four other future General Managers, H.A. Richardson, J.A. McLeod, H.F. Patterson, and H.D. Burns, were already in the Bank's service, having entered the Bank during the legendary Fyshe years.

NOTES

1. BNS Directors' Minute Book, April 4, 1882.
2. Quoted in BNS *Monthly Review*, Aug.-Sept., 1952.
3. "Paper Cities in the Northwest," *Monetary Times*, Toronto, Jan. 1882; also quoted in BNS *Monthly Review*, Aug.-Sept., 1952.
4. George Hague, *Banking and Commerce* (New York: The Bankers Publishing Co., 1908), pp.381-82.
5. David R. Forgan, *Sketches and Speeches*, Chicago, 1925, privately printed, pp.61-62.
6. *Ibid.*, p.62.
7. *Ibid.*, p.62-63.
8. Quoted in BNS *Monthly Review*, Aug.-Sept., 1952.
9. BNS Archives, Fyshe to E.H. Taylor, dated Halifax, Jan. 10, 1883.
10. *Ibid.*, James Forgan to Fyshe, dated Winnipeg, Feb. 8, 1883.
11. *Ibid.*, Feb. 27, 1883.
12. *Ibid.*, April 30, 1883; also quoted in BNS *Monthly Review*, Aug.-Sept., 1952.
13. *Ibid.*, Fyshe to Robert Steven, dated Halifax, Feb. 28, 1884.
14. *Ibid.*, Fyshe to the Agent, Wpg., dated Halifax, April 30, 1884; also quoted in BNS *Monthly Review*, Aug.-Sept., 1952.
15. *Ibid.*, Fyshe to James Forgan, dated Halifax, Nov. 5, 1884.
16. *Ibid.*, Fyshe to George McLeod, dated Halifax, March 11, 1884.
17. *Eastern Chronicle*, New Glasgow, July 1886; quoted in James M. Cameron, "The Pictou Bank," *Nova Scotia Historical Quarterly*, June 1976, p.131.
18. "Banking Review," *Monetary Times*, Toronto, Feb. 5, 1886; also quoted in BNS *Monthly Review*, Aug.-Sept., 1952.
19. BNS Archives, Fyshe to S.A. White, dated Halifax, Jan. 5, 1884; also quoted in BNS *Monthly Review*, Aug.-Sept., 1952.
20. *Ibid.*, Fyshe to Edward Trout, dated Halifax, Feb. 21, 1884.
21. *Ibid.*, Fyshe to George McLeod, dated Halifax, July 25, 1884.
22. *Ibid.*, Fyshe to Robinson, dated Halifax, Feb. 10, 1885; also quoted in BNS *Monthly Review*, Aug.-Sept., 1952.
23. *Ibid.*, Report of BNS Annual Meeting, Feb. 17, 1886.
24. D.L.C. Galles, "The Bank of Nova Scotia in Minneapolis, 1885-1892," *Minnesota History*, Minneapolis, Minn., Fall, 1971, p.270.
25. *Ibid.*
26. *Ibid.*, p.268.
27. James B. Forgan, *Recollections of a Busy Life* (New York: The Bankers Publishing Co., 1924), p.93.
28. *Ibid.*, p.96.
29. David Forgan, *op.cit.*, p.69.
30. BNS Archives, Report of BNS Annual Meeting, Feb. 17, 1886.
31. D.L.C. Galles, *op.cit.*, p.274.
32. *Ibid.*, pp.274-76.
33. BNS Archives, Circular No.535, June 28, 1893.
34. *Ibid.*, Fyshe to James Burnett, dated Halifax, Mar. 7, 1883.
35. *Ibid.*, Fyshe to J.S. Maclean, dated Halifax, Aug. 10, 1887.
36. *Ibid.*, Fyshe to T.V. MacDonald, dated Halifax, Feb. 17, 1888.
37. *Ibid.*, Fyshe to H.C. McLeod, dated Halifax, July 7, 1888.
38. *Ibid.*, Fyshe to John Paton, dated Halifax, Mar. 12, 1889.
39. *Ibid.*, June 3, 1889.
40. BNS Directors' Minute Book, June 18, 1897.
41. Quoted in *The Bank of Nova Scotia One Hundredth Anniversary, 1832-1932*, Toronto, 1932, p.76.
42. BNS Archives, Circular No.483, Jan. 15, 1892.
43. Thomas Fyshe, "The Growth of Corporations," *Journal of the Canadian Bankers Association*, Vol.XII, 1905.
44. BNS Archives, Fyshe to George McLeod, dated Halifax, Oct. 23, 1883.
45. *Ibid.*, March 11, 1884.

46. *Ibid.*, Fyshe to T.V. MacDonald, dated Halifax, June 4, 1889.
47. *Ibid.*, Fyshe to George McLeod, dated Halifax, July 27, 1889.
48. *Ibid.*, Fyshe to Robert Steven, dated Halifax, Mar. 17, 1883; also quoted in H.D. Burns, "Thomas Fyshe," *Canadian Banker*, Autumn 1951.
49. *Ibid.*, Fyshe to George McLeod, dated Halifax, Sept. 30, 1884.
50. *Ibid.*, Fyshe to Robert Steven, dated Halifax, Oct. 6, 1884.
51. James B. Forgan, "In Memoriam of Fyshe," *Canadian Banker*, October 1911.
52. *Ibid.*

BANK BUILDINGS THROUGH THE DECADES

The Bank's Head Office building, Halifax, N.S. (above), opened in 1931.

From grand structures in major centres to modest ones in small towns, Scotiabank's buildings reflect the diversity of styles and the economic development of the past 150 years. The following pages offer a brief pictorial tour through our history.

Living With the Past

Many of our older branches continue in use today. Concerns for customer service and a pleasant working environment for our employees necessitate change, but, whenever possible, existing branches are modernized rather than replaced.

Scotiabank opened in Pictou, N.S., in 1839 and acquired this building from the Pictou Bank in 1887. It is still in use, although a new wing has been added and the interior, shown here in 1932, has been modernized.

The Amherst, N.S., branch looks much the same today as it did in this 1910 picture.

Built in 1905, the Dundas & Brock branch, Toronto, was renovated in 1977.

This Petrolia, Ont., branch was built for the Metropolitan Bank in 1911.

College & Bathurst, Toronto, was renovated in 1977, but the exterior was preserved. The design won an Award of Merit from the Toronto Historical Board.

Fitting into the community is an important aspect of branch design. In the 1920s the Chester, N.S., branch (left) looked like one of the houses on the street. The current Chester branch (below) fits the streetscape in scale and architectural detail.

The neighbourhood – and the trees! – grew up around the Codette, Sask., branch shown here in 1926 (bottom), but the branch exterior stayed basically the same for decades. A new branch was opened recently.

The Lyle Buildings

John M. Lyle (1872-1945) endeavoured to define a Canadian architecture, principles of which he applied to several buildings for The Bank of Nova Scotia. The Ottawa and Calgary branches shown here, as well as the Halifax and Petrolia branches shown on previous pages, are examples of that work.

Ottawa Main branch (opposite page) was designed in 1925 in what Lyle called a "modern adaptation of the Grecian Doric" style. The Calgary Main branch (top and right), designed in 1930, was the first in which Lyle used Canadian motifs – wheat sheafs, oil derricks, sunflowers, and even cowboys – in place of traditional Greek decorative forms. Large skylights provide the major source of natural light in both the Ottawa and Calgary banking halls. The Calgary building has now been sold, but the Ottawa branch is still in use.

Serving the Frontiers

Sometimes, reaching the customer is what counts. In 1934 in Oxford Mills, Ont., the Bank operated in a store (below). A granary served Hinton Highway, Alta., until a real branch could be built (bottom).

In 1957 uranium miners lined up on paydays at the Spanish, Ont., branch (right). During the early 1960s, Scotiabank brought banking service to 76 locations in Newfoundland and Labrador through a branch aboard the S.S. **Northern Ranger,** *a CN coastal steamer (below).*

From Coast to Coast

The Canadian branches of Scotiabank comprise a variety of architectural styles to match the variety of the country itself. Inside the branches, though, one thing is the same from coast to coast: courteous, efficient service from friendly, professional Scotiabankers.

Coburg & Robie, Halifax, N.S.:

The Bank of Nova Scotia has had a branch on this site since 1919. This building was erected in 1964.

Florenceville, N.B.:

The branch acquired through amalgamation with the Bank of New Brunswick was destroyed by fire in 1933. The style of the new branch, however, is well suited to its location.

Sussex, N.B.:

There has been a branch in Sussex since 1882. This modern building was erected in 1974.

Port Daniel Station, Quebec:

Opened in 1911, Port Daniel was a sub-branch to Paspébiac until 1913. The branch moved into this building in 1980.

Port Dover, Ontario:

The branch moved to this new brick building in 1980, but Scotiabank has been in Port Dover since 1955.

The new Windsor, Ont., branch (above) opened in 1979.

Winnipeg Main branch and Manitoba and Northwestern Ontario Regional Office are located in this building (below) on the corner of Portage & Main.

*The new home of Saskatoon Main branch and
Saskatchewan Regional Office was completed in 1980.*

*There are more than 30 Scotiabank branches in Vancouver, B.C.
Pictured (below) is Granville & 12th Ave.*

Bank Towers

Scotiabank's varied homes include high-rise office complexes in major centres around the world.

Vancouver Centre opened in 1977 and the Main branch and the B.C. and Yukon Regional Office are located here. The 25-storey building at King & Bay in Toronto (opposite) houses General Office. Built in 1951, it was the Bank's first high-rise office.

Alberta Regional Office and Calgary Main branch (opposite) are located in Scotia Centre, erected in 1976.

The new offices of The Bank of Nova Scotia Jamaica Limited were opened in 1979 (top right).

The artist's rendering (below right) shows the headquarters of Scotiabank de Puerto Rico, which is now under construction.

Brunswick Square, opened in Saint John, N.B., in 1978, reflects the Bank's Maritime roots in its nautical decor. New offices reflect new trends, but our heritage is not forgotten as we build for the future.

6

The Move to Toronto 1897-1909

THE GENERAL OFFICE IS MOVED TO TORONTO

The new Cashier of The Bank of Nova Scotia, Henry C. McLeod, was a man of action. (The title of the operating head was changed from "Cashier" to "General Manager" in 1898.) In November 1897, five months after his appointment, he opened a branch of the Bank in Toronto. Then in January 1899, he reopened the Winnipeg branch. And, most important of all, under the date January 19, 1900, the Directors' Minute Book recorded that "The General Manager...submitted for the consideration of the Board the subject of the removal of the office of the General Manager and his Staff from Halifax to Toronto, which was thereupon unanimously decided to be done at such early date as he should fix."[1]

In view of the number of years which McLeod had spent in the Bank's service in Winnipeg, Minneapolis, and Chicago, it is not surprising that he was convinced that its centre of operations should be moved westward. The Klondike gold rush and the completion of the Canadian Pacific Railway had heralded the beginning of the greatest period of prosperity which Canada had yet known. If the Bank was to become a national institution and to participate fully in this new prosperity, its headquarters needed to be more centrally located. The connections which the Bank had established in Winnipeg, Chicago, Toronto, and Montreal required facilities free from the delay attendant upon correspondence between these points and Halifax, and, more specifically, required closer and more direct control.

THE BANK'S BOARD OF DIRECTORS

Interestingly enough, the members of the Board who unanimously supported McLeod's proposal for moving the General Office of the Bank from Halifax to Toronto were all dyed-in-the-wool Maritimers.[2]

Jairus Hart,
President, 1899

John Y. Payzant,
President, 1899-1918

John Y. Payzant was one of these Maritimers. He had been elected President in 1899 – a position he was to hold for eighteen years. A lawyer and financier and a widely travelled man whose interests ranged from literature and theology to fishing and sports, Payzant was of Huguenot descent. His forebears had settled in Nova Scotia in 1753 before the British conquest of Quebec.

Succeeding Payzant as Vice-President of the Bank was Charles Archibald, a mining engineer whose family owned a coal-mining and -shipping firm in Cape Breton; his father had been the first Bank of Nova Scotia agent in North Sydney. Another member of the Board was Robert L. Borden, who was already a Member of Parliament and who would become leader of the federal Conservative Party in 1901 and Prime Minister of Canada in 1911. As well, there were Hector McInnes, who was, like Borden, a prominent Halifax lawyer, and G.S. Campbell, a shipping man, and two merchants, J. Walter Allison and R.B. Seeton.

There was little comment in the Halifax press about the relocation of

Canada Life Assurance Building, King and Bay Streets, Toronto.

The Bank of Nova Scotia rented the basement of this building as its first Toronto office from 1897 to 1904.

the Bank's General Office in Toronto. The March 23, 1900, issue of the *Acadian Recorder* simply reported that "It has been definitely decided that the General Manager's office of The Bank of Nova Scotia is to be moved to Toronto. The staff who will leave here for Toronto on Monday are: D. Watters [sic], chief inspector; W. Caldwell, chief accountant; E. Crockett, J. W. Huggies, P. C. Robinson, C. S. Jenner, J. K. Wannamaker, W. L. Keith, S. W. Mahon, H. D. Burns."[3] The last name on the list was that of a young man, twenty-one years of age, who would eventually become President and then Chairman of the Bank.

In March of 1900, the General Office staff of the Bank was installed in Toronto in the Canada Life Building on the north side of King Street, near Bay Street – coincidentally, the site of the present General Office building of the Bank. McLeod himself came to Toronto in April, having sailed from North Sydney on his cutter *Gloria*, soon to be known as the fastest ship on Lake Ontario.

THE BANK'S NEW GENERAL OFFICE BUILDING

McLeod was soon on the lookout for a more permanent home for the Bank in Toronto. In April of 1902, he acquired two lots, numbers 37 and 39, on the south side of King Street, just east of Bay, and in June he approved the plans for a five-storey building on the site. Payzant laid the cornerstone in December and the *Monetary Times* remarked, "This is not a skyscraping edifice for a hundred office tenants, but primarily a structure for a bank and its whole construction and appointments are subordinated to that purpose."[4] Commenting further on the plans, the newspaper admired the tall, columned front, the great banking room with its walls of varied marbles and its floors of mosaic tiles and the massive security of the vaults. Also, the new building was to have some impressive modern features: a steam-electric generating system and "a system of heat and ventilation – under which the entire air of the banking room will be changed every ten minutes." The Bank moved across the street into its new General Office Building in April of 1904, and in the same month, McLeod wrote a letter to his Board of Directors, describing the banking room as "so beautiful that it is a revelation to visitors."[5]

EMPLOYEES' PROPER CONDUCT

Coincident with his belief that the Bank should be properly housed was McLeod's emphasis on the proper conduct of Bank employees. Thus, the 1902 Manual of Rules and Regulations stipulated that "Officers found guilty of immoral practices, of visiting gambling houses or saloons, will be dismissed. In this connection Circular No. 868 is specially referred to."[6] The circular in question stated that "Although gratified by complimentary remarks on the comparative sobriety and general good behavior of this Bank's officers, frequently expressed by the public, we regret to find that the improper use of intoxicants, long the primary cause of much loss to the Bank, is not so exceptional as a perusal of the reports on the staff would indicate.... we now state it to be our policy to eliminate from the staff all who drink in saloons or use intoxicants in any other way than in strict moderation.... Some may defend a visit to a bar-room for a friendly drink with a customer on the plea of securing business; and doubtless, the customer seeing that such conviviality makes his banker more pliant, is likewise convinced that a saloon attachment is a desirable addition to a banker's office. However, we have been taught that the customer generally has the advantage in such bibulous financiering ...."[7]

EMPHASIS ON EFFICIENCY

Furthermore, McLeod emphasized that the Bank's staff should be efficient. Thus, according to Circular No. 829, "In addition to examination prior to admission of junior clerks it is proposed to require each

The first Bank of Nova Scotia General Office Building was erected in 1904 on the south side of King Street West, Toronto.

officer to pass an examination after being three years in the service. The examination will consist of a series of verbal questions by one of the Inspectors, the questions having special reference to the clerical work of a Branch, the Bank's rules, and so forth. Our object is to obtain for the Bank all the advantages to be derived from careful selection of its officers, the intention being to retain only the most promising young men. Those who are incapable or too indolent to become proficient in their chosen profession, or who have acquired objectionable habits, or whose penmanship unfits them for good work will be recommended to take up another calling.... each officer occupying the position of accountant, or who aspires to such a position, will be required to answer questions relating to double entry bookkeeping, the law of notes and bills, the customs of bankers and traders, commercial law, and generally on all matters that should be known by a good business man."[8]

THE UNIT SYSTEM OF WORK

Carrying his ideas on efficiency a step further, McLeod inaugurated the "Unit System of Work" in 1901. This is thought to be the first cost analysis conducted by a Canadian bank. Under the system, each branch manager made an estimate of the work done by each employee during the preceding year; then the average cost of the principal branch functions, divided into twelve categories, was calculated and the averages converted into units of labour. Using these calculations, bonuses were paid to the most efficient employees.

It will have become clear by now that McLeod was a strong leader and a very exacting General Manager. He set the same high standards for the staff of the Bank as those he lived up to himself and he had no use for anyone who did not measure up to them. He was also short-tempered; one of his clerks remembered his pulling the telephone from the wall and hurling it across the room when he became exasperated by a manager. On the other hand, he was willing to reward employees who did a good job. And he supported those he thought were being unfairly treated.

WITHDRAWAL FROM THE CANADIAN BANKERS' ASSOCIATION

A case in point was McLeod's withdrawal from the Canadian Bankers' Association in September 1899, in protest against a motion of censure which had been passed by the local branch of the Association against the Winnipeg manager of The Bank of Nova Scotia. The estrangement between the Bank and the Association endured for more than four years; it was not until March of 1904 that McLeod considered that the apology tendered to the Bank by the Association was suitably phrased and that the Bank could therefore return to the fold.

C.A. Kennedy, the Bank's manager in Winnipeg, who had very

recently reopened the branch, was accused of "calling at the offices of customers of certain other Banks doing business here and soliciting their accounts," a course which "has always been considered unprofessional, improper and unsafe by this Association."[9] Kennedy denied the charge and John Pitblado, who was then manager of Toronto branch and who had formerly been a clerk in Winnipeg, reported on the incident to McLeod.

It was, in fact, at Pitblado's instigation that Kennedy had made a call on a Mr. Campbell, who was a customer of the Merchants Bank of Canada. Pitblado had previously dropped in to see Mr. Campbell, who was a friend of his. "I led the conversation around in a natural way to banking....I asked if he had met Mr. Kennedy, our Wpeg Manager," he told McLeod. When Mr. Campbell said that he had not, "I said, 'You will find him very agreeable and I will bring him in if you would like to meet him.'" Pitblado did acknowledge that he "asked about his present bankers...& said if he felt like making a change we would be very pleased to take up his business." Mr. Campbell replied that he would be pleased to meet Kennedy, but a few days later when Pitblado returned with Kennedy, the friendly atmosphere had evaporated. "...the air felt chilly....As soon as I got out of the door, I told Mr. Kennedy something was wrong,"[10] Pitblado reported. It turned out that Mr. Campbell had been in touch with the manager of the Merchants Bank, and the consequence was the passage of the motion of censure at the next meeting of the Winnipeg Sub-Section of the Canadian Bankers' Association on April 19, 1899.

CBA "MUST BE FREE FROM HOLLOW PRETENCE"

McLeod was incensed and sent off a letter to the Winnipeg Sub-Section: "The usefulness of the Canadian Bankers' Association would seem to depend on avoiding the use of its name to foster prejudice or for personal ends, on its manifestos being free from hollow pretence and simulation, and on its actions being neither arbitrary nor intimidating."[11] And when his demand "that the council of the Association cause the resolution of that Sub-Section...to be expunged"[12] was ignored, he announced that "this Bank will, on 1st September next, cease to be a member of the Canadian Bankers' Association."[13]

The Winnipeg Sub-Section did, in fact, expunge the "obnoxious resolution," but in a manner that was not satisfactory to McLeod. He stuck by his decision to leave the Association and at the Association's annual meeting in Montreal in October, it was noted that "Your council regrets to announce the formal withdrawal of the Bank of Nova Scotia from the Association as of 1st September last....your council exerted its powers in the effort to bring harmony, but without success."[14]

In the succeeding four years, the council of the Association continued to exert "its powers in the effort to bring harmony" – a harmony the Association was, on its part, anxious to restore because deposit-rate agreements made under its umbrella were showing signs of weakening, not only in Winnipeg but also in Halifax.

On December 2, 1903, the following communication was received by Kennedy in Winnipeg: "The members of the Sub-Section...express themselves ready and willing to accept your denial as to the alleged charge in connection with the solicitation of accounts of other Banks, and to rescind any clause or clauses in said resolution reflecting on your actions. The members also unanimously extend to you a cordial invitation to rejoin the Sub-Section."[15]

Kennedy thought that the apology was satisfactory and he answered, "While I hesitate to reply for the Bank, I feel I am safe in stating that this will be equally satisfactory to the General Manager."[16] How wrong he was! McLeod scolded Kennedy for his "most amazing acceptance of their left-handed apology, if the word 'apology' can be used....you were asked to accept the surrender which was looked for to be unconditional, and the result was so near to a capitulation that it was simply a staggering blow to our faith in your diplomacy and tact.... we shall not accept, and the weakness shown by you leaves us to keep up the fight."[17]

THE BANK RETURNS TO THE FOLD

However, the fight lasted only three months longer. On March 1, 1904, the incident was finally closed. McLeod received the unconditional surrender he desired in the form of a resolution stating that "The Canadian Bankers' Association, having taken into consideration the fact that on the 19th of April, 1899, the Sub-Section of the said Association at Winnipeg, passed a resolution of censure upon the Winnipeg Manager of the Bank of Nova Scotia, containing a threat to the Bank of withdrawal of friendly relations; that, although notices of the meeting were sent to all members of the Sub-Section, the object of the meeting was not stated to the Manager of the Bank of Nova Scotia; that despite the denial of Mr. Kennedy, who alone of those present had any knowledge of the facts other than hearsay, the resolution was adopted, and that the charges made against Mr. Kennedy, and upon the basis of which the censure was passed, are now admitted by all parties to be untrue.

"*Therefore be it resolved*: That this Association desires to express to the Bank of Nova Scotia its sincere regret that a Sub-Section of this Association should have taken the action hereinbefore referred to, and that in the opinion of this Association the attempt to deal with such a charge by a vote of censure and intimidation was indiscreet and wholly *ultra vires*.

"The Association also desires to express its satisfaction that the above resolution, with the accompanying statement of facts, has been accepted by the Bank of Nova Scotia and by Mr. Kennedy as a satisfactory adjustment of the estrangement due to the action of the Sub-Section."[18]

WESTWARD EXTENSION

Meanwhile, McLeod had important questions of policy other than his quarrel with the Canadian Bankers' Association to consider. Having moved the General Office to Toronto, the next logical step was the extension of the Bank's operations to western Canada, where development was rapidly proceeding.

The Canadian Pacific Railway had been completed in 1885. With the advent of the twentieth century, thousands of miles of branch lines were now spreading across the prairies, and immigrants from Europe, the United States, and eastern Canada were beginning to pour into the West. Problems arising from the growing of wheat in the prairie climate, with its short growing season and its extremes of temperature, had been mitigated by the development of Red Fife wheat, a hard and early-ripening variety. Also, the introduction of new roller methods meant that this hard wheat could be milled into good flour. World demand for Canadian wheat was expanding and world wheat prices were rising. Grain elevators and towns were sprouting up along the branch railway lines, and manufactured goods were flowing in from eastern Canada. British Columbia was enjoying a boom as well, because of the coming of the CPR, the Klondike gold discoveries, and the development of forest resources. And the port of Vancouver, the Gateway to the Far East, was coming into its own.

Indicative of the opportunities which were opening up for Canadian banks in the West was a remarkable proposition put forward in 1903 by the General Manager of the Canadian Bank of Commerce to the Minister of Finance. Acknowledging the Bank of Montreal's historic role as principal banker to the Government of Canada, he suggested that the Bank of Montreal should retain that position only in eastern Canada and that a "certain geographical area covering a considerable extent of the more recently settled part of Canada should be set aside for [the Commerce]." Under such an arrangement, he wrote, "the relations of the Bank of Montreal with the Dominion Government would be lessened very little indeed, and they would enjoy as a result of their long connection with the Government the business arising from the richest and most densely settled part of the country. We, on the other hand, would be content to await the development of the newer part of Canada, with the hope that twenty or thirty years from now we would have relations with the Government perhaps as important as those of the Bank of Montreal at the present time. We [suggest] that all of Canada west of Assiniboia and all the country north of the fifty-first parallel and west of Hudson Bay should be assigned to us."[19] Not surprisingly, this novel proposal was turned down by the Minister.

The Bank of Nova Scotia, with its business still concentrated in the

Maritimes and with only one branch beyond the Head of the Lakes, at Winnipeg, was not in a position to formulate any such grandiose schemes. In the same year, 1903, the Directors of the Nova Scotia made a more modest decision: that a proposed opening of a branch in Windsor, Nova Scotia, be deferred "In view of the importance of establishing some Branches of the Bank in the North West as soon as possible...."[20]

OPENING IN EDMONTON

Edmonton, on the North Saskatchewan River, was an obvious choice for a branch location. As a centre of the fur trade and a focus of river traffic, it had long been dominant in the economy of the Northwest. It had served as a supply base and transit point during the Klondike gold rush days and now that the gold fever was subsiding, settlers were beginning to settle the land around the town. On May 18, 1903, E.T. Hammett, F.W. Ross, B.P. Alley, and Morris Kinnear arrived in Edmonton to find quarters for a branch of The Bank of Nova Scotia.

At that time, the population of the town numbered about four thousand, and there was the usual prairie atmosphere provided by frame and false-front buildings and hitching posts and bars. Since branches of the Canadian Bank of Commerce, the Bank of Montreal, the Merchants Bank of Canada, the Imperial Bank, and the Union Bank had all been established, the choice of premises for the Nova Scotia was limited to a decrepit old store. It provided a narrow banking room at the front, together with a back room which was equipped with a Ping-Pong table. On days when there were not many customers, as was frequently the case throughout most of the summer, one of the staff kept watch while the others improved their game.

A low-level railway bridge across the North Saskatchewan linked Edmonton to Strathcona (now South Edmonton), the terminus of the line from Calgary. In June, Ross and Kinnear opened a sub-branch in a hotel in Strathcona; the Bank's space was part of the bar, which had been partitioned off. Declining an offer from the proprietor to exchange a tap to his beer keg for a key to the Bank's safe, Ross and Kinnear went in August to investigate the possibility of opening in Wetaskiwin, some forty miles down the railway line. The two men were there in early September when an urgent message called them back to Edmonton: the General Manager of the Bank, Mr. H.C. McLeod, the Vice-President, Mr. Charles Archibald, and two other Directors, Mr. G.S. Campbell and Mr. J. Walter Allison, were all arriving on a tour of the West.

THE DIRECTORS' TRIP TO WESTERN CANADA

The imposing party came to Edmonton in a large four-seated carriage, which jolted across the railway bridge from Strathcona, Ross recalled many years later. The ride was so rough that, on the return journey, a piece of luggage containing a copy of the Bank's cipher code fell from the carriage undetected. Although a diligent search was made, no trace of the suitcase was found and a new cipher code had to be drawn up.[21]

Ross's description of his own railway journey across the prairies to Edmonton is of interest: "From Moose Jaw to Swift Current was then for the most part a lone land; we scanned the far horizon and saw wolf, coyote, fox, gopher, duck, antelope – but little human habitation."[22] However, Regina and Saskatoon, circled by homesteads and miles of wheatfields, were now rising in the emptiness. And Calgary, built by ranchers and made prosperous by the railway, already had handsome streets and homes.

The Directors of the Bank were impressed by their glimpse of the prairies, and also of Vancouver, which they visited as well. On October 20, 1903, "the Directors present having returned from their trip through the Western parts of the Dominion... it was therefore decided to establish branches as soon as convenient, in the following places, viz: Vancouver, B.C., Calgary, N.W.T., Wetaskiwin, N.W.T. and Fort Saskatchewan, N.W.T."[23] Unfortunately, this early foray by The Bank of Nova Scotia into the West beyond Winnipeg turned out to be disappointing. Branches established in Strathcona, Wetaskiwin, and Fort Saskatchewan all proved to be unprofitable and were soon closed. Branches in Edmonton, Calgary, and Vancouver took many years to join the one in Winnipeg as money-makers. In 1906, following the creation of Saskatchewan as a new province, the Bank opened in Regina and also in Saskatoon. Three years later, expenses at Saskatoon were barely being recovered, while the loss shown at Regina was $16,000. Yet, these branches in the key centres in western Canada had to be maintained, even though they were expensive and difficult to staff.

Inadequate housing was an important factor in the staffing problem, as the following letter written in June of 1906 to the General Manager by the Saskatoon manager so graphically indicates:

> Since coming to this town, I have found it an absolute impossibility to rent a house, and, consequently, like a great many others, I have been obliged to live in a tent since last April.... The hotels here make no allowance for board by the month, and their prices are therefore prohibitive. Most of the houses in this town are, as yet, of the shack variety, but I have now an opportunity of obtaining one of very moderate proportions, for which the absurd rental of $45 a month is asked. I wish to say that with my living allowance, I am unable to pay this rent, my expenses for the past year, while living in a very modest manner, being somewhat more than my salary.... Having had sufficient of tent life, I wish to ask your consideration for an extra living allowance to enable me to take the house mentioned.[24]

The manager received a salary increase the very next month.

EXPANSION IN THE EAST

Meanwhile, a happier story of expansion was unfolding in the Bank's home territory of the Maritimes. Between 1897 and 1909, nineteen new branches were opened in Nova Scotia and New Brunswick. And four branches were added in Quebec, two of them in Gaspé fishing towns and one in Quebec City. Also, there were sixteen new branches in Ontario in this period. From Ottawa, Berlin (now Kitchener), and Arnprior at the beginning of the 1900s, the Bank moved into Hamilton with the development of the steel industry. Branches were opened in Peterborough in 1905, in London in 1906, and in St. Catharines in 1907. In the year 1908 alone, seven new branches were added in Ontario, with an emphasis on industrial centres such as Welland and Brantford. And in 1909, a connection with a pulp, paper, and lumber company took the Bank as far west as Rainy River, near the Manitoba border.

GROWTH IN THE WEST INDIES ACCOMPANIED BY PROBLEMS

The Bank had developed a solid and profitable business in Kingston, Jamaica, and building on that base, the Bank opened branches in Montego Bay and Port Antonio in 1906, in Mandeville in 1907, and in Port Maria and Savanna-la-Mar in 1908. But extension to Trinidad in 1906 proved to be an unhappy venture. E. T. Hammett, who had been sent from Edmonton to manage the new branch in Port-of-Spain, died within six months of yellow fever, and since the disease was endemic and therefore the rest of the staff was threatened by it, the branch was closed.

About the same time, the Bank turned its attention to Cuba. Having won its independence from Spain in the Spanish-American War of 1898, the island had embarked on a modernization and improvement program which was stimulated by U.S. investment. In consequence, its cane sugar and tobacco production expanded. In 1906, the Bank opened in Havana and a year later it entered Cienfuegos, the second city of the island. For F. W. Ross, another Edmonton banker now transferred to the Caribbean – to Havana – the sight of swarms of workers piling sugar cane onto oxcarts on the great plantations soon became a familiar sight.[25] So did the tobacco fields, covered over with cheesecloth to protect the plants from the sun and rippling like breezy lakes. Half a century later, Ross still had vivid recollections of the intense heat and the unfamiliar smells of the city, with its twisting streets and its barred and grilled houses. And he remembered the loneliness of this foreign country, whose language he did not know and where the constant fear of fever hovered over everything.

Paspébiac, 1915.

The Bank of Nova Scotia's second Quebec branch opened in Paspébiac on April 29, 1898.

Kingston premises six days after the earthquake in Jamaica in 1907.

EARTHQUAKE IN JAMAICA

It was a natural disaster in Jamaica, however, which posed the greatest single problem for the Bank in the West Indies in this period. On January 17, 1907, the island was struck by a tremendous earthquake which destroyed countless buildings, including the Bank's premises in Kingston; the branch was buried beneath layers of burning rubble. First reports of the disaster were relayed by ships at sea because cable lines had been broken. It seemed impossible that the Bank staff could have survived.

They had done more than survive, however, as McLeod learned four days later when he arrived in Kingston himself. The ruins of the branch were in the midst of a scene of desolation, but the building's "iron verandah with its pillars withstood the shock and saved the staff from annihilation."[26] Every member of the staff was alive and well, and they had all pitched in to help clear the buildings around their own blazing wreck. Later on, they had made their way back and had managed to find the door of the vault and to lock up the cash and ledgers. The next morning, returning with picks and shovels, they had cleared away the debris from the red-hot vault, which, after allowing to cool, they had been able to open. By the time McLeod arrived, the tired staff, armed with scorched books and the cash intact, had inaugurated

Two of the cottages of the Acadia Club in Kingston, which was built in 1908 at the direction of H.C. McLeod to provide housing and recreational facilities for the Bank staff.

emergency service from a room in Government House. Subsequently, long leaves and special holiday allowances were the order of the day for those who had worked so hard.

THE BEGINNINGS OF THE ACADIA CLUB

A crisis had taken McLeod to Jamaica. But when he was there, he was struck by the fact that the Bank was not coping with another problem of a very different kind: that of boredom and restlessness, particularly on the part of younger staff members. On March 5, 1908, he wrote a report on the subject to the Board. In the West Indies during 1907, the Bank had spent some $3,200 on staff transfers, most of which were returns because of ill health. "Young men sent from the North go to Kingston and have little to engage their attention after business hours. They become tired of reading at their boarding-house, and as there is but little society, they commence to complain that 'We have nothing to do, nowhere to go for amusement.' Naturally they apply to be removed North, generally sick."[27]

McLeod had a proposal which was aimed at making the leisure hours of the Bank's employees in Jamaica more enjoyable. He had engaged an architect to draw up plans for staff quarters to be built on a 143-acre piece of wooded property owned by the Bank just outside

Kingston. McLeod described the plans in the following terms: "These will consist of a dining room, billiard room and reading room....There will be a bungalow to accommodate about eighteen clerks;...The dining room will be used in common....We will put in lawn tennis equipment and also add three or four, or perhaps more, holes for golf playing. Furthermore, each clerk will be permitted to keep a pony, and where an officer is not able to purchase a pony, I would suggest that the Bank purchase one for him."[28] Such was the origin of the Acadia Club.

MCLEOD'S LOVE OF YACHTING

While McLeod might refer to billiards, lawn tennis, golf playing, and pony riding as suitable forms of recreational activity for his staff in Jamaica, his own particular avocation was yachting. It was sometimes said of him that he had moved the Bank's General Office to Toronto because he preferred yachting on the Great Lakes to that on the Atlantic! He would have been sympathetic to the opinion expressed by the Water Rat in *The Wind in the Willows* that "there is *nothing* – absolutely nothing – half so much worth doing as simply messing about in boats." However, McLeod would have ranked banking ahead of boating, and he didn't mess about in boats – he raced them.

In 1899, while he was still in Halifax, McLeod had designed the sloop *Minota* as a contender for the Canada Cup, in recognition of which he was awarded a life membership in the Royal Canadian Yacht Club when he moved to Toronto. The cutter *Gloria*, in which he sailed to Toronto in 1900, had been bought by him in Southampton. She was apparently too fast for his new Toronto sailing friends, since the RCYC barred her from competition. But McLeod had his sights set higher than racing on Lake Ontario; in 1909, his 98-foot *Amorita* won the New York-Bermuda yacht race.[29]

THE ARGUMENT ABOUT THE LIMIT ON THE BANK'S NOTE ISSUE

Not only did McLeod like to win yacht races but he also liked to win arguments about questions of principle. He had the satisfaction of scoring a total victory in his battle with the Canadian Bankers' Association. However, the outcome of another long-drawn-out dispute of a different kind with the Deputy Minister of Finance was still unresolved when McLeod resigned as General Manager in 1910. This argument concerned the legal limit on the Bank's note issue and the exaction of fines whenever that limit was exceeded.

McLeod agreed with Fyshe's characterization of one of the clauses of the 1890 Revision of the Bank Act as "a rotten law which has neither rhyme nor reason to it."[30] The clause in question limited the amount of each bank's note issue very strictly to the amount of its paid-up capital and required the payment of a stiff penalty if that limit should be exceeded even for one day. Even under the most favourable circumstances, keeping track of the amount of bank notes outstanding was a difficult task for banks with a large number of branches, and when the Canadian economy expanded around the turn of the century, the situation became almost intolerable. The rising cash requirements of the country strained the banks' resources to the limit. In an attempt to cope with the problem, they paid out their competitors' notes whenever they were available, and some banks (*not* including the Nova Scotia) wrote off older issues as lost, destroyed, or irredeemable for some other reason; such issues would thus not appear as a liability on the balance sheet of the bank in question, though in fact many of the notes might still be in circulation.

On July 4, 1901, in spite of careful bookkeeping and a daily exchange of telegrams with all major branches, McLeod had to report to the Deputy Minister of Finance that an exceptionally heavy amount of business that day had pushed The Bank of Nova Scotia's note circulation to some $15,000 above its legal limit. In view of the short duration and the immediate correction of the error, he requested "that you will treat the offence as lightly as possible."[31] The Bank was charged with a fine of $1,000 and the Bank paid it.

In November of the same year, however, McLeod wrote to the Deputy Minister complaining that "The Banks are now circulating one another's notes to such an extent that the advantages, protection and limitation afforded through competition bringing about daily redemption no longer exist....it would be easy for a small bank to circulate many times the amount of its capital...a condition tempting to the unscrupulous...."[32] The Bank Act had just undergone its periodic revision and the so-called "rotten law" pertaining to the limitation on bank note issues had been retained. McLeod suggested in his letter that the Bank Act should be amended again as soon as possible, so as to permit the banks to increase their note circulation up to an equivalent amount of gold deposited with the government. This suggestion was ignored by the Deputy Minister and also by the general managers of the other banks when McLeod put forward the idea to them.

The problem of an excessive note issue by The Bank of Nova Scotia arose again in 1907. Between March 30 and April 1 of that year, in the confused state of affairs existing after the disastrous earthquake in Jamaica, there was an over-issue of some $30,000 by the Bank's branch in Kingston. This transgression called for a $10,000 fine. McLeod asked that the error be overlooked, pointing out that the Nova Scotia, unlike other banks, listed its total note issue as a liability, although there were issues outstanding on which not a note had been presented for half a century.[33] The Deputy Minister was prepared to halve the fine, but McLeod flatly declined the offer. "We are not so much concerned over the amount as over the principle involved, and I regret to have to say that the suggestion is not a satisfactory solution of the difficulty,"[34] he wrote in May. In August and again in November, the Deputy Minister renewed his demand that the fine be paid.

Payzant and several other members of the Board came to Toronto in December and suggested to McLeod that the time to pay had come; L.D. Murray, who was the General Manager's clerk at this time, recorded many years later that he "heard snatches of raised voices as I opened the [Board Room] door."[35] But McLeod was stubborn and wrote his last word on the subject to the Deputy Minister in January 1908, "We feel that this Bank is not justly entitled to pay the fine mentioned in your correspondence, at least until other banks are compelled by your Department to pay the penalties so long overdue, and we, therefore, decline to accede to your suggestion in the matter."[36]

And there the dispute about the fine rested; it would be another three years before the succeeding General Manager, H.A. Richardson, would settle the matter. And two years after that, the 1913 Revision of the Bank Act included McLeod's idea for permitting the banks to expand their note issues on the basis of gold deposits with the government.

MCLEOD'S CAMPAIGN FOR EXTERNAL BANK INSPECTION

Another of McLeod's pioneering ideas about Canadian banking reform was that all banks should be subject to external inspection. This radical notion, popularly known as "McLeod's Fad," was prompted by the proliferation of bank failures; between 1895 and 1910 there were no fewer than nine failures of Canadian banks, five of them involving deposits of $1 million or more.[37] Nevertheless, it was not until 1924, the year after the failure of the Home Bank and two years before McLeod's death, that the office of Inspector General of Banks was finally created (though the mandatory shareholders' audit was inaugurated earlier – in 1913).

As early as 1901, McLeod wrote to the Deputy Minister of Finance that he was "anxious to have and will later urge a general inspection of all banks by the Department of Finance,"[38] a notion which he enlarged on and actively promoted in succeeding years. The seed of his idea, however, fell on stony ground in the banking world as well as in government circles. The notion was dismissed by eminent bankers (including Thomas Fyshe!) in the following terms: "What manager or director in control of any of our banks would be content to be taken charge of, like so many stupid, errant schoolboys, and twisted or guided or bullied into a condition of fitness, by irresponsible auditors or inspectors, carrying probably less weight than some of their own clerks?" and "Neither Government inspection nor compulsory audit can do for us what our trained bankers do....there are many forms of possible loss to shareholders which no Government inspection or audit by a chartered accountant could detect....In the last analysis a bank must be judged by its board and by the men who constitute its management, not merely at head office, but at its branches, and it is not so difficult as some would have us think to judge whether a bank is carefully officered and safely managed or not."[39] The November 10, 1906, issue of the *Monetary Times* commented that "There is one among the general managers of banks who approves of government inspection, but probably he stands alone."[40]

THE FIRST AUDITED STATEMENT OF A CANADIAN CHARTERED BANK

At that time, the "one among the general managers of banks who approves of government inspection," McLeod, decided that The Bank of Nova Scotia should no longer delay in having its affairs inspected by an outside agency. Accordingly, he advised the Board, "if we take the initiative in having chartered accountants verify our next annual statement I think we will still further entitle ourselves to the full confidence of depositors and of the public generally. I am today writing the Manager of the Royal Bank of Scotland, London, requesting him to put us in communication with the auditors that verify their statements, or with any others that he may think superior."[41] Accordingly, two Scottish chartered accountants, D.H. Huie and J. Maxtone Graham, arrived from Edinburgh in December. In January of 1907 the shareholders of The Bank of Nova Scotia received the first statement of any Canadian chartered bank to be verified by independent, external audit. And six years later, the 1913 Revision of the Bank Act made the shareholders' audit compulsory for all the banks, as has already been mentioned.

MORE STRINGENT CASH RESERVE REQUIREMENTS

Thus, two of McLeod's ideas for the improvement of the Canadian banking system – that a controlled expansion of bank note issues should be allowed and that all banks should be subject to external examination – were slow to gain acceptance. He was more fortunate with a third important reform which he promoted: that banks' cash requirements should be made more stringent. The average of bank cash reserves had declined from 13 per cent of their liabilities in 1885 to less than $7\frac{1}{2}$ per cent in 1901.[42] McLeod pushed for a legal reserve requirement of 10 per cent for all banks, and his campaign bore fruit. In 1909, he wrote, "Single-handed I advocated an enactment for increased Cash Reserves. The enactment did not carry but the same result was accomplished through action by the [Canadian Bankers'] Association, no doubt at the direction of the Finance Minister. In any case, I am satisfied with the result."[43]

REFORM: NOT A POPULAR STANCE

Not surprisingly, McLeod's pressure for reform, which he exerted throughout his tenure of office by means of a bombardment of letters and printed pamphlets, did not endear him to his banking confreres. He acknowledged his unpopularity with some members of the Canadian Bankers' Association. "I confess to a contempt for several features of the Canadian Banking System and perhaps am not sufficiently complacent to altogether hide that feeling when seeking to remove the objectionable features," he admitted to the Board of The Bank of Nova Scotia. But, he went on, "I will not be led by any banker or body of bankers in regard to any essential matter on which my judgment differs from the majority."[44]

THE "BANK INSPECTION" PAMPHLET

In November of 1909, after failing to realize "a faint hope...that the bankers would go on record in favour of some effective system of inspection," McLeod took the unusual step of circulating "to legislators, to bank shareholders, and to the public generally"[45] 60,000 copies of a pamphlet entitled *Bank Inspection: The Necessity for External Examination*. A circular accompanying the pamphlet stated that, "Since 1865 Shareholders in Canadian Banks have lost approximately $40,000,000 through bank failures....Banks should be stable; they should exist indefinitely; and failure through speculation and fraud should be made to practically cease....external supervision has been successfully adopted as a remedy in countries transacting more than three-fourths of the business of the world....I suggest your personal investigation of the subject, in the hope that you will use your influence towards legislation...."[46]

There was a prompt reaction from Aemilius Jarvis, a prominent Toronto stockbroker, a shareholder of the Bank's and also a customer (though a disgruntled one, as it turned out). He had been a personal friend of McLeod's – they were fellow yachtsmen – but their relationship had cooled in recent years. Also, Jarvis had been the last president of the Sovereign Bank, which had failed in 1908 and whose orderly liquidation the Nova Scotia, in conjunction with other banks, had helped to support.

In his capacity as a shareholder, Jarvis complained at length in a letter to Payzant written on December 7, 1909, "I fail to see why our General Manager should constitute himself the financial policeman for the Dominion....From Mr. McLeod's propaganda I am confident that our Institution will be attacked on an entirely different point from any which the Directors contemplate, wholly due to the aggression, unpopularity and what some consider unwarranted interference of our General Manager....I feel so strongly on this subject...that I shall be much obliged if you will be good enough to lay this correspondence before your Board."[47]

Payzant did as he was asked and also forwarded the letter to McLeod, who reacted with the remark "that so far as banking capacity is concerned Jarvis is an infant." And McLeod elaborated, "Since our

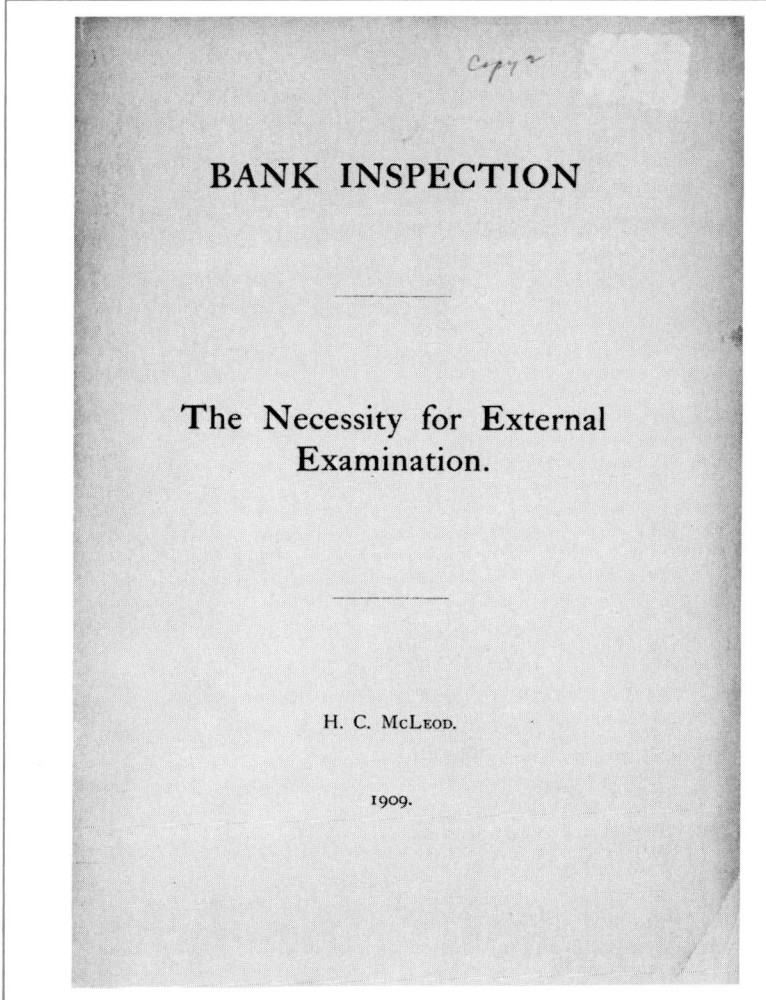

H.C. McLeod promoted his ideas on bank reform through pamphlets. This call for the external audit of banks evoked great controversy in banking circles.

refusal to carry [certain loans] Mr. Jarvis...has acted in a most unfriendly way. But vilification of those who oppose him is his most prominent characteristic." So far as Jarvis's arguments against bank inspection were concerned, McLeod concluded, "they are the arguments of B.E. Walker [the General Manager of the Canadian Bank of Commerce] and I look upon the whole scheme as an attempt to intimidate the Directors in order to produce friction between the Board and the Management."[48]

There was no doubt that by this time there was some friction between the Board and the General Manager, but it was not the result of a scheme perpetrated by Jarvis. McLeod was determined to carry on his crusade for banking reform, particularly for external inspection, while some of the Directors felt that he should concentrate his efforts on the business side of banking.

MCLEOD'S RECORD

"During the term of my management the Bank has been not only the strongest but the most successful from a profit standpoint,"[49] McLeod stated, perhaps somewhat defensively, as the year 1909 drew to a close. In response to his solid program of national expansion and also to the favourable economic climate of the period, the Bank showed good progress during McLeod's term of management: between 1897 and 1909, over fifty new branches were opened; total assets more than tripled (from $15 million to $48 million); and shareholders' equity rose from $3 million to $8½ million. And McLeod noted that the price of the Bank's stock had risen by over $80 per share, moving from fifth place in 1897 to first place among all Canadian bank stocks. He also pointed with pride to the rise in the dividend rate: from 8 per cent to 12 per cent of capital.[50]

But the time for McLeod's departure from The Bank of Nova Scotia had come. At the age of fifty-nine, he resigned as General Manager at the Bank's annual meeting on January 26, 1910. As might be expected, he took advantage of the occasion to fire off one last volley: "...I am not satisfied with banking conditions in Canada.... All the members of the Canadian Bankers' Association are opposed to changes that I have urged with the object of doing away with secretive management and they suggest no other remedy for the demonstrated weaknesses of our system.... Eventually the more important changes advocated will come. Secretive management must end. But I have not the patience to await these changes, nor the disposition to quietly tolerate banking practice that has produced so much loss.... Therefore, I have asked the privilege of retirement."[51] For their part, the Board treated McLeod generously, granting him a retirement allowance of $20,000 per annum for life, on the stipulation that "Mr. McLeod will not enter into the services of or become a director of any Bank doing business under the Bank Act."[52]

THE NEW GENERAL MANAGER: H.A. RICHARDSON

As his successor, McLeod had nominated Daniel Waters, who was then Assistant General Manager and who was the officer who had drawn up the Manual of Rules and Regulations in 1902. But the Board, in approving Waters's promotion from Superintendent of Branches to Assistant General Manager four years before, had stated that "such appointment shall not be regarded as in anywise affecting the future action of the Board in the selection of a successor to the present General Manager."[53] Now they selected instead the forty-eight-year-old manager of Toronto branch, H.A. Richardson, as the new General Manager.

NOTES

1. BNS Directors' Minute Book, Jan. 19, 1900.
2. James Douglas Frost, *Principles of Interest, The Bank of Nova Scotia and The Industrialization of the Maritimes, 1880-1910* (a thesis submitted to the Department of History in conformity with the requirements for the degree of Master of Arts), Queen's University, Kingston, Oct. 1978, pp.17-25.
3. *Acadian Recorder*, March 23, 1900, p.3, col.4.
4. *Monetary Times*, Dec. 5, 1902.
5. BNS Archives, General Manager to the Board, dated Toronto, April 6, 1904.
6. *Ibid.*, Manual of Rules and Regulations, 1902, p.11.
7. *Ibid.*, Circular No. 868, Nov. 8, 1901.
8. *Ibid.*, Circular No. 829, May 10, 1900.
9. PAC, RG 19, Vol.3193, file 11889: Resolution, Canadian Bankers' Association, Winnipeg Sub-Section, Apr. 19, 1899.
10. BNS Archives, J. Pitblado to H.C. McLeod, dated Winnipeg, Apr. 27, 1899.
11. PAC, RG 19, Vol.3193, file 11889, McLeod to Chairman, Winnipeg Sub-Section, Canadian Bankers' Association, dated Toronto, May 3, 1899.
12. *Ibid.*, McLeod to Secretary, Canadian Bankers' Association, dated Toronto, June 1, 1899.
13. *Ibid.*, July 17, 1899.
14. Canadian Bankers' Association, *Journal*, Vol.VI, Oct. 25-26, 1899.
15. BNS Archives, J.B. Monk, Chairman, Winnipeg Sub-Section, Canadian Bankers' Association, to C.A. Kennedy, Manager, The Bank of Nova Scotia, Winnipeg, dated Winnipeg, Dec. 2, 1903.
16. *Ibid.*, Kennedy to Winnipeg Sub-Section, Canadian Bankers' Association, dated Winnipeg, Dec. 5, 1903.
17. *Ibid.*, McLeod to Kennedy, dated Toronto, Dec. 21, 1903.
18. *Ibid.*, quoted in Circular No. 933, March 3, 1904.
19. PAC, RG 19, Vol.3207, file 12474, B.E. Walker, General Manager, The Canadian Bank of Commerce, to Hon. W.S. Fielding, Minister of Finance, dated Toronto, Feb. 7, 1908.
20. BNS Directors' Minute Book, March 31, 1903.
21. BNS Archives, F.W. Ross, "When the West Opened Up," Part II, BNS *Staff Magazine*, Winter 1955, p.1.
22. *Ibid.*, F.W. Ross to Betty Hearn, dated Winnipeg, Aug. 9, 1955; also quoted in BNS *Monthly Review*, Sept. 1955.
23. BNS Directors' Minute Book, Oct. 20, 1903.
24. BNS Archives, Andrew Mooney to General Manager, dated Saskatoon, June 23, 1906.
25. *Ibid.*, Ross to Hearn, dated Winnipeg, June 20, 1958.
26. *Ibid.*, *The Nova Scotian* (BNS Staff Magazine), Nov. 1907.
27. *Ibid.*, General Manager to the Board, dated Toronto, Mar. 5, 1908.
28. *Ibid.*
29. *New York Times*, June 9, 1909.
30. PAC, RG 19, Vol.3125, file 9145, Fyshe to J.M. Courtney, Deputy Minister of Finance, dated Halifax, June 4, 1897.
31. PAC, RG 19, Vol.3183, file 11493, McLeod to Courtney, dated Toronto, July 4, 1901.
32. PAC, RG 19, Vol.3185 file 11599, McLeod to Courtney, dated Toronto, Nov. 11, 1901.
33. PAC, RG 19, Vol.3252, McLeod to T.C. Boville, Deputy Minister of Finance, dated Toronto, Apr. 12, 1907.
34. *Ibid.*, May 13, 1907.
35. BNS Archives, L.D. Murray to Margot Dixon, dated Charlottetown, Feb. 27, 1968.
36. PAC, RG 19, McLeod to Boville, dated Toronto, Jan. 24, 1908.

37. A.B. Jamieson, *Chartered Banking in Canada* (Toronto: The Ryerson Press, 1953), p.370.
38. PAC, RG 19, Vol.3185, file 11599, McLeod to Courtney, dated Toronto, Nov. 11, 1901.
39. BNS Archives, quoted in H.C. McLeod, *Bank Inspection: The Necessity for External Examination*, 1909, Appendix, pp.29-32.
40. *Ibid.*, p.25.
41. *Ibid.*, General Manager to the Board, dated Toronto, Nov. 1, 1906.
42. *Ibid.*, McLeod to General Managers of Canadian Banks, dated Toronto, Apr. 24, 1902.
43. *Ibid.*, McLeod to the Board, dated Toronto, Dec. 15, 1909.
44. *Ibid.*
45. *Ibid.*, H.C. McLeod, *Bank Inspection: The Necessity for External Examination*, 1909, Preface to the Second Edition, Toronto, Nov. 26, 1909.
46. *Ibid.*, McLeod, Circular Letter, *To Bank Shareholders*, dated Toronto, Nov. 25, 1909.
47. *Ibid.*, Aemilius Jarvis to John Y. Payzant, dated Toronto, Dec. 7, 1909.
48. *Ibid.*, McLeod to the Board, dated Toronto, Dec. 15, 1909.
49. *Ibid.*
50. *Ibid.*, Report of BNS Annual Meeting, General Manager's Address, Jan. 26, 1910, pp. 16 and 22.
51. *Ibid.*, pp. 23-24.
52. BNS Directors' Minute Book, Jan. 26, 1910.
53. *Ibid.*, Dec. 12, 1905.

7

The Amalgamations 1910-1923

RICHARDSON AT THE HELM

H.A. Richardson had entered The Bank of Nova Scotia in 1879 as a junior clerk at Liverpool, Nova Scotia, and had progressed for twenty-one years through various Maritime appointments. Now, after ten additional years at the centre of affairs in Toronto, he had formed his own ideas about managerial techniques and the proper course for the Bank. Deceptively mild and affable, he had a resilient, steely toughness and a gift for dealing with people. Though never physically strong, he was renowned for his capacity for hard work. He also had a sense of humour, which his former chief had lacked. More than anyone else before or since, he brought the Bank to an enviable position of national strength.

SETTLING AN OLD QUARREL

As the inheritor of McLeod's quarrels, he was prepared to let them sleep, but when he roused one of them inadvertently, he had his own solution. On May 10, 1911, Richardson found himself in the uncomfortable position of having to report an overrun of the Bank's note issue to the Deputy Minister of Finance; its notes in circulation on Saturday, April 29, had exceeded the legal limit by $47,000. As Richardson pointed out, this was partly due to the fact that other banks had hoarded Bank of Nova Scotia notes and had chosen that particular day to unload them. Furthermore, in the vein of injured innocence which McLeod had made familiar, Richardson referred to the practice of competitors writing off portions of old note issues, emphasized again that The Bank of Nova Scotia did not do such things, and hoped "that the Department will accept this explanation as a settlement of the matter."[1]

As usual, the Department would not. Thomas Boville, the Deputy, was on better terms with Richardson than he had ever been with McLeod and was inclined to be sympathetic. But he had heard all the excuses before and he was there to administer the law. For its latest

H.A. Richardson,
General Manager, 1910-1923

103

offence The Bank of Nova Scotia was liable for a fine of $10,000. A more serious problem existed, however, in that the Bank was a defaulter on the books of the Treasury Board for the fine of $5,000 assessed four years earlier, which still remained unpaid. In view of all the circumstances, the Deputy Minister thought it possible that he might prevail on the Minister to accept $5,000 in payment of the original fine, plus $2,500 as a compromise on the new. Richardson replied appreciatively but still as the injured party. For an offence so totally involuntary, even $2,500 was a pretty stiff fine and would make it difficult for the new General Manager "to recommend a course so diametrically opposed to the recommendation of my predecessor."[2] He asked that the second fine be reduced to $1,000 and set off by train for Ottawa to expand on this plea in person.

When Richardson came back, he was in high good humour. "I went into his office and enquired how he got along," L.D. Murray recorded later; Murray had served under McLeod as General Manager's clerk and acted in the same capacity under Richardson.

"We paid the fine," he replied with a smile, "but they agreed to increase their free deposit [with us] by $1,000,000." It was an example, in Murray's view, of "Mr. Richardson's diplomacy,"[3] a quality which he would find scope for in a number of other fields as well.

THE BANK HAD TO GROW

In June of 1910, Richardson embarked on a six-week tour of western Canada, with expansion very much in mind. The country obviously excited him, from the twin cities at the Lakehead to the prairie wheatfields and on to the bustle of Vancouver. Yet, when he returned, it was to bemoan the cost of premises, the cutthroat ways of large, established competitors, and the eternal lack of staff. Of the fifteen branches opened in 1910, more than the Bank had opened in any previous year, not one was in western Canada and only one – in San Juan, Puerto Rico – was an advance into new territory.

For all the Bank's strength, it was still regional and still comparatively static, cut off by its lack of branches from many areas of growth. The cost of building and staffing, and the consequent long wait until branches began to pay, inhibited large and rapid expansion. Not surprisingly, most of the smaller banks were faced with the same problem. They had to grow at a pace they could not afford if they were to continue to exist at all. They could not accumulate deposits without extending their reach, which was very costly. And they could not make the best use of their deposits for lending without providing the widespread representation that the large borrower required. Only the few giants spread-eagled coast to coast were actually keeping pace with the country's progress. Bigness was being forced on all the banks, and it remained to be seen which banks would be squeezed out. On this subject, Richardson had ideas.

The Amalgamations, 1910-1923 105

"THE OLD BANK" – THE BANK OF NEW BRUNSWICK

In Saint John, New Brunswick, just across Prince William Street from the main branch office of The Bank of Nova Scotia, was the handsome head office building of the Bank of New Brunswick, the oldest Canadian chartered bank. Known as "the Old Bank," it was strong and much respected and it was also on good terms with The Bank of Nova Scotia. An ingrained conservatism, a fondness for old ways of doing things, and a reluctance to take chances were the dominant characteristics of "the Old Bank." The directors voted on discounts by using black and white beans and for years they had frowned on establishing branches. In 1885, with no branches and an excess of idle funds, the directors had simply voted to reduce the capital by half and to buy back shares of stock to that extent from the shareholders. Meanwhile, the bank continued to pay dividends on the funds that remained in use, and

Bank of New Brunswick Head Office, Saint John.

The dates on the building refer to the founding of the Bank of New Brunswick (1820), the year its original permanent premises were built (1826), and the year this building was completed (1878). The Bank of Nova Scotia took over this building in 1913 after the amalgamation with the Bank of New Brunswick.

life went comfortably on. The President carved the roast for the staff at the midday meal and generally took care of his "boys."[4]

The turn of the century ushered in some changes. In March of 1900 James Manchester, a Saint John dry goods merchant, became the new President of the Bank of New Brunswick. In December of that year, he hired William E. Stavert away from The Bank of Nova Scotia and installed him as General Manager. Stavert, it may be remembered, did an excellent job of building up the Nova Scotia's business both in Kingston, Jamaica, and in St. John's, Newfoundland. Stavert, as he had always done everywhere, swept out old cobwebs and generated new momentum in the Bank of New Brunswick. By 1905, when he moved on again for a more senior position with the Bank of Montreal, he had expanded business, opened some twenty branches, and attracted back the capital which the bank had previously returned. He was said to have told a local financial agent seeking to promote a merger with the Bank of Montreal that if it took over the Bank of New Brunswick at $350 per share it would be getting a good deal.

EARLY SUGGESTION OF MERGER

That statement, though it was never set down on paper or presented as a formal offer, became generally accepted as gospel by the directors of the Bank of New Brunswick. Robert B. Kessen, recruited from the Bank of Ottawa, became the new General Manager and for the next five years built on Stavert's work. The bank's assets and deposits continued to rise, and by the summer of 1910 it was operating twenty branches in New Brunswick, six in Nova Scotia, and four in Prince Edward Island. Nevertheless, it was in the course of that same summer that F.P. Starr, one of the senior directors of the Bank of New Brunswick, dropped in on Richardson in Toronto with a highly tentative proposal. Starr felt, though he had not consulted his colleagues, that the time was approaching for a marriage of the two banks. The Bank of Nova Scotia, if it was prepared to make an offer, might find the Bank of New Brunswick in the right mood to accept.

There was no doubt in Richardson's mind about the views of his own Board; the taking over of the Bank of New Brunswick would leave The Bank of Nova Scotia in an impregnable position in the Maritimes. There was not much doubt as to the reason for Starr's offer. "The Old Bank," which twenty-five years earlier had returned capital to shareholders rather than attempt to expand, was now losing out in its belated attempt to catch up. Like every small bank confined to a single region, it lacked the resources to grow and it could not afford to stand still. Pushed already to its limit, it was probably slipping back. Kessen, the General Manager, would have the answer and the man across Prince William Street might be able to get it out of him; C.H. Easson, manager of the main branch of The Bank of Nova Scotia in Saint John, was instructed to investigate and report.

THE BANK OF NOVA SCOTIA IN NO HURRY

Actually, Easson's work was easy, for Kessen proved co-operative and aware of what was in the wind. By December of 1910 Easson was forwarding some advance figures from the Bank of New Brunswick's forthcoming statement and putting forward the view that "we could not make a very serious mistake in offering $360 per share."[5] In January of 1911, as his friendship with Easson grew, Kessen himself volunteered the suggestion that an offer of $350 might be acceptable and should be made without delay. In Richardson's view, however, it would not be an acceptable offer to his own Board of Directors and delay was what was called for; "...standing pat for the present is not likely to do any harm," he wrote Easson, "especially as the competition for business will not be felt any lighter by them as time goes on."[6]

Almost a year later Richardson was sounding the same note, with a certain tinge of frustration. Not only the competition but some of its own people had weakened the Bank of New Brunswick's position. A director had gone bankrupt after heavy speculation. A defaulting manager in a suburban Saint John branch had been the cause of another scandal followed by a minor run. But the tough "Old Bank," having been in business for ninety-two years, persisted on its course. Richardson came to Saint John in January of 1912 and found Kessen doubtful that there would be a sale at all since the majority of the Board were still in a mood to oppose it. As for Starr, who had proposed the merger in the first place, Richardson wrote Payzant: "He feels that the time is not quite ripe to undertake successfully the consummation of the project that he himself agrees with me is in the best interests of his shareholders. In the circumstances the only thing to do is to keep up friendly relations and leave the matter to the logic of events, pulling any strings within reach from time to time."[7]

FURTHER COMPLICATIONS

Meanwhile, Richardson was installing a new manager to replace Easson, who had been transferred to Winnipeg. At the same time, Kessen was becoming restless at the Bank of New Brunswick; he wanted to resign, apparently under the influence of his wife, who disliked Saint John social life. Kessen's decision to leave led to the receipt by Richardson in February 1912 of a letter from W.H. Davies, the New York agent of The Bank of Nova Scotia. He, Davies, had been offered $10,000 a year to replace Kessen as the General Manager of the Bank of New Brunswick. He had, however, declined – much to Richardson's regret, since "it would help matters a good deal for us to have one of our men in charge."[8]

Within the next two weeks, however, there were similar offers made to The Bank of Nova Scotia's manager in St. John's, Newfoundland, its manager in Montreal, and the manager transferred from

Winnipeg to make way for Easson. After all three men declined, it was hardly surprising to receive a telegram from Easson himself. He had been offered the Bank of New Brunswick position, which, after twenty-five years with The Bank of Nova Scotia, he was most reluctant to accept. But he was finding Winnipeg expensive and "it occurs to me, in the event of my definitely refusing the Bank of New Brunswick offer, that you might consider some special inducement, either in the way of an increased salary or a suitable residence or something."[9]

"DRIVE A HARD BARGAIN WHEN THE TIME COMES"

That approach may have smacked of blackmail to Richardson and there were no inducements forthcoming. There were, instead, some strong words of advice and on March 13 a chastened Easson reported that he was, after all, remaining at his post and would "give the interests of the bank the benefit of the best that is in me."[10] That, Richardson informed Payzant, was a relief for him since it would be an embarrassment to have "our erstwhile manager at St. John...walk across the street and take charge of a competitive bank.... We might wink at that if there were any certainty of his returning in the course of a year or two, bringing the Bank with him, but there is no certainty of that as I feel that these people will drive a hard bargain with the highest bidder when the time comes."[11]

It was still necessary, however, to maintain friendly relations and Richardson recalled a prospect who was no longer on his staff. Two years earlier he had informed H.V. Cann, a friend of his Maritime days who had become an assistant inspector in The Bank of Nova Scotia, that he was to be transferred as manager to Winnipeg. Cann had flatly refused, since he wanted a Toronto posting, but Richardson had told him to go off and think about it. When Cann returned, having thought, he demanded a certain salary, the territory and title of Superintendent if he was to go to Winnipeg.

The result was a brusque though apparently not an acrimonious parting; Cann subsequently joined the Federal Reserve Bank of New York, and Richardson often lunched with him on business trips to that city. On March 21 Richardson reported to Payzant that Starr had called on him again in Toronto, still looking for a General Manager. "After thinking the matter over pretty carefully," Richardson wrote to Payzant, saying that he had decided to give Starr "...a letter of introduction to H.V. Cann.... We know of course that Cann is cold-blooded and in the event of our at any time making terms with the Bank Mr. Cann would not forget his own rights. However, I think that at heart he feels that his course with us was unjustifiable, and I would expect his early association with us to influence him in our favour in the event of their concluding to go out of business."[12]

MAINTAINING FRIENDLY RELATIONS

But Cann decided to remain in New York and Starr was again confronted with the problem of finding a General Manager. On July 9, 1912, Easson wrote from Winnipeg to Richardson: "I am advised by Mr. Starr that he has received assurance from you that my resignation as a member of the Bank's staff in order to accept the General Managership of the Bank of New Brunswick, is, under the circumstances, agreeable to you."[13]

Agreeable it was certainly not, Richardson retorted. He continued, "When Mr. Starr raised the question while I was in St. John recently I told him that it was anything but agreeable; indeed I pointed out that it would create a situation so anomalous as to be at first blush well-nigh impossible." Starr, however, had pressed hard and had done his best to reassure Richardson in his continuing effort to bring the two banks together. Thus, by the end of his letter to Easson, Richardson had come round to accepting Starr's argument: "In view of that, and as it seemed the step lay close to the hearts of our old B.N.B friends and yourself, I concluded it would be as well to allow the matter to take its natural course."[14] By August 12, 1912, Easson was installed as General Manager of the Bank of New Brunswick.

The manager of the Bank of New Brunswick's Saint John branch, located in the same building as the head office, was the elderly Arthur Macdonald, a close observer of events. He had, he confided to a friend, been half-heartedly seeking the General-Managership himself, but he was glad he had not got it, as he wrote in a letter in December 1912:

> Mr. Easson when confronted with [various bad debts and overdrafts] weakened & called on Mr. Richardson for succor and to deliver him from a situation that he was not able or inclined to deal with.
>
> He and Mr. Kessen exchanged a few remarks not complimentary before the latter took his departure....I think Mr. Easson intended to carry on the Bank when he came though probably there was an understanding that he would work it into the Bank of Nova Scotia later on, but his [Easson's] view was that the contingent reserve was gone and that the rest [account] would have to be broken into to the extent of $250,000 to take care of all the losses that he would insist on writing off and though his view was extreme and perhaps the amount exaggerated affairs were pretty bad and we did not realize how bad until an outsider came to point them out.[15]

AN OFFER IS MADE

In Macdonald's view, a good General Manager could still have brought the bank back to a sound footing. But Easson, Richardson, and the directors of the Bank of New Brunswick were not prepared to make the attempt. Starr, at last in the ascendant, won over his grudging colleagues one by one. Richardson, shuttling between Halifax and Saint John, had no difficulty with his own Board, and by October 18 he had an approved draft of the terms of amalgamation. On October 19, the Bank of New Brunswick submitted the terms to its shareholders, recommending acceptance. The change would mean an alliance with a strong bank, one which was 70 per cent owned in the Maritimes and one whose traditions and methods were familiar to the Bank of New Brunswick. Customers would feel at home in the new institution and shareholders would receive one share of Bank of Nova Scotia stock, plus $10, for each share of Bank of New Brunswick stock. Dividends, moreover, would increase from 13 per cent to the 14 per cent rate of The Bank of Nova Scotia.

Nevertheless, with Bank of Nova Scotia stock trading at this time between $250 and $275, and allowing for the proposed $10 premium, the Bank of New Brunswick shareholder would be receiving much less than the fabled $350. As soon as the offer was announced, meetings were held by dissident shareholders and by proxy-hunting investment houses, and, worst of all, another bank made an offer! This bank did not, however, prove to be one of the giants as Richardson at first feared; rather, it was the small but venerable Quebec Bank. "I saw their General Manager," Richardson wrote on November 16, "and let some light into his mind as to the consequences of their interference. This morning we received a letter from him stating that the Quebec Bank valued the friendship of the Bank of Nova Scotia too highly to enter into a quarrel with us."[16] Next, Richardson was able to convince the financial houses of the viability of the amalgamation and to isolate the dissatisfied shareholders. Thus, Richardson was able to telegraph the Board that night, "All organized opposition to our deal with Bank of New Brunswick has been disposed of."[17]

THE FINAL MEETING OF "THE OLD BANK"

The final meeting of the shareholders of the Bank of New Brunswick was held on December 9, 1912. In Arthur Macdonald's view, it "was somewhat in the nature of a funeral and at which a good many pertinent questions were *not* asked of the directors."[18] To the one inevitable question concerning the price of shares, the President of the Bank of New Brunswick had a categorical answer: "Never before had the Directors received a bona fide, unqualified offer."[19] The offer of The Bank of Nova Scotia, "if not generous is advantageous and shareholders will find their income increased through association with one of the strongest banks in the country."[20] It was enough to restore good humour and induce a touch of philosophy. "The day of the small bank is gone," observed one of the directors, "like the day of the wooden ship"; and the meeting adjourned with a vote of 8,966 to nil in favour of amalgamation.[21]

On December 11, 1912, the agreement was approved by the shareholders of The Bank of Nova Scotia. In Saint John, on Saturday, February 15, 1913, with all formalities completed, the books, records, cash, and fittings of the old main office of The Bank of Nova Scotia were transferred across the street to what had become the new main office. On Monday, with the combined office set up, "Joe Lewis our messenger, fitted out for the first time in a uniform with a round stiff hat, was stationed in the lobby to direct customers....Joe didn't mind the uniform but hated the cap, said it made him look like a monkey."[22]

"Our revered President," Arthur Macdonald wrote as he neared the conclusion of his letter to his friend, "still presides at the carving board with dignity and distinction....Poor old chap. He lingers like myself 'superfluous on the stage.'"[23] In point of fact, the prophecy was too dour. James Manchester served as a Director of The Bank of Nova Scotia for ten years after the amalgamation, though his other function of course disappeared; "...after our arrival which doubled the staff to perhaps 26 or so," records L.R. Crammond, one of the newcomers, "the job [of carving] was handed over to Tom Evans their caretaker. If you stood in well with Tom he would say, 'Let me give you some dish gravy.'" Arthur Macdonald himself, "who stayed on with us for a short time before retiring," is also remembered by Crammond in a pleasant twilight phrase. "[He] lived up Westfield way in the summer at least, had nets set out on the river, and when he made a catch we had salmon for dinner – we lived well in those days."[24]

ANOTHER DEAL WAS SHAPING UP

Even as the Bank of New Brunswick was settling into the fold, another deal was shaping up. On October 6, 1913, Richardson wrote to Payzant that at the next meeting of the Board, "The most important matter under discussion, as you understand, could not be referred to on our records."[25] A week later, the minute book for the meeting in question referred only to "further general discussion on the Bank's affairs."[26] One of those subjects was the taking over of the Metropolitan Bank. In that year just before the outbreak of war, a long-foreshadowed development was slowly working to a head.

The Metropolitan Bank had commenced business in Toronto on November 17, 1902, under extremely bright auspices. Its President was Alfred Ernest Ames, a thirty-six-year-old, successful Toronto stockbroker. Associated with him as Vice-President was the Reverend R.H. Warden, D.D., general agent of the Presbyterian Church of Canada, while the other directors were Chester D. Massey, President of Massey-Harris, Thomas Bradshaw, Vice-President of Imperial Life Assurance, and Samuel J. Moore, who was already well established as a manufacturer of sales books and business forms.

Samuel J. Moore,
President, 1927-1934;
Chairman, 1933-1945.

MOORE OF THE METROPOLITAN

In 1907, Moore had succeeded to the presidency of the Metropolitan Bank. A man of forty-eight by that time, he had come from England with his family to settle in Barrie, Ontario, when he was twelve years old. He had begun work with the Barrie *Examiner* as printer's devil, had moved on to become reporter and city editor, and had finally left his job. He later moved to Toronto, where he joined a printing firm which in 1880 became Bengough, Moore and Company and subsequently the Grip Printing and Publishing Company.

For Moore, who was by then the general manager of the Grip Printing and Publishing Company, a decisive moment came in 1882 when John R. Carter, a clerk in a dry goods store adjoining the printing plant, walked in with a brilliant idea. He was holding what looked like an ordinary pad of paper but which was actually a duplicating sales book with each original sales slip numbered, a similarly numbered slip behind it, and between the two a sheaf of "black leaf" or carbon paper. This ancestor of the counter sales book, which would replace the ponderous ledgers in the department stores of the time, was a simple idea which no one had yet thought of. Moore saw its potential, patented the idea with Carter, and scraped up money for printing. "Carter & Company" was formed, with Moore, Carter, and the Grip Printing and Publishing Company as equal partners, and within three months the Grip presses were producing Paragon Black Leaf Counter Books, the antecedents of today's Moore Business Forms.[27]

For the next twenty years, as demand outgrew production, the fledgling company followed its market and expanded into the United States. Frequently short of capital as he added presses, enlarged plants, and acquired subsidiary companies, Moore had to sell stock in order to finance his ambitious undertakings. Carter would have none of that; he considered the pace too fast. The solution was the break-up of the partnership, with Moore buying out Carter, though he still retained the inventor's name on the masthead. In 1888, Carter & Company took over the Grip interest, and shortly thereafter it acquired the company that made the Grip presses. An infringement-of-patent case in 1893 ended in a truce and a merger: Carter & Company (the complainant) joined hands with the Crume-Sefton Company of Dayton, Ohio (the defendant), with S.J. Moore as chief executive of the new Carter-Crume Company.

THE GROWTH OF MOORE'S INTERESTS

Another infringement-of-patent suit led to another merger in 1911. This time it was Moore's company which was the defendant – in a case that lasted for eight years. But again the Moore interests emerged triumphant, acquiring a majority holding in the American Sales Book

Company. Later, in 1919, the merger was extended to include Beardsley Press, New York Cash Book Sales Company, and Eastern Sales Book Company, all of New York City. Then, F.N. Burt & Company, "largest manufacturers of small paper boxes in the world," and the Pacific Manifolding Book Company of San Francisco were also acquired. Such were the events which put S.J. Moore at the head of a large international conglomerate; the mild-seeming, Baptist entrepreneur from Barrie, Ontario, had invaded the United States, taken on some of the big corporations, and cut them down to size.

Nor was this the limit of his interests. In Niagara Falls, New York, where his largest plant was located, he had met the young William A. Rogers, who in 1901 was making his living by selling silver spoons to tourists. There were possibilities in silver as there were in sales books; on the strength of capital raised through Moore's efforts, the William A. Rogers Company was born. And there were even opportunities in milk distribution. In Toronto, the City Dairy, which had been inaugurated by the famous Massey family, had been allowed to languish. S.J. Moore reorganized the company and set it on a paying basis.

Although he seldom attended public functions and was often away from Toronto, Moore's presence was felt where charity and religion met. He was described by the Toronto *Globe* in 1912 as "a prominent if not the most prominent lay member of the Baptist Church in Canada."[28] He continued to teach Sunday School at the Dovercourt Baptist Church whenever his travels permitted. In his role as President of the Metropolitan Bank and later of The Bank of Nova Scotia, his touch was light and his advice quietly given. He did not swear, smoke, or drink but could tolerate those who did; and, wearing his virtues lightly, he was at home with his outgoing right-hand man, William Donald Ross.

W.D. ROSS – BIG, GENIAL, AND OUTSPOKEN

W.D. Ross, born in Little Bras d'Or, Cape Breton, was big, genial, and outspoken, with a colourful Maritime vocabulary. In 1883, at the age of fourteen, he had entered The Bank of Nova Scotia and for the next seventeen years had followed in the steps of Richardson, who was six years his senior. In the process, as they moved from branch to branch in the Maritimes and from junior to senior appointments, the two had become fast friends. Then, at the turn of the century, when H.C. McLeod was General Manager, the time for parting came. Richardson moved to Toronto, while Ross set out for Ottawa to embark on a new career.

On the recommendation of Thomas Fyshe, Ross was going to become Deputy Minister of Finance, succeeding Fyshe's friend Courtney, who was retiring. Even McLeod concurred in the appointment, though he would be losing an able man and he was seldom a graceful loser. On December 27, 1901, he reported to the Board from Toronto: "We have sold at 237 to Mr. W.D. Ross, Ottawa, ten shares of the

Bank's stock.... while 238¼ has been steadily bid here for the stock, I think it desirable to have the future Deputy Minister of Finance on our list of shareholders, seeing that he knows something of the inside."[29]

It was soon apparent, however, that the $12.50 McLeod had invested in the good will of a civil servant was money thrown away. Ross, the rough diamond who could go anywhere and get along with anyone and who was to close his career as Lieutenant-Governor of Ontario, was not to persist in a career in the civil service. By November of 1902, he had resigned his post in favour of Thomas Boville, and had become assistant general manager of the Metropolitan Bank. Six months later, he had succeeded to the post of General Manager.

The Metropolitan, as its name implies, had been centred in, capitalized by, and designed to serve the interests of metropolitan Toronto. Toronto financiers had offered its stock at a premium, subscribed for most of it themselves, and allowed only three thousand of a total of ten thousand shares to be sold to the general public. Thus, closely controlled, it followed the growth of Toronto's expanding interests, but only within the province. Of the thirty-nine branches it eventually came to open, ten were located in Toronto and most of the others in the southern part of the province.

AN EASYGOING RELATIONSHIP

The Metropolitan Bank soon established an easygoing relationship with The Bank of Nova Scotia. Between 1903 and 1909, the two General Managers, McLeod and Ross, seemed to find ground in common when in opposition to the larger banks and yet enough ground between each other to avoid collision in growth. Harmonious competition became even more apparent when Richardson took over from McLeod. In that part of Ontario outside Toronto, the twenty-nine branches of the Metropolitan Bank and the twenty-seven of The Bank of Nova Scotia happened to be so spaced that not one was duplicated except in the city of Hamilton.

Richardson and Ross were close friends and neighbours during all their years in Toronto. They were drawn even closer by the death of Ross's wife. "When my mother died," Donald Ross, W.D. Ross's son, reminisced many years later, "Mr. Richardson practically brought me up. I remember almost every morning Mr. Richardson would come round in his big car, pick up my father and the two would drive downtown together."

All this the financial community noted, drawing its own conclusions. Newspapers later recalled the gossip of the street: the long-sustained intimacy between the Metropolitan and The Bank of Nova Scotia; the expansive tendencies that the Nova Scotia was showing; the pattern of branches in Ontario; and the flat rejection the Metropolitan made to the approaches of other banks. What the two men in the big car talked about is a matter only for conjecture, but each had similar or complementary concerns. The larger bank, forever pushed to expand, was appalled at the cost and the difficulties of opening new branches. Furthermore, with every advance it made, or was forced by competitors to make, the larger bank pressed on the smaller. How long could the Nova Scotia and the Metropolitan continue the idyll in Ontario? The larger bank, in justice to its own shareholders, had to move into every profitable point. For the smaller bank, expansion meant added capital, and capital was not readily to be had.

Bank shares had fallen out of favour with the failures of earlier years and the agitations which followed them. The low yield and the double liability were features that discouraged investors. "Bank shares," Richardson had written to the Board of The Bank of Nova Scotia in August of 1911, "are not at present popular with the investing public. At the present time our shares are offered here at 270, with no buyers."[30] If that was the situation with a bank whose shares had been selling at the highest price in Canada, what did it mean to the small banks? It meant decline and perhaps failure or it meant amalgamation. In Richardson's view, "the logic of events" had caused the Bank of New Brunswick to join The Bank of Nova Scotia. Thus had it made the best use of its resources and done the most for its shareholders, and so would the Metropolitan when it was persuaded to see the light.

THE METROPOLITAN WOULD SEE THE LIGHT

By September of 1911, Richardson was denying rumours. "About ten o'clock last evening," he reported to the Board on September 16, "the Globe newspaper rang up my house and stated they had received the news from Montreal that the Bank of Nova Scotia was about to take over the Metropolitan Bank. I informed them that the report was idle gossip."[31] Gossip it may have been, but idle it was not, though it was considerably premature. Ross had still to convince S.J. Moore, who was rarely present at meetings and whose hand was seldom seen. Donald Ross remembered Moore as "the man in the Bank my father depended on more than anybody" and he was a man who took his time. In February of 1912, Richardson reported to Payzant: "There is nothing very new in connection with our friend Ross, the difficulty at the present time being that his Directors are so scattered....Mr. Moore will be away for three or four months."[32] Mr. Moore returned and another year went by with a renewed crop of rumours. Then, on October 13, 1913, "the most important matter" which could not be referred to on The Bank of Nova Scotia records was discussed by the Board.

Three months later, as the annual statements of the chartered banks began to appear in the newspapers, a reason for the discussion of "the most important matter" became clear. The Bank of Nova Scotia, the Bank of Montreal, the Commerce, the Royal, and the Dominion – all had had the best year in their histories. In contrast, the Metropolitan's

Metropolitan Bank Branch,
Broadview and Danforth Avenues, Toronto.

This building was erected in 1909
and taken over by The Bank of Nova Scotia
in the amalgamation of 1914.

profits had declined from the year before. It was a well-managed bank in a rich region of the country but it was finding it increasingly difficult to compete with the larger institutions.

"THE AMALGAMATION IS DESIRABLE"

In these circumstances, negotiations ensued and a Memorandum of Agreement was completed in early May. In June, E.R.C. Clarkson, as an independent auditor of the Metropolitan Bank, submitted his report to Ross:

> Following the interviews between us during the last few weeks when you advised me, as auditor of the Metropolitan Bank, of the proposed amalgamation between it and the Bank of Nova Scotia – the terms thereof having been fully discussed between us – you have asked me to give you my opinion as to the equity of the agreement towards the shareholders of the Metropolitan Bank and its merits having regard to the prospects of the Bank for the future.
>
> In reply thereto would say that in my investigations of the Bank's affairs as its auditor I have made a careful and comprehensive scrutiny of its assets and am clearly of the opinion that the terms are fair and equitable to the shareholders of the Metropolitan Bank.
>
> With respect to the Bank's prospects for the future would say that with the difficulties met with by smaller banks in obtaining fresh deposits of volume (the Metropolitan Bank being no exception) and the increasing cost of doing business, I am of the opinion, in view of all the interests concerned, that the amalgamation is desirable.[33]

After all this, and in spite of the years of rumours, the word came to the Metropolitan's stockholders like a cheerful bolt from the blue. They went to bed on July 23, 1914, with shares valued at $205 and woke next morning to find them worth $232.50. Newspapers commented favourably on a union which "in fact will not do much more than cement a working arrangement which has been in effect for some years."[34] It was also pointed out that with the addition of 39 branches and $12,500,000 in assets, The Bank of Nova Scotia had become the fourth largest in Canada. In W.D. Ross and S.J. Moore, who were added to the Board of Directors, the Bank had regained an alumnus and acquired a future President. Finally and satisfactorily, as war rolled over the country, the Metropolitan's affairs stood up to examination. Its contingent reserve, Richardson reported to the Board of The Bank of Nova Scotia, would be quite ample to take care of its bad debts. And Richardson added, "I will be disappointed if we do not come out with a substantial part of that fund to the good."[35]

THE WAR – "BANKS AND GOVERNMENT PRACTICALLY ONE"

From August 5, 1914, when a staff circular suspended the holiday schedule, The Bank of Nova Scotia, like every other financial institution, was whole-heartedly involved in the war effort. The banks became agents of government. The Finance Act of August 1914 made bank notes legal tender and resolved at one stroke the old controversies about note circulation. New money was issued by the government as the needs of the war required and these needs were soon enormous. The banks worked closely with the government on the mechanics of war finance, and in the case of Victory Bonds they acted as salesmen as well, thus sparing the government from having to conduct a sizeable promotional campaign. Furthermore, the banks extended credit to individuals for deferred payments for Victory Bonds – a novel idea at this time, when loans for the purchase of bonds were generally made only to brokers.

Canadian bankers spent thousands of extra hours on the recording of the sales of Victory Bonds, the filing of loan returns for instalment purchases of the bonds, and the education of customers who had never before bought a bond. Senior bank executives became advisers of government, and juniors behind the wicket became part-time employees of government. Men left for the services and women came to replace them, still strictly on sufferance, in branches starved for staff. But the banks took their increased responsibilites in stride. Richardson, returning to his desk from one of the innumerable meetings in Ottawa, wrote matter-of-factly to the Board: "the Banks and the Government are practically one in whatever is done to finance Canada through this war, and we must sink or swim together.... The side that emerges from the struggle successfully will the more quickly work back to normal conditions.... for the defeated, the consequences may perhaps best be left to the imagination."[36] And Sir Thomas White, who was Minister of Finance during the war, subsequently commented that the Canadian banking system was "the most perfect instrument that a Minister of Finance could have at his hand in floating a national loan. Nothing like it in the world, that I know of.... What had I to do? Just call up on the telephone the President of the Canadian Bankers' Association. 'I want all the branch banks of Canada notified to do a certain thing' – It was done."[37]

During the four years of war, all the banks were drained of resources – resources of people and of facilities. Branches across the country had emptied themselves of youth, their elders had doubled up on the work, while "temporary" girls and women unravelled the mysteries of ledgers and counted the cash. Even so, in the last year of the war as the peak of the strain came, banks closed branches and awaited the return of their men. In the case of The Bank of Nova Scotia, eighty-two of the six hundred and twelve who had gone to war gave their lives and ninety-one were wounded. The majority of those able to return chose to rejoin the Bank's service. One of those who had been

H.A. Richardson, H.C. McLeod, and W.P. Hunt.
London, England, 1914

wounded and who returned to the Bank after the war was Capt. C. Sydney Frost, M.C., later to become General Manager and then President. He had an illustrious career in the Royal Newfoundland Regiment, in which he served from 1914 to 1919, joining up as a private, rising through the ranks, and winning the Military Cross in action near Passchendaele.

STAFF RELATIONS WOULD NEVER BE THE SAME

Now that the war was over, never again would the staff and staff relations be quite the same. The men who came back were different – more demanding and sometimes difficult, but absolutely essential to the resumption of peacetime banking and normal growth. By 1921, moreover, 450, or more than 20 per cent of a total staff of 2,014, were women. They had not been sent home, as some of the naive had fancied, when the days of "normalcy" had returned. Prewar normalcy, as Richardson had learned, was one of the many conceptions blown away with the wind. In its place were many questions to trouble a long future, but he saw the answer to one. "It is better," he wrote to Charles Archibald, the President, discussing salaries, "for us to satisfy the staff than to accumulate profits, inside or out, that are to be taken from us by the Government."[38]

Charles Archibald, President, 1918-1923

A POSSIBLE CONNECTION WITH ANOTHER INSTITUTION IN THE WEST?

By 1917, as staff shortages had become acute, the banks had agreed together that they would open no new branches. That was reasonable enough but it did not rule out an alternative which Richardson had in mind, and at a meeting of the Board in Halifax on October 17, he moved to clear his way. The Bank, he said, was in need of branches in the West but war conditions and the agreement with the other banks made it impossible to establish new ones. He was, therefore, "of the opinion that should an opportunity offer by which this Bank could make connections with another institution having branches already established in the west, such an opportunity should be taken advantage of." The Board, the record concludes, "approved of this suggestion."[39]

The bank with branches in the West which Richardson had in mind may well have been the Northern Crown, whose head office was in Winnipeg. He had approached it in 1911 with some tentative overtures and had had his eye on it since. In 1918, when it was taken over by the Royal Bank, Richardson was to profess himself chagrined and commented that "Apparently in their desire to outgrow both the Commerce and the B. of M., the Royal are not deterred by the question of price."[40]

THE THIRD AMALGAMATION

The third and most important of Richardson's amalgamations – with the Bank of Ottawa – came after the war, in April 1919. Its origins, however, went back two years or more. In April 1917, Richardson had written Payzant a chatty personal letter with a good deal to be read between the lines. It was a compliment to The Bank of Nova Scotia, he said, that some of its men were finding high positions with other banks, and he mentioned one in particular: "...the Bank of Ottawa appointed H.V. Cann Assistant General Manager. The General Manager, Mr. Burn, has retired and his assistant, Mr. Finnie, is about 67 years old, so that probably in about two years Cann will be in charge of the Bank. As he has us to thank for his appointment, he called a couple of weeks ago and I had a very friendly and satisfactory interview with him."[41] The man in New York who had earlier turned down the Bank of New Brunswick had accepted a better offer.

Bank of Ottawa Head Office, Wellington St., Ottawa.

This building was erected in 1883 and taken over by The Bank of Nova Scotia in 1919.

THE BANK OF OTTAWA

The Bank of Ottawa, with its symbol of a woodsman's axe and its motto "J'Avance," was a true child of lumbermen and the Ottawa Valley. Established in 1874 by some of the prominent families in the business – the Maclarens, Frasers, Gilmours, Blackburns, Brysons – it was as much at home on the Quebec side as on the Ontario side of the river. Indigenous to the region and a popular institution, it had built up strong resources of local support and trust. It had moved on from the white pine forests of the Ottawa Valley to the Huron-Ottawa tract, gone up round Georgian Bay, and entered the far west. It had opened fifty-four Ontario and fourteen Quebec branches, most of them in the Ottawa Valley, extended across the prairies with fifteen branches in Manitoba and Saskatchewan, and pushed on to the Pacific by way of Edmonton and Vancouver. The chain was widespread but the bank's strength lay in the Ottawa Valley.

The bank's directors had a genuine pride in the institution which, in many cases, their fathers had helped found. As time went on, however, according to T.A. Boyles of The Bank of Nova Scotia, who had known some of them in his youth and who would later become Chairman, "they recognized their need for additional capital. Also they felt that they had too many eggs in one basket, too much money in the lumber industry." George Bryson, the President of the Bank of Ottawa and the son of a former director, recognized familiar symptoms in frequently idle funds, declining commercial loans, and steadily reduced earnings. As one of the principal stockholders at a time when its shares were becoming unattractive, he was keenly aware of his bank's static condition and of some of the consequent dangers that held. All these problems were heightened, moreover, by the stress of war. The General Manager, George Burn, was President of the Canadian Bankers' Association at this time and was knighted for his efforts in promoting war loans. The work, however, exhausted him, a man who was then entering his seventies, and his health gave way. At the end of 1916, he resigned as General Manager and D.M. Finnie took over. But the replacement of a man of seventy by one of sixty-seven did not promise rejuvenation. It was clear that the bank could only regain momentum with an infusion of new blood, as well as capital.

COMPLEMENTARY INTERESTS

The stage was set at this time for the arrival of H.V. Cann, and it remains an interesting question as to how and why he came. Burn was a friend of Richardson's and the two had been closely involved for several years past in the work of war committees. It would have been quite natural for the friends to consult together on the dilemma of the Bank of Ottawa and on Finnie's need for an assistant. It would have been equally natural for Richardson, as he had with Starr in the case of the

Bank of New Brunswick, and with the same motives, to have recommended Cann. The Bank of Ottawa would be invaluable to the Nova Scotia, which had almost no representation in the Ottawa Valley and hardly any in western Canada. It would be easy to deduce from Richardson's letter to Payzant that he hoped Cann, like Easson, "would return in a year or so, bringing the bank with him."

The directors of the Bank of Ottawa themselves had a strong incentive in seeking a merger with a larger bank. They were not optimistic about the prospect of raising capital and setting the bank on a renewed course of expansion, and they knew they could not stand still. Obviously, they would get the best deal where their acquisition would mean the most. As they surveyed the financial landscape, the strong, aggressive Maritime bank, which was still a stranger in the Valley and not much known in the West, seemed promising. It could easily have been that Cann, when he took up his duties in Ottawa, had been nominated by one party and accepted by the other with complementary motives.

As to what happened exactly after his arrival in March 1917, Cann has left only a sketchy account. Richardson, he says, spent a great deal of time in Ottawa during 1917 and 1918 in connection with the war finance committees. "He often came to my house and I spent a number of week-ends with him in Toronto. He broached the subject of a merger between our banks on several occasions. But more than eighteen months passed before a definite proposal was made...."[42]

A PROPOSAL IS MADE

According to the terms of the proposal, which was formally put forward late in 1918, The Bank of Nova Scotia was to take over the Bank of Ottawa on the basis of four shares of its own stock for five of the other. A dividend adjustment was to be made so that Bank of Ottawa shareholders would get the same return on four shares of Bank of Nova Scotia stock as they had on five of their own. Seven directors of the Bank of Ottawa were to be elected to the Board of The Bank of Nova Scotia, and the executive officers and board of the Bank of Ottawa would continue to function from their own building in Ottawa for two years after amalgamation. All the staff was to be retained with all pension benefits and the question of compensation to such senior officers as might be retiring would be settled later.

By January 13, 1919, Cann was writing to Richardson with an urgent inquiry from Bryson regarding some of the details of the proposal. The concerns were not serious, said Cann, but he was anxious to have Richardson come down and talk them over with his Board. "They are a cautious lot," he wrote but hastened to add that as to the general reception of the offer, "Our people are keen for immediate action....Mr. Bryson said to-day, 'Unless this is closed up within the next week or so the whole deal may be off.' White must be made to see that quick action is imperatively necessary."**43**

QUESTION OF CABINET APPROVAL

"White" was Sir Thomas White, Minister of Finance, who would have to clear the way for Cabinet approval. He had, Cann wrote, agreed to a meeting in Ottawa to be held the next night, and the next night Richardson was there. But, first, Richardson spent the day with Bryson, ironing out "details," and then went on to an even more difficult two-hour session with Sir Thomas White. White was afraid of criticism not only from the financial press but also from the Ottawa Valley constituency when its old bank disappeared. He would approve nothing without Cabinet support and Bryson could approve nothing without a board meeting with all the members in attendance. Richardson returned to Toronto with everything still up in the air.

Five days, however, were enough to resolve everything. On January 19, as Cann resumes his account: "Our directors decided to accept the offer and instructed me to advise Mr. Richardson accordingly. I called him on the long distance telephone and gave him the information by means of words and phrases from the code book. He said the quick action almost took his breath away with surprise and asked me to hold W.N. Tilley, K.C., in Ottawa to draw up the merger agreement. Messrs. Richardson and Ross arrived in Ottawa by the next train and executed an agreement with our directors. They then departed for Halifax to have the document approved by their full Board."**44**

In Halifax there was no doubt about the Directors' enthusiastic approval of the main thrust of the agreement. As Richardson pointed out when he laid the terms before them on January 21, the two banks had a total of three hundred branches, which duplicated each other at only eleven points. And The Bank of Nova Scotia would be adding nearly $75 million to its assets, the greatest single gain it had ever made. Less warmly received were the details of the phasing-out of the Bank of Ottawa. It was to continue in its own city as a subordinate head office for two more years, with Cann in charge as Assistant General Manager. Also, to avoid the embarrassment of selecting only seven from the Bank of Ottawa's ten Directors, none of whom had seen fit to resign, it seemed like the best thing might be for The Bank of Nova Scotia to elect them all to its Board. They would be gone soon in any case, certainly within two years, and courtesy might save criticism. At the end of the afternoon, though still with some misgivings, the Board voted for courtesy along with the amalgamation.

Bank of Ottawa, Vancouver Branch.

In taking over the Bank of Ottawa, The Bank of Nova Scotia increased its representation in Western Canada, including this office in Vancouver.

BANK OF OTTAWA APPROVES

On March 4, the shareholders of the Bank of Ottawa gave their approval and on April 30, 1919, the Cabinet followed suit. Sir Thomas White braced himself for a barrage of public criticism, which largely failed to materialize. By the end of May, Richardson was contentedly reporting that the amalgamation had brought the paid-up capital of The Bank of Nova Scotia to $9.7 million and the reserve to $17.8 million. He asked for permission to transfer $200,000 from the profit-and-loss account to make the reserve an even $18,000,000.

He was as yet, however, not quite into the affairs of the Bank of Ottawa and he was far from out of the woods. As the auditors applied themselves to "boiling down" the assets they had taken over, the bad debts and hidden losses of the past twenty years were rising to the surface. At the same time, the ten Directors responsible for these liabilities were meeting weekly in Ottawa with weekly lists of complaints. In September, Senator George Gordon, as a representative of these Directors, called on Richardson to make their grievances known. They considered, said Gordon, that they were being given no voice in the management of the combined Bank and they proposed that a group of them should come to Toronto each week, meet with Richardson, and give all new business the close supervision it should have. The General Manager, fresh from briefings by his auditors, professed himself surprised. He had thought the ten Ottawa Directors – not seven, mind you, as agreed, but ten – were happy with what they were doing. He pointed out that in Toronto, in contrast, they had been constrained to mark time and "give our whole energies to liquidating Bank of Ottawa Bad Debts and otherwise digesting what we had taken over....the Ottawa Directors," he continued, warming to his subject, "having, as a result of their close management of the Bank's affairs practically landed the Bank of Ottawa on the rocks, I do not regard it as logical that they should agitate for a continuance of such supervision of the Bank's affairs."[45]

NO MEETINGS IN TORONTO

The Senator retreated somewhat cowed, and the next day Cann came down to Toronto. Bryson thought, Cann reported, that one of the Ottawa Directors should receive a Vice-Presidency. Vice-Presidents, replied Richardson, were not made in Toronto; they were made by the Board in Halifax. It was also out of the question for any Ottawa Directors to hold meetings in Toronto; it might be assumed that the full Board had moved its meetings from Halifax. If it was a question of information, the Ottawa Directors could have all they wanted – Richardson's cards were always on the table – but there would be no Vice-Presidency and no Toronto meetings. If any Director was dissatisfied, he had the option of retiring from the Board; or, on the other hand, if Bryson wanted a fight and went after proxies, Richardson would circularize the shareholders, showing "the plight in which Mr. Bryson and co-Directors as far as they were responsible had landed the Bank of Ottawa, and the amount of money it would still be necessary for us to find to liquidate their bad debts."[46] Like the Senator, Cann retreated to Ottawa and Richardson was left with a breathing space.

"THE GRACIOUS ACT ON OUR PART"

By December, he had had a considerable change of mood. The auditors were no longer bringing him red-ink figures; the condition of the Bank of Ottawa was not as bad as he had made it out to be and he had a better opinion of the Directors. He was more impressed with the wisdom of being on good terms with them and, as the time came to prepare for the annual meeting, he wrote to the President and the Vice-President in Halifax with a suggestion. By agreement, three of the Ottawa Directors were slated to retire, leaving only seven of their number on the Board. They were, however, having a difficult time among themselves since, though several professed a willingness to go, none would make the first move.

Richardson now felt that "the gracious act on our part of continuing to re-elect them until through the effluxion of time they retire, would be the best investment we could make as far as they are concerned. If there were any disposition on their part to be disagreeable, they would be in a better position to gratify it off the Board than on the Board.... these are generally speaking wealthy and influential men, and I apprehend that any of them who retire from our Board would shortly thereafter be importuned to join the Board of some other bank...." Furthermore, "...the whole character of our relationship has so radically changed since [September], and the desire shown at our recent meeting here by the Ottawa Directors to fall into line with us [is] so marked" and, in any event, "the number of Directors in Ottawa will steadily become less,...[that] in my judgment the custom should continue until it expires through the passage of time,"[47] he concluded.

That was all very well, but that was a Toronto view of the situation. There was also a Maritime view. In Halifax, John Y. Payzant was no longer a familiar of the boardroom. In 1918, in his eighties and in frail health, he had finally become insistent about a resignation he had offered for several years past. Charles Archibald had succeeded him and G.S. Campbell had followed Archibald in the position of Vice-President. Head of a large firm of steamship agents and customs brokers, Campbell had as wide interests and was as much a traveller as Archibald. He had also the mild manner and family tone of Payzant and Archibald in his correspondence with the Bank's executives, but he could be very firm.

On January 2, 1920, Campbell replied to Richardson's letter, apparently speaking for both himself and Archibald. What the man in Toronto seemed to be overlooking was the possible result of allowing ten Directors to continue regular Board meetings in Ottawa "which have no legal effect, and which in future may cause friction. If these meetings are to continue, we must recognize these gatherings as regular meetings of our Ottawa Board, and can't ignore any decisions they may come to. You may think we are conjuring up trouble that will never arise, but we can't ignore the fact that we have ten directors there who have openly expressed the opinion that the head office should be removed from Halifax, and who would vote for such a change if it were proposed tomorrow. If that change were in the interest of the bank I would vote for it too, but I don't think it is at present, whatever the future may bring forth. I can't help thinking you exaggerated the effect of asking them to carry out their contract.... I can assure you we don't wish to take a narrow gauge or sectional view of the matter. We are acting in what we consider to be the best interests of the bank."[48]

AN EXTREMELY UNCOMFORTABLE QUANDARY

By January 16, 1920, Richardson was in an extremely uncomfortable quandary. One of the members of the Bank's Board of Directors had just paid a visit to Ottawa and, knowing nothing of the correspondence between Richardson and Campbell, had said to his friends on the Ottawa Board that they would all be rejoining him at the next annual meeting. "In the circumstances," the General Manager complained to Campbell, "I do not know what to do. We must remember that the Bank has acquired seventy-five millions of assets and seventy branches and I have reasonable hopes that the franchise and good will of the Bank of Ottawa will cost us practically nothing. Mr. [Grant] Macintyre, who puts all his time on their bad debts, told me at the end of the year that he thought the $500,000 we had set aside for their losses would not be needed. I only fear now that we may take a step that will lose to us part of the good will for which I am satisfied either the Bank of Montreal, the Royal, or the Commerce would have paid two million dollars or more."[49]

Richardson was positive that there was no such thing in the minds of the Ottawa Directors as moving the Head Office or acquiring the Presidency; they had even given up any hope of a Vice-Presidency. "Further, they do not regard their little meetings in Ottawa as Directors' meetings; they are invariably designated in our correspondence as 'Committee' meetings and they consist of informal talks with Mr. Cann about credits to the branches under his charge and are really a sort of vehicle for keeping up a little interest in business life.... Mr. Cann said that they had no unfriendly criticism to make of us in any way, and he is satisfied that their intentions are honourable and they have not the slightest disposition to make any trouble; it is just that they cannot decide as to who is to retire." In Richardson's view, one Director who was in England and Sir George Burn, who was losing interest in remaining, could well be retired by the Bank. For the others, "they are

The Amalgamations, 1910-1923

all hoping for a reprieve. I have not the slightest doubt as to the wisdom of our granting the eight of them that reprieve."[50]

PROBLEMS FINALLY RESOLVED

Richardson won his point, and with the re-election of the eight, the debate on Directors closed. By 1924, after three additional retirements, the Ottawa "slate" would be down to five men who would serve the Bank with distinction for most of the next decade: the Honourable George Bryson, Russell Blackburn, the Honourable George Gordon, John B. Fraser, and Alexander Maclaren. In the meantime, in accordance with the terms of the merger, all executive functions of the former Bank of Ottawa were to be transferred to General Office, Toronto, at the end of 1921. Cann's post as Assistant General Manager of the Bank of Ottawa would be eliminated but another position would be found for him. (Richardson wanted to send Cann to London, England, where a branch had been opened after the war, but difficulties developed and he went instead to New York as agent.) There would be a general and final merging of all accounting records and there would be neither place nor purpose for the Ottawa Directors' weekly "committee meetings."

H.A. Richardson, on running-board.

In car, left to right:
H.D. Burns;
W.W. Watson;
G. Macintyre;
McIlroy (chauffeur);
unidentified.

SENIOR HELP FOR RICHARDSON

Having guided the Bank through its great expansion and having almost worn himself out in the process, Richardson urgently needed more senior help; his right-hand man, Waters, had retired in 1917. In 1923 H.F. Patterson was brought from New York (where he had been agent and was now replaced by Cann) to Toronto, where he was appointed as an additional Assistant General Manager. In New York Patterson had established himself as one of the best officers of the Bank and now, along with J.A. McLeod, who had been Assistant General Manager since 1917, he became a key member of the headquarters team.

AN EXTRAORDINARY RECORD OF GROWTH

In the thirteen years between 1910 and 1923, the Bank had increased the number of its branches from 97 to 306 and the total of its assets from $53.5 million to $227.8 million. Through the three amalgamations and its own laborious branch-building, it had strengthened itself in each of the nine provinces and extended growth abroad. It had added ten branches in Newfoundland, four in the British West Indies, three in the Dominican Republic, and two in each of Puerto Rico and Cuba, not to mention establishing an office in London, England. It had become the fourth-largest Canadian bank, with the weight of its representation shifting westward. Compared with 86 branches in the three Maritime provinces, it now had 127 in Ontario alone.

RICHARDSON REFLECTS ON THE PAST

In 1919, Richardson reflected on his years of hard work in a letter to Payzant and found that life was good. "It seems to me," he wrote, "that on the whole...we have been a very happy family."[51] It is apparent from anecdotes and the flow of his correspondence that he got along well with those around him, though like most members of his generation, he had some difficulty in adapting to the rapidly changing times, as the following letter to a branch manager illustrates:

> Your letter of 28th ultimo on the subject of motor cars received. I may say that hearing from some Manager on this subject is now almost a daily occurrence with us. I quite agree with you that "everyone" seems to have a car now-a-days. As I walk down University Avenue in the morning and home at night, myriads of them pass me, and I often reflect on the economic waste, not to mention the impairment in the general health of our citizens, who would be much better off financially and physically if they traveled on foot as their forefathers did. However, the thing is in the air and I suppose it must run its course....If, therefore, you conclude to purchase a car we will make you a loan, although I would point out that a loan of $2,000 reduced at the rate of $600 a year would hardly

be extinguished during the lifetime of the car.... Please understand, however, that if your desire for a car is very strong, you may so far as we are concerned gratify it without feeling that the Bank disapproves of your course. I am afraid that the wave of desire for beginning where our fathers left off that is sweeping over the country is a good deal like other epidemics – grippe, measles, etc. – and we can only become immune by passing through the ordeal.[52]

RICHARDSON AND MCLEOD

One of Richardson's most valued men was his Assistant General Manager, J.A. McLeod, whom he was said to have brought up to Toronto with the remark, "There he was sitting on his fanny over in Chicago while I'm working my head off."[53] McLeod did not wish to be caught in such a position, but a former colleague recalled one day when he was. He had received, after he arrived in Toronto, a very welcome gift of some apples and had brought a bag to the office. At lunchtime he and the colleague had drifted into a conference room and had begun eating apples. The session had become extended as talk of the Bank led on to yarns about Nova Scotia. Something like an hour had passed when the door was yanked open and Richardson stalked in. "McLeod," he said, "I have been trying to see you for over one hour but was informed that you were very busy." Then he stopped as his eyes fell on the bag and he grasped the situation. He grinned, picked up an apple, and walked out.[54]

Another anecdote about the two men was recounted by Murray, who, it will be remembered, was the General Manager's clerk. McLeod, who was "perhaps ultra-conservative," had written a long letter for the General Manager's signature, addressed to the Calgary manager, criticizing him for his handling of a certain loan. Richardson had signed the letter, added a small footnote, and left it on Murray's desk, where McLeod happened to see it. The footnote in Richardson's distinctive handwriting that "he should not pay too much attention to the above" leaped up at him. The loyal assistant stiffened and walked off uttering a familiar Maritime expression: "I might as well be pissing up the wind as writing him."[55]

THE HALIFAX EXPLOSION

Of all the disasters of the war, the one which came most nearly home to the Bank and to Richardson himself was the explosion which took place in Halifax on the morning of December 6, 1917. In Toronto, rumours had reached Richardson in the afternoon of the day and he had telegraphed to the Secretary of the Board: "Presume reports here greatly exaggerated."[56] The reply had come back to him at ten-thirty in the evening. There had been no exaggeration; the rumours were less than the fact:

Terrific explosion on munitions ship at nine o'clock this morning partially demolished every building in Halifax and Dartmouth. Business suspended to-day and possibly to-morrow. Hundreds of people killed. Our offices here will be repaired as soon as possible. Several of staff slightly injured.[57]

Other reports followed of what was up to that time the world's greatest man-made explosion. The French ship *Mont Blanc*, heavily laden with T.N.T. and picric acid and carrying a deckload of benzol in drums, had collided in Halifax Harbour with a Norwegian freighter. The collision had set off an earthquake, a tidal wave, and an air concussion which broke windows in Truro, sixty miles away, and which demolished the north end of Halifax. The tremendous pressure of air and a subsequent firestorm destroyed 6,000 homes, killed 1,630 people, and wounded thousands of others.

The Bank was comparatively unscathed and none of its people was seriously hurt, but it was treated as a family disaster that required

Devastation as a result of the explosion of the *Mont Blanc* in Halifax harbour, Dec. 6, 1917. The S.S. *Imo* is seen on the far shore where it was thrown by the blast.

CREDIT: JAMES COLLECTION, CITY OF TORONTO ARCHIVES

unstinting help. "Think we should lead in arrangements for contributions to relieve needy and amount contributed,"[58] Richardson telegraphed Payzant on December 7. (The Bank was, in fact, a leading donor to the Halifax Relief Fund; its contribution of $100,000 matched that of the province of Ontario.[59]) On December 8, Richardson went to Halifax to examine the situation himself. Ordinary business could wait, he wrote before he left. Then he continued, "I have had several telegrams from Halifax and they all indicate that the disaster there is stupendous...hundreds dead, thousands injured, and that most of the buildings...are wrecked....We are going through so many such experiences to-day that it perhaps takes some of the edge off this Halifax disaster; at the same time it is shocking and pretty nearly prevents one going on with one's work."[60]

THE STRAIN OF CONTINUOUS TRAVEL

"Going on with one's work," even in the prewar years, had entailed considerable effort. Richardson had come to office responsible for the development of a business with enormous territorial dimensions, dimensions which he further extended and filled out. With such a big constituency, he had perforce become familiar with all the discomfort of railway travel from one coast to the other – an aspect of his job which he did not enjoy.

He detested the sea voyages that took him to the Caribbean branches and appreciated associates who were of quite another mind. Both Archibald and Campbell, whether as Directors, Presidents, or just tourists on a busman's holiday, had been ready to go anywhere, scout a promising territory, and turn in a shrewd report, meanwhile enjoying it all. "Everything seems to agree with you," an envious, queasy-stomached Richardson had once written to Archibald, "even sea voyages when it is rough."[61]

With regard to one of his own voyages, Richardson has left a harrowing account of his return journey from Puerto Rico:

> Although the *Brazos* is a 10,000 ton ship, she is, as conducted at present, the most filthy thing I ever traveled on, and I have horrible recollections of the...Spanish, greasy, cold cooking. My room was over-run with cockroaches and my ankles are pretty badly bitten up – by what, I leave you to imagine. Owing to the running seas they battened down the windows so that my heated imagination is able to conjure up just about exactly what the Black Hole of Calcutta was like.[62]

The strain, the physical discomfort, and the difficulty of supervision were only a part of the growing pains that went with an evolving bank. The ever-expanding network required an administration that could divide responsibilities and answer to specific needs. During Richardson's term, at least a start was made. By 1922, he had both J.A. McLeod and H.F. Patterson as Assistant General Managers, as has already been mentioned. Under them were a Chief Superintendent and six Superintendents, two District Supervisors with a staff of thirteen Inspectors, all having specific regions or special responsibilities. Evolving little by little were the autonomy, the supervision, and the controlled flexibility which further expansion would require.

TROUBLES AHEAD

The Bank, however, was moving into a period when expansion would be slow and later cease. In 1922, the collapse of sugar prices in the West Indies and of fish prices in Newfoundland signalled what lay in store for the world. The Bank and the Bank's customers felt some of the shock. "Never in my mind have I doubted," wrote one of the men around Richardson, "but that the sugar fiasco, plus the bottom falling out of the Newfoundland Fish prices hastened the demise of H.A. Richardson."[63] From February of 1923 it was evident to those close to him that his strength was failing. By March, he was confined to his home and on May 18, at the age of sixty-one, he died.

He had been forehanded in providing for his own succession. J.A. McLeod took over as General Manager, with H.F. Patterson and H.D. Burns as Assistant General Managers. Burns, whom Richardson had recently moved from Vancouver back to Toronto, had been one of the original group sent from Halifax in 1897 to open the Toronto office. These three were left, thanks to their predecessors, at the head of a well-balanced, well-integrated, nationally established bank. It was only in western Canada that Richardson's hopes had not been realized.

NOTES

1. PAC, RG 19, Vol.3303, H.A. Richardson to T.C. Boville, Deputy Minister of Finance, dated Toronto, May 10, 1911.
2. *Ibid.*, May 22, 1911.
3. BNS Archives, L.D. Murray to Margot Dixon, dated Charlottetown, Feb. 27, 1968.
4. *Ibid.*, L.R. Crammond to Dixon, dated Saint John, N.B., Feb. 16, 1968.
5. *Ibid.*, C.H. Easson to Richardson, dated Saint John, Dec. 29, 1910.
6. *Ibid.*, Richardson to Easson, dated Toronto, Feb. 4, 1911.
7. *Ibid.*, Richardson to Payzant, dated Toronto, Jan. 26, 1912.
8. *Ibid.*, Feb. 12, 1912.
9. *Ibid.*, Easson to Richardson, dated Winnipeg, Feb. 29, 1912.
10. *Ibid.*, March 13, 1912.
11. *Ibid.*, Richardson to Payzant, dated Toronto, Feb. 29, 1912.
12. *Ibid.*, March 21, 1912.
13. *Ibid.*, Easson to Richardson, dated Winnipeg, July 9, 1912.
14. *Ibid.*, Richardson to Easson, dated Toronto, July 15, 1912.
15. *Ibid.*, Arthur Macdonald to Charles Tompkins, dated Saint John, N.B., Dec. 12, 1912.
16. *Ibid.*, Richardson to the Board, dated Toronto, Nov. 16, 1912.
17. *Ibid.*, Richardson to the Board (telegram), dated Toronto, Nov. 16, 1912.
18. *Ibid.*, Macdonald to Tompkins, dated Saint John, N.B., Dec. 12, 1912.
19. *Globe*, Saint John, N.B., Dec. 9, 1912.
20. *Ibid.*
21. *Ibid.*
22. BNS Archives, Crammond to Dixon, dated Saint John, N.B., Feb. 16, 1968.
23. *Ibid.*, Macdonald to Tompkins, dated Saint John, N.B., Dec. 12, 1912.
24. *Ibid.*, Crammond to Dixon, dated Saint John, N.B., Feb. 16, 1968.
25. *Ibid.*, Richardson to Payzant, dated Toronto, Oct. 6, 1913.
26. BNS Directors' Minute Book, Oct. 13, 1913.
27. *The Story of Moore, 1882-1982* (brochure), Moore Corporation Ltd., Toronto, 1982.
28. *Globe*, Toronto, Jan. 20, 1912.
29. BNS Archives, McLeod to the Board, dated Toronto, Dec. 27, 1901.
30. *Ibid.*, Richardson to the Board, dated Toronto, Aug. 16, 1911.
31. *Ibid.*, Sept. 16, 1911.
32. *Ibid.*, Richardson to Payzant, dated Toronto, Feb. 22, 1912.
33. *Ibid.*, E.R.C. Clarkson to W.D. Ross, dated Toronto, June 23, 1914.
34. *World*, Toronto, July 24, 1914.
35. BNS Archives, Richardson to the Board, dated Toronto, Jan. 1, 1915.
36. *Ibid.*, Nov. 5, 1915.
37. Merrill Denison, *Canada's First Bank: A History of the Bank of Montreal*, Volume 2 (Toronto: McClelland & Stewart, 1907), p.323.
38. BNS Archives, Richardson to Charles Archibald, dated Toronto, Sept. 7, 1918.
39. BNS Directors' Minute Book, Oct. 17, 1917.
40. BNS Archives, Richardson to the Board, dated Toronto, Mar. 22, 1918.
41. *Ibid.*, Richardson to Payzant, dated Toronto, Apr. 2, 1917.
42. *Ibid.*, H.V. Cann, *Pages from a Banker's Journal*, p.37.
43. *Ibid.*, Cann to Richardson, dated Ottawa, Jan. 13, 1919.
44. *Ibid.*, H.V. Cann, *op. cit.*, p.38.
45. *Ibid.*, Richardson to Archibald, dated Toronto, Sept. 26, 1919.
46. *Ibid.*
47. *Ibid.*, Richardson to G.S. Campbell, dated Toronto, Dec. 30, 1919.
48. *Ibid.*, Campbell to Richardson, dated Halifax, Jan. 2, 1920.
49. *Ibid.*, Richardson to Campbell, dated Toronto, Jan. 16, 1920.
50. *Ibid.*
51. *Ibid.*, Richardson to Payzant,

dated Toronto, Nov. 19, 1919.
52. *Ibid.*, Richardson to N.W. Berkinshaw, dated Toronto, May 5, 1920.
53. *Ibid.*, Murray to Dixon, dated Charlottetown, Feb. 27, 1968.
54. *Ibid.*, R.H. Hegan, Bank of the Manhattan Company, to H.D. Burns, dated New York, Mar. 11, 1946.
55. *Ibid.*, Murray to Dixon, dated Charlottetown, Feb. 27, 1968.
56. *Ibid.*, Richardson to the Board (telegram), dated Toronto, Dec. 6, 1917.
57. *Ibid.*, The Board to Richardson (telegram), dated Halifax, Dec. 6, 1917.
58. *Ibid.*, Richardson to Payzant, dated Toronto, Dec. 7, 1917.
59. *The Canadian Annual Review*, 1918, Chapter 7, p.40.
60. BNS Archives, Richardson to Cann, dated Toronto, Dec. 7, 1917.
61. *Ibid.*, Richardson to Archibald, dated Toronto, Feb. 9, 1914.
62. *Ibid.*, Richardson to Campbell, dated Toronto, Mar. 13, 1919.
63. *Ibid.*, E.L. Pequegnat to F.W. Ross, dated Toronto, Sept. 2, 1959.

8

Consolidation and Then...
The Great Depression
1924-1939

During the thirty years from 1890 to 1919, from the time the Bank first started moving out from the Maritimes until after the First World War, its average annual rate of growth had been 9 per cent in real terms. In the 1910-1919 period, the decade of the acquisition of the three banks described in the previous chapter, the growth rate had been even higher: 10^1/$_2$ per cent. In these few years, the Bank's assets had more than doubled in size and its geographic coverage was greatly extended.*

TURNING FOUR BANKS INTO ONE

A long process of consolidation was essential to turn four banks into one, and it is little wonder that a period of rapid expansion should have been succeeded by one of more modest development. In the twenties, which was a time of excitement and growth for many businesses and most banks, the Nova Scotia's progress was indeed modest – only about 2 per cent per annum. In contrast to some of the other banks, there were no more takeovers and few branches were added. A more aggressive policy might perhaps have been expected and the posture of the Bank was undoubtedly conservative. But at the same time, this conservative posture saved the Bank from entering the Great Depression in an extended position rather than in the strong situation in which it actually found itself. Richardson's acquisitions had made the Nova Scotia one of the big banks of Canada, and McLeod's conservatism brought it into the depression with the strength to withstand the storms that were just over the horizon.

---

*Comparisons of this kind, here and elsewhere in this book, must be regarded as approximations because of the virtual impossibility of making accurate corrections for inflation.

J.A. MCLEOD AS GENERAL MANAGER

As The Bank of Nova Scotia entered this period of slower growth, there were significant changes in its upper echelons. As has already been noted, J.A. McLeod became General Manager after Richardson's death in 1923. In 1923 also, Charles Archibald resigned as President and G.S. Campbell, who succeeded him, lived only until 1927. In that year, S.J. Moore became President. He was the first Upper Canadian, Toronto-based industrialist to be elected to that post, but any fears that less attention would now be paid to Maritime concerns proved groundless. At the same time, McLeod and Hector McInnes (the senior Director in Halifax) were both made Vice-Presidents. The record of correspondence between McLeod in Toronto and McInnes in Halifax indicates a continuation of the congenial relationship between the two centres which had characterized the Richardson regime. And in the previous year, the West had been included for the first time in the councils of the Board in the person of Sidney T. Smith of Winnipeg.

GOOD TIMES BUT SPECULATION A DANGER

By the end of 1925, the Canadian economy had recovered from the postwar slump. Good crops were again growing on the prairies and there was a general improvement in business in the East. McLeod characterized 1926 as the best year for Canada since the postwar deflation, and by the end of 1927, the West had had its third successive year of bountiful harvests and the industrial East was making impressive progress. The one cloud on the horizon, noted by Moore and McLeod at the Bank's annual meeting in January 1928, was the growth of speculation in the stock market. By May 1928, it had become a serious matter for the Bank, in McLeod's view.

> So widespread has speculation become [he wrote in a confidential circular to branch managers] that to-day we have an unhealthy, if not dangerous, situation confronting us. Everyone who can borrow money appears to be speculating.... Other banks as well as ourselves are overloaned against stocks and bonds, and as the supply of money which was coming from the United States has practically ceased owing to higher interest rates...the strain on Canadian banks is now beginning to tell. It is imperative for us to strengthen our cash position.... casual stock and bond loans are to be avoided.... Managers are cautioned to look carefully to their margins.[1]

Early in 1929, Moore sounded a warning to the Canadian public at the annual meeting in Halifax:

> The fever of speculation which marked the year 1927 continued, with occasional recessions, throughout 1928. Contrary to predictions and expectations no serious permanent decline in prices

Consolidation and Then . . . The Great Depression, 1924 - 1939 139

G.S. Campbell,
President, 1923-1927

occurred and the opinion of many seems to be that this condition can safely continue indefinitely. Therein lies a serious danger. The present market price of many stocks seems to be entirely out of line with what may reasonably be expected from them in the years to come.... Great discrimination, therefore, seems to be necessary if serious losses, involving a real hardship to many are to be avoided.[2]

But still the boom went on well into 1929. The Bank's own figures showed an unusually prosperous year with earnings at the highest level in history: $2.8 million, compared with $1.9 million in 1919 and $1.2 million in 1913. The truth was that the country had been enjoying a great boom in construction, with other industries responding to that stimulus and, as McLeod had pointed out at the beginning of 1929:

More buildings were erected, more metals were produced, more goods were manufactured and more trade conducted both at home and abroad [during 1928] than at any time since the war. For the fourth consecutive season the income from farm crops has been very large. At the same time the wages of factory workers have been well maintained, while employment and profits have been substantially increased. This even distribution of good times between town and country and rich and poor is, after all, the essence of real prosperity. It has brought a renewed feeling of content and confidence and vigor to the whole nation. It has resulted in greater industrial efficiency and in less social and political unrest. National unity has been strengthened accordingly.[3]

IMPOSSIBLE TO ENVISAGE SEVERITY OF DEPRESSION

Even a year later, after the shock of October 1929, it was impossible for the shareholders and their President and Directors, and indeed for most people, to envisage what the future would bring. Figures for the full year 1929, because they contained nine or ten good months, still gave the illusion of prosperity, though there had been some slackening shortly before the stock market crash and the prairie crops had been disappointing. Even as the year came to its end, with automobile sales falling steeply and railway earnings declining, and with business conditions worsening in the United States, no one expected the longest and deepest depression in history. The Canadian economy was bigger and stronger than ever before. The Bank of Nova Scotia, which had expanded only moderately in the twenties, was looking forward to significant growth in the thirties. During 1929, it had purchased the northeast corner of King and Bay streets in Toronto as the site for a new General Office building. Construction, it was planned, would begin in 1931. Of equal interest and more imminent was the prospect of a splendid new Head Office building in Halifax.

On January 28, 1931, the last annual general meeting of shareholders to take place in the old Head Office building was held to consider the statement for 1930. With assets, deposits, commercial loans, and profits all considerably lower, it was hardly a cheerful occasion. "At the beginning of 1930," said McLeod, "we knew that, following the great decline of stock market prices, industry must receive a set-back. But none of us realized how great that set-back would be."[4] Still less had anyone anticipated the blows that would be suffered by prairie farmers. Heat, rust, and high winds in the summer and late rains in the fall had all combined to reduce grain production. Worse still, a downward spiral of commodity prices was eroding the value of wheat. Number One Northern Wheat at Winnipeg, which had been 1.68^{1}/_{8}$ on August 3, 1929, had fallen by December 26, 1930, to 50$^{5}/_{8}$¢ per bushel. Cash income from the sale of farm products in the three Prairie provinces had dropped from $620 million in 1928 to $268 million in 1930, and everything pointed to still further declines.

TORONTO BUILDING PROJECT POSTPONED

In these circumstances, it was not surprising that the Bank postponed its largest building project – the new General Office building in Toronto – a postponement which, in fact, lasted for almost fifteen years. Meanwhile, however, in Halifax it was expected that the Head Office building would be ready to receive tenants by May 1, 1931, and that the main banking quarters would be completed three months later. "We join," said McLeod in January 1931, "in hoping that, when next we hold our Annual Meeting (which we expect will be in our new building), the celebration of the one hundredth anniversary of The Bank of Nova Scotia will occur amid conditions indicating trade recovery, with the promise of renewed prosperity to come."[5]

NEW HEAD OFFICE IN HALIFAX

His hopes for business recovery were dashed, but the successive steps in the occupation of the new building went as planned. On Monday, August 3, the building was opened for business, the staff having made the move from the old building on the previous Saturday; customers could walk in and do business during banking hours or they could join tours conducted by staff members from five to eleven in the evening. On Tuesday, August 4, following the first meeting of the Board of Directors in the new building, there was a brief ceremony in the banking room, at which both Messrs. Moore and McLeod made speeches. But there was no buffet luncheon, such as had been proposed by one of the Directors, the Hon. F.B. McCurdy; "he says," McInnes had reported to McLeod, "that his wife and my wife could look after it very well and see that the Lord Nelson Hotel supplied us with food."[6] Also, the suggestion that "a paper knife, suitably embossed or some such small but chaste article" be given away was not followed up.[7] The Commerce, McLeod recalled, had got itself into trouble by handing out souvenir postcards made in the United States for the official opening of its Head Office building. "...The same thing would apply in our own case if we got the suggested mementoes from Chicago," McLeod wrote. In any case, "in view of the present depression the less display and money spent the better."[8]

As far as the structure itself was concerned, nothing was stinted. Located on the northeast corner of Hollis and Prince streets, the building contained four floors of office space above the banking room. "In design, however," said its prospectus, "it does not present a purely office building but is distinctly a banking structure in which the architects have introduced a new note of distinctly Canadian character. Throughout the whole decorative treatment, whether in stone, wood, plaster, or bronze, this new Canadian motif is everywhere apparent and is worthy of study."[9]

"BUILDING SPOKE OF LUXOR"

The architects were John M. Lyle of Toronto in association with Andrew R. Cobb of Halifax. Lyle wrote later that he had found "a rich field of inspiration lying dormant in the fauna, flora and marine life of

Canada. We began three years ago to accumulate data in the form of Canadian flowers, fruits, trees, birds, animals, grain, marine life and Indian motifs. I sent a man to the Royal Ontario Museum to make colour drawings of Indian decorative forms.... We have adopted a new language or ornament based on Canadian forms, having in mind that they must all pass the test of beauty."[10] Thus were the Greek and Roman ornaments traditional to bank construction at that time replaced by Canadian themes. Sheaves of wheat, pine cones, Canada geese, dolphins, and dories all appear on the walls of this Maritime bank. And, as has already been mentioned, there is a mural of Cunard's *Britannia* over the main door of the banking room. The room itself has a thirty-foot ceiling rich in design and "warm and exhilarating in colour," from which hang handsome light fixtures. Grilles are of bronze, as are the splendid doors at the entrance, which had been on exhibition prior to installation and which had been much admired. The floors and counters are of marble, the walls of travertine stone, and eleven windows throw an "ample but softened light" over all. To one awed newspaper correspondent, the building spoke of Luxor.[11]

BANK'S ATTACHMENT TO HALIFAX

In that August of 1931, as admiring Haligonians passed through the new building, the Bank had some cause to be satisfied with its record in the city. It had been a good corporate citizen. Over the years the various members of the Board of Directors and of the staff had been contributors to local enterprises and they had enriched their home community. The Bank was proud of its association with Dalhousie College. Halifax's social agencies had been supported by Bank executives and their wives; and in the great disaster of the 1917 explosion, the Bank's people had pitched in whole-heartedly.

The Bank's attachment to Halifax and to Nova Scotia went deeper than purely commercial considerations would suggest. Lawson, Johnston, and Uniacke – distinguished names in the early history of the Bank – were also important in the political life of the province. The interests of the Archibalds and the Payzants extended from politics to the arts; Edith Archibald was a writer of distinction. The many-sided Anna Leonowens has been as well remembered in Halifax artistic circles as her son-in-law, Thomas Fyshe, has been in banking; the gallery at the Nova Scotia College of Arts bears her name. George S. Campbell was the son of Duncan Campbell, the author of several histories of Nova Scotia. In all this there was a sense of belonging and achievement which the Bank shared with the town.

Halifax as Head Office might now be something of a symbol; the regular Directors' meetings had been held in Toronto since 1929 and the executive group had been located there since the turn of the century. But Halifax was still of real meaning, as Upper Canadian and western Directors discovered, particularly during the trips by special railway car to the annual meeting. These journeys, which continued for more than fifteen years after the Second World War, gave the participants a chance to unwind and to share in the Bank's tradition. They found in Halifax a link with the pioneers from this great Atlantic port who had established a strong local institution which had broadened into an international enterprise.

The Nova Scotia had been first among Canadian banks to reach out along the traditional routes of Maritime seaborne trade. It was now leader in Newfoundland and had been overtaken only by the Royal, that other Halifax-born institution, in the West Indies. Its first venture into the western midcontinent, unfortunate in the case of Winnipeg, had been redeemed by the success of Minneapolis and Chicago. The offices in New York and London were well positioned to take advantage of any upturn in trade and foreign exchange business.

Main Banking Room, Halifax Main Branch, Erected 1931.

The mural over the main doors depicts Samuel Cunard's *Britannia* and commemorates the inauguration of regular steamship service between England and North America in 1840.

A DEPRESSING CENTENARY

The Bank at its hundredth year had 36 branches in its home province, 9 in Prince Edward Island, and 37 in New Brunswick, for a total of 82 in the Maritimes. It had 23 branches in Quebec, 134 in Ontario, 38 in the three Prairie provinces, and 6 in British Columbia, bringing the Canadian total to 283. In addition, there were 12 branches in Newfoundland, 12 in Jamaica, 8 in Cuba, and 7 other foreign branches, which made a grand total of 322 branches. The number of employees had settled at around 2,400, and this number would show little variation until the beginning of the Second World War.

Ahead, as the depression deepened, was one 5 per cent pay cut (10 per cent for senior officers), which would come in 1933. While there were some salary increases, particularly among the junior staff, the period from 1933 to 1939 was a very slow one. There were few promotions because there were few, if any, new jobs. However, the level of real income, as General Office circulars occasionally pointed out, did not fall on the average but actually rose to some extent as the cost of living declined; in that sense, some employees were ahead of the game. In urban centres, the junior, the ledgerkeeper, or the teller could look around him, and count himself lucky to be among the ones in mere possession of a job.

THE OLD WAYS – NOT A LEADER IN MECHANIZATION

Any bank that could envisage a picnic lunch managed by its Directors' wives as part of the opening ceremonies for a new Head Office had still within it a certain homey touch and a hankering for the old ways of doing things. Certainly the Bank retained its pervading tinge of Scottishness. "When I came to General Office in 1927," said Boyles, "with a lot of the people I had to deal with and report to I almost needed an interpreter." But perhaps that was because he was English!

The Bank was not yet a leader in mechanization. The adding machine was making its appearance slowly, and in fact, its introduction was resisted by some of the older managers who felt that it would reduce their officers' ability to add columns of figures. There were few regrets, however, when handwritten communications and the sponges and blurs of the letterpress book gave way to the typewriter and carbon paper. Under the old process, says Harry Freestone, who began his banking career in Campbellville, Ontario, and retired from it as manager of one of the London, England, branches:

> The manager's communications to Head Office were written out in longhand, then handed to the junior who was expected to take copies from them in the copying book – a bound book with leaves like tissue paper and a loose sheet of oiled cardboard that you put beneath the paper. Then you took a sponge, dampened the whole of the tissue paper over the oiled sheet, put the manager's communica-

Consolidation and Then... The Great Depression, 1924-1939 145

tion face down on the wetted tissue, placed another piece of oiled cardboard over that, put it in the letterpress, tightened it down and left it there for about a minute. When you opened it there was supposed to be a copy of the manager's communication on the tissue sheet while the original could go to Head Office. But occasionally you'd put on too much water – you'd have to take the blurred mess to the manager and he'd have to write his communication all over again. It was worse still with the branch returns which were often pages and pages of figures – and worst of all if it was the accountant's work because then you were almost sure to get a good cuff or a boot.

George C. Hitchman, recently retired as a Deputy Chairman of the Board, entered the Bank in its hundredth year at Woodbridge, Ontario, and is graphic on a junior's duties and the economics of depression:

Montague, P.E.I., 1922.

"A staff of 5,
a typewriter,
no typist, and
no adding machine"

The junior was responsible for the office in general and in particular a taker-out and a retriever of drafts....in those days all the stores bought their merchandise and the supplier didn't wait for a cheque to come in; he drew a draft. The supplier's bank would finance the supplier by discounting those drafts and then send the draft into the area where the store was. So the junior's responsibility was to take the draft down to the drug store or the clothing store or whatever and get it accepted. You had two days, generally speaking, to get the draft collected. I guess, looking back, this was one of the real fine ways of learning to become a banker because when you walked up and down the street people were educating you, particularly some of the old-timers in the stores who had very cute ways of testing you and keeping you from getting that draft back in forty-eight hours.

The writing up of the ponderous ledgers which the manager kept under lock and key is vivid in Hitchman's memory, as it is in that of everyone who was a junior in those days. "The teller in the branch was the boss guy. He taught you what you knew. About six months after being in Woodbridge, the economic conditions were such that the staff was reduced to two, the manager and me. I became junior, teller and all on a salary of $500 a year. Room and board was $7 a week and after paying $3 a month for a university course, I was left with $2 a week."

"You paid $3 a month for a university course at a time when you were making that salary? It was a course on banking?"

"Yes."

"The other $2 a week was to waste?"

"The other $2 a week was capital."

HEAD OFFICE COMMUNICATIONS

For H.R. Younker, who joined the Bank at Montague, Prince Edward Island, in 1925, life as a junior was much the same as for Hitchman. Montague had a staff of five, a typewriter but no typist, and no adding machine. Younker has recollections of the manager sitting down at the typewriter after the close of business to hunt and peck his way through a long communication: "I don't think he had the faintest idea that there was such a thing as paragraphing. He just started at the top and went right through." As a ledgerkeeper, balancing at the end of the year stands out in Younker's mind: "One December 31, I listed down by hand the savings account balances–then the interest, added on the interest, listed the new totals–and left at 4:00 a.m.–balanced."

Even more poignant is Younker's memory of a fire at the Montague branch and its unsatisfactory sequel: "...the insurance settlement, when received, included $50 to replace Younker's suit. The whole amount was credited to Head Office and it was expected they would credit us with $50. After forty-six years I am still waiting....I have figured that $50 with interest at, say, 6% compounded annually for 46 years comes to something over $1,200."[12]

C.E. Ritchie, now Chairman of the Board, and J.A.G. Bell, President, have a somewhat different opinion about the value of Younker's suit and they proposed another settlement in a Head Office communication sent, rather belatedly, in 1975:

> The Bank could, but it will not, question your assertion that in 1929 you did have in your possession a suit of clothing that, at some point in time previously, had had a value of $50. Let us not go into the subject of constant dollars, but one has to think about depreciated values and were we to think of a reasonable 50% annual rate of depreciation and assuming just for a moment that you had had the suit for five years, we would be thinking of a book value of $1.56 in 1929.
>
> In short, the enclosed cheque for $50 represents an astronomical return on investment.[13]

BANK WAS HUMAN

On some occasions, the hundred-year-old Bank was surprisingly human. Freestone, having been transferred to Timmins, tells of the problem he faced when General Office rejected a loan application from his manager: "The manager went on holidays and the day after he left, a communication came in from Head Office turning down a loan he'd asked for, which was beyond his discretionary limit. Well, I said to myself, if the manager comes back and finds this loan has been turned down and I haven't done anything about it, I'm going to be in trouble. There was only one thing to do – go right to the top. So I phoned Mr. Burns in Toronto.

"I said, 'Mr. Burns, you've turned down that loan to George Bartney.'

"'Oh? What loan was that, Mr. Freestone?'

"'Well,' I said, 'it's the loan the manager recommended before he went on holidays. We can't turn it down.'

"There was a kind of sigh on the line and something that just possibly might have been a chuckle and he came at me again. 'Now what's all this about?' And I explained it all.

"'Well,' he said when I finished, 'it wasn't me who turned down the loan. It was the General Manager. If you were the man on the spot, what would you do?'

"'I'd make that loan, Mr. Burns.'

"'You would?'

"'Yes. Because if we don't give George the money, Mr. Burns, he'll go right across the street and get it from our competitor and we'll lose a customer.'

"There was another long pause, another of those sounds on the line that might have been a chuckle, and he came through clear and crisp. 'Right. I'll go and tell the General Manager, Mr. Freestone, that you're the man on the spot and you're making the loan.'

"So I made the loan," concludes Freestone, "and in due course, George Bartney paid it back." It was a transaction characteristic of a time when it was still possible for a junior to know most of the people in a community, and when a senior executive could say, as Burns did, that he knew every member of the staff and many of their relatives.

IMPROVING ORGANIZATION

While not a period of marked expansion, the years after taking over the Bank of Ottawa in 1919 saw a number of significant changes in the organization of The Bank of Nova Scotia. As has already been noted, the general executive was strengthened by the appointment of H.D. Burns as an Assistant General Manager in 1923, who joined Patterson in this capacity. After Patterson became General Manager, the appointment of Edwin Crockett kept the number of Assistant General Managers at two. To meet the needs of the much larger organization resulting from the takeover of the three banks, most General Office departments were enlarged, including the Chief Accountant's Department and the Inspection Department.

The Chief Accountant's Department, the supporting arm of the general executive, also broadened its functions because banking was becoming more complicated. For better or for worse, there were more and more relations with governments, more forms, and more tax problems. Customers had tax problems, too, so the Bank began to help here as well. Accounting methods were improving and machines were being developed for posting accounts. And more detailed calculations with regard to costs had to be made in order to determine appropriate rates to charge customers, including governments. A.L. MacDonald, Chief Accountant during this period of change, was an astute and able man with a sense of humour which at times became frayed in his relationship with J.G. Rogerson, who was Secretary of the Bank. Rogerson, representing a competitive centre of power in the General Manager's office, was often in conflict with MacDonald, as everyone in the office knew; whoever was at fault, it was a continuing fact of life which created some amusement and probably also some inefficiency.

FORMATION OF THE INVESTMENT DEPARTMENT

One of the most important developments in the early twenties was the formation of an Investment Department to deal with the Bank's security holdings and the many transactions involved. With the advent of the depression in the thirties, government expenditures increased sharply while commercial lending declined, with the result that the

Bank ultimately found itself with more securities than loans on its books – a complete reversal of the relationship which characterized the twenties. Under H.J. Coon, a gold medallist from Queen's University, the Investment Department not only enlarged its scope but also became an important source of profit for the Bank. Coon had great ability and balanced judgment in financial matters and he worked closely and effectively with Patterson on the tough problems of depression. Subsequently, Coon left the Bank to become financial adviser to one of its important customers and was replaced by W. Keith Waters, who had had experience in the New York agency.

Loans and dealings with the investment community were an important part of the Bank's business in Toronto and Montreal, as well as in New York. It was generally profitable, though there were, of course, problems, particularly in the early years of the depression. Profitability depended not only on the managers of the big branches, but also on people closely involved in the business, like Basil Howard in Montreal, who worked directly in securities, and assistant managers like Donald Gordon and F.W. Nicks. The efforts and ingenuity that went into getting and keeping business were interesting to say the least, as, for example, when the Montreal office succeeded in attracting important securities business from U.S. citizens who were concerned about prospects in their own country in the thirties.

The Montreal branch, though not of the scale or breadth of the Toronto branch, was nevertheless a centre of major importance and was famous for some of its managers, such as N.W. Berkinshaw, who subsequently retired in 1948 in Toronto, where he was an Assistant General Manager. He ran the Montreal branch like a sergeant-major. People who did not obey orders promptly and visibly were in trouble. He was not at all popular, yet one of the staff was heard to remark after Berkinshaw's departure from Montreal that he was "happier in the old guy's regime than under the new manager who didn't seem to take much interest in you."

THE NEW ECONOMICS DEPARTMENT

Another significant development at headquarters was the decision made to publish a *Monthly Review* of business conditions, beginning in January 1927. It was to cost $5,000 per annum – not a very lavish budget even in those times. The editor of the *Monthly Review* and the Supervisor of the new Statistical Department* where the *Monthly Review* was to be prepared was to be Gilbert Jackson, a keen, interesting, and rather opinionated Englishman, who was the director of the Commerce Course at the University of Toronto. Devoting only part of his time to the project, Jackson began to look around for staff. First, he

---

* Though it was called the Statistical Department until 1942, it did the work of an Economics Department from its beginning.

MONTHLY REVIEW
THE BANK OF NOVA SCOTIA

Vol. 1   January, 1927   No. 1

WHEAT IN 1926

BY CONTRAST with the violent and unpredictable disturbances of 1924 and 1925, the price of wheat has been stable in 1926, and at a level satisfactory to the producer. The present position is illustrated, in relation to former years, by the chart on page 4. Opening in the New Year at $1.57 (Fort William basis), No. 1 Manitoba Northern has moved within limits of $1.58 and $1.29½, and is now selling at a few cents above the latter figure.

No less important than the market price is the size of the crop; and until the harvest is well advanced an element of anxiety will remain however excellent the market.

In the season now closing the farmer laboured under a series of handicaps. Rain was constant and heavy. Grain was badly damaged in the fields. Manitoba was visited early by snowstorms. In Ontario the weather was especially harsh. Nature herself at times seemed to fight against the harvester. The serious labour shortage on the prairie was an additional handicap. A despatch to London, published in early November, expressed "apprehension that the weather has dealt the Canadian West one of the worst blows in its history." Signs of pessimism multiplied.

A small crop, with an unusually large proportion below contract grade: these were the possibilities before the country. The realization of them would greatly narrow the home market; and since the bulk of Canadian manufactures must inevitably be sold in Canada, this would involve consequences no less serious to the cities than to the farmers of the countryside. Poor harvests imply closed factories.

Within a surprisingly short time these forebodings were dispelled. Damaged wheat quickly dried. Estimates of the crop volume were revised upwards. It is now clear that the number of bushels harvested is within a few millions, at least, of last year's figure. The percentage falling short of contract grade is larger than that of last season, but the difference is not a great one.

During November, wheat was exported in great volume and flour in quantities somewhat larger than those of the corresponding month in 1925. Ice on the Great Lakes abruptly checked the movement in December. Vessels attempting to trans-ship a last cargo before the close of navigation were compelled to return to the Bay Ports. Storage holdings increased abruptly.

Prices, meanwhile, were weakening. Australian and Argentine wheat crops were reported to be ripening better and earlier than usual. Freight rates, in consequence of the Coal Strike, were still high. Expecting that they would soon be lowered, European importers hesitated to charter space on ocean vessels. Rumours of a large Russian export—improbable, to say the least, since the clean grain of pre-war Russia came mostly from the grandees' estates that have been broken up, and not from peasant farms—were nevertheless disturbing.

On the threshold of a new year the wheat outlook is always uncertain. In the last few weeks uncertainty has been rather more marked than usual. Official estimates of the world's export surplus in the current season place it at 880,000,000 bushels. Estimates of the world's import requirements vary between 865,000,000 bushels and 705,000,000. The question which of these estimates comes nearer to the truth is one of no small consequence to the farmer as well as to the trader.

Recently the market has been a little firmer. Millers' stocks, both in England and on the Continent of Europe, are said to be low. Higher prices in the near future are therefore expected.

In his provisional estimate of crop values for the present season the Dominion Statistician takes $1.09 as the average price per bushel likely to be received by the farmer at the point of production. This is three cents less per bushel than the figure for last season.

If the wheat crop as a whole be reckoned as 405,800,000 bushels, its value to the farmer should therefore be $442,700,000; a decrease of $16,500,000 as compared with the preceding crop. The prairie farmers' aggregate income from wheat is calculated to be $411,100,000, a decrease of $12,300,000 on the same comparison. For their wheat, oats, barley and rye together, they should receive $556,200,000 in 1926-7 as compared with $580,900,000 in 1925-6; a decrease of $24,700,000.

If, in fact, the farmers of the west receive some 5% less for their grains this season than last, this is roughly balanced—perhaps a little more than balanced—by the fall of other commodity prices which has occurred in the last twelve months and is discussed elsewhere in this Review. Their purchasing power, in other words, is not adversely affected.

January 1927 Monthly Review, *First Issue.*

The Statistical Department began publishing the *Monthly Review* in January 1927 and the Economics Department carries on this tradition today.

hired D.C. MacGregor, one of his brightest students at the University of Toronto; he stayed for a year and then left to go to Harvard. When the class of 1929 graduated, Jackson chose one of its women, Betty Ratz. In 1931, she was joined by J. Douglas Gibson, who was also a Toronto graduate in political science and economics, and who later became General Manager of the Bank (and who is one of the authors of this book).

One of the Economics Department's problems, then and in the years that followed, was the high quality of its personnel, which made them unusually mobile. Betty Ratz interrupted her stay at the Bank to return to the University of Toronto on a teaching fellowship under Professor Harold Innis, and Jackson himself went to the Bank of England in 1935, leaving Gibson in charge with the part-time assistance of D.C. MacGregor (now a Professor at the University of Toronto) and Professor J.F. Parkinson. MacGregor pioneered research on the national income in the mid-thirties, an account of which appeared in the *Monthly Review*, while Parkinson responded to developments in Alberta by preparing two issues on social credit.

A succession of economists came and went, many of them going on to important careers elsewhere: E.R. Clark, who became President of the Industrial Development Bank; T.L. Avison, who was head of the Investment Department of the Canadian Imperial Bank of Commerce; E.H. Heeney, who became Chairman of the National Trust Company; and Morgan Reid, who was General Manager for Planning of Simpsons-Sears. Over the years, Betty Ratz (later Mrs. Hearn) carried out much original economic research, concentrating latterly on developments in Canadian economic history, and also on the history of The Bank of Nova Scotia. She also established the Bank's Library and Archives.

The office of the *Monthly Review* was the apartment of the former janitor, located by the dome above the banking room of Toronto branch and reached by a catwalk. The door to the office opened on bare floors, peeling wallpaper, and a blatantly exposed bathtub; a move to another building improved working conditions only moderately, since the roof leaked there and the typist was known to have worked under an umbrella. Nevertheless, the early issues of the *Monthly Review* as well as the flow of statistical data to senior executives of the Bank justified the existence of this department.

By the mid-1930s, not only the *Monthly Review* but also the reports of annual meetings were widely read in Canada and the United States. The day had long passed when the comments of a President or a General Manager would be summed up as "a few desultory remarks." Shareholders received from the President a wide-ranging survey of national and world conditions and from the General Manager a statement relating to the degree of progress made by the Bank.

DISASTER IN THE WEST

Meanwhile, the chill winds of depression were sweeping across the world. On January 27, 1932, as the Bank began its second century with "the first annual general meeting of Shareholders to be held in our beautiful new Head Office building,"[14] there was nothing in the recent past and less in the immediate future that offered grounds for optimism.

On the prairies, the elevators were choked with a huge surplus of wheat which could not be sold in a world where other countries (both exporters and importers) were expanding production; importing countries were imposing quotas and other trade barriers and exporting countries were putting Canada at a competitive disadvantage by depreciating their currencies. The price of Number One Northern Wheat was declining further; it hit the all-time low of 39 $\frac{3}{8}$ ¢ per bushel on the Winnipeg Grain Exchange in December 1932. The farmer lost money on every bushel he grew and the very soil that had produced the great surpluses seemed to be blowing away before a rainless prairie wind. In many of the worst areas of heat and drought there was hardly a green sprout to be seen in the acres of flour-fine, brownish-black dust.

In 1929 the Wheat Pool, which as marketing agent for the Manitoba, Saskatchewan, and Alberta Pools handled over 50 per cent of the Canadian wheat crop, had borrowed from the banks as usual to pay farmers a first instalment of $1 per bushel on the crop about to be sold. By February 1930, however, with a huge, unsold carry-over and falling prices, it was evident that the Pool could not maintain the 15 per cent margin which the banks required for security. The provincial governments initially stepped into the breach to prevent collapse of the Pool, providing funding for the 1929 crop by issuing twenty-year bonds. When the situation failed to improve in subsequent crop years, the federal government provided guarantees to the chartered banks on their loans to the Pools – a situation that continued until the formation of the Canadian Wheat Board in 1935.

DEPRESSION IN THE FINANCIAL MARKETS

Meanwhile, industry in eastern Canada was also in serious trouble. At the same time that the prairie market for domestic manufactures was deteriorating rapidly, export markets for base metals and forest products were collapsing, and construction activity was drying up. The Bank of Nova Scotia's plan for a new General Office building in Toronto was only one of many such projects abandoned at this time. Stock and bond prices reflected a distrust and apprehension which became even worse after September 20, 1931, when Great Britain went off the gold standard and a dozen nations followed. By the morning of September 21, Canadian banks and stock exchanges, after a series of all-night meetings, had agreed that though the exchanges should open, trading would be restricted. Short selling was prohibited and no transactions would be permitted at prices under those registered at the close of the previous week. These floor prices were extended for months and then gradually removed, the last in mid-1932. Meanwhile, the exchange rate on the Canadian dollar fell sharply, and in October three important Montreal brokerage houses with sizeable call loans in New York were forced to close their doors. By December, the Canadian dollar had fallen to a 20 per cent discount in New York.

In a market where government bond prices had dropped considerably and quality stock prices were being pounded down to levels much below book value, the banks, like other institutions with large security portfolios, were concerned about their balance sheet positions. The temporary floor under stock prices was of some help and on October 27, 1931, the federal government, led by R.B. Bennett, provided a further measure of support in the form of an Order-in-Council authorizing the banks to value their securities, bonds as well as stocks, either at book value or at the price prevailing at the close of business on August 31, 1931, whichever was the lower. The Inspector-General of Banks reported later that the banks made only limited use of the measure, since, by the end of 1931, they were in a position to make reasonable allowances for depreciation in all their investment securities. It is interesting to note that The Bank of Nova Scotia did not need to take advantage of the authority of the Order-in-Council at all.

In fact, the Canadian branch banking system as a whole weathered the storm very well indeed, unlike its unit banking counterpart in the United States, which a little more than a year later came to a complete standstill. On March 4, 1933, the day all U.S. banks were ordered to close, the Canadian Minister of Finance issued the reassuring statement that "the Canadian banks are in a very strong and exceptionally liquid position, and wholly capable of meeting any demands made upon them." Furthermore, as A.B. Jamieson has described in his authoritative work *Chartered Banking in Canada*,[15] officers of Canadian banks played a constructive role during the depression. Not only did they manage their own institutions in a way that ensured their solvency – there was not a single failure – but also they helped their customers deal with their problems by giving advice, extending loans where possible, and helping to work out reorganizations. Most banks had designated a senior officer, or often officers, supported by credit men to give special attention to customers in trouble. In the Nova Scotia, the man concerned was Grant Macintyre, who had an excellent record as a troubleshooter and problem-solver. Macintyre originally came from the Metropolitan Bank, and, it will be remembered, was responsible for sorting out the accounts of the Bank of Ottawa after The Bank of Nova Scotia took it over in 1919. He was appointed Assistant General Manager in 1943.

CRITICISM OF BANK DIVIDENDS

A sore point at this time was the critical attitude of the public towards bank dividends. Through 1931, The Bank of Nova Scotia had maintained its dividend rate at 16 per cent on a nominal share value of $100. Since the market price of the share, however, was in the neighbourhood of $300, the real return on investment was less than 6 per cent. The 16 per cent rate had shrunk in 1932 with the lowering of the dividend rate to 14 per cent at midyear, but the reduction was less than that of some of the other banks and it was not enough for the times.

> ...I am afraid [McLeod wrote to McInnes on April 27, 1933] that we will have to come down another 2%. The large Banks have now reduced their dividend disbursement 6%, including the 2% bonus.
>
> There are two reasons for a further reduction. First, our earnings have been reduced to a low ebb, with little prospect of any improvement this year. We have now over $13,000,000 of loans on which we are not taking the interest into profits, for the reason that on the bulk of the loans no interest is paid, and where it is collected we are reserving the amount on account of the doubtful condition of the loans involved....
>
> There is a second reason. We are held up as a shining example of the enormous dividends paid by Canadian Banks. On this point Mr. Bennett spoke to me last fall and suggested that we reduce our reserve fund so as to make capital and reserve of an equal amount. I pointed out that this could not be done under the Bank Act, but he volunteered to put through the necessary legislation to that end. Of course we would not consider such a step, but I give you this information because our large dividend is somewhat embarrassing to all the Banks. It is useless to try to convince the public that the amount we pay on shareholders' funds is relatively small. They consider the 14% in relation to capital only. Here and in the West it has often been repeated that Banks should not be paying dividends at all, but that interest rates should be brought down to give the governments, municipalities and other borrowers cheaper money.[16]

QUESTION OF REDUCING "OUTSIDE RESERVES"

Even more exposed than the banks to that line of argument was the harassed Prime Minister, faced with the political storms growing out of the disaster in the West. Later on in an eventful 1933 which saw the coming to power of Franklin D. Roosevelt in the United States and the establishment in Canada of the Royal Commission on Banking and Currency, McLeod wrote again to McInnes, enlarging on his opposition to the idea that the banks should reduce their reserves:

On Tuesday [the General Manager reported to McInnes on November 16, 1933] all representatives of the Banks were in Ottawa for a conference with the Prime Minister on matters of general interest, but particularly the advisability of reducing outside reserves. The Prime Minister has put it up to the Banks as a national necessity for he was quite satisfied in his own mind that no bank had sufficient inside reserves to see them over another crisis.... All Banks are holding an unusual proportion of investment in bonds. This, with the uncertainty in the fluctuation of currencies, made it necessary, in the view of the P.M., that the Banks should strengthen up inside. While he did not say that he requested this action, nevertheless he put it in such a way as to indicate that he wished it done. Of course it is well known now that three institutions will be obliged to take such action before they close their books on the 30th of this month.... But it is felt that if all the Banks should take similar action, on the ground that it is a conservative move, the effect on the public mind would be lessened rather than if one or two institutions had to do it alone.

There was another matter stressed by the P.M. and that is that the West has the impression that the Banks have been making too much money out of the public. They point out that many firms and corporations have had to take substantial losses, that no doubt the Banks have had to make provision for doubtful debts, and if they can do this from the inside then their charges to the public have been more or less exorbitant. If it is pointed out that the Banks have had to encroach on their outside reserves, that might create the impression in the mind of these people that after all they have not exacted interest rates beyond what was necessary.[17]

Six of the nine banks did in fact reduce their outside reserves. The Bank of Nova Scotia was one of the three that did not. But around this time, the focus of public attention was shifting to the Report of the Royal Commission on Banking and Currency, which had recommended the establishment of a central bank.

REVISION OF THE BANK ACT

In late 1932, with the Bank Act due for revision the following year, the government decided that an inquiry into the workings of the whole monetary system, and not just the legislation directly affecting the banks, was necessary. It was soon apparent what some of the findings might be. Conservatives, Liberals, and the newly born CCF were all in favour of the establishment of a central bank. The idea had been discussed periodically in Canada ever since the inauguration of the Federal Reserve System in the United States in 1914, but the issue had become confused by the introduction during the depression of a host of competing theories about what the proper role for a Canadian central

J.A. McLeod,
General Manager, 1923-1933;
President, 1934-1945;
Chairman, 1945-1946.

bank should be. There were advocates of a government bank to compete with chartered banks. Others saw a Bank of Canada as a new source of credit. And to still others, it was simply to be a supplier of printing-press money.

In November of 1932, McLeod became President of the Canadian Bankers' Association and, in his address to the annual meeting of the Association, he voiced a number of the misgivings he and his colleagues had about the establishment of a central bank:

> There is a risk today, that the Bank Act may be drawn into politics, and that the creation of a central bank for Canada may become a political question.... From the standpoint of security the Canadian banking system has successfully stood the strain and passed the severest test.... There has been a great deal of misapprehension as to what they [central banks] can do.... Without wishing to be flippant, I may fairly say that it suddenly became fashionable after the war, for governments to create central banks.... but whether a central bank, when once created, can control credit, can stabilize business and lessen the strain of economic depression – that is another question.... It may be questioned whether in any country that is a debtor country the central bank can possess effective power. For a central bank that does possess power, to bring its influence to bear without shock to the financial business structure, it should be functioning in a sensitive money market and, if possible, a market which creates bills of exchange in its own currency.... Canada fulfills none of these conditions.... She does not possess a sensitive money market. Although she has a strong financial structure, it is essentially simple. While the businessman, as a matter of routine, discounts his bills with his banker, there is no market within this country for dealing in bills of exchange, and no machinery for dealing in them, such as exists in London and New York....if we were to create a central bank in Canada, it would inevitably rouse extravagant expectations in the minds of a great many people. Most of these expectations would be doomed to disappointment....[18]

PRESSURE FOR CENTRAL BANK

There were other considerations that struck nearer home. The chartered banks would be required to maintain deposits with the central bank: cash reserves. The central bank would take over the note-issuing privilege from the banks, thus depriving them of an important source of revenue. It would also require the gold of the chartered banks as a reserve to support the currency. All this, in McLeod's view, would be the outcome of the Commission's findings. "I do not think," he was later to write McInnes, "that any arguments the banks can present will influence the Commission so far as a central bank is concerned. Confidentially, I think it was decided before Lord Macmillan left London that some kind of a central organization shall be established in Canada."[19]

There was, however, some comfort to be taken in the fact that the Prime Minister, having decided on a Royal Commission, had gone to considerable pains to secure a good one. The chairman was the Right Honourable Lord Macmillan, an eminent British jurist who had already headed a major inquiry into British finance. Sir Charles Addis, also British, was a prominent banker and financier. Sir Thomas White, a former Minister of Finance and a former Vice-President of the Canadian Bank of Commerce, and Beaudry Leman, General Manager of the Banque Canadienne Nationale, were the Canadian banking experts. And J.E. Brownlee, then Premier of Alberta, would be able to provide from a province highly interested in monetary affairs a rigorous analysis of the system. The academic side was covered by an economist, A.F.W. Plumptre,* who was the Assistant Secretary.

MCLEOD'S PRESENTATION

The Commission began its work in July 1933 and at the outset McLeod, as President of the Canadian Bankers' Association, gave a succinct account of the development of the Canadian branch system, its present role in the country, and its contribution to the strength of the Canadian economy, and he was well prepared for difficult questions. "In order to present the position of the bankers in an orderly manner,..." stated a memorandum written for the General Manager in 1932, "it is suggested that the representatives of the Bankers' Association would be well advised, on the first appearance before the Committee, to file with it certain carefully prepared memoranda which would represent their considered views on various issues likely to be raised."[20]

The Bank of Nova Scotia's presentation to the Commission was delivered by H.J. Coon of the Investment Department. The main objection on the part of the Nova Scotia, he said, was a fear of politics and a reluctance to experiment at a time when most countries of the world were off the gold standard and when large sections of Canada were suffering acutely from the depression. Coon continued, "An error in the policy of a commercial bank has a limited influence, but an error in the policy of a central bank would permeate the whole structure of the country....our considered view is that in the present extremely disturbed state of business it would be most unwise to experiment with an organization entirely new to this country...."[21] He perhaps realized as he spoke, however, that the argument was lost and so did McLeod by the time the hearings concluded.

Incidentally, at the Commission's last session, McLeod received what must have been a very gratifying compliment from Sir Charles

---

* Plumptre was later to write *Central Banking in the British Dominions* (University of Toronto Press, 1940), which contains a comprehensive discussion of the events leading up to the establishment of a central bank in Canada.

Addis, who was acting as Chairman in the place of Lord Macmillan:

> Mr. McLeod, I am proud of my profession. You have been subjected to a searching questionnaire and you have given us a straight reply. You have refuted many ill-informed and, I may add, in some cases malicious charges which have been levelled at the banks. You have done so with a dignity, with a moderation and with a frank sincerity which compel conviction. I believe that your document will stand as an historical defence of the Canadian banking system. If this Commission should do nothing more than to elicit this response it would not, in my judgement, altogether have failed in the task allotted to it.[22]

THE COMMISSION'S RECOMMENDATIONS

As expected, the Royal Commission did recommend that a central bank be established, but the new institution was to have a reasonably familiar shape. The new Bank of Canada would control the currency, issue all bank notes, and regulate credit in the interests of the Canadian economy. It would also, under the Minister of Finance, manage the public debt and carry out foreign exchange policy. It would not compete with the chartered banks. The banks, however, would be required to carry minimum cash reserves with the Bank of Canada – a provision which would enable the central bank, through securities transactions, to expand or restrict the availability of bank credit. Buying securities would increase cash reserves of the banks and thus liberalize credit, while selling would tend to constrict it. The interest rate – the bank rate – set by the bank would signal its view of economic conditions.

THE NEW BANK OF CANADA

In 1934, when the regular decennial revision of the Bank Act was carried out, a companion bill, the Bank of Canada Act, set up the new central bank. The establishment of the Bank of Canada was accepted with good grace. The chartered banks, required to deposit their gold reserves with the Bank of Canada, did so with some legitimate grumbling over the price allowed them. The banks' note issue, curtailed year by year, was to be down to 25 per cent of their paid-up capital by 1944, and at that time another revision of the Bank Act would provide for the abandonment of all note-issuing privileges by 1950.

Since the original Bank Act of 1871, the chartered banks had been limited to a maximum rate of 7 per cent interest on loans or discounts. The 1934 revision provided for penalties for exceeding that maximum. At The Bank of Nova Scotia's annual meeting in January of 1934, H.F. Patterson, the General Manager, complained about "the limitation in the rate of interest – not a new feature of The Bank Act, but now made

H.F. Patterson,
General Manager,
1933-1941;
Executive Vice-President,
1941-1943.

rigid as never before....But it should be realized...that the maintenance of banking service in remote areas is not made easier, but more difficult than before, by these changes."[23] Yet, both he and McLeod had a high respect for Graham Towers, the first Governor of the Bank of Canada, and for J.A.C. Osborne, who had come from the Bank of England to be Deputy Governor. Donald Gordon, moreover, the new Bank's very able and energetic secretary, had been assistant manager of the Toronto branch of The Bank of Nova Scotia.* "As from now," pronounced Patterson, "the Bank of Canada becomes an integral part of this country's financial structure. Needless to say, The Bank of Nova Scotia will co-operate cordially with it."[24]

THE NEW EXECUTIVE – PATTERSON, GENERAL MANAGER

At the annual meeting of the previous year, in January of 1934, S.J. Moore, at the age of seventy-four, had stepped up to the newly created post of Chairman of the Board, and J.A. McLeod, succeeding Moore as President, had become the first man in the Bank to rise through the ranks to that office. H.F. Patterson had taken over as General Manager.

A shrewd, down-to-earth man with a sense of humour, Patterson had the gift of keeping his composure in difficult situations and of making good decisions – qualities which he needed greatly in the years of depresssion and war which were his lot. Of average height, with an engaging smile, he had a wide circle of friends and an excellent reputation as a knowledgeable banker. Unlike McLeod, who was rather reserved, Patterson was approachable and affable. Edwin Crockett had joined H.D. Burns as an Assistant General Manager. Like Burns, Crockett was one of the ten original men who had opened the Toronto office at the turn of the century, and since then he had enjoyed a wide experience, mainly in the area of credits.

ECONOMIC SITUATION STILL WEAK

The world economic situation in 1935, though past its worst, was still weak and trade was restricted as never before. The world was still lurching from crisis to crisis and political tension was rising. In Canada, some one million people out of a population of eleven million were, in

---

* It is of interest to note that Donald Gordon nearly left the Bank prior to his joining the Bank of Canada. In the depths of the depression, his pay low and family responsibilities burdensome, Gordon was offered a job on far more attractive terms by an American institution. He was sorely tempted and, had his pay not been increased, he might well have left. He was highly regarded in the investment community and it was suspected that one or two of its members, entirely on their own initiative, had pressed the Bank to keep this unusual man in Canada.

Consolidation and Then... The Great Depression, 1924-1939

varying degrees, on relief. There were some signs of recovery, but the disastrous state of affairs in the prairies – and Canada was still a "wheat economy" – cast a shadow over the whole country. Between 1933 and 1935, the Bank closed nineteen branches, reducing the total to 303, while profits dropped from $2.3 million in 1932 to $1.8 million in 1935. The dividend rate, which had been lowered from 16 per cent to 14 per cent, declined further to 12 per cent, yielding an actual return to shareholders of less than 4 per cent.

PROBLEM OF COSTS IN A SLOW RECOVERY

Meanwhile, costs stayed fixed or, in some cases, even increased. The complex of nation-wide services still had to be maintained; and the Bank, which distributed $1,440,000 in dividends, also paid out $1,160,000 in taxes. The regular pictorial calendar had been omitted in 1933, and there had been a circular from General Office enjoining young officers against the temptation to buy cars. In 1935, Patterson was moved to object to "an impression that, in some mysterious manner, banks and bankers are immune from the lot of ordinary mortals and ordinary corporations in periods of depression."[25]

The Bank's troubles were not confined to the Canadian scene. Business in Newfoundland rose fitfully in 1934 and then went into a deeper slump. Jamaica had good crops and was weathering the depression fairly well; but in Cuba, labour troubles and political agitation made prospects uncertain. The Bank was hard hit in Santo Domingo because of the poor state of the sugar industry, and in Puerto Rico a deteriorating political situation complicated the outlook. Above all, not yet quite in the forefront but haunting people's minds, was the rise of Fascism and Nazism, and the threat of world war.

HOCKEY HELPED IN DEPRESSION

But all was not gloom in this generally depressing atmosphere. One of Patterson's diversions was an interest in bank hockey. It was an interest shared by D.A.Y. Merrick, then manager of Toronto branch, and a large number of the staff who turned out to support their favourites. According to Harry Bartlett, captain of the Nova Scotia team, "the Toronto Bank Hockey League in the thirties was the best thing next to the National Hockey League." However this may have been, some interesting planning went into producing good teams, not least by the Nova Scotia, who won the pennant three years in a row. Bartlett, the captain, who was also an able banker, eventually retiring as manager at Charlottetown, was moved from Fredericton to Toronto. He had earlier felt the pull of his hockey ability in the Maritimes when H.L. Enman, then Eastern Supervisor, had tried to resolve Bartlett's conflicting interests in banking and hockey. Another able player who came a long way – from

A bright spot for bank staff during the depression was provided by the Toronto Bankers' Hockey League. The Bank of Nova Scotia team were the champions in 1932-1933.

Consolidation and Then... The Great Depression, 1924-1939 163

Calgary – was J.A. Cranstoun. He ultimately retired as Western Supervisor. C.J. Ash, who was later to be an Assistant General Manager, was transferred from Peterborough. Somehow or other, Joe Worters, an outstanding goalkeeper, brother of the famous goalie of the New York Americans, joined the Bank in Toronto. The day after each game, Patterson would call Bartlett in for a post-mortem. All this was good for morale when things were slow and difficult.

Bartlett, Ash, and Boyles – who was manager of the hockey team – and some of the other team players would lunch at a big table in the lower dining room, where the Bank provided a free lunch designed to ensure that its employees had "at least one good hot meal a day." Over several years F.W. Nicks, later President, Chief Executive Officer, and Chairman, J. Douglas Gibson, F.J. Finlay, later Secretary of the Bank, and W.S. Bond, who became an Assistant General Manager, also sat at the same big table, where, needless to say, the conversation was lively.

MONEY WAS SHORT, MARKETS WERE WEAK

All over the country, money was short and markets were weak. In Woodbridge, Ontario, Hitchman recalls that in the depths of the depression "Money was practically non-existent. The only source of income was really from selling milk or from selling a cow or a pig." Auction sales were held by and for people without money, and it became the job of the bank manager to generate funds on the spot. "When the farmer had a sale the manager would go out and literally buy the notes that the people had brought, whether it was for a cow or farm implements or whatever.... the buyer with no cash would give a note which the local manager would approve and discount and give to the auction sale." Yet the manager at Woodbridge could make no loan in excess of $300; when Hitchman was moved to the Danforth & Greenwood branch in Toronto he found almost no loans at all being made there, and on a transfer to London, Ontario, he discovered that no deposit in excess of $2,500 would be accepted because there was no use for the funds.

DROUGHT AND DEPRESSION COMBINED

F.W. Ross was Western Supervisor during the thirties and he later chronicled his impressions of those days as he did of the period early in the century when he first went to Edmonton. For a number of years, "hardly a blade of green grass was visible" throughout the area affected, he said, writing of the southern regions where the drought was worst. "No crops were harvested and the farmers who remained in the districts were reduced to accepting charity. Lakes and streams dried up.... Dust storms and soil drifting added to the devastation, ruin and discomfort. It was said that children of seven or eight years of age who had never seen rain, ran terrified to their mothers when rain finally did come. It was a common sight to see wagon after wagon load of farmers and their

Nanton, Alberta, 1932.

Drought and depression in the thirties combined to make conditions in the Prairies doubly hard. Bankers worked hard to help their customers through the crisis years.

families trekking North in search of new land. All their worldly possessions were piled high on carts or so-called 'Bennett Buggies' – these were old cars with the engine removed – ... or wagon boxes attached to the chassis of abandoned automobiles. The carts were drawn by a half-starved, spavined horse or two, followed on a drag-rope by an equally scrawny, crippled cow."[26]

The history of the Bank's branch in Spring Valley, Saskatchewan, about forty miles south of Moose Jaw, provides an example of some of the problems arising from such conditions. Opened in 1919, it lost money steadily from the beginning of the 1930s but was not closed until 1937. In those last seven years, the region had had only one fair wheat crop and the price obtained for that one was less than the cost of production. Each year the farmer ended up a poorer man than before; notes for seed, feed, and living expenses piled up in the Bank's portfolio, while the prospects of repayment dwindled. Yet, when the branch finally closed, its customers wanted to stay with the Bank and special arrangements were made for them in Avonlea and Moose Jaw.[27]

FROST'S EXPERIENCES IN SASKATOON

C. Sydney Frost was manager at Saskatoon in the 1930s. It was a grim period for manager and customer alike, but there were also satisfactions. "What I did," he says, "I took my motor car and I went long distances and called on all these people. I didn't ask them to pay their notes – I knew they couldn't pay, because I sometimes even had to give my lunch to the kids. They were poverty-stricken in a lot of cases, but they were all friends of mine....There was one family, they hadn't much but they had a vegetable garden near their house and they shot prairie chickens and caught fish – well, they came through. They didn't declare bankruptcy, they didn't go through the family credit arrangement or anything. They just hung on, four sons and a couple of daughters, all working the place with their father and mother. Well, I was out in Saskatoon a few years ago and I asked about these people. They had $60,000 in the bank and they owned three sections of land, clear. That account paid off.

"Then there was the chap who bought land before the drought came and owed the Bank about $30,000 on it and couldn't pay off a cent. As his debt got up to about $40,000, I said, 'Well, what if we cut it in half?' I wrote to Head Office and made it strong and they came back with an arrangement. 'We will cut the loan down to $21,000 and in years when the crops are under five bushels per acre there will be no payments and no interest.' If the crop went to ten bushels he paid five per cent, if it was fifteen bushels six or seven per cent, and on up from there. Well, it came out all right and a few years ago the manager in Saskatoon wrote me, 'You will be glad to hear that Ernie paid off the last of his note.' That was the kind of thing that made one happy at work."

THE RISE OF "SOCIAL CREDIT"

Such incidents stand out in the general gloom which shrouded the prairies in the depression years. It was perhaps inevitable that some sort of demagogue should come to the fore and in this case it was William Aberhart, teacher, gospeller, and Premier of Alberta from 1935 until his death in 1943. He was a high school teacher turned evangelist and he was one of the first to discover the power of radio oratory. By the early thirties, he had attracted a huge audience for his Sunday religious broadcasts all across the prairies. He became attracted by the theory of "Social Credit," as expounded by one Major C.H. Douglas, an Anglo-Scottish eccentric. Douglas had developed the idea that under the current economic system there was a chronic shortage of money, which must be made good by the state. The issuance by the state of additional money, sometimes called the "social dividend," would be based on the goods and services which the society was potentially able to produce. The state must first assume complete control of the monetary system, it must issue its "social credit," and it must establish a just price for all goods and services. This theory, which the Bank's *Monthly Review* at that time described as "Banking in Wonderland," never seemed to be entirely clear even to its author; it baffled the members of the Royal Commission on Banking and Currency when Douglas presented it to them. Yet, while it was a mixed-up approach and quite

Monthly Review, May 1935.

In 1935, the Social Credit Party swept to victory in Alberta. The party was built on the monetary theories of Major C.H. Douglas, and the Bank used the pages of its *Monthly Review* to analyse these extraordinary theories.

unworkable, it struck a highly responsive chord in the general public with its emphasis on the shortage of purchasing power. In a very real sense, most people were indeed short of money. In 1935, the Social Credit Party, built on Aberhart's broadcasts, swept to power in Alberta in a landslide election.

"BANKING IN WONDERLAND"

Since the new Social Credit government needed the banks as agents to put their monetary theories into effect, and since the banks neither knew how to, nor would, co-operate, they were soon under relentless attack. "Hon. William Aberhart...," A.B. Jamieson has written, "is unlikely ever to be forgotten by chartered bank men who had anything to do with the operation or supervision of branches in Alberta while he was in office."[28] On coming to power, Aberhart proceeded with evangelical fervour to put the banks and the "money interests" into what he conceived to be their proper place. To that end, a procession of acts was passed by the Alberta legislature. Each branch of each bank doing business in the province was to be required to pay a licence fee of $100. The management of each branch was to be taken over by a local committee consisting of three persons appointed by a Social Credit Board and two appointed by the bank, thus removing from the banks control of their own policies. In addition, each employee of each bank was to be licensed. The employee of an unlicensed bank was to be deprived of the right to bring any civil action in an Alberta court. Banks were to be forbidden to appeal against any statute without the permission of the provincial government.

Most of these measures remained inoperative, since the British North America Act specifically provides that "banks and banking" come under federal, not provincial, jurisdiction. Nevertheless, the Alberta government took its case to the Supreme Court of Canada and finally to the Privy Council – a long-drawn-out process which added to the difficulties of the banker's life in the West. All across the prairies, the banks were accused of profiteering, ruthlessness in collecting loans, closing branches, and unfair restriction of credit in favour of their large eastern accounts. The banks responded to this attack – perhaps not forcefully enough – with statements at annual meetings which were not widely read, or widely understood when they were read. In 1937, the Canadian Bankers' Association sponsored a series of radio broadcasts on "Facts About Canadian Bankers" which endeavoured to explain the fallacies of Social Credit theory. The Bank of Nova Scotia, for its part, put forth its views in the *Monthly Review*. In June 1934 "The Nature of Credit – Mystical Notions and the Hard Reality," in May 1935 "'Social Credit' – The Douglas Proposals," and in June 1935 "'Social Credit' and the Canadian Economy" introduced more clarity and good humour to the discussion than was common in those bleak and bitter times.

What perhaps helped the banks most in the long run was the branch system itself, since local managers were themselves members of suffering communities. They, too, were hard up in the face of static salaries and slow promotion, and were all too evidently not eastern exploiters. They were fighting along with their customers against impossible conditions to achieve livable solutions.

PARTIAL RECOVERY BY 1939

Gradual but uneven revival, sparked by the mining industry and marred by continued drought in large areas of the West, characterized the four years from 1936 to 1939. By the end of the thirties the country, with the exception of the western drought areas, had achieved a considerable recovery from the depths of the depression but still had not caught up to the level of activity of the late twenties and was still afflicted by a high level of unemployment and under-employment. The national income as calculated by the Statistical Department of The Bank of Nova Scotia had recovered to $4,800 million in 1939, compared with $3,225 million in 1933, the worst year of the depression, and $5,900 million in 1929, the peak of the boom.[29]

The young Bank of Canada was gradually developing its operations to regulate "credit and currency in the interests of the Canadian economy" and, it should be pointed out, was doing an excellent job of providing an even flow of monetary resources. Coincidentally, the new central bank was building a nucleus of financial and economic leadership which would be needed all too soon in the days of conflict ahead. Meanwhile, the Royal Commission on Dominion-Provincial Relations (the Rowell-Sirois Commission) was busily engaged in the first major examination of the workings of the Canadian economy in its federal framework; its Report would provide an approach which helped the country to set an effective course in the immediate postwar period.

ONE OF THE STRONG BANKS IN CANADA

The Bank of Nova Scotia came to the end of 1939 firmly established as one of the strongest banks in Canada. Total quick assets – cash, securities, and immediately realizable loans – amounted to 68 per cent of public liabilities. This, of course, was too high a ratio from an earnings viewpoint but it certainly indicated strength. Between 1935 and 1939, the Bank's total assets had increased from $289 million to $343 million, but the average rate of return on loans and investments had continued its long decline. From almost exactly 6 per cent in 1928 the return was down to 3.76 per cent by 1938. Low yields had pushed the rate paid on deposits down to $1^{1}/_{2}$ per cent, and the same condition had necessitated increases of pension fund contributions both from the Bank and from individual officers. As Patterson reported in 1938, expenses were difficult to prune; "Nor has it been practicable to reduce salaries."[30] At the same time, the volume of work continued to increase, forcing the Bank along with other banks to institute a long-overdue system of service charges. The Bank ended the decade with 297 branches and a staff of 2,537.

LOANS STILL LOW, SECURITY HOLDINGS HIGH

By 1938, though the depression had been at least partly overcome, the banks were faced with one of its long-term effects. The decline in economic activity had been accompanied by heavy government borrowings – municipal, provincial, and federal – to provide funds for relief. Patterson pointed out that in 1928 commercial loans had made up 35 per cent of the assets of the chartered banks and security holdings 16 per cent, but in 1938 the positions were almost reversed; commercial loans were only a little more than 23 per cent of bank assets and securities 43 per cent.[31] Very largely as a result of the depression, securities, which were mainly loans to governments, had displaced higher-yielding commercial loans as the principal item on the asset side of the balance sheet.

There was a wider aspect to the problem which was more disturbing. In this time of depression, Thomas Fyshe's view of the business cycle, "Bad times – good times – bully times – collapse," was sometimes wryly recalled. Less quoted but of more present significance, however, was the article he had written in 1905 in which he had raised questions about the general future of banking.*

At the annual meeting to consider the statement for 1938, Patterson followed the trend foreseen by Fyshe through its modern ramifications. "The diminished importance of commercial lending," he told the shareholders, "...cannot be entirely ascribed to the influence of the depression."

> It is in part a long-term tendency, which has been in evidence for a quarter of a century, not only in Canada but also in the United States and to some extent in Great Britain.... Perhaps the most important [factor] has been the growth in the size of the business unit, evident...in the trend toward consolidations and mergers.... the big corporation finds it easier to obtain capital on the market than the small concern. With the development of domestic facilities for corporate financing – stock exchanges, the bond market and investment banking houses – the large enterprise has been able to obtain a greater proportion of its total capital requirements on a long-term basis than was the case in pre-War days. Moreover, big companies in particular have often tended to plow in profits, and establish large reserves, thereby further lessening their need for bank loans. As industrial processes have been speeded up and transportation has

---

* See page 75.

become more rapid, requirements for working capital have been correspondingly reduced, while the declining cycle of commodity prices from 1920 to 1933 was working in the same direction. In addition, the banks have been faced with a certain amount of competition in the commercial lending field, largely of an indirect character. One aspect of this has been the financing of Canadian subsidiaries of American corporations through the parent company in the United States and another has been the development of finance companies which are now an important factor in the short-term lending field.[32]

VAST SEGMENT OF BANKING UNTOUCHED

A vast segment of the short-term lending field, still almost untouched by the banks, was that of consumer credit. It lay waiting the plough; if the producers of consumer goods now had less need of credit in the productive process, they were soon to have more need of consumers for their ever-mounting flood of goods and of credit to support that consumption. Nor was the banker of the late thirties, fortunately for himself, given the foresight to see what persistent continuing inflation would do to the demand for bank loans.

But much more was to happen before these possibilities could be realized. In January 1940, as the shareholders gathered for the annual meeting in Halifax, Patterson was an overworked, ailing man and his address was read by Burns. It was already an account of war measures. The Bank's staff was working long extra hours to cope with a flood of new and unfamiliar requirements. Foreign exchange control was in effect, a Foreign Exchange Department had been set up, and thirty-seven men had already left the Bank to join the armed forces.

NOTES

1. BNS Archives, Confidential Circular, May 18, 1928.
2. *Ibid.*, BNS Annual Report, 1928, Chairman's Address, p.10.
3. *Ibid.*, President's Address, p.12.
4. *Ibid.*, BNS Annual Report, 1930, General Manager's Address, p.14.
5. *Ibid.*, p.17.
6. *Ibid.*, Hector McInnes to J.A. McLeod, dated Halifax, July 28, 1931.
7. *Ibid.*, July 3, 1931.
8. *Ibid.*, McLeod to McInnes, dated Toronto, July 7, 1931.
9. *Ibid.*, *The Bank of Nova Scotia Announces the Opening of Its New Halifax Building, August 3rd, 1931* (brochure).
10. John M. Lyle, "Canadian Ornament Goes Native," *American Architect*, Dec. 1931, pp.36-7.
11. *Evening Mail*, Halifax, Aug. 3, 1931.
12. BNS Archives, Speech by H.R. Younker at a BNS staff meeting, Halifax, Dec. 11, 1975.
13. *Ibid.*, J.A.G. Bell and C.E. Ritchie to H.R. Younker, dated Toronto, Dec. 12, 1975.
14. *Ibid.*, BNS Annual Report, 1931, Chairman's Address, p. 14.
15. A.B. Jamieson, *Chartered Banking in Canada* (Toronto: Ryerson Press, 1953), pp.80-1; also, pp.72-86 have been extensively drawn upon in the description of the Great Depression.
16. BNS Archives, McLeod to McInnes, dated Toronto, April 27, 1933.
17. *Ibid.*, Nov. 16, 1933.
18. *Ibid.*, Address by J.A. McLeod, President of Canadian Bankers' Association, at Annual General Meeting, Toronto, Nov. 10, 1932; quoted in "Does Canada Need A Central Bank?" By a Canadian Banker, reprint by *The Financial Post*, Toronto, p.28.
19. *Ibid.*, McLeod to McInnes, dated Toronto, Aug. 25, 1933.
20. *Ibid.*, "Memorandum [for the General Manager] with Reference to the Coming Revision of the Bank Act," 1933.
21. Royal Commission on Banking and Currency, *Proceedings*, Ottawa, Sept. 1933, Brief presented to the Royal Commission on Banking and Currency by Investment Department, The Bank of Nova Scotia, p.3381.
22. *Ibid.*, Comment by Sir Charles Addis on Brief presented by J.A. McLeod, President, Canadian Bankers' Association.
23. BNS Archives, BNS Annual Report, 1934, General Manager's Address, p.20.
24. *Ibid.*, p.21.
25. *Ibid.*, p.22.
26. *Ibid.*, F.W. Ross, "When the West Opened Up," *BNS Staff Magazine*, Winter 1955, p.2.
27. *Ibid.*, BNS Inspection Report on Spring Valley, Sask., branch, May 20, 1937.
28. A.B. Jamieson, *op.cit.*, p.92.
29. BNS *Monthly Review*, Sept. 1940.
30. BNS Archives, BNS Annual Report, 1938, General Manager's Address, p.26.
31. *Ibid.*, p.23.
32. *Ibid.*, pp.24-25.

9

The Second World War
1939-1945

H.D. Burns,
General Manager, 1941-1945;
President, 1945-1949;
Chairman, 1949-1955.

PATTERSON'S LOT: DEPRESSION AND WAR

The Bank, whose growth had been slow in the twenties and which, like other banks, had been severely restricted in the thirties, now entered a new and different kind of restriction in which private ambitions had to be put aside for national purposes. Through much of the period, management had little or no opportunity to build on the enlarged base resulting from the amalgamations of 1913–19. McLeod could have been more aggressive from the time he became General Manager until the depression set in six years later; but he did run the Bank with ability and distinction. Patterson had nothing but depression and war with which to cope. There was one crisis after another, and few if any opportunities for profitable growth. He had little chance to show the leadership that might have been expected of him in happier times. He, however, did a fine job in very difficult circumstances, which unfortunately took a heavy toll of his physical strength.

BURNS BECOMES GENERAL MANAGER

H.D. Burns became General Manager late in 1941, though before that his responsibilities had been increasing as a result of Patterson's deteriorating health. Burns, a big, impressive man, had been manager at Vancouver, as well as at the main Toronto branch. He was popular with the business community. He was an omnivorous reader and loved to quote Shakespeare and the Bible. He was not above showing off: at luncheon in the Bank he would quote from either of these distinguished sources and then turn to Gibson, whom he would describe as "a university graduate," asking him to identify the quotation. Seldom could Gibson rise to the occasion.

Frost said of Burns that he was the last of the conservative bankers and in a sense he was. He liked stability and order, and he laid great emphasis on traditional values. In one of his annual speeches to the shareholders, for instance, he gave a short lecture on the old-fashioned virtue of thrift. "The man or woman who saves...is usually a better citizen for the restraint and self-discipline which saving requires,"[1] he asserted. He had an avuncular attitude towards the staff; as has been already noted, he prided himself on his acquaintance with not only individual staff members but also their families, and he even knew the family backgrounds of many of the Bank's customers. He was neither a driver like Enman nor an innovator like Nicks. Yet, the same Burns was the man who took the risk of bringing in from the Maritimes an aggressive man to be his successor – Horace L. Enman. When he handed over the reins to Enman, the Bank was in good shape and ready to begin its next leap forward.

WARTIME CLIMATE – MORE WORK, FEWER MEN, AND MORE WOMEN

The war set the current climate for banking. It restricted the use of men, equipment, and buildings – the wherewithal needed to provide more services. At the same time, it greatly expanded the demands for a wide variety of banking services. These increased demands had to be met by fewer men using very little additional equipment. Surmounting these handicaps, the banks responded admirably indeed over the war period, and succeeded in raising their physical output of services by probably three-quarters. The main factors in this remarkable record were the great influx of women and the improved productivity of the whole work force. As the armed services and war industry grew, there was a tremendous movement of people into the cities. The enthusiastic entry of men into the services and heavy industry created an insatiable demand for replacements, who were primarily women, many of whom had never held a commercial job before.

One of the first restrictive measures taken by the banks was that they simply stopped opening new branches. Then, as a group, they cut back the number of existing branches. In the case of the Nova Scotia, the number of branches declined from 297 at the outbreak of the war to 275 by 1944. From the very beginning, the drain of men created many administrative problems. For instance, when a branch lost its accountant (the office manager) – an administrative level particularly hard hit by enlistment in the armed forces – the manager had to do the accounting work himself or extend some of the office management duties to people further down the line, or more usually, both. The difficulties were compounded by the next person down the line probably joining up as well. When branch managers went to war, the problems became even more difficult because many of those who would normally replace them – assistant managers, accountants, and inspectors – had gone to war too. Fortunately, many competent women were already on the staff who were fully capable of taking on increased responsibilities.

By October 1944, there were 834 men and 18 women of The Bank of Nova Scotia involved in active war service. The male staff then numbered 1,251, compared with roughly 2,000 at the outbreak of the war. The female staff had increased by nearly four times over the same period, from 487 to 1,866. The staff was larger than before the war – at a total of 3,117, it was up by almost one-quarter – and in the process, the proportion of women had risen to 60 per cent from 20 per cent. While there were considerably more people working in the Bank, there were far fewer experienced bankers.

DEALING WITH A HUGE FLOOD OF PAPER

Fortunately, the increase in the demand for bank services during the war was not in the commercial lending area. Peacetime business was restricted and wartime business was frequently financed by the government rather than by the banks. The main banking growth was in lending to the government and in financing war contracts, which did not call for much more staff, and in dealing with a huge flood of paper, which did. More and more cheques and vouchers, a vast quantity of ration coupons, documents in connection with sales of Victory Bonds and War Savings Certificates, and entries covering loans and payroll deductions to finance them were the principal elements. At this time when offices were not much mechanized, a typewriter and an adding machine were the sum total of an average branch's equipment; only in the larger branches would there be a current-account proof machine. Thus, the efficient handling of this ever-rising flood of paperwork was a remarkable achievement. Hard work, good morale, and better organization made it possible.

Walter S. Bond, who later became Assistant General Manager in charge of Administration, was the accountant at the Rideau & William branch in Ottawa at the outbreak of the war. He recalls that "our male staff declined fairly quickly from 14 to 3 in number and the volume of work went up enormously. The girls did wonders. Despite the intense pressure of the time and crowded working conditions, we had the best morale in town," and, it might be added, not only one of the best accountants, but also one of the best managers (W.B. Snow).

VARIETY OF WARTIME NEEDS

Most, if not all, of the increase in the volume of work resulted from the government's needs. Foreign exchange control was the first major step towards a war economy. The Canadian dollar was pegged at 91¢ U.S. With the pegging came a complex system controlling the use of foreign exchange, the banks acting as the principal agents under the direction of the Bank of Canada. When it came to government financing, tellers' wickets and accountants' desks became sales outlets for Victory Bonds, War Savings Certificates, and War Savings Stamps, and managers and senior officers participated in almost continuous bond sales campaigns, which raised a total of some $12 1/2 billion for Canada. The banks also provided payroll deduction services and lending facilities which were financed by the interest on the bonds.

Then, as the war continued, came rationing and the need for a coupon-banking system. This the banks, with their national branch system, were able to provide, though not without added strain and effort. Approximately fifty million coupons a week were processed by this system, and it was a real tribute to the overworked supervisors and to the hastily trained staff with their inadequate, old-fashioned equipment that it worked so well. The ration coupon accounts might not have balanced every night, but they came close. In addition, the banks distributed milk and butterfat subsidies and they also acted on behalf of the Custodian of Enemy Property, particularly in regard to deposit accounts and securities owned by enemy aliens. The circulars of instruction came thick and fast from General Office – more and more paper to handle more and more paper. As someone was heard to remark at the time, "Nobody is making money and everyone is overworked."

SCOTIABANKERS' WAR RECORD

By 1944, 70 per cent of the male staff of military age had joined the armed forces; some of them were promoted to senior ranks entailing a lot of responsibility and many were decorated for bravery. Of a total of 950 men and women of the staff of The Bank of Nova Scotia on military service in the Second World War, 81 lost their lives.

It is always difficult, in a book of this nature, to single out individual accomplishments but perhaps it is appropriate to mention a few who had outstanding war records. For instance, E.J.S. Dudley rose to the rank of lieutenant-colonel in the First Saskatoon Light Infantry, was mentioned in dispatches in the Italian Campaign in 1944, and subsequently served in Ottawa as Chairman of the Dependants' Allowance Board. Also in the Army was H.W. Caldwell, who became a major in the Royal Regiment; he commanded an infantry company in northwest Europe and received the Bronze Lion from the Netherlands government. Another army decoration – the Distinguished Service Order – was won by Major H.R.S. Ellis, "for gallant and distinguished services in the field." And many Scotiabankers remember "Cap" H.G. Boyd, a messenger attached to General Office in Toronto, who went on active service with his regiment, the Toronto Scottish, on September 5, 1939, and who received his commission in 1941 even though he was forty-five years old by then; "he's a born soldier" his commanding officer wrote to Burns. Others who held commissions in the army were C.M. Fraser, G.E. McCracken, G.F.H. MacIntosh, P. Cox, and W.L.

Robinson, the latter two winning the Military Cross and the M.B.E. (Member of the Order of the British Empire), respectively. And G.C. Hitchman served in the U.S. Army and was awarded the Bronze Medal.

Some men joined the Navy: A.H. Crockett, who, like Hitchman, recently retired as a Deputy Chairman of the Board, rose to the rank of lieutenant-commander, while T. Young, P.B. Coombs, and A. McPhedran were all lieutenants.

But the most popular of the armed services was the Air Force, where fourteen members of the staff of The Bank of Nova Scotia won the Distinguished Flying Cross. Two of these – Squadron-Leader W.R. Moseley-Williams and Flight-Lieutenant A.G. Rowe – sadly were later reported missing and presumed killed. But other DFCs, D.A. Beresford, P.D. Bluethner, J.D. Johnston, E.A. Mowatt, I.M. McGregor, T.A.T. Rhodes, G. Slocombe, and H.A. Walker, all returned from the war, as did P.W. Dennis, who was awarded the Distinguished Flying Medal. Flight-Lieutenant A.G. Brown was awarded the Czechoslovak Medal for Bravery. Johnston not only was decorated, but also was wounded twice and was a prisoner-of-war. A number of other employees were also prisoners-of-war, including W.H. Milne (now Secretary of the Bank) and the younger D.A.Y. Merrick (son of the earlier D.A.Y. Merrick).*

THE BOOK OF REMEMBRANCE

After the war, Frost, who was then General Manager, took great interest in preparing an appropriate record of those who had given their lives for their country during both world wars. This took the form of a Book of Remembrance beautifully illuminated by A. Scott Carter.† As Frost said, the dedication of the Book "brought about the fulfilment of a long-cherished plan to honour our War Dead and is a lasting profession of our pride in their devotion and of sorrow in their sacrifice – '*At the going down of the sun and in the morning we will remember them.*'"[2]

The Book of Remembrance contains the names of all members of the staff of The Bank of Nova Scotia and also that of the Bank of New Brunswick, the Bank of Ottawa, and the Metropolitan Bank, who died in the two world wars. The names are inscribed by hand on vellum pages, with two names on each page. In both wars, the very young age of the casualties is striking and sad. In the Second World War, of the total of 81 staff members who were killed, 57 per cent were twenty-five years old or younger, with an average of only three years' service in the Bank. Those killed in the First World War were even younger: of the 94 who died, nearly 80 per cent were twenty-five years of age or less, and

---

* There are a number of former staff members who distinguished themselves in the war but whose records are no longer available, since they did not return to the Bank or else stayed in the Bank's employ only a short time thereafter.

† Mr. Carter also designed the Bank's coat of arms.

The Second World War, 1939 – 1945   177

The Bank of Nova Scotia's Book of Remembrance records the names of all those of the Bank's staff who lost their lives in the line of duty during the two world wars.

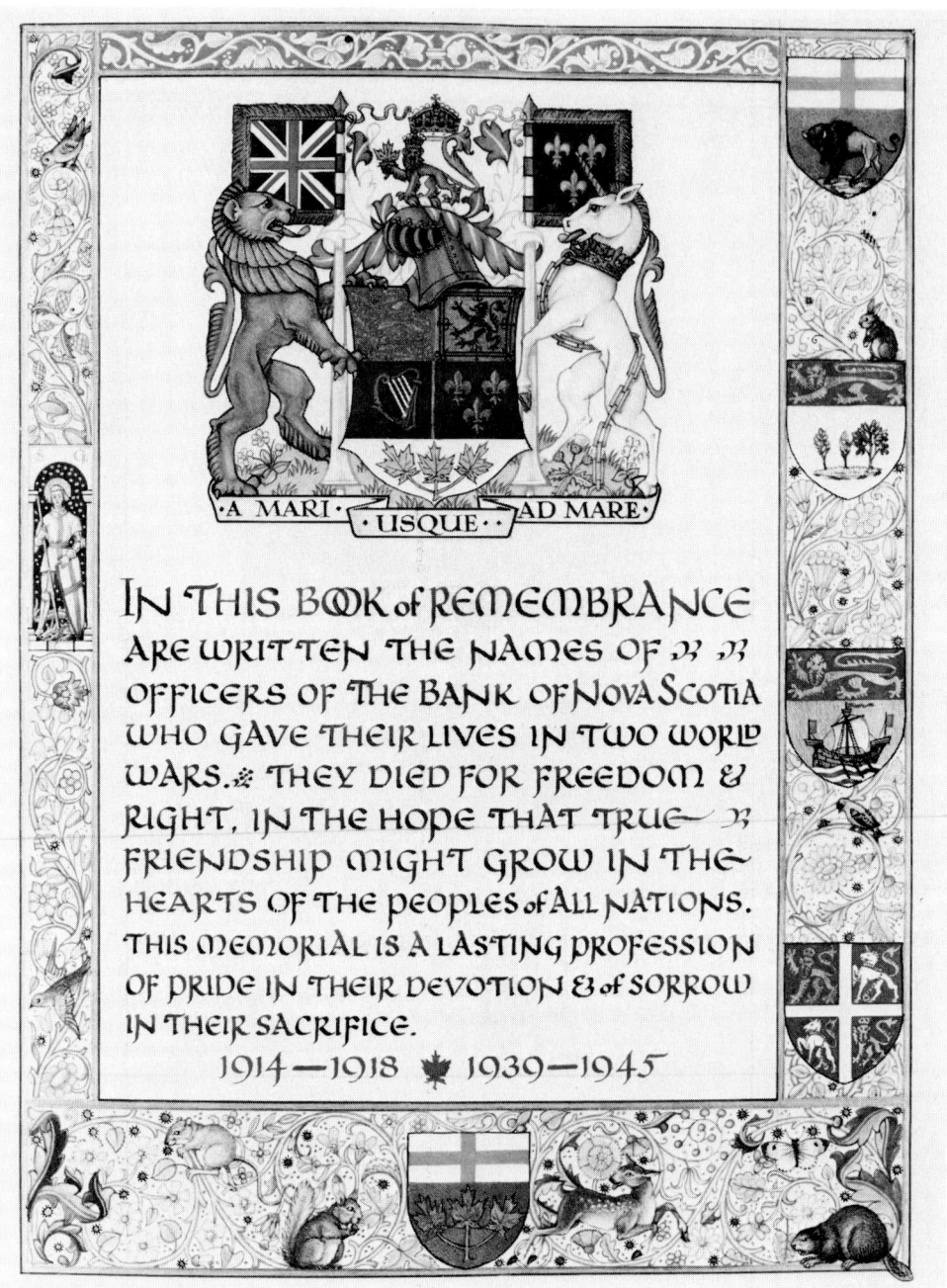

Opening Dedication in the Book of Remembrance.

The illumination was done by A. Scott Carter, who also designed the Bank's coat of arms.

The Second World War, 1939-1945

they also had an average of three years' service. Most of the First World War casualties were in the Army. Famous battles such as Amiens, Arras, Passchendaele, Mount Sorrel, Vimy Ridge, and Ypres took their toll. In the Second World War, more than three-quarters of those who died were in the Air Force, with the words "reported missing, presumed dead, following air operations" appearing after many of the names.

FITTING IN THE VETERANS

For those who returned to the Bank, the policy was to make appropriate appointments after a suitable interval for settling in and adjusting had passed. Officers' positions in the Pension Fund and their Group Insurance had been maintained during war service, and on return their salaries were increased in line with what they would have been had they not enlisted. Six hundred and forty-six bank employees had returned by October 1945, which, when allowance was made for those who died or who were otherwise unable to return, meant that about three-quarters came back to the Bank. John Young, then Supervisor of Staff, said, "It wasn't easy to fit everyone in. They came back even faster than they went out and it took time to fit people into appropriate jobs. There was inevitably some waiting and some mistakes. People had changed and some wanted rather different jobs. Some of the men who did well in the war felt they should have more responsibility than could be given, at least for the time being. The Bank did lose some good men. But it was a big adjustment and we were reasonably successful in making it."

The women also had done a fine job. They had shown that they were as reliable as men and with similar training could do many jobs as well as or better than men. They were loyal and had proven a willingness under pressure to carry their share of the load. They were no longer temporary employees in any real sense, though it has to be admitted that their status as "emergency" employees was not changed until 1948.

Sample Page from the Book of Remembrance

ASSETS UP SUBSTANTIALLY

At the end of the war, the total assets of the Bank were $614 million, 87 per cent higher than at the beginning. Deposits were up similarly, amounting to $541 million. There are two very interesting points about this expansion. The first is that it was largely real, rather than inflationary. Inflation as measured by the cost-of-living index was 23 per cent over the six-year period of war. Thus, while the end-of-the-war dollars were somewhat less valuable, the real growth in the assets of the Bank was still nearly 50 per cent. This was a notable achievement in six years of war. As McLeod said at the annual meeting at the end of 1944, "No important inflation has developed, though all previous experience would suggest that inflation was inevitable in such circumstances as have prevailed. Canada has managed to devise an anti-inflation policy that has worked, and produced results which compare favourably with those achieved by any country."[3]

The other interesting feature about the increase in assets was that it was entirely in securities – mainly federal government securities. In 1945, securities represented almost 50 per cent and loans only 20 per cent of total assets. The shift away from commercial lending had gone even further than in the days of depression as the government's needs for financing the war grew and grew, as civilian business declined, and as war production was increasingly financed out of war contracts. Thomas Fyshe would certainly have been concerned about the trend of the thirties; he would have been doubly worried – with good cause – by the extreme position reached by the banks at the end of the Second World War. Yet, as sometimes happens, bankers' fears were not realized and Canada moved into a new era of expansion, which transformed the chartered banking figures and, indeed, the banking business as a whole.

PROFITS RESTRICTED

Needless to say, profits were restricted during the war. They were slightly lower in 1945 than in 1939, despite the notable increase in assets. They were kept low by the high level of taxation, which by 1942, with the excess profits tax, meant that profits available for dividend payment could not exceed 70 per cent of average taxable profits in the four years 1936 to 1939. When the war broke out, the Bank was paying a nominal dividend of 12 per cent – nominal because the 12 per cent was calculated on paid-up capital only. With the inclusion of published reserves and undivided profits, the actual rate of return came to $3\frac{7}{8}$ per cent. At the end of 1942, when the nominal rate was reduced to 10 per cent, the actual return on the Bank's stock was little more than that available on Victory Bonds. These low earnings, however, were accepted by the Bank's management, directors, and shareholders as a necessary consequence of the war.

NATIONALIZATION NOT BONE OF CONTENTION

While the willing and vigorous co-operation of the banks in the war effort helped defuse criticism of the banking system, the advocates of nationalization again took up their cry when victory seemed assured. Both McLeod and Burns defended the banks' position at the annual meeting of The Bank of Nova Scotia early in 1944. Because the Bank of Canada was now responsible for the volume of credit, it was naive to attack the banks in this area. The banks had shown their mettle during the war by doing an effective job in a number of areas. Burns made perhaps the most telling point of all: "Nationalization of the banks would remove the very important element of competition and substitute a government monopoly. What effect it would have on banking practice and privacy in the customer's affairs is a matter for conjecture. However benevolent and well-intentioned such a monopoly might be, the Canadian public would have to accept its decisions and would have no recourse except through the ballot box or political influence. I cannot believe that this would be an improvement over the existing state of things where the Government exercises supervision and control over monetary policy generally, but leaves the particular conduct of banking to ten competing banks."[4]

As it turned out, the question of nationalization was not a bone of contention when the Bank Act received its regular decennial revision in 1944. However, the banks' right to issue notes was finally terminated: bank note circulation was further reduced and it was to cease entirely by 1950. Another change, the implications of which were not taken very seriously at the time, was a reduction from 7 per cent to 6 per cent in the maximum interest rate that could be charged on loans. The Hon. J.L. Ilsley, the Minister of Finance, suggested that the 7 per cent might be left available for short-term discounted notes to enable the banks to enter the small-loan field. But political opposition was great and the proposal was dropped. Telling people, particularly bankers, that they must *not* do something which might possibly be sinful had much more political attraction than leaving opportunities open which might encourage them to do something worthwhile. In any case, with Canada bonds selling at 3 per cent and the prime rate at 4^1/$_2$ per cent, there was no obvious or immediate reason to be concerned about whether the permissible maximum rate was 6 per cent or 7 per cent.

On the other hand, there were some constructive changes in the new Act. The all-important Section 88 was broadened in its application to lending to farmers, and security requirements under the Section were simplified. Furthermore, with the aim of making the ownership of bank stocks more widespread, provision was made for the reduction of the par value of bank shares from $100 to $10 per share. As well, the share qualifications for one-quarter of the members of the banks' boards of directors were reduced sharply.

CONTINGENCY RESERVES

The question of contingency reserves was discussed at great length. These reserves represent a bank's estimate of the amount it might need to meet losses which might be incurred in unfavourable conditions – these reserves being over and above the normal provisions for doubtful accounts. Suppose there was a financial crisis or another depression, said the banks; contingency reserves had certainly helped the banks through the Great Depression. Since contingency reserves were put aside for possible – though not probable – use in the future, they were not taxed. Critics felt that these reserves should be brought out into the open and taxed, on the grounds that they might not be needed. The banks felt that they were best able to assess to what extent contingency reserves might be necessary. The question was settled for the time being by having the banks report their detailed operating earnings and expenses to the Minister of Finance through the Inspector-General of Banks and by requiring the Minister to report on what he might regard as excessive appropriations.

Looking to the postwar period, the government also passed legislation for Farm Improvement Loans and a new Home Improvement Plan, both incorporating a fixed rate of interest, a maximum amount and term, and a government guarantee against losses, up to a modest percentage of the loans outstanding. It also set up two new institutions which, after rather lengthy growing pains, were to add significantly to the effectiveness of the financial system – the Industrial Development Bank and the Export Credits Insurance Corporation. Aimed at assisting small and medium-sized businesses, both directly and by stimulating competition from the banks, the I.D.B. (now the Federal Business Development Bank) has certainly promoted industry and trade while the E.C.I.C. (now the Export Development Corporation) has provided a government-guaranteed insurance facility which was urgently needed in the highly competitive export business.

GOVERNMENT AND BUSINESS WORKING TOGETHER

Perhaps the most important development of the wartime period was the striking demonstration of how well business and government could work together. The relationship between the banks and the government was only one facet of this, but a vital one. Senior bankers worked in harmony with the bureaucrats and the government. They understood the government's problems, supported its policies, and contributed a good deal to the implementation of those policies. A working committee of the banks, chaired by Boyles, examined the details. As Boyles said: "This was not a group trying to defend itself against the government, but completely the opposite. We were trying to find the best way to get the needed job done."

The top bankers understood the necessity of very high taxes, of almost continuous borrowing, and of a complete system of controls. Early in 1941, McLeod observed that the country was accepting, open-eyed, a "controlled economy in which individual rights and individual initiative are for the time being limited by the state. When, as at present, we can all agree on one pre-eminent objective, there are great and obvious advantages in unified control and direction."[5]

At the annual meeting early in 1942, McLeod returned to the subject of controls. Canada's economy was now almost completely controlled and its citizens were faced with far-reaching regimentation.

"There are few who like such regimentation for itself, but nearly everyone recognizes the necessity of widespread controls in these times of emergency, and it should be emphasized that the business community generally has not only accepted them with good grace but has actively co-operated in making them successful."[6] With price control under great pressure a year later, McLeod strongly urged the persistence of the battle against inflation "with unabated vigour and determination."[7] He pointed out that there was no question that the huge demands of war were reducing living standards and he went on to say, "the only question that has ever been at issue is how the burden of reduced civilian output is to be distributed. The way of rising prices and rising living costs is demoralizing and inefficient. It sets in process an ever-broadening struggle for compensation among all the group and individual interests of society, in which only the strong and unscrupulous can gain or maintain position, and in which most citizens and the nation are the losers."[8]

DECONTROL SHOULD BE GRADUAL

At the beginning of 1944, McLeod discussed the matter of decontrol. He dismissed the idea of full decontrol at the war's end as ill-conceived. "...Wartime controls should be removed as the shortages they were designed to combat are relieved and overcome. A few specific controls have been relaxed already. Many others may well be relaxed before the surrender of our enemies, while still others may be needed for varying periods after the close of hostilities....It is possible that the threat of inflation may remain for some time after the fighting has stopped, and in such circumstances price control might be one of the last to be entirely removed."[9] It is perhaps more than a coincidence that these ideas bore some resemblance to those of Donald Gordon, Chairman of the Prices Board, since Gibson had been loaned by the Bank to the Prices Board, where he served as its economist throughout the war.

Commenting on the possibility of achieving full employment in peacetime, McLeod observed that it would certainly be more difficult than during the war, and would depend on a unity of purpose and degree of co-operation seldom seen in peacetime. "To approach full employment, government and free enterprise will have to play complementary and not conflicting roles. For if Canadians fail to work together and waste their strength in social conflict, there will be no hope of attaining the better society which is desired."[10] The amazing thing is that for nearly twenty years after the war, Canadians did in fact make great progress towards this better society. The economy worked efficiently and people generally and particular groups in society managed to work and associate together tolerably well, or at least better than at most times in the past.

McLeod became Chairman of the Board in October 1945, and died only a few months later. He was reserved and very careful. Everyone

Edwin Crockett,
Executive Vice-President,
1945-1947

seems to have referred to him as *Mr.* McLeod, and in his letters in the Bank's Archives, there is only one correspondent who addressed him otherwise; his nephew called him "Uncle Jack." He was a good citizen, and a good churchman. He had a great sense of responsibility. Furthermore, with his neatly trimmed beard, he looked the part of an imposing banker. Burns's three-year-old grandson thought McLeod was Santa Claus when he saw him seated at his office desk in Christmas week! Burns now became President and E. Crockett, Vice-President, completing the long chapter which began when they left Halifax in 1897 with H.C. McLeod. And Enman entered the scene as General Manager.

NOTES

1. BNS Annual Report, 1948, Chairman's Address, p.18.
2. BNS Annual Report, 1953, General Manager's Address, p.26.
3. BNS Annual Report, 1944, President's Address, p.11.
4. BNS Annual Report, 1943, General Manager's Address, p.28.
5. BNS Annual Report, 1940, President's Address, p.21.
6. BNS Annual Report, 1941, President's Address, p.19.
7. BNS Annual Report, 1942, President's Address, p.18.
8. *Ibid.*, pp.17-18.
9. BNS Annual Report, 1943, President's Address, p.14.
10. *Ibid.*, p.15.

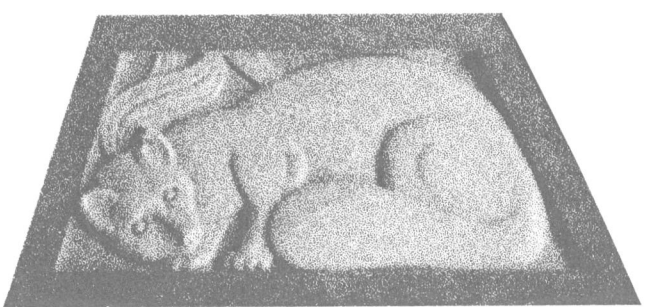

10

Filling Out a National Bank 1945-1960

CANADA EMERGED FROM THE WAR
WITH A HEALTHY ECONOMIC SYSTEM

At long last, the times were ripe for growth. Canada emerged from the Second World War a strong, united nation, perhaps stronger and more united than ever before or since. In the early fifties she was the third or fourth trading nation of the world and the sixth country in industrial production. The giants, Japan and Germany, would catch up and more than regain their relative positions, but that would not happen for some years yet. There was no doubt that Canada was becoming a force to be reckoned with and, as Canadians believed profoundly, a force for good. Canada saw herself as a middle power with the rather special assignments of promoting Anglo-American co-operation and of working out effective policies of aid to the less developed countries.

What was more, Canada came out of the war with a healthy economic system and a high degree of accord regarding political and social aims. She was probably more successful in combating inflation than any other country, taking off wartime controls gradually rather than suddenly as in the United States, and deliberately raising the exchange rate so as to reduce the impact of higher external prices. Despite the widespread fears that a difficult period of readjustment would follow the war, as had been the case after the First World War, there was no real postwar depression. On the contrary, the far-sighted Marshall Plan undertaken by the United States, with additional support from Canada and a few other countries, laid the basis of postwar recovery in Europe and created a very large demand for American and Canadian exports. In turn, the worldwide need for industrial raw materials promoted exploration and development of Canadian resources, which was to bring about a wider sharing of the larger national income. Even the Korean War, which did inject some added inflationary pressure into the picture, did not undermine the basis of prosperity, and the success of the United States and the United Nations in stopping aggression established world peace for many years to come.

H.L. Enman,
General Manager,
1945-1949;
Executive Vice-President,
1947-1949;
President,
1949-1956;
Chairman,
1955-1959.

ENMAN TAKES OVER

Into this propitious environment stepped the new General Manager, Horace L. Enman. Just over sixty years of age, he was certainly not a young man when he took over, but he was strong and energetic and he had been waiting a long time. Born in Moncton in 1884, he had graduated from Moncton High School and had started as a junior in that city at the age of fifteen when H. D. Burns, six years older, was teller. Five years later, now a teller himself in Halifax, Enman was discharged; he and his fellow teller were each $10 out, one over, the other short. They balanced by swapping the differences and this was discovered by an inspector – "a martinet," according to one informant. In any case, the manager of Halifax branch, though he could not question the decision, is believed to have written to W. D. Ross, General Manager of the Metropolitan Bank, recommending young Enman for employment.

Enman did join the Metropolitan Bank in Toronto in 1904, and within three years he became its Chief Accountant. Eight years later, he was appointed manager of the important Queen & McCaul branch in Toronto and in that capacity rejoined The Bank of Nova Scotia when it took over the Metropolitan in 1914. After the sudden death of his wife, Enman was sent to Calgary as manager in 1917. He found it hard to settle down in the West and Richardson brought him back to Queen & McCaul. This was an interim appointment until a better outlet for the man's restless energies could be found. In 1920, he became a superintendent of branches in Toronto, and in 1926, now remarried, he was appointed Supervisor of eastern branches in Saint John, New Brunswick. There for nineteen years he effectively promoted and expanded the Bank's business. He was an excellent judge of character and he gained a number of new customers, particularly when, during the depression, their current bankers lost confidence in them. One such case was that of Roy Jodrey of Hantsport, Nova Scotia, who swore by Enman and later became a Director of the Bank. When his friends had banking problems of their own, he would say, "Go see Enman." Fred Manning was one who took his advice and ultimately Manning too became a Director.[1] Seldom has one banker supervised an area more effectively than Enman did, and he accomplished this at a time when the Bank's operations were still closely controlled by General Office in Toronto.

As the years went by, Enman had his ups and downs and he felt himself banished from the centre of power in Toronto. Finally, in late 1945, as Burns moved up to the presidency, Enman came to Toronto as General Manager.

ABSOLUTELY DEVOTED TO BANK

Enman had great confidence in himself. His manner was rather formidable and he was usually noticed. He was a very able banker who, in addition to being familiar with balance sheet details, laid great stress on the character of the borrower concerned. He took an active interest in his customers and always had an eye open for opportunities which might be of use to them. He was absolutely devoted to the Bank. The introduction of Saturday morning closings in the 1950s – to which he was bitterly opposed – simply gave him additional time to get in his car and look for branch sites. When he built himself a summer place at Ingonish Beach on Cape Breton Island, a branch was opened in the nearby village, where he was said to play branch manager on his holidays.

Generally he was liked by the staff and in many cases he stimulated and inspired them. He had a strong will and a very powerful personality. He spoke quietly, but with an intensity and clarity that made his intentions more than clear. He usually got his way. He could be difficult and stubborn on those rather rare occasions when he turned out to be wrong. He could be interesting, and indeed charming, and much of the time he was. He was handsome and meticulous about his appearance.

Like most strong men, he did not arouse feelings of approval in everybody. He was rather outspoken at times and some people found him abrasive, perhaps a little arrogant. He loved his position of power; sometimes he could not resist pushing people around or showing something less than charity to those who could not keep pace. But, overall, he was a remarkable man who must rank with Fyshe, Richardson, Nicks, and Ritchie as major architects of the Bank's development.

Immediately under Enman were D.A.Y. Merrick and E.S. Crawford, the two senior Assistant General Managers now that Edwin Crockett and Grant Macintyre had retired. Merrick had been manager of Toronto branch and also Vancouver, and Crawford had been Supervisor of Cuban branches. As well, coming up quickly in the organization were two younger men of wide banking experience, C. Sydney Frost and Robert L. Dales. Frost, who had followed Enman as Eastern Supervisor, was later to follow him as General Manager. Dales, who in turn took over from Frost as Eastern Supervisor, soon moved to Winnipeg to replace F. L. Graham, the retiring Western Supervisor, and subsequently returned to Toronto to be an Assistant General Manager. Below them were F. William Nicks, Reid J. Smith, J. Douglas Gibson, Thomas A. Boyles, and Arthur H. Crockett (not related to Edwin Crockett). The senior staff for the big step forward was in place.

BECOMING A TRULY NATIONAL INSTITUTION

The prospect before Enman was an exciting one and one which he accepted with delight. To extend the Bank and make it a truly national institution and to improve the shareholders' returns were tremendous challenges. A great deal had to be done. In relation to the job ahead, the Bank was under-loaned, under-branched, under-equipped, and under-manned. It was also too conservative.

Thus, the first step, which Enman took very naturally, was to attack the deeply ingrained conservatism which stood in the way of progress and change. His attitude was positive and aggressive. He believed in going after business in an intelligent and persistent way and he had no patience with negative attitudes. He was not afraid of innovation, though as a man passing sixty it did not come naturally to him. He could perhaps most accurately be described as an aggressive but still traditional banker.

In any case, his appearance as the "boss" enhanced the hopes for the future which opened up at the end of the war. A new spirit was abroad. The staff, after long years of depression and war when advancement was at best very limited, began to feel that the Bank was going

R.L. Dales,
Executive Vice-President,
1958-1964;
Deputy Chairman,
1962-1964.

places. General Office was showing some signs of being able to say "yes" as well as "no." In some of the managers, Enman deliberately stirred up hopes of getting their lending proposals, even when a little unorthodox, through the credit department. He encouraged managers to push their proposals and fight for them.

BANK LENDING RECOVERS

Loans did in fact turn strongly upward when the war was over, in response both to favourable economic conditions and to less conservative management. From October 31, 1945, current loans in Canada by The Bank of Nova Scotia rose in successive stages from $105 million to $136 million in 1946, to $192 million in 1947, and to $272 million by 1950 – between two and a half and three times the end-of-war figure. Something very similar happened in the Caribbean, where the Bank's current loans in response to better markets for sugar and other produce rose even more sharply. After almost twenty years, the Canadian banks were again becoming commercial banks rather than government-financing banks. In the Nova Scotia's case, current loans in Canada and abroad which were less than 20 per cent of total assets at the end of the war had risen to 39 per cent by 1950. Security holdings were down from 50 per cent to 33 per cent. For the first time in sixteen years, loans were larger than securities and the Bank no longer took pride in having a statement whose conservatism vied with and even on occasion surpassed that of the Bank of Montreal.

Most of the increase in loans was of a regular commercial character, but some of the increase was related to government programs designed to encourage farm lending and home improvements. The Farm Improvement Loans program was not a great success, though perhaps it should have been. However, its potential was grasped by a few men, the most notable of whom was J. S. Burchell, manager of the Brooks, Alberta, branch, who, with one exception, had the best record in lending of all the chartered bank branches in Canada, under this federally sponsored program. He approached his job with enthusiasm, looking for opportunities, and where they did not seem apparent, he diligently looked for and found them. A striking example of his initiative occurred when one of his customers in Brooks found his cattle stuck in a gully surrounded by deep snow with no way of getting feed to them. A small airplane was the only chance. Burchell provided the funds to rent the airplane in Calgary and that saved both the cattle and his loans. He did not request permission of the regional office because he was sure it would sound too risky and he would be turned down.

NEW BRANCHES IN THE WEST

The job of filling out the Bank, and particularly of developing an adequate network of branches in western Canada, could not be done until substantial progress had been made in fitting in the returning veterans, and until many branches were reorganized and brought more nearly up to date. It is interesting indeed that in the first four years after the war, 165 existing branch premises had to be altered in a major way while 75 new branch buildings were opened. In terms of the number of branches, it took the Bank until 1949 to catch up to the position in which it had been in 1930. Such was the heritage of the depression and the war.

Nevertheless, by 1950 over 90 new branches had been opened and the total, while only a little higher than twenty years earlier, was much better distributed. Richardson's hopes of covering western Canada were at last on their way to fulfilment. Of the 90 new branches, half were west of the Great Lakes, mainly in British Columbia and Alberta. In these two provinces, where there had been only 15 branches at the end of the war, there were now 54. In another decade the representation would double again!

Enman took a vigorous interest in these activities. Robert E. Peel, who was then working in Vancouver branch on business development, remembers Enman at a meeting in 1949, demanding 60 new branches in the next eighteen months. For all of Canada? No! For British Columbia? Yes! While this extraordinary objective was only partly achieved, the Enman approach persisted, as exemplified by the following conversation in Toronto a few years later on a *Friday* afternoon:

> Enman to Harvey M. Dagg (Supervisor of Business Development): "Do I understand that that man Muir is going into Peace River soon?"
>
> Dagg: "Yes, sir, the Royal Bank is opening on Monday."
>
> Enman: "Well, see that you open before them. We should have been there by now."
>
> Dagg: "With respect, sir, I don't see how it is possible at this time. We might get it done by Wednesday."
>
> Enman: "That won't do at all. I want it open on Monday before the Royal. You can fly to Edmonton right away, rent a plane there tomorrow morning, get the manager, and be up there tomorrow. Maybe you will have to use a trailer, but get that branch open."

The 40-odd new branches opened by 1950 in the rest of Canada were spread widely. There was a highly desirable increase in the number of branches in Montreal and Quebec City; the province of Quebec was the other serious weak link in the chain of the Bank's representation across the country. Elsewhere, the rise in the number of new branches was more gradual, and clustered around the big cities. In the Caribbean, though business was good, only two new branches were opened at this time, both in Jamaica.

RE-EQUIPMENT AND STAFF PLANNING

That the Bank was under-equipped at the start of the postwar period is a gross understatement. When the war broke out, only 30 of the 300 branches were equipped with ledger-posting machines, these being located in the larger offices. A few of the big branches also had proof machines for sorting and listing cheques and similar cash items for clearing purposes. But, for the most part, the adding machine and the typewriter were the only machines in the office and few more machines were available until well after the war. Meanwhile, existing machines, though nursed tenderly, wore out, and an acute shortage of personnel for servicing developed.

Throughout 1946 and 1947 new machines were beginning to be delivered by the manufacturers and a new division of the Chief Accountant's Department was set up to handle the purchase and maintenance of machines and to review systems and methods in use at the branches. A fortunate development which occurred at this time was the appearance of a new "baby" posting machine which was just about ideal for the average-sized branch. These machines were rapidly brought into use in the Bank with the result that by the late forties the mechanization of ledgers had reached the point where only about 30 branches in Canada were not using them. This complete reversal of the postwar situation gave the Bank a notable competitive advantage. And the success of this section of the Chief Accountant's Department, in both mechanization and improved methods, led to its separation as a new department, Methods, headed by George MacDonell.

There was also every indication that the Bank was undermanned at the end of the war. However, with fair success in retaining the returned veterans – the proportion of nearly three-quarters was good but the loss of some very able men was not – the acute manpower shortage was easing by 1946 and 1947. The male staff rose from about 1,500 in 1945 to 2,400 in 1947 and 2,800 by 1950; while the number of female staff, after falling from its wartime peak, gradually increased again to around 1,850. Women were there to stay. Though they were no longer regarded as "emergency" staff, they were not yet accepted in the regular pension fund arrangements. By the beginning of the fifties, the Bank may have had an adequate number of people on its payroll, but it had very few trained people to cope with the rapid growth of branches and new business that lay ahead.

THE NEW GENERAL OFFICE BUILDING

And now to regress and digress a little. In 1855, William Cawthra, a prominent Torontonian, had built a handsome stone house on the northeast corner of King and Bay streets in Toronto. In 1931, this property, together with adjoining properties on King Street and on Bay Street, was bought by The Bank of Nova Scotia from the Canada Life

The north-east corner of King and Bay streets, Toronto, circa 1948, showing Cawthra House (left) and the Canada Life Assurance Building. On this site, General Office was erected in 1949-1951. The Bank's original Toronto office had been in the Canada Life Assurance Building.

Assurance Company. Interestingly enough, one of the buildings on this site housed the first Toronto branch of the Bank; the branch opened there in 1897 where it remained until 1903, when the new 5-storey building at 39 King Street West, accommodating the executive offices as well as the branch, was completed.

Plans for a seven-storey General Office building were drawn in 1931 by John M. Lyle, the architect of not only the Head Office building in Halifax, but also Ottawa branch and Calgary branch. Because of the depression and the Second World War, the construction of the General Office building was postponed. In 1946, A. S. Mathers and E. W. Haldenby were hired to take on the project, Lyle having died in the

Originally designed by John M. Lyle in 1931, the General Office building in Toronto was not constructed for fifteen years. Lyle having died, Mathers and Haldenby took over the project in 1946. The new General Office building opened in 1951.

interim. A building of only seven storeys at the most important corner of Toronto had no appeal for Enman, who saw the building as the headquarters of a major Canadian bank. Not every member of the Board agreed with him and the final decision was delayed about a year while the hole was being dug. Finally, Enman won the day and a handsome 25-storey building was opened in 1951. It could truthfully be said that the Bank's need for a new General Office building was acute by this time; since 1903, the premises on the south side of King Street West had gradually been expanded, taking in four neighbouring buildings and becoming a catacomb of corridors and stairways linking more and more office space.

The main banking hall continues the use of Canadian motifs which Lyle had introduced in the Bank's Calgary and Halifax buildings. The marble bas-relief at the north end of the banking hall, carved by Jacobine Jones, symbolizes the Bank's participation in the Canadian economy (shipping, fishing, lumbering, and manufacturing) and in the Caribbean.

Lyle had first introduced Canadian motifs into the design of Calgary branch – an idea which he greatly enlarged upon in the Head Office building in Halifax. Similarly, the Toronto branch banking room is dominated by a marble bas-relief which has a real Bank of Nova Scotia flavour. Carved by Jacobine Jones, it depicts not only typically Canadian economic endeavours – lumbering, fishing, mining, agriculture, construction, and manufacturing – but it also portrays the Bank's business in the Caribbean, in the person of a Jamaican girl carrying a bunch of bananas on her head. According to a press release issued when the building was opened, the banking room is approximately the size of the ice surface of Maple Leaf Gardens.

The wall of the entrance lobby looks back at the Bank's history; there is a sculptured replica of The Bank of Nova Scotia's seal and also of the seals of the four banks that were taken over: the Union Bank of Prince Edward Island, the Bank of New Brunswick, the Metropolitan Bank, and the Bank of Ottawa. Also, there is a carved dedication to "the men of vision and integrity who in the year 1832 founded this bank in the city of Halifax, Nova Scotia and to those who throughout the years have guided its destiny, served it faithfully and nurtured its growth westward to the Pacific, northward to the frontier outposts and south to the islands of the Caribbean."

THE OPENING CEREMONY

Burns laid the cornerstone of the new building on May 10, 1949, and he also was the one who opened the doors with a golden key on September 25, 1951. Present on the platform at the opening ceremony were two provincial premiers, Angus L. Macdonald of Nova Scotia and Leslie Frost of Ontario, the Mayor of Toronto, the Governor of the Bank of Canada, the Minister of Finance, the Lieutenant-Governor of Nova Scotia, the President of the Canadian National Railways (Donald Gordon, one of the most accomplished Bank of Nova Scotia alumni), and of course Enman, Frost, and the architects.

In addition to the "live" speeches by some of the platform dignitaries, including the two premiers, there were recorded speeches by the premiers of the other provinces. These messages established some sort of a record in brevity for speeches by politicians. As *The New Yorker* magazine pointed out, "Nine speakers had only seventeen minutes among them." On that account, the magazine commended the Bank's opening ceremonies program: "Any institution that can whittle down a speaker – or rather nine speakers – to something under two minutes... has our whole-hearted admiration. We wish we lived in Toronto and could favor The Bank of Nova Scotia with our checking account."[2] In its coverage of the opening, *Time* magazine singled out the Mayor's comment that the ceremony symbolized Toronto's new position as "the economic and financial centre of Canada"; this was the Mayor's way of taking a pot shot at Montreal, but perhaps a true statement nevertheless.

Over a thousand people were invited to the opening; naturally enough, most of the guests were from the Toronto area, but some came long distances for the occasion. The Bank brought in senior officers and a few senior pensioners from across Canada and abroad, and customers came from as far away as Jamaica. All the staff in the Toronto area had had a chance to look at the new building at an open house prior to the official opening. And perhaps more memorable for some was the Bank dance held a few months earlier. Fifteen hundred employees and their spouses and escorts accepted with much pleasure Mr. and Mrs. Frost's invitation to a buffet supper and dance, for which the entire convention floor of the Royal York Hotel was rented.

FROST BECOMES GENERAL MANAGER

By this time, Frost had entered the centre of the stage, or, if not exactly the centre, at least a prominent position near it. Actually, Frost became General Manager in December 1949 and Enman became President. In those days the title of Chief Executive Officer was not used in banking but, if it had been, Enman would have wished to retain it. He was by no means ready to retire and he had a good deal more that he wished to do. He was aware that some people thought he did not like Frost, but he is

C. Sydney Frost,
General Manager,
1949-1954;
Executive Vice-President,
1955-1956;
President,
1956-1958.

known to have said there was no foundation whatever for any such view. In a sense, Frost, who was an active and progressive person himself, had the bad luck to be caught between two driving individuals – Enman right ahead of him and Nicks just behind. Frost felt strongly that the Bank could be improved and expanded. He had an aggressive attitude towards obtaining business and a number of ideas about strengthening bank management. He also believed strongly in retirement at the age of 65; this belief was not shared by Enman.

Frost came from Yarmouth, Nova Scotia, where he entered the Bank in 1908 and where there is a pleasant park named after him. As has already been noted, he had a distinguished military career in the First World War. He received most of his early banking training in Newfoundland at the St. John's branch and elsewhere as a manager

Filling Out a National Bank, 1945-1960 197

and inspector. It was a happy coincidence for Frost, with his Newfoundland background, that his adopted country should join Canada at the time he became General Manager; and his interest in Newfoundland, more specifically the Royal Newfoundland Regiment, never waned. He spent a considerable amount of time in Winnipeg and in Saskatoon, where he learned to love the West and to do his best for his customers under the very difficult circumstances of the depression. After serving as a credit Supervisor at General Office in Toronto and as Eastern Supervisor in Saint John, he became an Assistant General Manager in 1946 and General Manager in 1949.

The new General Manager was a man of integrity and courage. A tall man, with more than a hint of military bearing, he was disciplined and efficient. To some he seemed perhaps a little cool-one of his associates felt he had never really left the army. But to his friends he was a good fellow who enjoyed bridge, golf, and good conversation, as did so many of his banking forebears. He was particularly interested in the staff and his reputation for fairness was well deserved. He stood for orderly and sensible ways of doing things and he believed in training to this end; this view had apparently been engraved in his consciousness by his experience in the Bank, if not in the army.

He was a good banker and he got along particularly well with James Fiott, the professional credit man who was the executive assistant to the General Manager. Frost was almost a workaholic. No job was too difficult for him and there were times when he appeared to be driving even harder than a man of his strength and determination should have done.

STAFF RELATIONS AND DECENTRALIZATION

During his tenure Frost directed his energies particularly towards better staff training and co-operation. He believed strongly in working closely with the man in the field-the manager-and, during his time as General Manager, he visited almost all of the Bank's 500-odd branches in Canada and the Caribbean. The purpose of these calls was to become acquainted with the manager and his customers. The fact was, however, that the Bank was becoming too big for this type of personal relationship between top management and all the local managers and their customers. The stage was now set for decentralization. The Bank had to be divided into effective operating units which were not too large for good management and for good relations with customers. In addition, attention had to be paid to the growing resentment evoked by "General Office decisions in Toronto" as opposed to those of the man in the area.

Decentralization was very clearly called for in western Canada with its rapid growth and enormous distances. When Frost was last working in the West in the late thirties, there were only 39 branches in the huge area stretching from Manitoba to the Pacific coast. By 1949 there were

74 branches – 26 of which were in British Columbia, a very long way from Winnipeg. Dales, who, it will be remembered, had followed Frost in a number of senior appointments and who had done much to build business, particularly in Calgary, continued as Supervisor of the three Prairie provinces, while Guy Penney became Supervisor – a new senior appointment – in British Columbia. As time went on, a regional office was established for Alberta in 1963, and another for Saskatchewan in 1973. But the process was gradual. It did not and could not occur overnight, if for no other reason than an insufficiency of trained people. At first, the main function of the regional offices was credit supervision, though the regional offices did have some say in hiring junior staff. In 1951, staff offices were established in each region and, as time went on, additional functions such as the responsibility for acquiring, developing, and maintaining branch premises were included. Thus the regional offices gradually took over more General Office functions, leaving to the General Office the large credits, the senior appointments, and the new buildings, in addition to the central planning and information job involved in steering the Bank on a promising course.

THE CREDIT MEETINGS

Though decentralization did lessen the relative burden on General Office, the marked growth in business and the process of review involved what still seemed a large expenditure of time on the part of the senior officers. At the daily credit meetings, which not infrequently ran for most of the morning, the General Manager presided, and the President sat on his right. Assistant General Managers could attend and of course did so when credits from their areas were up for review. The chief credit supervisor in effect acted as secretary of the meeting, while the credit officer who was directly responsible for the particular credit under discussion made the presentation.

This was a rather awesome gathering in terms of both position and credit experience. Before Frost's time, Enman conducted the meetings and Burns sat on his right. Every once in a while Burns, drawing on his vast knowledge of the Bank's customers and friends, would inquire about the family connections of the people involved in the credit, more often than not drawing a complete blank on the part of the credit officer concerned. The question might have been meaningful, but it was usually beyond the officer, who, having otherwise presented a well-balanced case, would have to go off and try to find information about somebody's uncle.

Credit officers seemed like soft-spoken gentlemen at the credit meetings, not at all like the ogres who were known to have written peremptory messages which infuriated branch managers. They did not look as though they would be "appalled and astounded at the temerity" of a manager in making such an "absurd" loan application. Nor did they seem like officers who would begin a letter, "With reference to the state of confusion which always exists in your branch..."

The credit meeting was an excellent training ground. It not only set high standards in credit presentations, but gave credit officers the opportunity of hearing presentations, questions, and criticisms from more experienced practitioners. But because of the time involved, Frost decided to have only the credit officers directly involved at the meetings rather than have them all there to see the show.

It is also true to say that in the fifties there was some shift in emphasis in the analysis of credits. As had always been the case, the current position, the quality of inventories and receivables, their relationship to current liabilities, and management, received due attention, but in addition earnings prospects were stressed more than they had been in earlier times. This reflected to no small degree the increased number of term loans, some of which were so designated and others of which, though described as regular working-capital loans, were, at least in part, of a capital nature.

TRAINING AND PROMOTION

The effective operation of a rapidly growing bank was clearly going to involve training for managers and prospective managers. Such a course, which concentrated strongly on credit, was introduced in 1951 and among its first lecturers was Dales, and among the first students, Crockett, one of the promising men of the future. The course, which was of six weeks' duration at the start, was later cut to three weeks. In fact the Bank appears to have been slow to adapt its staff training to its much increased size and rapid growth. The path to the top was reasonably discernible but the preparation of those likely to be successful was still rather old-fashioned in concept. It was evident, for example, that the jobs of assistant manager or accountant in a large branch were excellent in providing basic experience so absolutely necessary farther up the ladder. Similarly, being manager of a big branch (particularly Toronto) opened the door to the executive group. With only two exceptions, every manager of the main Toronto branch from 1940 to 1960 became an Assistant General Manager, and three of the six became General Manager. Another way up the ladder has been to acquire experience in New York and/or London. Patterson followed this route and more recent examples are Crockett, Hitchman, C. G. Webster, and J. A. G. Bell (the latter now holding the position of Deputy Chairman, President, and Chief Operating Officer).

The shortage of staff became acute as more and more branches were opened. Promotions in the Nova Scotia became rapid indeed and some people were catapulted into positions which were beyond their capabilities. The Staff Department was at its wit's end to find people to fill the many new jobs that were opening up. Successive efforts were made to fill the gap by importing people from the United Kingdom, particularly

Scotland, with some success, though a good many succumbed to the blandishments of other employers after arriving and settling in Canada. One very positive development was the hiring of finance company personnel to build up Scotia Plan, the Bank's consumer credit program which was inaugurated in 1958. This new group not only filled an immediate need but they also were a source of "new blood" in the Bank, many of them going on to become managers and supervisory personnel. The shortage of staff produced many problems and some inefficiency. But, on balance, the Bank was lucky. It endured this time of stringency remarkably well and some able senior employees were found in the process.

THE FIFTIES – A GOOD TIME FOR BANKING

The fifties, even more than the late forties, were a good time for banking. In the early years after the war, there was much catching up to be done, both in the physical sense of repairing a badly worn machine and in the reorientation of its functions to the varied business of commercial and individual banking as contrasted with the mass production of government financing and ration banking. As Frost noted at the 1950 annual meeting, the long period of low and controlled interest rates was coming to an end. It was heralded by an increase in the official bank rate from 1½ per cent to 2 per cent, a change which would scarcely be noticed today, but which in late 1949 was highly significant.[3]

The outbreak of the Korean War in 1950 aroused new fears of inflation and led to some credit controls. By the end of 1951, though the initial upthrust of prices had subsided, Enman devoted his address to the shareholders to the theme that "underlying inflation calls for more thoughtful attention."[4] In assessing the picture, he not only pointed to the consequences of increased defence spending but to longer-range influences such as the world shortage of many basic commodities: "Though this provides a welcome impetus to Canadian development, it is none the less a factor working on the side of inflation." Enman went on to say that another influence "of a menacing nature is the increasing evidence of lack of confidence in the future value of money.... Too many people are inclined to feel that inflation is inevitable." And, as he saw it, an additional long-term inflation-producing factor was "the natural desire for more leisure and shorter hours without any reduction in earnings." As well, a mounting pressure was the "widespread demand on governments for additional service and for social security."[5]

NORTH AMERICA SHOULD BE ABLE
TO COPE WITH INFLATION

Enman wondered "whether a free society is really capable of coping with the problem of inflation" and expressed the view that the answer ought to be "yes" for countries so favourably endowed as Canada and the United States.⁶ The events of the fifties tended to support this encouraging assessment. The North American economy was remarkably productive and inflation, while not overcome, was kept in check.

The great Canadian resource boom gathered strength, making available new sources of wealth right across the country, and spread in a way that the more exposed and less favoured regions benefited notably – Alberta with oil and gas, Saskatchewan with oil and uranium, Quebec-Labrador with iron and hydro-electric power, New Brunswick with base metals, and British Columbia with hydro-electric power and minerals – to name only a few in the impressive list of resource developments. Then there was the great improvement of transportation facilities as the much-enlarged St. Lawrence Seaway was completed and as the TransCanada gas pipeline was built. A great flood of immigrants poured into the country, mainly into the big cities and above all into Toronto. The Bank grew rapidly and, as might be expected in such circumstances, again strikingly in western Canada, and around the big cities. In the first half of the fifties, another 95 branches were added, 40 of them in the West and 25 around Toronto. The assets of the Bank at $1,193 million in 1955 were well past the billion-dollar mark. Loans had reached almost half of the total assets, while securities were about 25 per cent – a much better and more profitable relationship than that which had prevailed for many years.

Another important development for the Bank was the movement to a floating, or market-determined, exchange rate under the continuing pressure of heavy capital inflows. With many resource developments attracting foreign capital and with growing U.S. interest in this country, the Bank of Canada, in maintaining a fixed rate in accordance with the generally agreed rules of the time, was offering a nearly certain exchange bet which in itself attracted more capital. The official rate had had to be changed, up in 1946, down in 1949, and it was again under pressure in 1950 – underlining the difficulty of setting a fixed rate that would remain appropriate for long. And so, reluctantly, and with special dispensation from the International Monetary Fund, the Bank of Canada in late 1950 moved from a fixed rate to a floating rate. Thus, after ten years of a fixed rate, an open market for the Canadian dollar appeared again and the Nova Scotia was not slow to rebuild its exchange trading skills. These capacities turned out to be a vital adjunct to the Bank's entry into foreign wholesale banking.

Just how promising Canada's outlook appeared to be at this time is indicated by the subject of a *Monthly Review* issued in 1953: "Twenty-five Million Canadians."⁷ (The Canadian population was then only 15 million.) Prepared by Dr. Lucy Morgan, soon to become Supervisor of the Economics Department and the first woman of that rank in the Bank, her population forecast for 1980 turned out to be quite accurate – her estimate of 25 million compares with the actual figure of 24 million. It must be noted, though, that the author had not foreseen what a

Dr. Lucy Morgan, Supervisor, 1957-1960.

An economist, Dr. Morgan was the first woman to be appointed to the rank of Supervisor in the Bank.

CHANGES IN LEGISLATION IN 1954

In 1954 the Bank Act came up for its decennial review, as did the Bank of Canada Act, while a new National Housing Act was passed. An important change was that the banks were now permitted to make mortgage loans under the National Housing Act. This change opened up a large area of lending to the banks with their established and widely dispersed system of branches. A mortgage department was set up by the Bank and it gradually acquired a substantial portfolio. Towards the end of the decade, however, money became tight and it was only possible to maintain an effective operation in this field by developing a secondary market for mortgages, principally among the pension funds, so that sales could be made to provide the funds for new purchases. There were other difficulties, including the question of the applicability of the 6 per cent lending-rate ceiling, as mortgage rates rose. Under the direction of W. H. McDonald a flexible policy was pursued which allowed the Bank to stay in this area of business and thus in a position to take advantage of the opportunities which were to arise in the sixties.

Another change in the Bank Act which was to prove of special importance to The Bank of Nova Scotia a few years later, when Scotia Plan was inaugurated, was the power given to the banks to take chattel mortgages, thus making it possible for them to move into the area of individual automobile and household loans. Neil McKinnon, President of the Canadian Bank of Commerce, had presented a persuasive case for this important change before the Banking and Commerce Committee of the House of Commons. An additional change in the Bank Act was the widening of lending powers so as to permit security to be taken against hydrocarbons in the ground – a reflection of the fact that Canada was becoming a significant oil producer.

The cash position of the banks was also the subject of new legislation giving the Bank of Canada power to vary the banks' cash reserve requirements. Later, there was an agreement by the banks, at the direction of the Bank of Canada, to maintain a minimum secondary-reserve ratio (over and above the cash ratio) of Treasury bills and day loans amounting to 7 per cent of Canadian deposits.* These actions were closely related to the broadening of the money market through the issuance of more Treasury bills and through the inauguration of day loans, which are payable on demand and largely backed by Treasury bills.

---

* Ultimately, the Bank Act of 1967 gave the central bank formal power to vary this secondary-reserve ratio.

SEARCH FOR MORE DEPOSITS

As money became less readily available and as the Bank found new uses for it, an increasing effort was made to attract deposits. Unwilling to get involved in direct rate competition, the Bank looked for new deposit contracts that would bring in additional funds. A real innovation, worked out by Nicks, just before he became General Manager, was the PSP – the Personal Security Program – an insured savings plan. The depositor would state a savings target of up to $2,000 (later raised to $5,000) and would undertake to deposit one-fiftieth of it each month. If he lived he received the target plus interest, but if he died before the fifty payments were made, his heirs received the full savings target. This did bring in a sizeable amount of new business, but what was more important was that it gave the tellers and other members of staff something to sell that was different from other banks. It was in a real sense the opening gun in a continuing deposit campaign, which, for the first time, attempted to engage the full energies of the staff. As a matter of interest, the PSP idea came from the Bank of America, with whom the Nova Scotia had had fruitful mutual relations for years past.

Selling new services put emphasis on public relations and advertising, and further developments occurred in this area; though differences in view as to what ought to be done, and more fundamentally as to what were the Bank's objectives, meant that progress was only gradual. Robert E. Oliver, who was Supervisor of Public Relations during the late fifties and early sixties, made a significant contribution in clarifying the Bank's thinking about its image and objectives. A related development was the beginning of the publication of the new staff magazine in 1952; it carries timely articles of interest to the staff and it also records such staff activities as sporting events, branch and department parties, moves, retirements, and vital statistics. An early issue showed a photograph of Boyles, then manager at Ottawa, pitching a softball to Charlotte Whitton, the Mayor. "I hit her right on the backside and she came at me with the bat," he commented.

The Personal Security Program, an insured savings plan, was part of the increasing effort to attract deposits in the early 1950s.

THE NEW GENERAL MANAGER – F. W. NICKS

At the end of 1954, F. W. (Bill) Nicks became General Manager of The Bank of Nova Scotia. He was born in Winnipeg, and was the first non-Maritime General Manager; this was an indication of the increasing Canadianization of the Bank, now with three-quarters of its branches outside of the Atlantic provinces. Standing beside his successor, Gibson, at the reception after the annual meeting in Halifax four years later, he said, "Don't tell them you are from Toronto! Haven't you relatives in Tatamagouche?" In any case, the day was passing when it could be argued that the strength of the Bank lay in its reliance on recruiting staff from the Maritime provinces; many Upper Canadians and Westerners liked working for the Bank too.

Nicks joined the Bank in Winnipeg as a summer worker at the age of sixteen. He enjoyed his job so much that he stayed on, against the advice of his father, who wanted him to finish school and go to McGill University; his father was not prepared to admit that the boy had made the right decision until he became manager at Halifax some twenty years later.

Nicks brought to the Bank a fresh approach. He had on occasion been known to speculate on what he would do if he ever found himself in a position to do things his way. Now he had his chance. He held no brief for old ways of doing things if there were new and better ways. He could see no good reason why banking should be confined to certain kinds of financing, if it could perform other functions in a useful and profitable way. As Harry Randall, who was then Chief Accountant, said later, Nicks's "greatest genius was that he sensed the timing and having sensed it and grasped the opportunity he had a single-mindedness about it.... His mind would focus on that thing and it would stay focussed with an intensity that I have never known anybody to match and it really exhausted you just to keep pace."

He was of course an experienced banker, having worked as assistant manager and manager in both Halifax and Toronto, and as manager in Montreal. Earlier, he was also accountant in Montreal and Halifax and on leaving the latter job he expressed the hope to a colleague that he would be able to serve with him again some time in the future, to which the colleague replied, "Oh, no! You are destined for much more important positions than I could ever fill." He had served in the Inspection Department, where he had worked with, among others, F. J. Finlay and W. C. McKinnon. Finlay described him as a restless fellow who had to be on the go and who could not face a weekend stuck in a hotel. So they would take trips, in one case to Moosonee, in another to Kapuskasing, just to see the sights. One night on an inspection assignment, McKinnon went on working past midnight and Nicks, who had been wondering how long the session would continue, apparently said to himself, "If this fellow can work all night so can I." So they went right through till morning. Nicks got along well with the financial community and went out of his way to cultivate the friendship and respect of its members. He procured a great deal of business, and in Halifax made his first connection with the Greek shipping industry, which was to become an important area of business in future.

NICKS'S TEAM

He was immensely anxious to show what he could do – he wanted to break new ground – he liked what he described as "firsts." But he knew he had to be right. With this in mind, he gradually gathered around him a small but competent group. Randall, the Chief Accountant, as the central source of information for the General Manager, was of course

F.W. Nicks,
General Manager,
1954-1958;
President,
1958-1970;
Chief Executive Officer,
1960-1972;
Chairman,
1962-1972.

the first member; there has seldom been a more determined and enthusiastic worker. The rest of the group consisted of C. W. Jameson, who followed Randall as Chief Accountant and who ultimately worked full-time for Nicks; W. Scott McDonald on the international side; and later on, to some extent, Cedric E. Ritchie as Chief Accountant. These men worked on Nicks's various projects, obtaining information from others in the Bank, seconding some staff members to do special jobs, and hiring outside legal and accounting help as needed.

Nicks's team thought a lot of him and they worked hard and with ingenuity and dedication. Their products included PSP insured deposits, term notes, Scotia Plan credit, gold dealings, and trust company arrangements in the Caribbean. Nicks would try out his proposals in discussion in his office, Dales being a constant attendant and to a lesser degree Gibson and Boyles. He wanted to be sure that his plans were

Advertisement of the Bank's 125th Anniversary in 1957

right and that they would benefit the Bank. Yet he had already worked them over and over with his assistants and he was not always happy with questions from those who had not been through the long process of developing the plans and whose comments might be poorly based. For this reason, actual criticism was sometimes muted or indirect.

Nicks was quite a big man and he had a strong presence. There was something almost courtly about his manners as he met visitors in his rather small but elegant office. He was polite and usually serious. When annoyed or challenged, his face would become noticeably red. He was essentially a shy person. He did not like social gatherings whether of a Bank or an outside nature. He preferred to spend his weekends at home without guests, when he was not travelling abroad. There was a great intensity about him and he drew heavily on his store of nervous energy, probably too heavily. He was absorbed in his various projects and it is small wonder that he had not the time nor the energy to carry out many of the formal duties expected of a man in his position. Some of his colleagues found him difficult to communicate with, or even to see, and most wished that as the head man he could be less distant and more visible to the staff. Yet, like many shy people, he was generous and thoughtful in his relations with a few friends and associates, and he did a number of kindly things that few people knew about. So far as the printed record is concerned, he was the first General Manager to thank the pensioners and the Directors for their services to the Bank. He did not have much sense of humour. If he had, he would have taken his job less seriously, less intensely – and perhaps accomplished less.

Enman, who had described Nicks as the "crown prince" when he was still manager of Toronto branch, stayed on as President while Frost became Executive Vice-President in 1954. In 1955, Enman assumed the position of Chairman as well as President, and Burns, now in his late seventies, became Honorary President, with Frost becoming President the following year. Dales became Vice-President and a Director in 1954 and the group under Nicks then consisted of Reid J. Smith and Fiott and three new Assistant General Managers: B. R. Calder, who had been executive assistant; T. G. Adams, formerly Chief Supervisor; and Gibson, from the Economics Department. A number of able men had recently retired: Crawford, who had been one of the senior Assistant General Managers in Toronto and before that in charge of the Bank in Cuba; Penney, from his empire in British Columbia; G. F. Hinchcliffe, Assistant General Manager in Toronto, who had had long experience in the Caribbean and New York; and Merrick, the other senior Assistant General Manager in Toronto.

CONSUMER CREDIT – LEADING EVENT OF THE LATE FIFTIES

Without question, the most important development of the late fifties was the entry of the Bank into consumer credit. This was the second act in the revolution in domestic banking which brought the banks into a closer lending relationship with the general public; in 1954, the banks had been allowed to make mortgage loans for the first time. Now, the entry of the banks into the consumer credit field was what increasingly brought them out to shopping centres in the suburbs, and made life more complicated for the finance companies and trust companies. Interestingly enough, the banks had been permitted to take chattel mortgages ever since 1954 – the same year that mortgage loans were allowed for the first time – but they had delayed their entry into personal lending on a large-scale basis for several years.

The Bank of Nova Scotia had done most of its homework on consumer credit by 1955,* but as the year went on, money tightened, the Bank of Canada requested restraint, and it therefore seemed inappropriate to start a major new program. Moreover, as President of the Canadian Bankers' Association from mid-1955 to mid-1957, Nicks was not inclined to introduce a program which he knew some of the banks regarded as undesirable.

The biggest problem, however, was the 6 per cent ceiling on the rate of interest charged by banks under the Bank Act, which would have made consumer credit quite uneconomic for them. Since personal loan and sales finance companies were not subject to such a restraint, they were charging much more, say from 14 per cent to 20 per cent. The banks calculated that they needed roughly $10^1/_2$ per cent to 12 per cent, rates which would obviously result in considerably cheaper credit for the consumer. However, there was no political prospect in the offing that the 6 per cent ceiling would be removed, even though it was perfectly evident that the public interest would be served by allowing the banks to levy rates higher than 6 per cent on this type of loan. Thus, what the Nova Scotia did was much the same as what the Canadian Bank of Commerce had done earlier – it required customers to make monthly payments into a bank account which would produce enough to pay off the loan at its due date, charging interest at 6 per cent. Since the Bank would have on deposit over the term of the loan an average balance approaching half the amount of the loan, the true rate of interest would turn out to be a good deal higher than the nominal rate of 6 per cent, probably around 11 per cent, depending on the term.

As part of its 125th Anniversary, the Bank ran a series of advertisements focussing on famous names in Canadian history.

"A DIFFERENT KIND OF CAT"

To head up consumer credit, outside experience was needed. Large-scale consumer lending was something new for a bank. As Nicks put it, "a different kind of cat" was required. So W. J. Dixon, with extensive experience in the personal loan and sales finance business, was hired to head up Scotia Plan credit and together with William Lawson, from a

---

* Again, as had been the case with PSP, The Bank of Nova Scotia received help from the Bank of America, which had already developed a major consumer lending business.

The move into consumer lending became an important and successful part of the Bank's retail business.

personal loan company, and Hugh Kinsman, formerly assistant chief accountant, the preparations were made to put the new plans into effect. It was no doubt propitious that a second William Lawson, a namesake of one of the Bank's founders, should be involved!

On October 1, 1958, the new plan went into effect. Experienced consumer credit people were hired in substantial numbers from outside companies, approximately one hundred being taken on by the Bank within the first year. What this meant was that an experienced consumer credit person was on deck quite early at virtually all of the larger branches and at certain other locations such as large shopping centres. Elsewhere, training programs were in progress for existing staff. When outstanding Scotia Plan Loans passed $100 million in the second year, it became evident that the program was a great success, and as time went on it developed into a major contributor to the Bank's earnings. Because of the program's early start and vigorous development, the Bank has maintained to this day much more than its proportionate share of this important type of business.

An interesting sidelight on the introduction of Scotia Plan was the fact that Randall's secretary, Sally Monnot, had been typing drafts and memoranda for a couple of years before Scotia Plan went into effect and, needless to say, knew all about The Bank of Nova Scotia's intention of entering the consumer credit field. Her father happened to be a senior officer in a small-loans company and was very surprised to read the newspaper announcement that his daughter's employer was about to become a formidable rival. For Monnot, just as it is for all the secretaries in the Bank, the necessity for discretion is simply one facet of a demanding and interesting job. It is, of course, impossible to include the names of all these invaluable secretaries in a history such as this, but a few senior secretaries who have had long careers in the Bank should be mentioned: in General Office in Toronto – Marguerite Burke, Beatrice Witt, Isobel Ironside, Olive Chapman, Muriel Baptie, and, last but not least, Betty Chalklin, whose brother, George W. Chalklin, was Secretary of the Bank and then a branch manager until he had to retire early because of ill health. And elsewhere in the Bank, Mae Froats (in Ottawa), Helen Mullan (in Vancouver), Blanche Tapley (in Saint John), Rita Munn (in London, England), Alice Mitchell (in New York), and Gloria Perez (in San Juan, Puerto Rico) have all served devotedly for many years and, in particular, have helped to provide a sense of continuity for a succession of "bosses."

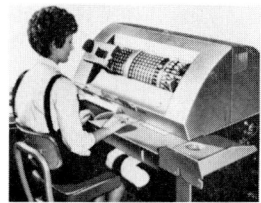

This 1959 advertisement announced the introduction of the new posting machines in the Bank's Winnipeg office. The latest development in bank automation, the machines had been introduced earlier in Toronto.

MONEY TIGHTENING AGAIN

During 1959, it was becoming evident that money was getting tight again. How could the Bank keep Scotia Plan going? The answer lay in building up deposits, while running down liquidity as low as was reasonable. The Deposit Development Department, headed by Neil Speicher, stimulated the drive. Deposit incentives, competitive programs – the whole gamut of modern selling – were employed in the effort by an imaginative, cheerful man who had the gift of making everybody an enthusiastic member of the team. Also, the Bank went after money with a new instrument – the term note, the term ranging from one to six years. In this new area, formerly dominated by the finance companies and trust companies, the Bank was able to compete quite well. By such means, the Bank lived through the money squeeze without seriously restricting its new initiatives in lending.

It was no accident that at around this time the Investment Department was modernized and turned into more than a mere cash-balancing unit with sizeable holdings of government issues. In 1957 the head of the Department, Keith Waters, died and Robert M. MacIntosh, who had moved from the Economics Department to be Waters's understudy, now took over in the Investment Department. In the next few years, MacIntosh improved cash management and set himself the task of developing a small trading group and of representing the Bank's interests in major financial developments. One of these developments was the government's controversial Conversion Loan of 1958, which accomplished the turnover of much of the war-accumulated debt through a considerable lengthening of term and some increase in interest rates. The Bank managed to emerge from this sobering experience with some, but not an undue, increase in the average term of its security holdings.

MECHANIZATION AND COST REDUCTION

Meanwhile, mechanization was becoming more and more important as a means of reducing costs and the Methods Department came up with delayed posting arrangements, which added substantially to the efficiency of the branches. A delay in posting until the following morning, rather than the traditional system of posting several times throughout the day, resulted in a sharp reduction in the time and costs involved in carrying out the posting operation. Moreover, another big advantage came from the great reduction in posting errors that resulted from the fact that the work was being performed in the morning before opening time when the operators were fresh and undistracted. In the words of W. C. Meek, Chief Accountant at the time, "the posting is now being performed when the operators' seams are straight and their powder is dry!" In a similar jocular vein, Enman referred to "this new-fangled system, where branches are now allowed to post ledgers on the walls, the ceiling or anywhere they please."

The great expansion in Canada limited what could be done abroad until the late fifties and sixties. Nevertheless, in the islands of the Caribbean, the Bank's operations did increase substantially. After the war, with a strong demand for sugar, rum, molasses, bananas, and other tropical products, and with the development of bauxite, and a boom in the tourist trade, economic conditions improved considerably. Unfortunately, political conditions did not; there was unrest in most of the islands, and in one island, Cuba, the unrest developed into revolution. For the Bank, there were disappointments and difficulties, though to a substantial degree effective adjustments were made to the new environment.

DISAPPOINTMENT IN CUBA

The greatest disappointment occurred in Cuba, where the Castro government nationalized the banks at the beginning of 1961. Since early in the century The Bank of Nova Scotia had built a good business in Cuba, which continued to grow after the war. It was developed and managed by men who, like J. A. McLeod, F. L. Graham, E. S. Crawford, and D. L. Lindsay, went on to make their further contribution in Canada and by some who, like Victor Cox, became absorbed in the Spanish-American atmosphere, or C. E. Tanner, who prior to the revolution had decided to make Cuba his permanent home. In the early days, Canadian bankers in Cuba, as in Santo Domingo, frequently spoke English, even though Spanish was often the language of commerce. As time went on, more and more of them learned to speak Spanish, in some cases fluently; for instance, young Fred Finlay, who came from Scotland to Santo Domingo in the early twenties, learned to speak Spanish well. Nationalism in Cuba, as in other Caribbean countries, meant that fewer and fewer Canadians were employed and that more and more Cubans were hired.

Tellers' Cages, Havana, Cuba.

Building erected 1913.
The office was closed in December 1960, and the
nationalization of the Bank by the Cuban government
was formally concluded in January 1961.

The Bank adapted to this process quite well, a process which was just as evident in Jamaica. But living under a communist regime was another matter.

While leaving Cuba was not a disaster for the Bank, it was unfortunate to lose the accumulation of experience and ability which the Bank had developed there. Also it was upsetting to have to sever the ties which the Bank had established with its Cuban employees. The Bank had taken root in Cuba. The manager of Havana branch, M. J. Betancourt, was Cuban and there were few Canadians left, of whom Lindsay and R. M. Taylor were among the last. What had been built was a productive institution contributing significantly to Cuba's economic welfare. But the structure into which it fitted, consisting in the main of privately owned business and private individuals, was superseded by a state-owned system in which all the decisions and financing were undertaken by the state. As the nature of the system became apparent, as the Bank's business customers were taken over or closed by the state, it became evident that there was no future for commercial banking in Cuba. In point of fact, the two Canadian banks in Cuba, the Royal in addition to the Nova Scotia, were among the last of the foreign banks to be taken over, and it appears that they emerged with a considerably better deal than did many other foreign banks.

The takeover was peaceful, and indeed the Cuban government continued to keep sizeable foreign balances with the Bank. Over a year elapsed from the time of the revolution which brought Castro to power to the time of the final nationalization of the Bank. During this period the banks were open for business part of the time. However, more and more business customers were being taken over. As Frank Irvine, assistant manager at Havana, said, "We were at a point where we were not going to lend any more money and we could not collect the existing loans. So, we were just more or less at a standstill.... Once the government put its man in, that was pretty hopeless because that meant the owners had gone – probably to the United States – and the new man in charge frequently did not know much about the business." Safety deposit boxes had been sealed by the government, and the communist unions in the Bank were feeling a new sense of power, which did not improve the service. Business was slow and confused. Though Bank personnel had to stay in their homes on occasion, they were not molested. And considering the fact that there was a great deal of doubt as to what was supposed to be done and that there were many young revolutionaries on the loose, conditions were better than might have been expected. This is not to suggest there were no problems. Victor Cox, formerly the Bank's head man in Cuba and then the director of the central bank representing the foreign banks, was put in jail. Finally, on appeal from the Bank and the Canadian government, he was released and later allowed to leave the country.

The closing of the deal for nationalization took several months, not because of detailed bargaining but probably because of the inexperience of the government, which had so much work on its hands and so few trained people to deal with its problems. The Bank received approximately the book value of its investment in Cuba in U. S. funds and the Canadian employees who owned property received compensation. G. A. Griffiths and E. A. Mowatt signed the document on behalf of the Bank in January 1961. And so ended a colourful and interesting chapter in the Bank's history. A significant source of revenue had disappeared, eight branches were gone, and over 200 people no longer worked for The Bank of Nova Scotia. By and large the Bank's record in Cuba was a good one and the Bank's closing was a matter of regret.

FURTHER GROWTH IN JAMAICA BUT NO FEDERATION

In Jamaica with its British tradition the postwar story was very different, though there were also disturbing undercurrents of a political nature. Because of the disruption of shipping, Canada had replaced Great Britain as Jamaica's principal supplier during the war. After the

The Bank opened in Kingston, Jamaica, in 1889. In 1908 it built these premises at 35-45 King Street.

In 1961, the King Street office in Jamaica was expanded to deal with growing business.

CREDIT: NOEL A. HO-SHUE

war, with improved demand for Jamaican products, and growing Canadian and U.S. interest in bauxite, Jamaica experienced considerable economic growth. The Bank participated in that growth, almost doubling its representation – from eleven to twenty branches – and strengthening its leading position on the island to over 40 per cent of the total banking business. What had started as a modest venture abroad in 1889 was in the 1950s a sizeable operation employing about 400 people and occupying a position of importance. Until the founding of a new central bank during this latter decade, the Nova Scotia was the government's banker. After the central bank was established, The Bank of Nova Scotia co-operated closely with it and with the government in matters of monetary and economic policy, and from time to time it lent the country money as well as advice. As a matter of interest, it may be noted that Gilbert Wainwright, who had retired in Jamaica in 1932 after his service there in the Bank as head man, served the Jamaican government during the Second World War and was honoured with a knighthood.

With the passage of time, the Bank gradually became more Jamaican as local people assumed more responsibility. The earlier arrangements, which provided for northerners doing most of the skilled work and living in the Acadia Club on the outskirts of Kingston, gradually gave way to a broader approach as education and internal training allowed Jamaicans to move up in the organization. A growing number of the managers were Jamaican. During much of this period, Thomas

Evans was the head man. Though he was finally moved to Vancouver, the goal of so many retiring bankers, he liked Jamaica so much that he moved back and retired there.

In the early fifties, it began to look as though there might be a Federation of the British West Indies. With this thought as well as more local considerations in mind, the Bank returned to Port-of-Spain, Trinidad, and later opened in San Fernando. It also opened in Bridgetown, Barbados. The Federation was in fact established in 1957, but Jamaica opted out in 1961 and the Federation formally ended in 1963. From many points of view this was a pity; however, the Bank's branches in Trinidad and Barbados were successful and in the sixties were followed by others in the area which was once to have been that of the Federation.

ADAPTING IN THE DOMINICAN REPUBLIC

In the Dominican Republic another set of problems faced the Bank, again basically political in nature. The Trujillo dictatorship established before the Second World War continued into the early sixties, when it was overthrown. The Bank's local commercial activities had grown materially and in addition, towards the end of the period, the Bank had become involved in what is known as wholesale banking in the form of loans to the central bank. These loans, which in effect were backed by U.S. dollars, were of a complicated nature and, while well secured, their documentation in a regime where customs and methods were unfamiliar created some problems. In turn, lending to the central bank had an interesting by-product in that it opened the door to lending to the government agency which had nationalized the country's sugar companies; these loans were made against the cane in the fields during the growing season.

The loans in the Dominican Republic can best be described as an early stage in the search for external business which Nicks initiated. At the time they were made, some of the senior staff were less than enthusiastic about them. Other banks showed no interest in competing for them until it became apparent that they were good business. Randall did much of the legwork and broke the ice in an absolutely new field. The early loans were followed by a further arrangement in which the Bank sold Dominican gold coins abroad.

Following the overthrow of Trujillo, there were several regimes and then, in 1966, a rebellion which led the Americans to move in. E. D. Hunter, who had become manager in the Dominican Republic in 1958 where he had lived since 1946, had developed an unusual understanding of the country. While there was a strong sense of insecurity during the dictatorship – "political opponents tended to disappear" – the Bank was able to expand visibly in the period after the rebellion. During the American occupation, it so happened that the Bank's main office was in the surrounded rebel enclave in the centre of the city. It was closed and theoretically cut off for six months. However, Hunter did in fact keep an eye on it, particularly the vault, visiting it several times a week without interference by the rebels. His experience in the Dominican Republic no doubt was of value to him in later years when he ran the Bank's branch in Beirut under fire.

The list of senior bank officers in the Dominican Republic bears a close resemblance to those in Jamaica, Cuba, and Puerto Rico. Hinchcliffe, manager in the Dominican Republic in the thirties, was in Puerto Rico in the forties and then was senior agent in New York. Hunter moved from the Dominican Republic to Puerto Rico and then through the Middle East and Athens to New York, also as senior agent. G. A. ("Bonzo") Griffiths, later killed in an air crash near Montreal, moved to Puerto Rico from the Dominican Republic. Crawford, in charge in Cuba in the halcyon days of the twenties (and also in the thirties), got earlier experience in Puerto Rico. Lindsay spent much of his time in Cuba but was also manager in the Dominican Republic, and moved on later to head up the Caribbean Region. In other words, southern experience had a special quality about it which often kept a man in the international service.

OTHER DEVELOPMENTS IN THE CARIBBEAN

In Puerto Rico, one more branch was opened in the period up to 1960 and business grew, though it was very difficult to obtain permission to open new branches. In a somewhat different way, and with far less unfortunate consequences, this island was suffering from the same unrealistic rise in expectations which affected the other islands of the Caribbean.

The opening of the branch in Nassau, Bahamas, in 1956 can be regarded not only as a development in international banking but also as an attempt to obtain local deposits and loans. It ties in with the later action in 1958 of establishing The Bank of Nova Scotia Trust Company (Bahamas) in partnership with British financial interests. This new company made possible the carrying out of certain offshore deals and trust operations which were not open to a Canadian bank. In 1959, the new trust company was registered for business in Jamaica and Trinidad, and The Bank of Nova Scotia Trust Company of New York, this time a wholly owned subsidiary, was formed to round out the external fiduciary services performed by the Bank.

Although the Bank was doing quite well in its Caribbean branches, it was also true that the rise of nationalism was limiting the opportunities for participating in local deposit business: local banks were to be protected or, if there were none, foreign banks were to be domesticated. And this threatened policy of domestication was carried out later in some instances. Therefore, it was logical that the Bank should turn towards international business of a wholesale, rather than retail, character and this was what was beginning to happen.

ENTRY INTO GOLD

One of the early manifestations of this new emphasis on international wholesale banking was the Bank's entry into the gold business. Nicks was looking for new business, for ways of breaking into the international sphere, and the removal in 1956 of the restrictions on trading in gold by residents and non-residents in Canada led him to investigate this area. Randall, with help from a gold expert whom the Bank hired – Jerome F. Forman – went to work. In the process the idea of gold certificates developed and the firm of Samuel Montagu, with its long experience in the London gold market, was approached. What emerged was a partnership arrangement with Montagu whereby the Bank would sell gold certificates redeemable in Toronto or London, depending on where they were purchased. A location in North America, in addition to that in London, was desirable because of the high cost of moving gold in settlement of contracts. Such a North American location could not be in the United States, since Americans were prohibited from holding gold in their own country. Thus, Toronto was a logical choice for a gold market centre on this side of the Atlantic.

A persistent effort was made to establish a source of supply of gold bullion from Canadian mines. By offering a very competitive deal and through Samuel Montagu's success in getting a London stamp of approval for the Canadian refiner, such a source was gradually developed. Knowledge of the gold business led to a number of interesting opportunities in the future.

LONDON AND NEW YORK

The Bank's branch in London, England, was to play a major role in the emerging international business. It had been opened just after the First World War, because London was regarded as such an important financial centre and because the other major Canadian banks were already there. Foreign banks were not supposed to compete with British banks for British business, but they could handle and invest the sterling from their operations abroad, as the Bank did, particularly in relation to Jamaica. It was also regarded as cricket that foreign banks approach British companies that might be setting up in Canada. In any case, The Bank of Nova Scotia's London operation was run on a conservative basis under the first manager, E. C. McLeod (another McLeod from Prince Edward Island), and his assistants, who had been recruited mainly from the Royal Bank of Scotland. During the very trying circumstances of the Second World War, they worked between the branch in the City and a house outside London where they kept their records.

Early in the postwar period a series of new managers – all men who were getting experience and going somewhere – enlivened the London branch; first, C. G. ("Buzz") Webster from New York, who subsequently returned to New York with an even broader comprehension of the Bank's international connections; then, Hitchman (the same Hitchman who described banking in a little village in Ontario in the depression), followed by J. D. Hubbert, who was succeeded by Crockett.

Hitchman developed a system of making calls on the Continent, as well as in Britain, looking for business with companies who might be developing Canadian interests; and he improved an already good connection with the Midland Bank. Crockett had the good luck of being in London when Nicks was endeavouring to develop European business. From the middle of the fifties to the end of the decade, and indeed after that, Nicks went to Europe usually twice a year and included London in one of his trips. His first official trip was with Enman. Peel, who succeeded Crockett as manager in London, usually accompanied Nicks on the continent, as Crockett had done before him. In the mid-fifties some important relationships were established in West Germany and Holland with firms who were developing connections in Canada. Indeed, in West Germany, a senior officer of a German bank, August Lenz & Company, by the name of Baron Karl Max von Hellingrath became the Nova Scotia's representative in that country. Persistent and repeated calls by Nicks on top officers of European companies – one-to-one calls at which he excelled – followed up by Crockett and others gradually bore fruit and helped to build a base for future international growth. Competition became tougher and in Britain some of the old rules or, more accurately, conventions fell by the wayside. Calls on British businesses became less circumscribed, and what were felt to be unreasonable conventions about restrictions on deposit interest paid by foreign banks were no longer adhered to.

In New York, The Bank of Nova Scotia agency developed a large call-loan business and during the fifties expanded its foreign exchange activities when the Canadian dollar was allowed to float. The agency was still interested and active in grain financing. And a system of making calls on large companies was developed, which was to produce remarkable results in the next ten to fifteen years. In reviewing the Bank's progress during 1960, the new General Manager, Gibson, observed, "We have gained a good deal of experience and know-how in the area of international banking.... We are quite confident that this aspect of our business will grow, probably very substantially, over the years."[8]

Towards the end of the fifties, the Bank's management changed considerably. Enman, who in Nicks's words was "one of the top architects of our remarkable growth," retired as Chairman of the Board. He died in 1960, as did Burns, who had had an association with the Bank lasting sixty-five years. Frost retired as President for reasons of health, while Nicks became President and Chief Executive Officer. Dales was appointed Executive Vice-President.

J. D. Gibson,
Chief General Manager,
1958-1964;
Executive Vice-President
and Deputy Chairman,
1964-1965.

GIBSON BECOMES GENERAL MANAGER

Douglas Gibson was the new General Manager. Gibson was an economist, something unusual in the top echelons of a bank. He had helped build up the Economics Department, which was widely known for The Bank of Nova Scotia's *Monthly Review*. During the war and for some time thereafter he was chief economist of the Wartime Prices and Trade Board, as has already been recounted. Returning to the Bank in 1947, after the wartime controls had been almost completely removed, Gibson continued as an economist until 1955, when as an Assistant General Manager he was made responsible for western Canada.

Under the broad direction of Dales and with the help of J. O. Walsh, one of the best credit officers in the organization, Gibson was given a practical course in bank credit. Introduced by Dales to his former constituency in the West, he travelled western Canada with the regional supervisors – with C. L. Bowlby through the Prairie provinces (and later with H. W. Caldwell at Winnipeg and A. McPhedran at Calgary) and also with J. S. Clinch (and later with C. V. Hutchinson) in British Columbia. Visiting almost all of the branches and many customers over a period of four years, Gibson became acquainted with the most rapidly growing part of Canada and of the Bank, and caught some of the enthusiasm which had already inspired people like Dales and Hitchman.

Gibson was particularly interested in improved management techniques and personnel planning. His appointment as General Manager, while apparently unanimous, had in fact encountered a real difference on the Board of Directors. Enman did not think that Gibson's compressed training in bank credit had been sufficient and felt strongly enough to advocate Boyles, who had had training in the large branches of Ottawa and Toronto. Nicks supported Gibson's appointment. After some discussion, Enman acceded to the majority view. Boyles was made Deputy General Manager.

Gibson was quite different from Nicks; he believed in the new management methods, whereas Nicks with his driving energy and ambition was in many ways an old-fashioned tycoon. Nicks had tremendous determination, he inspired loyalty, and he demanded and got results. An interesting illustration of the difference between the two men was Nicks's lack of interest in, if not hostility to, Gibson's setting up a management committee where policies and developments could be discussed freely. This committee was composed of top management personnel and it met weekly to cope with emerging problems and to keep one another informed. In the mind of one man it served a major and obvious purpose, while in that of the other it was unnecessary.

OTHER NEW APPOINTMENTS

Boyles, the new Deputy General Manager, had had an interesting banking career. Coming from London, England, as a young man, he joined the Bank in the Ottawa area in 1921. He turned up in General Office in 1928 where in time he became Chief Accountant and very well informed concerning the Bank's operations. Enman made Boyles his executive assistant in 1946 and later told him that he should get some direct banking experience. "Which branch would you like?" Enman inquired. Boyles replied, "Ottawa," so that he could become better acquainted with the government people concerned with finance. He did much to promote the Bank's interest. Returning to Toronto as manager of the main branch, he then moved upstairs to become an Assistant General Manager in 1956.

At the end of 1958, in addition to a General Manager and a Deputy General Manager, there were now eight Assistant General Managers, indicating the growing size and increasing complexity of the organization. Five of the AGMs dealt with credit and each had a region. They were B. R. Calder (foreign), Hitchman (Quebec), C. L. Bowlby (the West), G. J. Touchie (the Maritimes) – later to become General Manager – and C. J. Ash (Ontario). Webster from New York was also promoted to this rank, as was Randall, now in charge of the International Division, working closely under Nicks. W. S. Bond, a new entry to the executive group, became Assistant General Manager, Administration, with responsibility for personnel and premises. Other interesting appointments in 1960 were Jameson as assistant to the President, Peel as Supervisor, International Department, and Ritchie as Chief Accountant.

FIFTEEN YEARS OF SOLID GROWTH

In the fifteen years since the war the Bank had changed a great deal. It was much bigger and better balanced. It had filled in the gaps in its national representation. Though the province of Quebec was still not adequately covered, there had been a notable improvement in Montreal. The Bank had overcome its unduly conservative background and was spreading its wings abroad. It had 8,500 employees, two and one-half times as many as at the end of the war. More than half these employees – 56 per cent – were women and, while their turnover was high, a substantial number were becoming permanent staff of the Bank. The Bank's foreign business was growing rapidly and the base had been built for further growth.

The number of branches had increased to 574, nearly twice as many as at the end of the war. In the West there were now 154 branches, compared with 37 in 1945. It might have been cheaper and faster to buy another bank than to build this huge additional structure almost from scratch. Had such a course been followed, the fit could not have been nearly as good but the cost might well have been less. In fact, there were some approaches and skirmishes in the direction of amalgamation which never came off, on the first occasion because one of the bankers primarily concerned appears to have been doubtful, and on the second, which had been thoroughly prepared, because of the long delay resulting from the difficulty of getting a decision from Ottawa.

From the standpoint of the shareholders, the record of the fifteen years was an improving one. While earnings per share were low in 1945 because of wartime taxes and restrictions, they recovered to a somewhat higher than prewar rate by 1950, when they reached $1.91 per share. From 1950 to 1960 there was a notable gain to $2.95. Dividends increased more or less in line with the growth in earnings. The proportion of earnings to shareholders' equity in the last half of the fifties was between 6 per cent and 7 per cent, which was better than in

1950, when the rate was 5¾ per cent, and much better than in 1945, when it was 3½ per cent.

The growth of the Bank necessitated substantial increases in capital. There were three stock issues during the period from 1945 to 1960 and some additional appropriations to the reserve fund or rest account. In any case, paid-up capital rose from $12 million to almost $27 million, while the rest account grew proportionately more, from $24 million to $87 million – a total of $114 million in 1960, or 6 per cent of deposit liabilities.

A LARGER BUT THOROUGHLY ACTIVE BOARD

The composition of the Board of Directors had changed with the Bank. There were now 32 Directors as compared with 22 at the end of the war. All but one of the Directors who might have been said to represent the banks taken over in the Richardson regime had passed from the scene. The representation from the West had increased from 2 to 5 and from Quebec from 2 to 3. Half the Directors came from Ontario, while the Maritimes representation, still numbering 5, had declined proportionately. A new development was the election of two Directors from overseas; this tied in with Nicks's plans of international expansion.

Of the 32 Directors, 17 might be described as representing active business and commercial connections of the Bank. There were also 4 lawyers and 2 financial men. There were 2 who might be called elder statesmen and maybe 4 who could be classified as old friends and connections. The remaining 3 were management people. While discussion is usually inhibited by such a large Board, the frequency of meetings and the many opportunities for personal conversations, plus the variety and interest in such a rapidly growing institution, promoted a good deal of effective communication.

This was an able Board, representative of the business community in the broadest sense. It brought to bear the entrepreneurial and market experience of people like Max Bell, W. C. Harris, Percy Gardiner, and Roy Jodrey; the business acumen of the Shermans, Norman McLeod, D. G. Willmot, and Harold Rea; the skilled legal approach of Donald McInnes, William Macklaier, and Senator Hayden; and, last but not least, the broad views of Norman Mackenzie, J. Y. Murdoch, and Ralph Bell. These were strong men with their own individual characteristics. For example, the story is told of Roy Jodrey by C. F. Gill, now Senior Vice-President, Eastern Canada, that when Jodrey came into the Windsor, Nova Scotia, branch, "you could always catch his mood by the tune he was humming – a light tune if all was well, a hymn if there were problems, and 'The Old Rugged Cross' if things were really tough."

The practice of having a banker rather than a businessman as President was now well established and the president was the Chief Executive Officer. At the same time, two non-banker Directors were made Vice-Presidents with some regional connotation – J. Y. Murdoch of Toronto and R. P. Bell of Nova Scotia. The earlier practice of the train trip to Halifax for the annual meeting was beginning to break down under the pressure of other demands on Directors' and officers' time and the existence of better alternative air transport. So, a rather useful and pleasant social event which had brought Directors and senior staff together in a relaxed atmosphere came to an end in the early sixties.

REID J. SMITH MAKES HIS CONTRIBUTION

One of the difficulties about history is that it is a story of change – the activities that progress more or less along the same lines get little or no attention no matter how well they are done, but the things that progress in a different manner get a lot. So it is in a bank history that the men who do the regular jobs well, like running a branch or supervising credit or inspecting branches, attract little attention. The same dictum applies even to people who do play a part in change but who are not close enough to the top to be noticeably visible. Sometimes, too, this observation applies to very senior people.

A good example is Reid J. Smith, who was a good banker and a character to boot. After some experience in smaller branches, Smith became assistant manager at Halifax, assistant manager at Montreal, manager of the Foreign Relations Department in General Office, manager at Halifax, and manager at Toronto. He ended his Bank of Nova Scotia career as an Assistant General Manager, retiring from that post in 1956. He preceded Nicks in his jobs in Halifax and Toronto and he was a close associate of Boyles. On one occasion Boyles, who as manager, Ottawa, reported to Smith, sent him a press clipping which made the point that The Bank of Nova Scotia's main branch in Ottawa was the easiest place in town in which to cash a cheque. Smith replied that he assumed Boyles regarded this publicity favourably or he would not have sent the clipping to him; however, he pointed out, it could not be favourable, for it simply showed that Boyles was an easy mark!

EXPANSION IN MONTREAL

Another problem in writing history is that big expansion, like great changes, gets the principal attention. Much has been said about Toronto and the West, and yet Montreal has been almost overlooked. However, there was much expansion in Montreal, particularly in the late fifties under Hitchman and then Crockett, each of whom had earlier played a business-building role in London, England. Between 1954 and 1960, 11 new branches were opened in Montreal, bringing the total to 25 branches. It was a time of strong growth and the Bank succeeded in enlarging its base, though not much in the predominantly French-speaking areas.

NOTES

1. See Harry Bruce, *R.A.: The Story of R.A. Jodrey, Entrepreneur* (Toronto: McClelland & Stewart Ltd., 1979), pp. 191-98, for a fuller treatment of these matters.
2. *The New Yorker*, New York, Nov. 17, 1951.
3. BNS Annual Report, 1950, General Manager's Address, p.17.
4. BNS Annual Report, 1951, President's Address, p.9.
5. *Ibid.*, pp.10-12.
6. *Ibid.*, p.12.
7. BNS *Monthly Review*, June-July, 1953.
8. BNS Annual Report, 1960, General Manager's Address, p.15.

A SELECTION OF BANKNOTES

The Bank of Nova Scotia   £5
This note was part of the Bank's First Issue, August 6, 1832. The £5 and £10 notes in this series bear dates from 1832 to 1870. This example is dated June 2, 1834. Colour: Black with no tint.

The development of trade and commerce in Canada is linked to the history of bank notes. Issued by banks to borrowers who paid interest on their loans or discounts, the notes provided a convenient form of money and commercial credit from the 1820s to the 1940s. With the establishment of The Bank of Canada in 1934, the note-issuing powers of the banks were sharply curtailed and the 1944 Bank Act ended the practice altogether and called for a phasing out of all bank-note circulation by 1950. Thus, responsibility for the issuance of paper money was switched to The Bank of Canada.

The notes of The Bank of Nova Scotia and its amalgamated banks serve as a record not only of the growth of the Bank, but also of the early economic development of Canada.

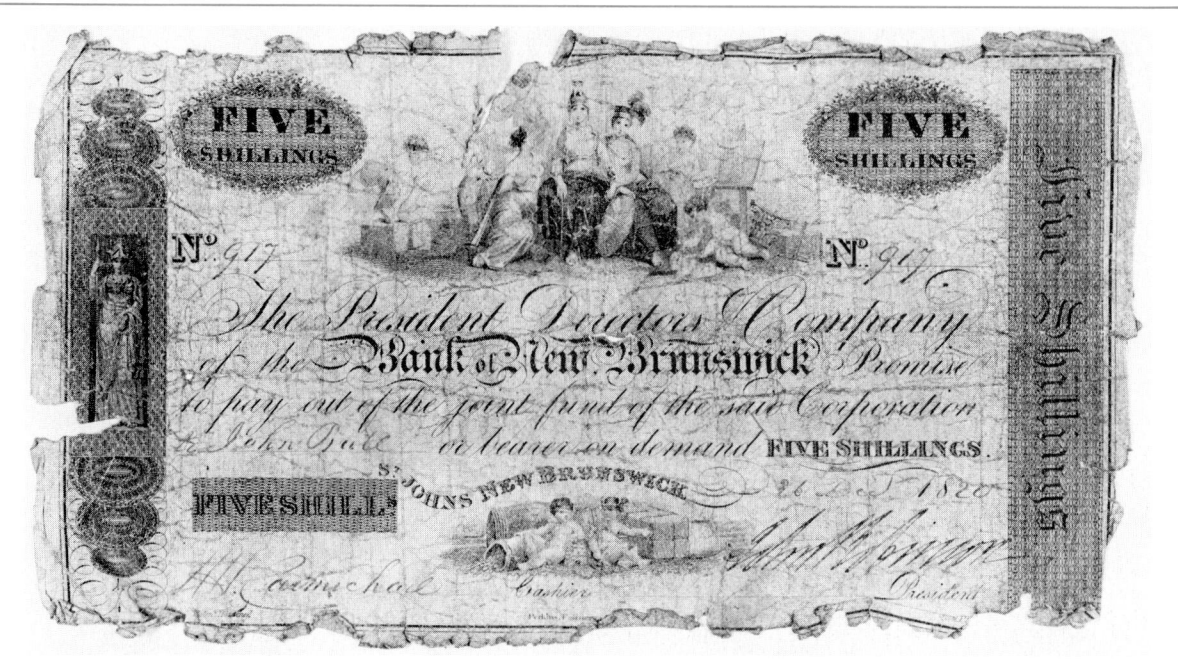

Bank of New Brunswick   5s

This 5s note is part of the First Issue of the Bank of New Brunswick, December 26, 1820, the first chartered, or public, bank in Canada. The instruction to pay to "John Bull or bearer" was typical of early notes. Colour: Face is black with no tint; back is blue.

The Bank of Nova Scotia $4
*With the Sixth Issue, July 1, 1870, notes changed from Pound to Dollar denominations. This issue was also the first to have printing on the back of notes.
Colour: Face is black with green tint; back is printed in green.*

Union Bank of Prince Edward Island $1
*The dollar notes issued January 1, 1872, by the Union Bank of Prince Edward Island were basically unchanged in design from earlier notes, but some varieties, like this example, were overprinted with the words ''Canada Currency.'' Prince Edward Island joined Confederation in 1873.
Colour: Black with no tint.*

Bank of Ottawa $5
An example of the First Issue of the Bank of Ottawa, November 2, 1874, this $5 note shows the Hon. George Bryson, a director of the Bank from 1874 to 1895, and James Maclaren, the President from 1874 to 1892.
Colour: Face is black with green tint; back is green.

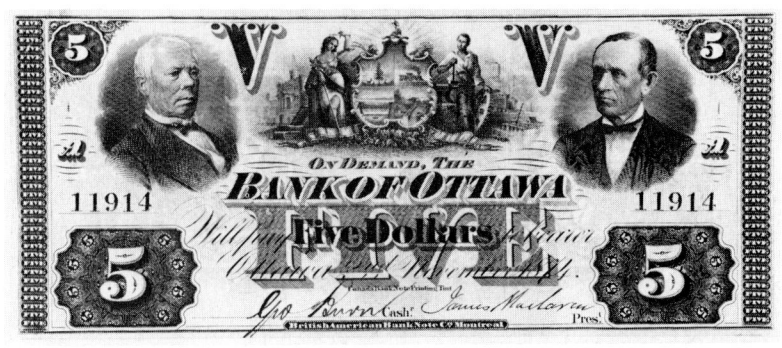

Bank of Ottawa $5
In its 1880 note issue, the Bank of Ottawa chose a logging-scene design suited to the bank whose founders were pioneers in the Ottawa Valley lumber industry.
Colour: Face is black with olive tint; back is brown.

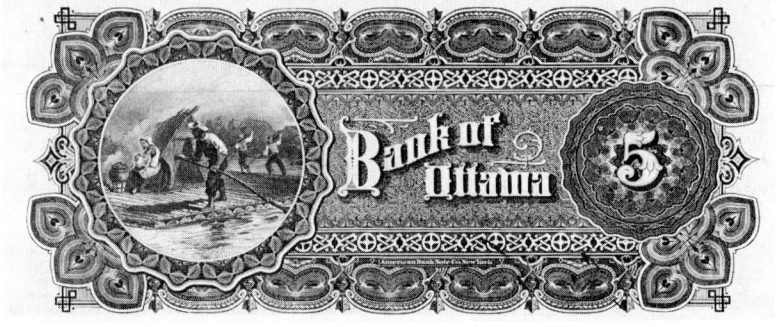

The Bank of Nova Scotia $5
The $5 notes in the Seventh Issue, July 2, 1881, depict Joseph Howe on the face. This example is also overprinted ''Winnipeg'' and marks the opening of the Branch in that city.
Colour: Face is blue tint with red overprint; back is green tint.

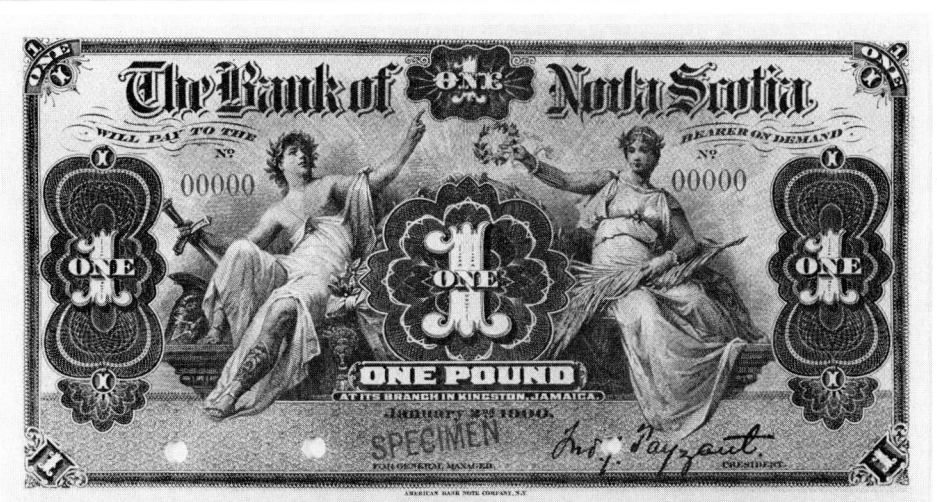

The Bank of Nova Scotia Jamaica £1
*An Act of Parliament passed in 1899 enabled Canadian banks to issue notes in British colonies outside of Canada. This is a specimen of the £1 note design dated January 2, 1900.
Colour: Face is black with green and yellow-green tint; back is green.*

Metropolitan Bank $5
*Five-dollar notes such as the one shown were part of the First Issue of Metropolitan Bank notes, November 5, 1902. This variety was signed by S.J. Moore, then President of the Metropolitan and later President of The Bank of Nova Scotia.
Colour: Face is black with yellow and red tint; back is green.*

Metropolitan Bank $100
*This $100 note, issued November 5, 1902, by the Metropolitan Bank, depicts a mining scene. The bank used the same design on subsequent issues of this denomination in 1909 and 1912.
Colour: Face is black with yellow-green and red tint; back is slate.*

Bank of
New Brunswick
$5
This note, dated January 2, 1904, is an example of the last $5 notes issued by the Bank of New Brunswick. It features a view of Saint John, N.B., and a likeness of James Manchester, President of the Bank from 1900 to 1913. The back depicts the Head Office of the Bank of New Brunswick. Colour: Face is black with yellow-green and rose tint; back is green.

The Bank of
Nova Scotia
$50
The Thirteenth Issue, May 1, 1906, was the Bank's first issue of $50 notes. Colour: Face is black with red and olive tint; back is green.

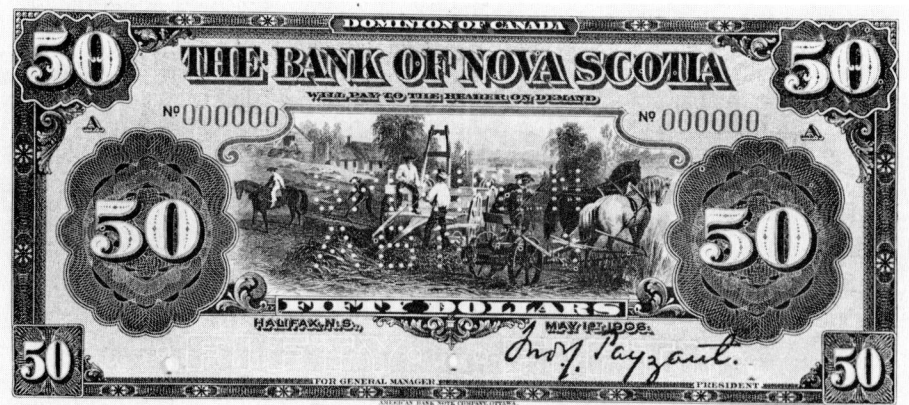

The Bank of Nova Scotia $5
There were two varieties of notes in the Fourteenth Issue, September 1, 1908. The example shown here is of the first variety, distinguished by orange V's at the top. Colour: Face is black with yellow-green and orange tint; back is olive.

Bank of Ottawa $10
The Ninth Issue, September 1, 1913, included the last $10 notes of the Bank of Ottawa. Colour: Front is black with green tint; back is green.

The Bank of
Nova Scotia
$5
*J. Payzant
(President of the
Bank from December
1899 to January 1918)
and H.A. Richardson
(then General Manager)
were depicted on
the Seventeenth Issue,
July 2, 1918.
Colour: Face is black
with green tint;
back is green.*

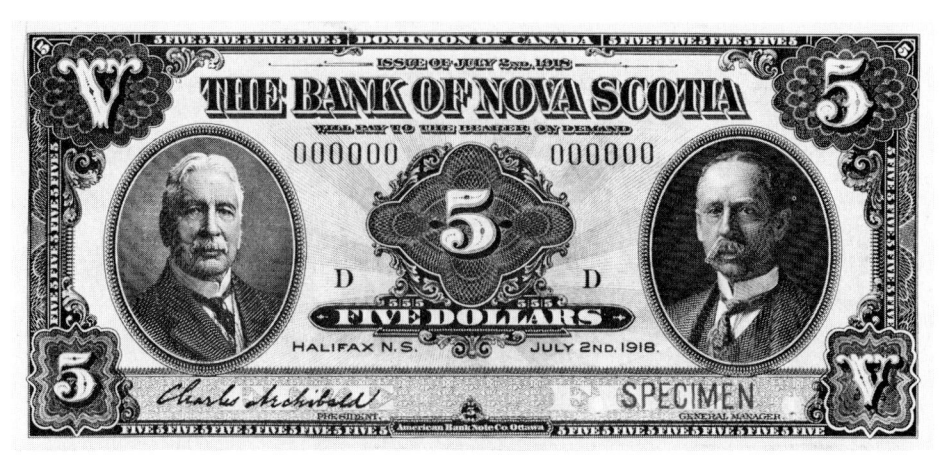

The Bank of
Nova Scotia
$100
*This note was part
of the Twenty-second
Issue, January 2, 1929,
the last issue which
included $100
denominations.
Colour: Front is black
with yellow-green
and rose tint;
back is brown.*

The Bank of
Nova Scotia
Jamaica £1
*The notes issued by The
Bank of Nova Scotia for
Jamaica, January 2, 1930,
were physically smaller
than those of previous
Jamaica issues. The design
of the notes reflected
the agricultural trade
base of the Jamaican
economy.
Colour: Face is black with
green, blue, and yellow
tint; back is green.*

11

More Growth and the Management Revolution 1960-1965

GROWTH WITHOUT INFLATION

Though there was some recession in 1959 and 1960, business began to improve during 1960 and the economy then enjoyed five consecutive years of growth without inflation. Looking back today, tight money and slowed growth for a year or two were a small price to pay for subduing expectations of inflation and for almost bringing price rises to a halt. Admittedly, the atmosphere at the time was anything but calm. The dispute between the Governor of the Bank of Canada and the government, the later run on the Canadian dollar, not to mention the Cuban missile crisis, did not suggest the kind of solid economic progress which was actually occurring. But the fact was that the Bank's Canadian dollar assets rose slightly faster in real terms – 7 $\frac{1}{2}$ per cent per annum – in the first half of the sixties than they did in the second half, when inflation began taking over again.

As Nicks put it in his speech at the annual meeting in 1962, the Canadian economy was now in a favourable position to move ahead. "There is no longer undue preoccupation with the fear of inflation nor on the other hand are there unrealistic expectations in the business community of what easier money may do." The Canadian dollar had been fixed again, at 92$\frac{1}{2}$¢ U.S., "down enough to put Canada in reasonable adjustment with the world economy." Rising cost pressures in Europe and Japan were also helping "to skate us on-side." Furthermore, Canada had built up her managerial talent and a considerable range of technical know-how.[1] In 1963, Nicks summed up the situation by saying that "the Canadian economy is in the best position that it has been in in years, not only to work towards a sounder internal base but also to contribute more actively to vital international programs." He drew attention to "the generally favourable economic trend throughout most of the Free World economy" and pointed out that "the U.S. economy has continued to move ahead, with gains spread over an impressively broad front...."[2]

The international side of the Bank's activities grew even more rapidly than the domestic, developing from the base that had been built in the fifties and steadily expanding as the decade progressed. Growing at a real rate of 11 per cent per annum from 1960 to 1965, foreign currency assets reached a level of over 40 per cent of Canadian dollar assets in 1965, and, indeed, by 1967 they were half as large as the domestic figure.

THE DRIVE FOR DEPOSITS

Because the Bank had been so successful in the consumer credit business, it started the decade of the sixties with the acute problem of obtaining an adequate flow of Canadian dollar deposits. Furthermore, in addition to Scotia Plan's needs, there was a growing demand for mortgage money and the prospect of there being a larger volume of term loans to smaller businesses. With the national money supply growing only modestly and with such expanding opportunities for lending, an aggressive policy of deposit development was the natural course to follow, and branch expansion was a key element in this program. Between 1960 and 1965, 104 new branches were opened in Canada (as well as 27 abroad), bringing the Canadian total to 643. A great many of these new branches were in the suburbs; the Bank was moving out into the big new shopping centres close to where people lived or where they could at least park their cars.

The suburban branches were in fact retail banking centres – taking deposits, making personal loans, and also making some moderate-sized commercial loans. Of the 104 branches opened in the five years, about two-thirds were of this character and they were concentrated around the big cities, particularly Toronto, Montreal, Edmonton, and Calgary. These new branches were bright and pleasant, just as the new style of banking was friendly and cheerful. The old forbidding banking rooms with their iron cages and grilles and their austere atmosphere were pretty well gone. It was hoped that Stephen Leacock's graphic description of his banking experience no longer applied: "When I go into a bank I get rattled. The clerks rattle me; the wickets rattle me; the sight of the money rattles me; everything rattles me."[3]

In such ways the Bank's physical plant was undergoing a radical transformation. The challenge was to engage the interest of existing customers in new services, and most of all in deposits, and to attract new customers. New instruments such as term notes, certificates of deposit, and six-year savings certificates played an important part. The staff became members of a promotional team and, as a result, the Bank managed to enlarge its share of the total Canadian savings pool. Indeed, from 1960 to 1965, the Bank increased its personal savings deposits by almost 50 per cent, the highest percentage rise of any bank in Canada.

More Growth and the Management Revolution, 1960 – 1965 227

Teller's Cage, 1950, Toronto Main Branch.

During the early 1960s the familiar cages and grilles began to be replaced by the more open design of modern branches.

Open-Plan Branch, 30 King St. W., Toronto, 1974

PACEMAKER IN PERSONAL DEPOSITS

That The Bank of Nova Scotia was the pacemaker in the personal deposit area was in no small measure due to Speicher's enthusiastic approach to deposit development. As he put it, referring to all members of the staff, whether senior or junior, "If each one of us continues to promote our services with enthusiasm and imagination and if we continue to display thoughtfulness and courtesy in our dealings with customers, our Bank will continue to grow at a rate second to none."

The incentive program inaugurated at the end of the fifties was intensified. Campaigns were so designed that the team in any branch could qualify for rewards and any manager, no matter how small the branch, could lead his team to a President's Award. In setting growth objectives for deposits, some of the regional officers chided Speicher by saying that "before long you will want us to establish objectives for loans." To which he replied, "Don't knock it. That day will come." And it did, the following year. As one of his friends said, "Neil Speicher could have run the Maple Leaf hockey team with his promotion of team spirit." He fully understood the psychology of co-operation.

DEPOSIT CAMPAIGNS INVOLVED ALL THE STAFF

In their recollections of the deposit campaigns, the former heads of the various regions all emphasize the quite radical change which these campaigns brought to banking. Though A. McPhedran (at that time the AGM for Alberta) notes that the more conservative managers were not keen on the deposit campaigns and J. M. Hayman (then the AGM for New Brunswick and Prince Edward Island) expresses a certain regret "to see tradition, prestige, and dignity cast aside in favour of more modern methods of doing business," all agree that the results were impressive. Says D.A.Y. Merrick (the AGM for Nova Scotia, Quebec, and British Columbia at various times), "the campaigns...did engender a sense of striving and loyalty with many, but not all, of the staff...and those motivated were for the most part the better members." H. W. Caldwell (the AGM for Manitoba and Saskatchewan and later for New Brunswick and Prince Edward Island) believes that the "deposit campaigns introduced a tremendous change by involving all the staff. Suddenly there was a new yardstick in the evaluation of employees at all levels. We discovered talents that were never in evidence before."

As C. I. Archibald (the AGM for Nova Scotia and later Quebec) puts it, "It was not easy to have the rank and file in the various branches actively solicit new business, but the deposit campaigns provided the vehicle for the manager to stir up the staff and the Assistant General Manager to stir up the managers." Competition between branches of similar size, sometimes in different regions, helped greatly. "You had to fire up inter-branch and inter-province competition," says Merrick and a "certain feeling of triumph" did result, in the opinion of McPhedran.

Archibald had a striking habit of writing notes in red ink to each branch on its progress. In one case, such a note led one of the branch staff to go to the manager in the early afternoon before the special deposit dinner with the AGM that evening, suggesting that they start moving right away and "get the rest of the $100,000 and shove it down that ——'s throat with his coffee to-night." In Caldwell's view, the campaigns, successful as they were, "contributed to the awareness of the need for more staff training," a side effect which did gradually exert its influence.

ARCHAIC RESTRICTIONS ON BANKING

Thus, in addition to their direct results in the form of greatly increased deposits and numbers of deposits, the deposit campaigns had an important effect on banking practice. Moreover, they enabled the Bank to get through a time when, particularly because of the 6 per cent maximum on lending rates, it was at a competitive disadvantage in relation to the so-called near-banks, specifically trust companies, finance companies, and credit unions. It is true that the personal loan business, now actively engaged in by all of the banks, was not so handicapped. But most other types of lending were, and, as interest rates moved up, it was obvious that the banks' competitive position would deteriorate further. It was becoming clear that the inability to charge market rates for loans limited the rates which the banks could pay on deposits. In 1963, when The Bank of Nova Scotia went out and obtained the money it needed, its margin was so squeezed that profits showed little increase despite a considerable rise in the volume of business. The deposit drives and the new savings instruments naturally helped to sustain the flow of deposits, but at the cost of a considerable decline in margins. Not until 1967 was the lending-rate ceiling at last removed.

ROYAL COMMISSION INVESTIGATES

In 1962, a Royal Commission on Banking and Finance was appointed by the government to study the whole Canadian financial system, with a view to recommending appropriate changes in the Bank Act and the Bank of Canada Act, both due for revision in 1964. The purpose of the Royal Commission was to carry out a broad review, rather like that performed by the earlier Macmillan Royal Commission, which in 1933 had recommended the establishment of the Bank of Canada.

There were seven commissioners from the main regions of Canada, some with special professional abilities, as in the case of Dr. W. A. Mackintosh, the highly respected economist and former principal of Queen's University. Another member was Paul Leman, senior officer of a multinational corporation with headquarters in Montreal, and interestingly enough the son of Beaudry Leman, a member of the Macmillan Commission. Then there were Thomas Brown, investment man and Rhodes Scholar from Vancouver; Jack MacKeen, Nova Scotia industrialist; Gordon Harrold of the Alberta Wheat Pool; and the chairman, the Hon. Dana Porter, Chief Justice and former Treasurer of the Province of Ontario. Gibson was also a member of the Commission – he was the sole banker – and it absorbed about half of his time during the next two and one-quarter years. When the government asked for Gibson's services, the Bank wished to co-operate and, for himself, Gibson was keenly interested in being part of such a fundamental study. Furthermore, on the staff of the Commission was a group of some of the best economists in the country. Among them were W. C. Hood as research director, H. A. Hampson as secretary, and such other able men as the late John H. Young, the late Harry Johnson, and the still-very-much-alive Grant Reuber, Jacques Parizeau, Robert Johnstone, Gilles Mercure, and Donald Daly.

The Royal Commission conducted its hearings across the country from Charlottetown to Victoria. It used its strong team of economists to study extensively the whole Canadian financial system. It received submissions from individuals and associations, not least the Canadian Bankers' Association, and it requested a number of distinguished experts, Canadian and foreign, to appear as witnesses, including Louis Rasminsky, Sir Denis Robertson, Paul Samuelson, and Marius Holtrop. Finally, in February 1964, it produced its report.

The report came out strongly for a competitive system – for getting rid of restrictions to the free flow of funds in the financial structure – in short, for letting the price system work. Because of the banks' large size individually and their dominant position as a group in the financial system, the report did recommend some restraints – the banks were not to buy up other financial institutions, or indeed any other Canadian institutions, as a proposed restriction of 10 per cent ownership in other companies indicated. However, in the case of useful innovations, it was thought that the Treasury Board might make exceptions and the banks were to be permitted to form subsidiary companies in areas in which they did business; for example, they could start a mortgage company. But the banks were not to enter the trust business, which in effect was to be reserved for the trust companies in Canada. Nor were rate agreements among banks or interlocking directorates between banks and trust and loan companies to be permitted.[4]

RESTRICTIONS SHOULD BE REMOVED

But apart from these exceptions, the restrictions should be removed. There should be no ceiling on interest rates; the ceiling "impedes the flow of credit to some borrowers and – by driving them to higher-cost lenders – frequently harms the very people it is designed to help. Moreover, the chartered banks are unable at times to pay as high returns on their liabilities as they otherwise might."[5] The Commission also recommended a change in the cash-reserve requirements for the chartered banks to permit a 4 per cent ratio, as against the existing 8 per cent, on deposits subject to genuine notice (which did not include regular savings deposits). It was also proposed that savings banks and trust and loan companies be permitted to compete for commercial and personal lending business, provided that they also be subject to the same cash reserve requirements as the banks. In addition, it was proposed that the banks be allowed to take mortgage security, thus opening to them the conventional mortgage market and making practicable medium- and longer-term loans to business customers. To improve the mortgage market, the rates on NHA mortgages were no longer to be determined by government but by the open market, and it was also proposed to raise the maximum loan-to-value ratio for first mortgages in the conventional market to 75 per cent from the former two-thirds.

BUT GOVERNMENT DELAYS ACTION

However, the government of the day did not act on the important recommendations made by the Commission. Its proposed bill for the revised Bank Act did not remove the 6 per cent ceiling, nor did it adopt the cash reserve proposals which would have been of some help to the banks in competing for term deposits, and perhaps of some help to the trust and loan companies in entering the commercial lending business. Nicks could not resist pointing out at the Nova Scotia's annual meeting in 1965 that while the Bank was trying to meet its opportunities "with both vigour and common sense," in Canada it was "shackled by an outdated structure of financial regulations."[6] An election was called before the bill was passed; and so the old legislation was simply extended.

"A MAJOR STEP IN THE RIGHT DIRECTION"

It was not until 1967, three years after the submission of the report, that Mitchell Sharp, who was a trained economist and who was now Minister of Finance, took the bull by the horns and presented a new bill. Hearings were again held by the appropriate Parliamentary Committee, and finally a revised bill emerged after long discussion and argument, and was passed by Parliament.

The new legislation did not contain any ceiling on lending rates. It lowered the cash-reserve requirement for term and savings deposits to 4 per cent while increasing the reserve requirement for demand deposits to 12 per cent. The net result of these changes was a moderate reduction in cash requirements for the banks. The recommendation that similar cash-reserve requirements be applied to the near banks was not adopted. In addition, the recommended provisions concerning the taking of mortgage security by the banks were passed, the NHA rate was related to the prevailing market rates of interest on federal government securities, and a higher percentage valuation on first mortgages was permitted. Thus, finally, a more competitive financial system emerged. It was not entirely what the Royal Commission had proposed, since it failed to agree on a definition of banking which might have broadened the banking system and provided a basis for dealing with the problem of foreign banking. But it was very definitely a major step in the right direction.

The new Bank Act did contain the 10 per cent restriction on the ownership of other business which had been recommended by the Royal Commission. This affected The Bank of Nova Scotia's plans for close relationships with certain trust companies. In their function as trustees, these trust companies performed activities directly related to banking and, in fact, at least two of the large banks had well-established relationships with trust companies. In 1963 the Nova Scotia had helped to bring together under its control the Eastern Trust Company and the Chartered Trust Company to form the Eastern and Chartered Trust Company. In 1965, in light of the then-proposed legislation, the Eastern and Chartered Trust Company amalgamated with the Canada Permanent Trust Company (then controlled by the Toronto Dominion Bank), with the result that the interests of each bank in the new trust and mortgage company – the Canada Permanent – were sharply reduced, and in due course brought down to the permitted 10 per cent. Similarly, the Bank reduced its interests in Markborough Holdings and the Mortgage Insurance Company of Canada, both of which companies had been founded by the Bank in partnership with the Aluminum Company of Canada and Greenshields and Company.

SCOTIA PLAN SURGES UPWARD AGAIN

As noted earlier, the strongest factor behind the Bank's growing need for deposits was the remarkable success of Scotia Plan. Since the interest rates charged were substantially below those of small loan and finance companies, the demand for Scotia Plan Loans expanded dramatically. While slacker business in the early sixties dampened the increase, in 1964 and 1965 the rapid upward surge resumed, and, by the latter year, outstanding Scotia Plan Loans were more than three times what they had been in 1960 – they were now well over $300 million.

This impressive growth reflected good management by Dixon, the AGM in charge of the whole operation, and good co-ordination by Kinsman with the large group of outside professionals who had been hired from consumer loan and finance companies. Without the help of these professionals, the development of Scotia Plan would have been much slower and more difficult. To start with, there was an understandable resistance in some quarters of the Bank to the small-loans business. Some managers did not think it their job to lend people money to buy cars and furniture. But as was soon demonstrated, Scotia Plan was profitable, it was helpful to the customer, and it brought new customers into the Bank for other services.

Perhaps the most important contribution of the outside professionals was in supervision and training. While managers and accountants were equipped, of course, with an explicit set of instructions to guide them in the proper handling of consumer credit, which was quite different from that of traditional bank lending, the direct assistance provided by supervisory officers was what helped most. These officers hammered home the importance of the customer's equity and of the prompt follow-up on payments, and the need to accept applicants as they are rather than as the lending officer would like them to be.

The hiring of professionals from outside the Bank gave rise to some personnel problems. Some of the newcomers were paid more than Bank staff of the same seniority. But with ad hoc adjustments and with the introduction of job evaluation (which began in 1964), there was a relative increase in the pay of a number of important Bank positions and this went a long way towards correcting the problem. All in all, the influx of consumer credit officers was a good thing for The Bank of Nova Scotia, not only for Scotia Plan staff but for the fresh approaches that came with these officers.

NOTABLE DEVELOPMENT OF MORTGAGE ACTIVITY

The growth in the Bank's mortgage business in the early sixties was less spectacular than that in Scotia Plan credit. The demand was not as great and at that time Scotia Plan received a higher priority. Nevertheless, mortgage holdings did rise by an average of 10 per cent per annum from 1960 to 1965, to a total of over $100 million. Furthermore, the activity of the Bank in the mortgage area was in fact larger than this figure would suggest, because it was also taking on mortgages and selling them to customers and buying and selling mortgages in the developing secondary market. In addition, as has already been mentioned, the Bank had pioneered with two partners in the establishment of the Mortgage Insurance Company of Canada. This company provided mortgage insurance on conventional mortgages, thus permitting higher-ratio mortgage loans and reducing the need for expensive second-mortgage financing. With the same two partners, the Bank had also founded Markborough Properties, a real estate company, and Central Covenants Ltd., a mortgage-financing company.

Meanwhile, Canadian business loans, still the Bank's largest lending category by far, rose substantially in 1962 in response to huge crops and the development of a wheat surplus. As business gained momentum in 1964 and 1965, loans rose materially, but as money became tighter a special effort had to be made to accommodate regular customers, particularly those whose size was not sufficient to allow them access to the bond market. Those who could go to the bond market or the short-term money market were encouraged to do so.

NO MORE CONCERN ABOUT REDUCED LOAN DEMAND

In the first half of the sixties, the Investment Department had developed a money market capability, which meant that it could handle day loans and Treasury bills efficiently, as well as Government of Canada bonds. The Bank knew what it was to sell long-term bonds at a loss, and MacIntosh was determined to maintain a more flexible position in future. Under the pressure of increasing loan demand, security holdings had been declining and the fears expressed by Patterson in the late thirties, as well as those which had concerned Fyshe even earlier, had vanished.* Indeed, the problem now was really the reverse – that of maintaining a suitable liquidity ratio. At the beginning of the sixties, the liquidity ratio (defined as the ratio of liquid assets to major Canadian assets) was a little over 30 per cent. By 1965, it had declined to 28½ per cent, and as time went on it decreased further, in line with the general trend.

There were no major changes in the Bank's organization in 1961 or 1962. Nicks received the title of Chairman of the Board, a function which he had been performing for some time, and he also continued as President. Gibson became a Director and John S. Proctor joined the Bank as Deputy Chairman of the Board and Executive Vice-President, the same title as that held by Dales. Proctor's appointment was something new – in Nicks's words "a first" – in that he had been a senior officer in another bank, the Canadian Imperial Bank of Commerce. It was not a generally accepted practice among the banks then or now to employ executive officers from other banks. It was not unknown, however; in the more distant past Stavert had worked for three banks, Cann for at least that many, and Fyshe moved on to another bank from his position as Cashier of The Bank of Nova Scotia.† Proctor brought to the Bank a wide range of experience, including many connections in mining and across Ontario.

MAJOR REORGANIZATION

A big change, however, did occur in 1963 when a major reorganization was carried out, involving a radical upward adjustment in the world of titles. The Bank had grown so much that many jobs had become more important than their titles indicated; also, some titles were not in tune with outside practices. The head of each region now had a great deal of authority, and yet his title of "Supervisor" cut no ice with the public, failing as it did to indicate the importance of the job. Similarly, the heads of most General Office departments were also "Supervisors" and some

J.S. Proctor,
Deputy Chairman and
Executive Vice-President,
1962-1971

CREDIT: MILNE STUDIOS

---

* See Chapter 8, pages 168-69 (Patterson), and Chapter 5, page 75 (Fyshe), where concern was expressed that corporations might become largely self-financing and that bank loans would then become a relatively small proportion of total bank assets.

† See Chapter 7.

of them were doing highly responsible and often complex work. As a result, the heads of the regions, some of the senior credit men, and a number of the departmental heads were made "Assistant General Managers." In addition, this title, already held by the senior agent in New York, was given to the then managers of the main branches in Toronto and in London, England.

Above this group of 28 people of Assistant General Manager rank were four Deputy General Managers – Ash, Hitchman, Randall, and Touchie – all of whom had been Assistant General Managers earlier. Boyles and Gibson now had titles of General Manager and Chief General Manager, respectively. Nicks was jubilant about the new arrangements, which, as he said at the annual meeting in 1963, were "aimed mainly at assigning greater responsibility and authority to individuals" and which would provide "more scope for achievement, and more sense of fulfillment."[7] Gibson added, "In this kind of highly competitive world, we must have first-class specialists who can produce ideas and services that will help our front-line men – the branch managers – to produce results. The branches bring the Bank business which produces its earnings. The headquarters and regional offices provide service, direction, and investment and money management. There is a continuous interaction, and good planning is an essential ingredient of success."[8]

PROFIT PLANNING INTRODUCED

Along with this reorganization came a system of profit planning designed to improve efficiency and profits by relating business decisions all the way through the Bank to market forces – or profit and loss. Starting with the branch, the manager was called upon to make his best estimate of profits or losses for the coming year, bearing in mind not only his past results but also the opportunities open to him and his staff to obtain new lending and deposit business and to reduce costs.

He had to estimate his loans and deposits in some detail. If the Bank needed deposits, as it usually did, the rate of interest which the branch was allowed on deposits surplus to its lending needs would provide a good incentive to build up the deposits. If the branch lent more than it received on deposit, it would pay for additional funds from headquarters at a rate higher than its average cost of deposits, but not so high as to make lending opportunities unattractive. These rates were changed from time to time in accordance with market conditions and the Bank's needs. The manager's plan was not to be drawn up in a casual way, but was to represent a genuine goal on the part of the whole branch.

Moving up the line, the branch plans were to be sent into the appropriate regional office and, if they were accepted as reasonable, would be incorporated into the regional plan, but not until after the regional office had assessed the position of the region, bearing in mind economic conditions, the position of larger customers, and the opportunities as seen from the regional office. After discussion with the branches concerned, there might be some revision in the individual branch estimates, perhaps because of differences in assessing the economic conditions or perhaps because the branch's estimate was regarded as reflecting, on the one hand, an insufficient effort or, on the other, an unrealistic degree of optimism. Then the headquarters group would make their best estimate for the whole Bank, using data from the Economics Department and other sources, and comparing it with the estimate built up from the figures supplied by the branches. Ultimately a forecast, broken down by regions and branches, for the annual profit plan for the whole Bank would emerge.

GOOD PLANNING PAYS OFF

At first, of course, some of the plans were a long way out. To some of the managers, and indeed to some of the regional heads, the new system with all the additional forms and extra demands on valuable time seemed a questionable one. Archibald, like Saint Paul, was initially very negative but subsequently became a converted enthusiast. McPhedran also was at first inclined to regard profit planning as an added chore levelled at the regional offices and managers, but he too was converted. Merrick thought there was too much emphasis on profit to the exclusion of common sense. Visits from R. M. Taylor, the senior officer responsible for the implementation of the new program, together with a lot of work and thought, helped win support for the new approach. As any good budgeting exercise will confirm – and profit planning is essentially a budget exercise – the effort involved in making a good plan and working out the appropriate use of staff and resources to realize it will show up in the results. After an initial difficult start, the mechanics of the planning process improved and profit planning became an integral part of the Bank's operations.

There is no doubt that the introduction of profit planning gave an added fillip to Scotia Plan. Managers and regional heads, when they set out to see how they could improve their individual profits and particularly when they began competing directly with other branches and regions, could not fail to appreciate the possibilities in consumer lending. Some of the regions pressed to receive more specialized help from headquarters, and some regions, such as Nova Scotia, went ahead and procured it themselves; as Archibald says, "We went out and recruited finance-company trained lenders and, after a short indoctrination at one of our branches, placed them in areas where they were well known. The results in nearly every case were spectacular." Profit planning also provided a continuing stimulus to deposit building because it translated the need for funds to lend into the rates and efforts made to obtain deposits right down at the branch level. And it undoubtedly put more emphasis on improving procedures and keeping costs down. There was a danger, which Merrick and others perceived, that too much emphasis might be put on profit in the current year at the expense of future profits. Managers and regional heads, for example, might fail to hire and train the staff needed for healthy growth and thus weaken the branch's or the region's future development. Improved supervision and methods gradually overcame this potentially serious problem.

Profit planning was perhaps the key move in the decentralization of banking. As Caldwell puts it, it made "decentralization feasible by producing a system of accountability." It made possible meaningful comparisons between branches and regions, and encouraged competition between them. Absolute and relative results now meant something and profit planning became a useful additional guide in assessing managerial achievement, which, with the development of job evaluation, could now be measured in a more accurate and effective manner.

Along with profit planning came the development of a marketing approach. The Bank was no longer a passive institution, ready to provide its traditional service when required. If that were all it was, it would steadily lose ground. The challenge now was to find out what the customers needed and wanted and to give it to them in a helpful way at a competitive price. Bankers could not be certain, as some thought they were, that they knew just what the customer wanted. They could only know for sure if they made a serious and organized effort to find out.

IMPROVEMENT IN PERSONNEL MANAGEMENT

Meanwhile, the need for more effective personnel policies was becoming urgently clear. All the new branches had to be staffed, ideally with people of ability, energy, and enthusiasm – a tall order indeed as there were hardly enough men and women already on staff to run the existing organization! In some jobs the rate of turnover was high and remuneration was sometimes lower than in competitive companies. More than that, because of the shortage of trained people, some were promoted too rapidly, with unfortunate consequences for everybody. Methods that worked when the Bank was a small organization were not appropriate to a big corporation of over 10,000 employees, stretching across a continent and developing overseas.

It was in these circumstances that the decision was made to turn to job evaluation, using Hay Associates as consultants. The Hay system provided a tool for measuring the relative importance of each job by giving points for know-how, problem solving, and accountability. Each job was worth so many points and, with the point values, the importance of one job could be quantitatively related to that of others. By applying the point system to all positions in the Bank, it was possible to have an *internally* consistent system whereby people could be paid in relation to what they did, and also an *externally* consistent system whereby pay in the Bank would be reasonably aligned with levels of remuneration in other companies.

COMMITTEE TO ASSESS JOBS

Thus the first task to be carried out under R. M. Brown of the Staff Department (now General Manager, Canadian Commercial Banking), with the help of some of the Hay people, was to describe a number of significant or benchmark jobs in the Bank. This was done by interviewing a variety of people and their superiors. These job descriptions were then reviewed and points were assigned to the jobs. This work, which began in 1964 and continued into 1965, was the responsibility of a committee of senior management including Gibson, Touchie, Hitchman, Archibald (who at that time was the regional head in Quebec), Meek (the regional head of western and northern Ontario), W. H. Kent and Brown from the Staff Department (Brown acting as secretary), MacIntosh (Investments), Speicher (Deposits), Dixon (Consumer Credit), and R. M. Taylor (Comptroller and later General Manager, Personnel); the Hay people guided the discussion of the benchmark jobs.

The committee met about every three weeks for over a year, with Taylor and then Dixon acting as chairman later on. Its task was more difficult and revealing than had been expected. It was revealing because it showed that the importance of some jobs had been underestimated, and that the significance of a few had been overestimated. For example, accountants generally, but particularly in the larger branches, were found to be relatively underpaid–underpaid in relation to their performance, responsibilities, and skills.

The committee also found that there were differences between some emerging job descriptions and what senior officers thought the jobs were supposed to entail. One of the interesting developments was the problem of describing the job of the second man in a region–the Supervisor under the Assistant General Manager in charge. Was he simply a senior credit man or did his supervision extend to include other matters concerning the branches within his purview? In other words, was he responsible under the Assistant General Manager for the whole area or only a specialized part of it? The committee was not unanimous in its view, and, though as time went on the Supervisor tended to develop as the line man under the regional head, the picture was still fuzzy rather than clear. Decentralization gradually carried the day, but certainly not to the point of moving all the staff jobs from headquarters to the regions. Indeed, as banking became more complex, the staff functions of headquarters grew too and new departments, such as that of taxation, were established to meet new needs.

THE SYSTEM OF JOB EVALUATION

Out of all this preliminary improvement in personnel management and job description and assessment came the present system of job evaluation. The Bank had to decide what it wanted. How much authority was required to achieve the performance expected? Was the incumbent of a particular job using the authority he had been given? The Hay system required spelling out what was wanted and providing the authority to do it. These fundamental questions could no longer be left vague and ill-defined. It was no longer good enough for senior management to hope that the bright and determined would figure things out for themselves and rise to the top. As in profit planning, management had to sort out its thinking and be as specific as possible about it.

Along with job evaluation came an improved method of salary administration based on the points system and on the external comparisons which job evaluation much facilitated. Salary ranges were set up for each job with a minimum, mid-point, and maximum, the bottom and the top being usually 20 per cent below and above the mid-point. As part of this system, salary changes were considered on a percentage rather than on a dollar amount basis.

It took quite a while to introduce these new arrangements and it is probably fair to say they were not in full operation until 1968. There were some difficult job descriptions, especially in General Office. The points did not always add up correctly in the eyes of management or sometimes in the eyes of the employee. But there is no doubt that job evaluation brought into play a more orderly and fairer system of pay and promotion. It certainly raised salary levels in some key areas in which the Bank would otherwise have had difficulty in keeping, let alone attracting, personnel. In the process, job evaluation led to an improvement in morale and laid a better basis for enlarging the number of trained people who would be increasingly needed.

STAFF TRAINING ARRANGEMENTS

While job evaluation was taking place, staff training arrangements were also being more actively pursued in The Bank of Nova Scotia. There was a new school of practical banking for young accountants – 350 were "back at school" in 1961. There were new managers' associations and accountants' clubs. An interesting development was the use of a management training team which visited regional centres and exposed managers and regional officers to a group of experts from General Office. The team, whose composition varied from time to time, consisted of senior credit officers, and experts on such specific subjects as staff, deposits, business development, methods, and, later, profit planning, and sometimes tax matters, premises, and investments. The meetings gave ample opportunity for exchange of views, including the normal complaints about head office.

While the more routine forms of training were probably quite well handled, there can be little doubt that until the seventies, training for management and other senior posts was inadequate. The big changes in management methods which were initiated in the first half of the sixties would have been more effectively and promptly applied had they been supported by appropriate training seminars. For example, R. M. Taylor carried most of the burden of explaining profit planning, a revolutionary innovation for the Bank, to the regional heads. There were no conferences at which to express one's ideas and to compare notes until considerably later.

MANPOWER PLANNING TAKES TIME

Another development of fundamental significance was the beginning of manpower planning in 1964. The Bank, of course, had always planned its manpower in the sense of moving its existing staff into appropriate positions as they became available and of moving employees from job to job to give them experience and to enable management to assess their capabilities. But the idea of looking ahead and planning to obtain and train the number and kind of employees that might be required in the future was certainly not an established practice, and the truth is that the Bank had been fortunate in achieving such marked growth with so little planning.

By the mid-sixties, however, the need to look ahead had become urgent, and manpower planning was obviously an essential management tool in the developing environment. For a number of reasons to do with personnel and the difficulty of the task, manpower planning was slow to develop in the Bank. It is very difficult to forecast future needs for personnel in a world where change is so rapid and growth far from even. As an exercise in arithmetic, such planning leaves much to be desired. At the same time, attracting competent employees has a great deal to do with the growth of the Bank, so it was deemed wise to plan for substantial recruitment of able and flexible people. As Nicks put it, the Bank was "more and more looking to young men and women with advanced education or special training suited to the more specialized and complex service we must provide." The new recruits should be "receptive to new ideas."[9] Moreover, with changes in attitudes about moving, and with the increased proportion of female employees, recruiting had to be considered more and more on a regional basis.

CENTRAL POSITION OF THE CHIEF ACCOUNTANT'S AND STAFF DEPARTMENTS

Work in the Staff Department in the first half of the sixties was anything but easy, though it was certainly very exciting. This group and a group in the Chief Accountant's Department were at the centre of the management revolution. The Staff Department also had to keep up with social change, and of course with the growth in the number of employees, which amounted to 25 per cent between 1960 and 1965. There was a notable improvement in pension arrangements, including the vesting of rights after an appropriate period of service, and in 1968 the admission of women to the pension fund. Longer holidays came into effect and medical insurance improved. Perhaps the most interesting development, and very much a top-level decision, was the appointment for the first time of a woman as branch manager – two women, in fact. The social revolution had come to stay, and economic realities were at last being recognized.

During this period, the Chief Accountant's Department under Ritchie did much of the work involved in profit planning, particularly after R. M. Taylor had become head of the Staff Department. The Chief Accountant's Department, in addition to its normal function as information and planning centre for senior management, developed and established a section on taxation. In the late fifties, A. B. McKie, a tax expert from Britain, had joined the Chief Accountant's Department to work on the Bank's tax problems. When he was interviewed by Bell in England, Bell wondered out loud why the Bank might need a tax man on staff. "After all," he said, "when we have a tax problem we go to our auditors and get their views." "Ah," countered McKie, "but how do you know when you have a tax problem?" Ever since, McKie has been finding tax problems and working on them, not just for the Bank, but for its customers and particularly those customers in the international sphere. As such problems became more complicated, involving many of the Bank's loan and security transactions, and as the international side of the business developed, the tax function grew and a group developed under McKie.

In the early sixties, McKie was moved to the Business Development Department, where sophisticated tax services combined with international trust operations and the vigorous pressure of Nicks and his group brought the Bank a good deal of new business. Part of the tax group stayed in the Chief Accountant's Department, concentrating on the Bank's direct tax interests. In 1965, the two groups were again reunited under McKie as a new department. All tax matters were then focussed at one point with a view to preventing duplication and making it clear where tax assistance was to be sought.

PROBLEM OF RISING COSTS

With all this growth, costs tended to increase. Greater decentralization carried functions out into the regions, not always with an equivalent reduction in head office activities. General Office had to see that the regions were doing their new jobs correctly in the good old head office tradition that "father knows best." With new services and new techniques, new head office departments began to appear on the scene, with more specialists to man them. In these circumstances, the Bank brought in outside management advisers to review its general office organization. A number of interesting proposals came out of their study, one of the most important being, in the words of Ritchie, that "international banking as a major operation could not be superimposed on a domestic organization." Thus, the international banking division emerged as an operating unit. A number of other changes were made, and an organization called the General Office Methods Group, or GOMG, of which more will be said in the next chapter, was brought into existence to follow through on these changes.

ACCELERATING GROWTH IN FOREIGN BUSINESS

Despite the loss of Cuban business, the foreign-currency business of the Bank grew more than the Canadian from 1960 to 1965 – at an annual rate of 14 per cent in terms of dollars, compared with 9½ per cent for Canadian dollar assets. And even after correction for rising prices, the annual increase was 10½ per cent, compared with the Canadian figure of 7½ per cent. Lost retail business in Cuba was more than offset by expanding operations in other parts of the Caribbean. Meanwhile, a growing business with the central banks of other Latin American countries, based in part on the experience gained in Cuba and the Dominican Republic, together with a healthy growth in the United States and Europe, resulted in mounting totals of wholesale deposits and loans.

Even though the Federation of the West Indies did not hold together, the Bank continued to expand its operations in what were the former British West Indies and the Bahamas. Two more branches were added in Jamaica, maintaining the Nova Scotia's leading position there with 22 branches in all. The Jamaican operation gained more autonomy, becoming a regional division of the Bank like the divisions in Quebec or Nova Scotia. There was notable growth in Trinidad, bringing the total from 2 to 6 branches in what was perhaps the most prosperous of the islands. Branches were opened for the first time in Antigua, Grenada, and St. Lucia. And in the Bahamas, three more branches were opened in Nassau and one in Freeport. Branches were also opened in the U.S. Virgin Islands, a convenient point of entry into United States financial markets.

A NEW APPROACH TO THE CARIBBEAN

At this time, the Bank was looking to the future of the Caribbean area, which obviously was no longer in sugar. The old plantations which had been the largest employers of labour and the source of substantial profit were in fact a declining industry; in some cases they had been taken over by the state and in others they had required substantial government aid. While there were some new resource industries, in particular bauxite in Jamaica and the Dominican Republic, and while there was

More Growth and the Management Revolution, 1960 - 1965 243

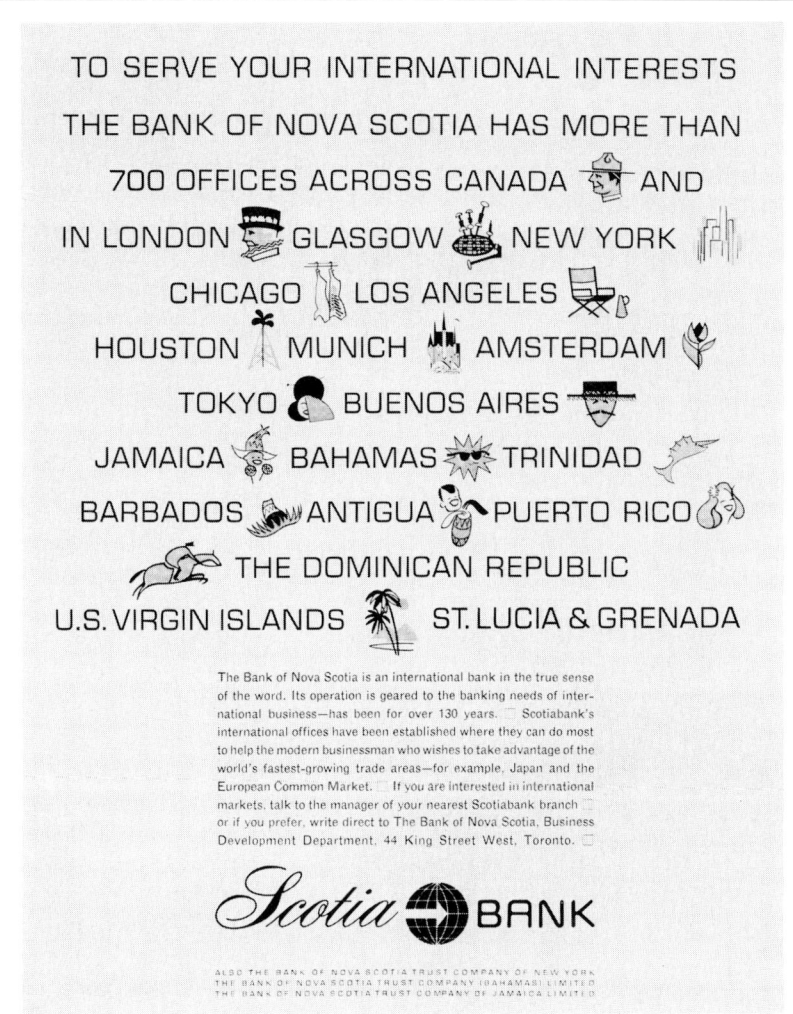

1964 advertisement listing Scotiabank locations around the world.

some industrial development sponsored by the state as in Puerto Rico and Jamaica, the most promising new industry was the tourist trade. Because of this upsurge in tourism, the Bank embarked on hotel and resort financing with mortgage security frequently on a five-year basis in such places as the Bahamas, Jamaica, and Antigua, in addition to continuing its usual local and tourist business. In societies where such forms of banking were previously unheard of, the Bank had a very real advantage over its more conservative competitors.

Meanwhile, through the efforts of Edgar Felsenstein, the Bank's representative in Latin America (Buenos Aires at that time), and Harry Randall, the Bank obtained substantial deposits largely from the central banks in that area. These banks were not always using their U.S. dollar

When, in 1958, it became legal for Canadians to hold gold, the Bank began developing this line of business, which includes gold certificates as well as coins and bullion. The Bank worked to establish a Canadian source of gold bullion.

and gold reserves to full advantage and the Bank was in a position to offer very competitive rates on U.S. dollar deposits.

THE EXCITING WORLD OF GOLD

The Bank had also developed professional know-how in the exciting world of gold. Gold, as Randall put it, "threw a fascinating sidelight on human nature." Some large deals were carried out. A number were turned down, including some on or over the edge of legality, and others which were just plain crazy.

All sorts of people wanted to buy gold for all sorts of reasons. Perhaps most revealing was the attitude of a European who insisted on seeing Randall in Toronto, wanting to invest his thousand dollars of capital in gold. Randall said he should not put his whole capital into

The Bank of Nova Scotia opened in Glasgow in 1964 and was the first foreign bank to operate in Scotland. The Province of Nova Scotia tartan was used for vests worn by the staff and for the draperies in the branch.

gold; for one thing, he would get no interest. To which the European responded, "Mr. Randall, I can afford to lose the interest, but I cannot afford to lose the capital." Such a statement throws much light on the motivations of gold buyers.

BANK OPENS IN GLASGOW

Meanwhile, Nicks was busy in Europe pursuing prospects on a personal basis, and opening new branches. The Bank opened a third branch in London, England – in Berkeley Square – and, what was really a first, it opened in Glasgow in 1964. This was the first bank from any other country that had opened in Scotland and strangely enough, despite the Nova Scotia's very Scottish background, it did not appear to be altogether welcome. Indeed, there was for a time a question about the

Bank's use of the Glasgow clearing arrangements, which was fortunately sorted out; in time, the chilly reception was followed by a friendlier atmosphere. Also in 1964, a new office was opened in Amsterdam (later in 1965 moving to Rotterdam and becoming a branch).

In addition to developing further German business (an office was opened in Munich in 1962), Nicks met more leading people in the Greek shipping business. This was partly a result of his friendship with a leading shipping figure in London who introduced him to other Greek shipowners and to the Governor of the Bank of Greece (the central bank). It also resulted from his earlier connections in Halifax when at the end of the war some Greek shipowners showed interest in the Canadian government's proposals for disposing of excess wartime tonnage at very reasonable prices in exchange for building new ships in Canada. Nicks's various contacts with Greek shipping magnates in turn led to the growth of shipping loan business for the Bank and finally to the establishment by the Bank of a banking and lending business in Greece itself.

MOVING AROUND THE WORLD

A first entry into the Arab world, long before the oil shortage and the formation of the Organization of Petroleum Exporting Countries (OPEC), was made in 1965 in Beirut. What was even more significant, the Bank opened a business office in Tokyo in 1962, headed by a former Japanese-Canadian, George Korenaga. Though the Tokyo office did not turn into a branch until 1981, it was of great value in developing loans to large Japanese companies, which were a major avenue for U.S. dollar loans in the early sixties.

Nicks's trips took him farther and farther afield. He made two trips to the Soviet Union in an endeavour to develop trade-financing business. He also made a point of attending the meetings of the International Monetary Fund and the World Bank, particularly those held outside of Washington every third year. He liked to take advantage of the opportunity of travelling abroad, where he could meet with a great variety of bankers, many of whom were customers or prospective customers, and where he could explore new possibilities.

BUILDING A BASE IN THE UNITED STATES

While the new efforts abroad were of importance, the most significant development in wholesale banking in the early sixties, and indeed of the whole decade, was the building of a base in the United States. Right next door, speaking the same language and doing business much the same way, with an open door and a friendly attitude, was the richest country on earth and therefore by far the greatest market opportunity

In the early 1960s, the Bank's expansion in international centres was highlighted in an advertising program. This example ran in 1965.

for international banking. Moreover, the currency of this same country was the dominant medium of exchange in the world and, because the United States was then running, and until recently was still running, a large balance-of-payments deficit, its money was available almost everywhere and in almost any quantity. Because the largest supply of U.S. dollars was obviously in the United States, the Nova Scotia, like other large banks, and rather earlier than most, went to the source and established offices to seek out deposits and, in some directions, loans. Foreign banks were, and still are, subject to a number of restrictions in taking deposits in the United States, but they could do so outside the United States – in the Bank's case usually Toronto – and carry out the transactions through their New York agencies. At the same time, they were not subject to U.S. interest rate restrictions or reserve requirements and in this respect had a competitive advantage over U.S. banks.*

On the lending side, the dollars obtained in the United States could be used anywhere until the U.S. balance-of-payments guidelines came into effect in 1965, though when used in the United States, as a matter of practice they tended to be concentrated in certain areas where the American banks were not keenly interested, such as finance companies. Sizeable amounts went into call loans against stock exchange securities; substantial amounts went abroad both to Japan and to U.S. companies requiring finances for new operations in the Common Market or elsewhere. Moreover, when money was tight, the American banks were generally quite content to see Canadian banks supplement loans to their customers.

NEW OFFICES IN THE WESTERN UNITED STATES

Thus, early in the sixties the Bank opened offices in the western United States – one in Los Angeles and one in Houston – thereby extending its American representation from New York and Chicago (the latter office having been reopened in 1955). The money was there. The problem was to staff the offices with the kind of men who could go to the treasurer of an international corporation (often a Harvard Business School graduate) and show him how he could earn an extra dollar for his company or obtain more suitable financing of his company's needs, perhaps in Europe or Canada. The Bank was quite competitive in the area of deposits, particularly when they replaced short-term investments in Treasury bills, which many of the big companies carried. It could also offer effective overseas financing. As time went on, it provided international tax services through McKie and his group, which was described by a banking friend in the United States as the "Nova Scotia's secret weapon."

DEDICATED DOOR-KNOCKING PAYS OFF

The Bank's representatives in each office would try to cover the major companies in their area by calling on them twice or more a year and by scanning the news for developments that might open up a deal, such as a new plant in Frankfurt or Edmonton. They would usually call on the treasurer or assistant treasurer, or perhaps the officer responsible for international finance. They would also turn up at various banking meetings where these men were to be found. It was slow work and

---

* This advantage has pertained to U.S. banks using their own domestic funds but not to U.S. banks obtaining U.S. dollars abroad and lending to residents of the United States from an overseas office, as many do.

often discouraging, particularly when some good-hearted vice-president would open the conversation with "And how are things in Halifax?" or "The last time I was in Halifax was when our ship came in to be refitted during the war." But this does not happen often any more because as Hugh McGinn, long a practitioner in the art of acquiring U.S. business, puts it, "At the big-business level, they know the world-class banks. Having our name associated with a locality does not hurt any more, just as it does not hurt the Bank of Tokyo or the Bank of Montreal." Calls by the Chief Executive Officer of the Bank – by Nicks or today Ritchie – were and are of great importance, particularly in the case of big companies, where the head man is often more receptive than the treasurer. Dedicated and intelligent door-knocking pays off, especially when the CEO pitches in.

In 1965 the United States, because of increasing pressure on the dollar, put a system of voluntary balance-of-payments guidelines into effect. At first this program reduced the U.S. funds available to the Bank. But since there was a large surplus of U.S. money available abroad and a large demand by American companies for loans in their foreign operations, the market for U.S. dollars domiciled outside the United States (Eurodollars) grew rapidly and the Bank's wholesale business soon resumed its strong upward trend.

SOME EXECUTIVE CHANGES

In the Bank's headquarters, new developments were also taking place. Gibson had been back full-time for less than a year after his work on the Royal Commission on Banking and Finance when he was promoted to the position of Executive Vice-President and Deputy Chairman. He was unhappy about this promotion, since it took him away from the job he had been doing on management methods, and he was further concerned by Nicks's explanation of his new job as one of "keeping in touch with the Bank of Canada and following economic matters." Boyles took over as Chief General Manager and Gordon Touchie as General Manager.

TOUCHIE BECOMES GENERAL MANAGER

Touchie, a good-natured, shrewd Maritimer, brought a long and thorough experience in branch banking and an outstanding ability in credit to his new job, having run such branches as Hamilton and Toronto. "He," as Ritchie puts it, "was an excellent manager in the sense of being a 'people' man, tough but very fair." For example, when Touchie was given reports on staff performance he would always satisfy himself that the officer commenting on the performance had discussed the weaknesses of the employee concerned with that employee personally, and had suggested corrective action. He had worked under Nicks as senior assistant manager in Toronto branch and they had made an

T.A. Boyles,
Chief General Manager,
1964-1966;
Executive Vice-President,
1966-1972;
Deputy Chairman,
1969-1972;
Chief Executive Officer,
1972;
Chairman,
1972-1974.

effective team, though not without some strain on Touchie's nerves.

When he became General Manager, he had not been to western Canada, so he took a holiday in the West. Clad in casual dress, he went from branch to branch as an informal visitor. Walking into an Alberta branch, he introduced himself to the manager as "Touchie from General Office." He lost no time in asking the manager how he was getting along with the credit department in Calgary – what sort of people were they? how were they to live with? The manager really exploded about "those characters" and how they made his life miserable and spoilt his opportunities. At which point, stopping suddenly he said, "Who did you say you were – Touchie?"

GIBSON RESIGNS

In November 1965, Gibson resigned from the Bank. While he had stayed on in his new capacity and continued to carry on some activity in job evaluation and manpower planning, he saw no prospect of making an effective contribution. He admired Nicks's strength of will, drive, and ability, but he did not think much of his management style. In his letter of resignation, Gibson said, "Policy is seldom discussed as such, whether it relates to responses to changed monetary conditions, to lending policies in Canada or abroad, or to priorities and objectives in our growth. Problems are dealt with as they come up on an ad hoc basis, and innovations, some of which have contributed greatly to the growth of the Bank, are introduced from time to time." This was not an acceptable assessment either to Nicks or to the Board. In the circumstances, the Board had little choice but to accept Gibson's resignation – a development which in a sense was another "first"!

FOUNDATIONS LAID FOR MARKED EXPANSION

The Bank had accomplished a good deal in the first half of the sixties. Its assets had risen substantially – in real terms by 50 per cent – and it was now a very sizeable bank, still fourth in Canada but narrowing the gap between itself and number three. Internationally, it was gaining increased recognition. Because it had had to make a substantial investment in new approaches and methods as well as in new representation and facilities, and because it had had some catching-up to do in improving parts of the salary scale, profit growth was less impressive. The average annual increase in profits per share in the five years was only 3 per cent and, even if the Cuban business had not been lost, the increase would still have been quite low.

But the foundations were now laid for marked expansion. The investment in the international side flowered in the late sixties as the Eurodollar market grew to unimagined size, while the improved domestic organization produced better results.

More Growth and the Management Revolution, 1960-1965   251

NOTES

1. BNS Annual Report, 1962, President's Report, pp.4-8.
2. BNS Annual Report, 1963, President's Report, p.4.
3. Stephen Leacock, "My Financial Career," originally published in *Literary Lapses* (1910) and subsequently included in *The Best of Leacock* (Toronto: McClelland & Stewart, 1957).
4. *Report of the Royal Commission on Banking and Finance* (Ottawa: Queen's Printer, 1964), pp.560-66.
5. *Ibid.*, p.562.
6. BNS Annual Report, 1965, President's Report, p.12.
7. BNS Annual Report, 1963, President's Report, p.6.
8. *Ibid.*, Chief General Manager's Report, p.20.
9. BNS Annual Report, 1963, President's Report, p.8.

12

A Full-Fledged International Bank
1966-1971

From 1966 to 1971, the growth of the Bank accelerated as a result of marked expansion in its international activities. During the six years following 1965, foreign currency assets increased at an average annual rate of no less than 20 per cent. By the end of 1971, just before Nicks died, the Bank's foreign currency business was almost two-thirds as large in dollar amount as its Canadian business. Out of seven and a quarter billion dollars in total assets, those assets in foreign currency accounted for almost three billion dollars. Even when allowance is made for renewed inflation, the annual growth rate in foreign currency business came to 16 per cent.

Meanwhile, the Bank's Canadian dollar assets continued to grow at a real annual rate of about 7 per cent. This rate had persisted ever since the middle fifties and was to continue into the seventies. But because of the improvement in efficiency, earnings were significantly higher domestically than in the early sixties and, because of the notable upsurge in volume, much higher internationally.

RECORD RETURNS TO SHAREHOLDERS

Indeed, the combination of efforts to control costs, of bigger volume, and of somewhat better margins internationally led to a marked growth in earnings per share averaging 16 per cent per annum over the six years, and bringing the return on shareholders' equity to a new high of 12.3 per cent in 1971.* This was the best performance that the Bank

---

* As noted in Chapter 14, page 324, after the 1967 Bank Act revision balance of revenue after taxes as a percentage of shareholders' equity plus accumulated appropriations came to be regarded by some analysts as a more appropriate measure of bank profits than the relationship of profits to shareholders' equity. On a balance-of-revenue basis, the rate of return was 14 per cent in 1971, compared with 12.3 per cent on a profit basis. In the 1980 Bank Act revision, this terminology was dropped.

A Full-fledged International Bank, 1966-1971

had recorded up to this time and it was to set the standard for the decade of the seventies. It did not reflect cutting back the rate of investment in the banking business – there were many new branches (an all-time record in 1969), and two new computer systems. Nor did it reflect any failure to build up reserves against loans, which, despite the necessity of making substantial taxable provisions, remained over 2 per cent. To some extent, it did reflect a lower capital ratio – a decline in the ratio of shareholders' equity to deposits from $4^{3}/_{4}$ per cent in 1965 to 3.9 per cent in 1971.

THE EURODOLLAR MARKET

Nicks was fairly optimistic about the Canadian economic outlook in 1966, though he was concerned about the mounting rate of government spending. However, he was more concerned about the international economic picture, particularly the large American payments deficit. Paradoxically enough, it was this deficit which built up the Eurodollar market, which in turn added so much to the Bank's growth. The world's willingness to accept U.S. dollars as official international reserves as well as a store of ready cash meant that the U.S. dollar was the international currency. The fact that more and more of this money was available outside the United States provided the basis for international banking. On the one hand, there was a world-wide demand for dollars, and, on the other, a huge supply arising from the American payments deficit resulting from the large corporate investments in the Common Market by U.S. firms and, as time went on, from the tremendous outlays for the Vietnam war. The wheel had come full circle. In contrast to the dollar-short world of the first ten or more years after the Second World War, dollars were now in plentiful supply, though still welcome in most quarters.

These dollars which accumulated outside the United States were known as Eurodollars – meaning simply dollars not resident in the United States but identical in every other particular with any other U.S. dollar.* The large banks, particularly the American, British, Canadian, European, and Japanese, were not slow to enter the business of marrying the supply of American dollars outside the United States with the very large demand for U.S. dollar loans which was developing all over the world. Thus, the banks would compete for the supply and endeavour to match it to lending opportunities; or more commonly, they would find borrowing customers and try to match deposits with loans at a reasonable margin. They would have a book or books to which they added or subtracted and in which they marked off one opportunity against another. In contrast to domestic banking, where the competition for loans was one operation and that for deposits

---

* "Eurodollar" is really a misnomer. The term applies not just to U.S. dollars in Europe but to U.S. dollars anywhere outside the United States.

This 1966 advertisement highlighted changes in the Bank's representation abroad.

another quite separate activity, international banking involved a continuous process of marrying the two.

A WORLD-WIDE BANKING SYSTEM WAS DEVELOPING

Prior to the imposition by the U.S. government of restrictions designed to strengthen the U.S. balance of payments in 1965 and later, there was no real difference between a Eurodollar and an ordinary U.S. dollar. With balance-of-payments restrictions, however, movement of U.S. dollars out of the United States for investment purposes was subject to some restraint, while there were no restrictions whatever on dollars located in other countries – Eurodollars. Thus the Eurodollar business grew and grew. The demand was there. The big banks accepted and collected U.S. dollar deposits everywhere and lent them out to each other and to borrowers in all parts of the world. In fact, a world-wide banking system was developing. If liquid assets were needed by big companies or governments, they could be obtained in the Eurodollar market. If money was tight and expensive at home, it might be more readily available in Eurodollars.

EURODOLLARS CAN GROW BY THEMSELVES

A number of European countries complained that this market was a vehicle for exporting inflation from the United States; and their concern was heightened by the fact that the Eurodollar market had the capacity to grow within itself. The reason for this was that the Eurodollar market was not subject to government requirements for cash reserves. Thus, the familiar multiplication of credit that occurs in a domestic banking system was not limited by the need to hold a fixed percentage of deposits as cash reserves in the form of national currency and central bank deposits. The result was that as time went on there were far more Eurodollar assets and deposits in existence than those provided by the payments deficits of the United States.

The expansion was modified of course by the quality of loans available and by the practice of the large commercial banks of keeping 40 per cent or more of their assets in the form of deposits with other large banks, the theory being that the risks they took on their loans were balanced to a degree by the high quality of their deposits with other banks. It is true that this practice results in diversification of risk. It also discourages the taking of undue risks for fear that the sight of weak loans on a bank's balance sheet might dissuade other banks from making deposits with it and thus lessen its growth and weaken its position. But the practice also gives some impression of taking in one another's washing and it does not provide a firm check on the growth of Eurodollars.

GROWTH IN LATIN AMERICA

Thus, though he was concerned about the U.S. payments deficit and growing world inflation, Nicks's alertness in building up foreign business connections and branches resulted in the Nova Scotia's acquiring a disproportionate share of foreign currency loans and deposits in relation to other Canadian banks. The Bank's earlier experience in Cuba and the Dominican Republic, its trading in gold, its strong New York and London connections, and its persistent efforts to develop foreign business all bore fruit. In Latin America, Felsenstein called repeatedly on all the central banks of that area and by the late sixties had deposits from most of them. He was able to procure for these banks a relatively favourable return on their U.S. dollar resources by taking their U.S. dollars for, say, two years, subject to a change in rate every 90 days, and depositing them in other banks or perhaps putting them into the New York call loan market.

LONDON, ENGLAND, BECOMES REGIONAL OFFICE

The London operation grew substantially, and in 1968 it became a regional office under R. Marsman as General Manager, with the branches and offices in Europe and Beirut reporting to him. Another branch was opened in London, another in Scotland, this time in Edinburgh (the ice had been broken earlier in Glasgow), one in Belfast, and also one in Dublin. On the Continent a branch was established in Brussels and two in Greece, one in Athens and one in Piraeus. An office

Athens, Greece.

The original office in Athens opened in 1969 in the Grande Bretagne Hotel, but with the growth in business the Bank moved into these larger premises after a few years.

Dedication ceremonies for the Branch in Piraeus, Greece, in 1969. F.W. Nicks, then Chairman, is shown speaking.

was also opened in Frankfurt, fulfilling Nicks's desire for better representation in Germany to provide a stronger financial bond with that country.

THE GREEK CONNECTION

The entry into Greece was the culmination of Nicks's association with Greek shipping companies and with the Greek central bank, through which the Nova Scotia had made Greece a sizeable loan subject to two-year adjustments in interest rates. Nicks was in Athens in the Grande Bretagne Hotel having his Bloody Mary in the cocktail bar when formal approval arrived for the opening of a branch in Athens. It suddenly struck him. "What better place for a branch than the bar of the Grande Bretagne, frequented by businessmen from all over the world and in the very centre of Athens?" Rather reluctantly his Greek friends, including the owner of the hotel, assented to this proposal, and, indeed, at the opening of the new branch in 1969 the Archbishop of Greece blessed the premises. There the Bank operated for several years until it moved into a modern and much larger branch in the area.

As a matter of interest, Nicks was given an order by the Greek royal family for his services to that country – Commander of the Royal Order of the Phoenix. Since the Government of Canada does not approve of orders from other countries, Nicks asked for its view on this honour, which he found embarrassing to refuse. Receiving no reply, he accepted the order. It is also of interest that in the late sixties a Greek seamen's pension fund used the PSP (Personal Security Plan) savings arrangements, introduced in Canada back in 1954, because of the life insurance feature built into the savings target. Whether or not it comforted the seamen, the sign of The Bank of Nova Scotia at Piraeus could be seen fifteen miles out at sea.

TOUR OF THE MIDDLE EAST

Nicks continued his trips to Germany, Britain, and Holland, as well as to Lebanon, where some Arab business was developed. He also went back to Japan, where the Bank continued to make substantial loans to some of the big international companies. Accompanied by Peel, in 1966 he toured the Middle East, including Cairo, Amman, and some of the Arab sheikdoms. On this trip he showed signs of weariness. It seemed that the strain of always pressing to keep ahead was beginning to tell. But he kept moving, taking his annual trip to London and then going on to Greece, Italy, and Germany, with European and Middle Eastern variants in his itinerary from time to time. For instance, he developed a good relationship with the Vatican, where he called periodically. During his 1970 trip he had a breakdown in Paris on his way home. Peel was able to get a doctor at the American Hospital whom Nicks much respected, and a major and successful operation was performed. Late in

The San Francisco Agency opened in 1968 to support an expanding wholesale banking business in the United States.

CREDIT: JULIUS SHULMAN

the year he returned home, had a long rest, and by the spring of 1971 appeared to have recovered fully.

Meanwhile, the wholesale banking business in the United States continued to grow, and was further strengthened by an agency in San Francisco. Though the Bank was now prevented by the Johnson guidelines from taking more money out of the United States, it could still lend deposits obtained in the United States and registered in Toronto to borrowers in U.S. markets. Also, it could still obtain deposits, through U.S. head offices, of their subsidiaries anywhere else in the world. Thus, despite balance-of-payments restrictions, the United States remained a very important source of U.S. dollars – either plain U.S. dollars or Eurodollars.

A Full-fledged International Bank, 1966 – 1971

INTERNATIONAL OPERATIONS INCREASINGLY COMPLEX

The Bank's international operations had become increasingly complex, so much so that, in the words of Ritchie, "it is virtually impossible to summarize the variety of influences which affect our affairs outside Canada."[1] The picture was made up of differing operations in many countries upon which converged such broad forces as the U.S. balance of payments, the creation of U.S. dollars through the Eurodollar market, the varying rates of inflation, and international economic and political pressures. The amalgam of all these things, combined with the Bank's own vigorous efforts, resulted in marked expansion in foreign currency assets in the latter part of the sixties. While consistently upward, and averaging 20 per cent annually from 1965 to 1971, the increase was quite uneven, reaching a peak of over 40 per cent from 1967 to 1968 and slowing to around 7 per cent in 1970 and 1971. Margins were squeezed in 1969 and early 1970, when Eurodollar rates were at very high levels. In 1971, interest rates again rose sharply for a time, but to quote Ritchie once more, "Interest rates were at such levels in the Eurodollar market that we were relatively cautious in taking on liabilities at that time. At the same time, we concentrated our efforts on improving our overall foreign currency margin, and we were rewarded with very considerable success in that endeavour."[2]

BETTER ORGANIZATION OF "INTERNATIONAL"

The organization of the international operations of the Bank improved notably in the late sixties. In 1965, as mentioned earlier, credit applications for wholesale operations went to a new international credit department rather than through Toronto branch, correcting a situation that was becoming difficult and inefficient. In 1967, Randall, as General Manager of the whole international division, had under him four Assistant General Managers stationed in Toronto: two in charge of credit, W.H. Kent and H.A. Murcell, one in charge of the Caribbean regional office, Lindsay, and the other in charge of business development, Peel. Two AGMs were located in New York: McPhedran, who was senior agent, and Webster, who continued his work on business development; and one in London, Marsman.

RITCHIE HEADS "INTERNATIONAL"

In 1968, Ritchie became head of the Bank's international operations with the title of Chief General Manager, International. Since up until this time the title of "Chief General Manager" had been reserved for the operating head of the whole Bank, it was now clear that the International division had come of age, as had the young man who joined the Bank at Bath, New Brunswick, in 1945 at the age of eighteen.

C.E. Ritchie,
Chief General Manager, International, 1968-1970;
Chief General Manager, 1970-1972;
President and Chief Executive Officer, 1972-1979;
Chairman and Chief Executive Officer, 1974 to Present.

With his early work in Maritime branches and illuminating experience on the inspection staff, Ritchie had developed a capacity for making the best of things as they were and finding the most effective way of sizing up and solving a problem. His further experience in Toronto branch as accountant and assistant manager was in his view invaluable, and like many other senior officers before and since, he felt that this was one of the best parts of his career. His next post, as Chief Accountant (in which position he first appears in this history), led on logically to Assistant General Manager, Administration, to Chief General Manager, International, to Chief General Manager of the Bank, and ultimately to Chairman and Chief Executive Officer. With his interested and open approach, he has the gift of looking for the positive side of every issue, of finding a way to do things effectively. As they now say in banks, his "people" relationships are good – straightforward and friendly and, what is of particular importance to subordinates, clear, leaving little doubt as to what is expected and giving appropriate latitude to do the job.

IMPROVED ORGANIZATION

At the same time in 1968, Randall formally retired but continued as a consultant for two years. Ritchie added a banking division to International, as the whole group was now called. This was an organized effort to bring together the finances and to match efficiently the assets and liabilities of a large and growing operation working in a number of different currencies and widely separated physically. The foreign exchange and money market functions under H. R. Wong and M. Lennon had become increasingly important in quoting competitive lending and deposit rates – in doing business in the right currency at the right time.

Another important change was the formalization of credit procedures in International to allow the more efficient use of time by the senior credit officers. Instead of dealing with major credits as they turned up, a regular meeting was held first thing in the morning and decisions were forthcoming by 11 a.m., unless in Ritchie's judgment the credit applications should be referred to the Executive Committee of the Bank consisting of Nicks, Boyles, Crockett, Hitchman, and himself. International now also had its own Comptroller and Personnel Officer. In accordance with the much increased volume and complexity of the work, titles were improved, Kent, Marsman, Lindsay, and Peel becoming General Managers.

A TIME OF RAPID CHANGE

It was a time of rapid change as well as growth, and, looking back, Ritchie points to the active and well-directed drive of Scott McDonald and Peter Godsoe (Godsoe having joined the Bank in 1966) in building

W.S. McDonald,
Executive Vice-President,
1972-1980;
Senior Executive Vice-President,
1980-1982;
Vice-Chairman,
1982.

CREDIT: V. TONY HAUSER

up the U.S. business, and "the competence and adaptability of the Bill Kents, Don Lindsays, Harvey Murcells, and others, without which I could never have run International." Ritchie certainly had his problems, an example of which was the financing of a Canadian airplane sale to a Latin American country. The credit had been authorized by cable and inadvertently there was no reference to certain security which was to be pledged. He referred this omission to Nicks, who agreed "he had a problem" and pointed out that there was a plane leaving Miami for the country concerned late that evening. Ritchie did succeed the following day in obtaining an undertaking to provide the security at a later date and then he phoned Nicks, whose response was, "That's fine, I suggest you go to bed now." After this incident there were fewer mistakes in regard to security and documentation in International.

MCDONALD TAKES OVER "INTERNATIONAL"

In 1970, when Ritchie became Chief General Manager of the whole Bank, W. Scott McDonald took his place as head of International with the title of Deputy Chief General Manager. (He now has the title of Vice-Chairman of the Board.) His immediately preceding job was Executive Assistant to the President, where he had long experience under Nicks in preparing plans and projects in the international area and where he became thoroughly familiar with the growth and problems of International. A thoughtful, rather reserved man of great intelligence, he was a graduate of the University of Toronto and the Harvard Business School. Serious but pleasant in demeanour, and also endowed with a sense of humour, he would weigh the evidence, hear the views, and reach a decision. Another significant appointment in the late sixties was that of Donald Fleming, a former Minister of Finance of Canada, as Managing Director of The Bank of Nova Scotia Trust Company (Bahamas) and its subsidiary trust companies – Jamaica, West Indies, Cayman Islands, and Caribbean.

"THE BANK OF NOVA SCOTIA JAMAICA LIMITED"

By this time, the Jamaican operation had become a separate bank, The Bank of Nova Scotia Jamaica Limited, in which 25 per cent of the stock was held by Jamaicans and of which 4 out of 10 directors were Jamaican. At the time of the changeover, 1967, the capital of the new bank was £2,500,000 and its staff numbered approximately 550, manning 24 branches and 7 sub-branches. The stock issue in Jamaica was over-subscribed and later in 1969 another 5 per cent of the stock was sold on the island, bringing the local holding to 30 per cent. There were only a few northerners left on the staff, including the Managing Director, J. A. G. Bell, who had done much to make the bank Jamaican. The new bank became part of the Nova Scotia network of foreign associated and subsidiary companies. Political and economic developments made further progress towards the target of 50 or 51 per cent local ownership impracticable.

In Trinidad, however, a similar policy of gradually handing over majority control to local residents, which started in 1971, has since been accomplished at just over 50 per cent.

FILLING OUT IN THE CARIBBEAN

In the Caribbean in the late sixties, most of the expansion was of a retail-banking nature. The Bank filled out its representation in Trinidad with 7 new branches, making a total of 13. Two more were added in the Bahamas, two in Barbados, one more in St. Lucia, and new representation was established in British Honduras, later Belize (2 branches), Guyana, the British Virgin Islands, and the Cayman Islands, the last

Scotiabank Jamaica.

In 1967 the Jamaica operations became a separate bank. This photograph, taken in 1976, shows the entrance to Scotiabank Centre in Kingston.

named having tax-haven implications. In the Dominican Republic, two new branches were opened, and one new one started in Puerto Rico. The Bank's representation in the U.S. Virgin Islands was raised from 2 to 5 branches. A branch, in the form of an incorporated company, was opened in St. Maarten, Netherlands Antilles. With its far-flung branch network, its interest in the Bermuda National Bank which was started in 1969, its trust companies, and its merchant banking connections, The Bank of Nova Scotia now thoroughly covered the Caribbean area. With its associate in Jamaica, it had a good retail business and all the offshore facilities to complement its wholesale banking business in continental North America.

BUILDING A WORLD-CLASS CANADIAN BANK

Nicks died of a massive heart attack at his home at the beginning of 1972. In addition to his achievements in domestic banking, which included Scotia Plan, he was the chief architect of the international business of the Bank. On the basis of the existing business in the West Indies and the structure in New York and London, he built an edifice which turned The Bank of Nova Scotia into a world-class bank. Earlier than most, he saw the likelihood of great economic growth internationally. He was enthusiastic about the Marshall Plan, foreign aid, the

Common Market and the importance of Britain joining it, the co-operation of central banks, and above all the part that Canada could play in the world economy. He foresaw the increasing cohesiveness of the important countries of the western world and he was determined that the Bank would take advantage of it. As he put it in 1963, "It is incumbent on us to press our services vigorously into the international financial scene."³

While Nicks did not foresee the enormous development of the Eurodollar market, mainly because he had hoped that the major countries would deal with inflation more effectively, he did construct an organization which was thoroughly able to respond to international opportunities as they developed. In the Bank, Nicks built up a staff of people who were a mixture of seasoned bankers of the "old school" and graduates of the modern business schools and universities and who were able to carry enthusiastically many of his goals and aspirations into the future.

G.J. Touchie,
Chief General Manager,
1966-1968

CHANGES IN THE EXECUTIVE

While all these major developments were taking place in the International division, at the executive offices Boyles moved up to the position of Executive Vice-President in 1966, and Touchie became Chief General Manager. Ritchie's title of Assistant General Manager, Administration, was raised to Joint General Manager, involving a broadening of responsibility rather than a change. In a similar way, MacIntosh's title was raised to that of Joint General Manager, again involving a greater area of responsibility. In the next few years, these two men were to make significant contributions to updating the Bank's operations and to keeping its costs in hand. Hitchman, who previously had the title of Deputy General Manager, joined the group of Joint General Managers, as did Jameson, who was previously executive assistant to the President.

The new title of "Joint General Manager" provided some innocent amusement. How could a Joint General Manager, presumably sharing his general-managership jointly, be senior to a plain General Manager, with nothing qualifying his title? But there it was on the roster of executive officers – the Joint GMs were above the GMs. As the March Hare said to Alice, in *Alice in Wonderland*, "Then you should say what you mean." "I do," Alice hastily replied, "at least – at least I mean what I say – that's the same thing you know." "Not the same thing a bit!" said the Mad Hatter. "Why, you might just as well say that 'I see what I eat' is the same thing as 'I eat what I see'."

At the next annual meeting in 1967 there was only one change – Younker became a Deputy General Manager in recognition of his major role in credit supervision. Everyone else's title remained the same – the Joint GMs' ambiguous titles were confirmed.

However, this confusing state of affairs could not last, and in 1968

A.H. Crockett,
Chief General Manager, 1968-1970;
President, 1970-1972;
Deputy Chairman, 1972-1982.

the list of senior titles was changed again. Gone were the "Joint General Managers," now replaced by "Deputy Chief General Managers." They were the same people, with the exception of Ritchie, who, as mentioned earlier, became Chief General Manager, International.

CROCKETT IS CHIEF GENERAL MANAGER

In 1968, Crockett moved up to occupy the position of Chief General Manager. His name, along with that of Ritchie, has already cropped up a number of times in this chronicle; he is another Maritimer, from Pictou County, Nova Scotia. He entered the Bank's service in 1934 and gained experience at various places in the Maritimes, particularly Charlottetown. He served in the Royal Canadian Navy from 1941 to 1945, as has already been noted. During the war he met Nicks in Halifax branch and, just before his discharge, while assessing job opportunities in Toronto, he called on Nicks, who persuaded him to return to the Bank in Toronto branch. With subsequent experience in New York, London, England, and Montreal and with the not uncommon background for a top executive position, manager of Toronto branch, as well as a long spell in the executive offices, he was ready for the new job. He had an attractive manner and in addition to being an energetic, driving worker he was gifted in the art of persuasion. In 1969, Crockett also became President of the Canadian Bankers' Association, a job which added substantially to his workload. Touchie had long planned to retire at 60 and did so just a little ahead of schedule at the annual meeting in 1968.

General Managers, as contrasted with Chief and Deputy Chief General Managers, were now no longer included in the small executive officer group. However, the title of General Manager was still one of importance and in 1968 there were nine GMs, three in Corporate Administration in Toronto, four as Canadian regional heads, and two as heads of external regions. Another interesting event which took place in 1968 in top management was the return of Bell to the executive offices from Jamaica. He had received an attractive offer from a major international corporation but had decided to stay with the Bank, even though at that time he did not enjoy Nicks's highest regard. On his return he was made General Manager, Metropolitan Toronto Region. Then as Deputy Chief General Manager, he was first in charge of Personnel, where the prescription for the job was for a "strong line man"; and later, in addition, in charge of Administration. Bell was used to hard work and this was hard work with a vengeance.

MANAGEMENT IN PLACE FOR A DECADE

Events moved quickly, and in 1970 Crockett became President, while Nicks remained Chairman and Chief Executive Officer. As noted earlier, Ritchie moved up to become Chief General Manager and McDonald became head of International. As a matter of fact, when

Nicks died at the beginning of 1972, the top management for most of the rest of the decade was in place, with the exception of Ritchie and Bell moving up a notch further.

CONTINUED SOLID GROWTH IN DOMESTIC BUSINESS

During this period of six years, from 1965 to 1971, the Bank's domestic business continued to grow at the average real rate of 7 per cent noted earlier, despite the drag resulting from the delay until 1967 in revising the Bank Act. To some extent the removal of the 6 per cent ceiling had been anticipated in the sense that the banks narrowed their margins in some cases in an effort to retain business until the change came, and margins did improve after the revision was enacted. The increase in rates offered to depositors after the Bank Act was revised was substantial and immediate. As Touchie put it, "With provisions for removal of the unrealistic lending rate ceiling and for a net lowering of non-earning cash reserve requirements, the banks were able to introduce a more competitive structure of deposit facilities and rates."[4]

The economic climate was quite favourable except for mounting inflation. In 1966, Nicks expressed the view that Canada could keep inflation reasonably in hand but, as time went on, the acceleration of government spending undermined his confidence and suggested to him that Canada might experience the worst of both worlds: rising prices and slow growth. Had it not been for the pressure of the Vietnam war on the U.S. economy, it might have been difficult to sustain the value of the Canadian dollar.

However, a few years later, in 1969, restraint was strongly applied in the monetary field, and to a significant degree in government spending. In 1970, Nicks questioned whether restraint could be sustained without incurring unacceptable costs of both a social and a political nature. He went on to observe that "We thus had to return to expansive policies before we could be fully sure of convincing the general public that it is not possible to get 10% per annum wage and salary increases out of an economy whose productivity goes up about 3% per year. Even in recent months, large unions have continued to press for excessive wage and salary settlements at a time when friends and neighbours have been out of work because of economic pressures set in motion by inflation itself."[5]

SCOTIA PLAN: THE PACE SETTER

Scotia Plan set the pace in the growth of the Bank's Canadian assets in the mid-sixties. There was some slackening in the rate of increase in 1969 and at the annual meeting that year, Crockett pointed out that in keeping with anti-inflation policies "we have not advertised our very efficient Scotia Plan Loan facilities through press, radio or T.V. for more than two years."[6] Scotia Plan growth picked up nicely again in 1970, making a five-year average gain of 17 per cent per annum. At the 1970 annual meeting Ritchie added, "It is our feeling...that relatively low-cost consumer credit" – and it was low at that time – "is just as much a mainstay of the modern economy as commercial credit, because there would be no adequate market for consumer durable goods in the absence of appropriate credit facilities. This Bank has been, and intends to remain, one of the dominant factors in the consumer credit market in Canada."[7] And so it did, accounting for well over 20 per cent of the consumer credit loans provided by the banks in this country.

Residential-mortgage lending also increased notably in the late sixties, rising more rapidly on a percentage basis than Scotia Plan lending and reaching a total by 1971 almost half as large. "Mortgage lending has caught on with our branch managers, and one of our great problems this year was to accommodate to the best of our ability the tremendous pressure put on us by our branches and regions for funds to supply their local markets," said Ritchie at the 1971 annual meeting. "During the year we revised upwards our allocations for the mortgage market on a number of occasions, and we have entered the new fiscal year with a declared intention to maintain the pace of our activity."[8]

EMPHASIS ON LENDING TO PEOPLE

Actually, the Bank's lending to individuals (including Scotia Plan, mortgages, and other personal loans) grew considerably more than its loans to business, and in contrast to the banking system as a whole, the Nova Scotia in its domestic operations was lending more to people at the beginning of the seventies than to businesses. As for business lending, growth was moderate from 1965 to 1970, but the proportion of medium and smaller loans to the total increased while that of larger loans – over $5 million each – declined. This probably reflected the Bank's efforts to develop its term lending to smaller business. As Touchie put it at the end of 1967, "The withdrawal of the distorting influence of the lending rate ceiling together with new authority to accept mortgage security under the revised Bank Act have enabled us to move towards a more rational balancing of all our costs and charges and as well to undertake much-needed improvements in our commercial lending services."[9] The following year, Crockett announced "a carefully planned program of term lending, which should improve our ability to meet the financial needs of borrowers, particularly those who do not yet require term funds in amounts normally obtainable through public issue."[10]

A SATISFACTORY LIQUIDITY RATIO

By 1971, it was true that the Bank's liquid asset ratio, applicable to its Canadian business, was relatively low compared with most of the banking system – about 25 per cent compared with an average of 30 per

The 1967 Bank Act revision opened the way for greater bank participation in the mortgage market and Scotiabank expanded this aspect of its personal banking services.

cent, or in 1970 about 26 per cent as against 28 per cent. With its lower ratio of large corporate loans and, what really matters, its lower ratio of large corporate lines of credit which are available on demand, potential calls on liquidity were relatively less than those in the whole system. Moreover, with a growing cash flow from repayments on its large portfolio of Scotia Plan loans and mortgages, the Bank's liquidity position was really better than comparison of the crude figures would suggest. Corrective action was therefore not considered necessary.

BRANCH GROWTH SPURTS IN 1969-1970

Branch expansion carried on at about the same rate in the latter part of the sixties as earlier, though it shot upward for two years, 1969 and 1970, at least partly in response to the enthusiasm of the new Chief General Manager, Crockett. Indeed, the number of branches opened in 1969 constituted a record, 55, of which 44 were in Canada and 11 were abroad. The head of a competing bank phoned Crockett and said, "How did you do it? You must have scraped the bottom of the barrel." "Yes," said Crockett, "we surely did," and proceeded to open 38 more in the next year.

Following this spurt, branch openings slackened again, settling at their earlier rate of around 25 a year. Many of the new branches were additional branches in the larger metropolitan areas: from 1965 to 1971, Montreal and Calgary were up 6 each; Edmonton 5; Winnipeg and Hamilton 4 each; Regina and Saskatoon 3 each; and Vancouver, St. John's, Victoria, and Windsor, Ontario, 2 each. The largest advance, as usual, was in the greater Toronto area, with 24 new branches, which carried the total for this metropolitan area to over 130 branches. In terms of economic regions, Ontario, Alberta, and British Columbia led the expansion, but there were sizeable advances in Quebec, Nova Scotia, and Newfoundland as well.

COSTS PUSHING UP

Adding more branches, while helpful, was not the only key to profitability. Costs were inexorably pushing upward. Though inflation made the total figures much bigger, it gradually tended to compress margins, partly because the proportion of current-account free balances and low-interest savings accounts to total deposits was decreasing notably, and partly because customer resistance to service charge increases seemed to grow as inflationary pressures intensified. In any case, there was a great need to improve efficiency. Better management and the most effective use of computers were at the top of the list.

GENERAL OFFICE METHODS GROUP

As noted in the previous chapter, an organization known as the General Office Methods Group (GOMG) had been set up in 1964 with Gibson's support and Ritchie's strong approval when the latter was Assistant General Manager, Administration. This group, which was advised by outside consultants, was examining the basic organizational structure of the Bank in depth. They were not merely looking at better ways of carrying out existing routines. Rather, they were trying to determine the objectives and functions of each department, and to see not only whether the objectives were still appropriate to the needs of the Bank, but also whether, even if they were appropriate, they were being carried out in an efficient manner and in the right part of the organization. The Steering Committee of GOMG consisted of Ritchie, MacDonell (Methods Department), and W. P. Meinig (then Chief Accountant, later Comptroller, and now Senior Vice-President, Ontario), and the working group of J. B. McCaig, L. A. Shaw (later Senior Vice-President, Canadian Commercial Banking), G. W. Thompkins, and B. E. Falle.

One of the first things the group proposed, and which was implemented, was the establishment of an International Credit Division. Then they took a look at the split in the Chief Accountant's Department between the accounting function and the variety of special activities which the Department had taken on in the preceding ten years. They also considered the possibility of putting together the Chief Accountant's and Comptroller's Departments, and proposed a way of doing so, only to be frustrated by the lack of any strong support for such action now that Ritchie had been promoted to head up International and was no longer in charge of Administration. As a matter of interest, the recommendation was finally carried out in the mid-seventies.

Another major proposal, which was postponed for almost a decade because of high-level differences and inadequate support from the senior executives concerned, was that of bringing about closer co-ordination between the money market operations of the Investment Department and the money market and foreign exchange activities of International. A study was made of the Mortgage Department and as a result improvements in organization were implemented.

BUSINESS DEVELOPMENT IN THE FIELD

The big challenge was the organization of the credit function on a regional basis. The idea was to inject into credit a marketing thrust: the important job of going out to call on customers, or the business-development aspect. This was to be the responsibility of each region, along with its responsibility for credit. This was the origin of the district manager system – the division of regions into districts with their own leaders – which is now largely in effect. When the system was started, it was tried out in certain areas and the district managers were given responsibility for credit as well as business development. This proved to be too much of a workload, and business development suffered, with the result that the system that has now evolved assigns credit supervision to the regional offices, rather than to the district managers.

The General Office Methods Group (GOMG) was disbanded in 1969 simply because there was not the will or the drive to take it further. Jameson, who followed Ritchie on Administration, was so overloaded with special work for Nicks that GOMG appears to have become a rather low priority. Moreover, there was little active support higher up for some of the important changes suggested. It was not strong opposition that led to the closing down of GOMG, but rather a lack of willingness at the top to effect changes against the normal opposition of vested departmental interests. But the approach was a good one, and, despite its failures at the time, GOMG accomplished much. Moreover, some of the major issues which were not resolved then were eventually settled, generally as had been recommended.

LEARNING TO USE THE COMPUTER

Overlapping these moves to reduce costs and improve efficiency was a long-continued effort to make effective use of the computer. Computers did not provide immediate cost reduction because they were expensive, and, as the Bank and other businesses discovered, they required a lot of time and more than a few mistakes if the know-how to use them well was to be developed. But there was no dodging the need for computer development, since it was quite clear that without mastery of these machines, the time would come when a bank would no longer be competitive and would be faced with fearful costs in trying to catch up.

The first act in the computer drama was the setting up of a committee in 1964, an internal committee of the departments most interested, with the addition of a highly regarded outside expert. The Bank already had a small computer for certain specialized jobs, but it had now decided it wanted a large one for more general use. The committee's job was to recommend the purchase of the most suitable hardware. After a considerable period of investigation and discussion, a proposal was made and the Bank made the purchase from one of the leading manufacturers. The next act in the computer drama was the hiring of an expert computer man to head up the operation. Things did not go as well as had been hoped, and, for a variety of reasons, the expert left and another expert was hired. When the curtain next went up on Act III, a new computer manufacturer had come onstage and a difficult and expensive changeover was in progress. In the next act the second outside expert left. During the whole period of change, there was serious delay in arriving at profit-and-loss figures, as well as delay in getting good computer systems working in the Bank.

MAJOR CHANGES IN SYSTEMS

In 1969, in the final act of the play, computer operations were relocated in a new centre in Don Mills, Ontario – an essential move to procure the space needed and to set up a properly functioning organization. Then, in 1970, outside advisers were hired to work with a Bank group to straighten out the systems problem. At this time MacIntosh was in charge of systems planning and Meinig had been appointed General Manager, Systems. The exercise carried out was an exhaustive and exhausting one, mornings, afternoons, evenings, and most weekends, extending over the greater part of a year. The result was a Bank group, led by Meinig, who understood the problems and potentialities of the computer system in a way that had never been appreciated before. The exercise was also associated with one more change in the hardware manufacturer and service. Then came the decision to centralize processing in one big operation in Don Mills, and hook the regional computers into it with telephone lines. As future events demonstrated, there were a number of good decisions made at this time.

Looking back at the series of problems and mistakes, Meinig reflects

Automation has enabled Canada's chartered banks to provide their customers with one of the most efficient cheque-clearing systems in the world. High-speed cheque-sorting machines were introduced in the 1950s and newer models like the 3890 in the photograph can sort over two thousand items per minute.

CREDIT: HAROLD ARMITAGE

that "the mistake we made, initially and subsequently, was to try to bring in all the expertise and not try to train our own people. We should have been sending people out to systems schools and programming schools, people who understood the Bank and what the system was intended to do.... Our approach to managing systems design was lacking in terms of user support and user involvement in the design process.... I think the feeling was that you could hire outside expertise to get you from A to B. Ultimately, this problem was recognized and strong efforts were made to involve the user to the extent that the user now has final responsibility for acceptance of the final product."

BRANCH PERFORMANCE

One of the essentials of branch management, and indeed of profit planning, is to have some means of measuring how well a branch is using its staff. There had long been such a system, originally started by H.C. McLeod.* The backbone of this performance-measurement system now consisted of a quarterly staff return which endeavoured to keep track of the major components of work in a branch, and, when appropriately weighed, gave some idea of a branch's efficiency in its use of people. In 1966, it was decided to see if this system could be upgraded and outside consultants were hired. They investigated several branches, examining the details of various kinds of work and of customer service, and came to the conclusion that there were considerable economies to be made. This resulted in the Bank's decision to apply the consultant's standards in British Columbia. There was a lot of initial criticism, with the result that an audit was made of the system, which confirmed its suitability. Admittedly, efficiency was affected by the rate of turnover of staff and the experience of employees. But as a general test the system has been applied and has become an effective and important guide in management and consequently in contributing to earnings.

CANADIAN INSTITUTE OF BANKERS

MacIntosh's computer and investment responsibilities were only two of a number of his activities. With his background as an economist and his education at McGill and Cambridge, he was a frequent spokesman for the Bank on economic matters and he was involved in the education of bankers, placing a great deal of emphasis on the necessity of knowing about the society in which we live. He could be quite outspoken and seldom indulged in the kind of reserve for which bankers are known. In any case, he was one of the founders of the Institute of Canadian Bankers and was its first Chairman. What the Institute did when it came into being in 1967 was to define the educational needs of young

R.M. MacIntosh,
Executive Vice-President,
1972-1980

CREDIT: V. TONY HAUSER

* See Chapter 6.

bankers and to sponsor suitable courses in each university. The Institute has received co-operation from most Canadian universities and 10,000 students a year are now registered – much the largest adult-education group in the country.

A NEW DRIVE IN QUEBEC

The operating head of the Institute in its early days was a French-speaking Canadian from Laval University, André Bisson. He and MacIntosh worked well together and the result of that excellent relationship was an invitation to Bisson to become the regional head of the Bank in Quebec. In his annual speech in 1970, Nicks had emphasized the Bank's interest in Quebec and had commented on "the difficult set of interlocking social and economic problems with which that province is confronted." He admitted that "this Bank is generally considered to be an English-speaking institution," but he went on to point out that "the fact is that we have over seventy branches in the Province of Quebec, over half of which are managed by French-speaking officers. We are actively planning the development of new branches and it is our intention to acquire and train an increasing proportion of our staff in Quebec from those of the French language."[11]

Bisson accepted the invitation to join the Bank and he is now Vice-President and General Manager, Quebec. At the next annual meeting, in 1971, Ritchie noted that the Bank's share of the Quebec market was "somewhat less than proportionate to our share of the whole Canadian market." Then he went on to say, "As evidence of our serious intentions, we have this year engaged a highly regarded French-Canadian as senior officer in the Province of Quebec, and he is charged with the responsibility of greatly improving our bilingual capacity throughout the Province."[12]

QUALITY CONTROL OF LOANS

In the central realm of credit administration, probably the most important change was the development of what might be described as quality control of the regional credits. In 1965, Younker started his reviews of regional credits going right down to $40,000 or $50,000 and visiting each regional centre. Later on, other senior men, often former regional heads, like Hutchinson and Archibald, would also do the job. It was a quick review designed to find the weak accounts and followed by on-the-spot discussion of the reviewing officer's report with the credit supervisors concerned. For weak accounts, monthly reports of action taken and progress made were required until the problems had been corrected.

Another significant change was the union of eastern and western credits in one location in General Office under Younker. This improved administration and led to the opening of a special-projects desk under

G.C. Hitchman,
Executive Vice-President,
1972-1974;
Deputy Chairman,
1974-1981.

CREDIT: V. TONY HAUSER

J. W. Chisholm, which dealt with larger credits of an unusual or particularly difficult character and, as time went on, the desk also generated new lending plans.

CREDIT MEETINGS

The credit meetings continued as before, though the personnel changed. In his time, Nicks presided at only some of the meetings, with Calder or Boyles often taking his place. In Gibson's time, Gibson was away a good deal and Hitchman, Touchie, and Ash were permitted to make decisions jointly, unless they felt the decisions should be referred to Gibson or Boyles. By the late sixties, Hitchman was chairman of the meeting, with Younker as his first lieutenant.

Hitchman had become the Bank's senior credit man and indeed may be said to have occupied that position from the middle sixties until his retirement in 1981. An enthusiastic and hard worker, he enjoyed a remarkable capacity not only for judging credits but for putting them together in a way that would result in success for the customer and for the Bank. There were few if any bankers whose judgment could be trusted more. His experience in Montreal, western Canada, and indeed all over the country with most of the Bank's larger customers combined with his native shrewdness and perception to produce an unusually able banker.

In the realm of personnel, the Bank was making progress with its problems in the sense that the shortage was less acute and the organization a good deal better. Late in the sixties, the personnel function became a double-headed arrangement, much as it is today when day-to-day operations are the responsibility of one person and manpower planning that of another. Better procedures were put in place for obtaining staff from the universities and business schools and more attention was given to their development on joining the staff. There was still a real problem of absorption, of which more will be said in the next chapter.

GROWTH OF ECONOMICS DEPARTMENT

In the Economics Department, F.L. Rogers succeeded Dr. Lucy Morgan, who had died suddenly in 1960. A thorough worker, well balanced in his approach, Rogers developed an excellent reputation in Canada as a business economist and expanded the Economics Department to meet the growing need for its services, not least of which were the increasingly complex and detailed requirements of profit planning and the widening needs of International for country and financial information. Indeed, these international needs and the better possibility of employing qualified personnel led to the establishment of an economics position in London, England, and the hiring by Rogers of a number of able British economists who have since done well in the Bank.

A Full-fledged International Bank, 1966 – 1971

REVIVING THE PAST

In this era of change, one successful effort was made to revive the past. The Financial Hockey League of Toronto, consisting of teams from all the large banks and the National Trust Company, renewed its activities in 1964 and the Bank proceeded to win the championship in the first year. Among the Bank's outstanding players were W.D. Armstrong, now district manager, Toronto Suburban Region; G.N. Hway, who has become Assistant General Manager, Canadian Commercial Banking; and D. R. German, recently appointed agent in Atlanta.

NOTES

1. BNS Annual Report, 1970, Chief General Manager's Report, p.17.
2. BNS Annual Report, 1971, Chief General Manager's Report, p.17.
3. BNS Annual Report, 1963, President's Report, p.10.
4. BNS Annual Report, 1967, Chief General Manager's Report, p.15.
5. BNS Annual Report, 1970, Chairman's Report, p.7.
6. BNS Annual Report, 1969, Chief General Manager's Report, p.16.
7. BNS Annual Report, 1970, Chief General Manager's Report, p.16.
8. BNS Annual Report, 1971, Chief General Manager's Report, p.16.
9. BNS Annual Report, 1967, Chief General Manager's Report, p.16.
10. BNS Annual Report, 1968, Chief General Manager's Report, p.19.
11. BNS Annual Report, 1970, Chairman's Report, p.13.
12. BNS Annual Report, 1971, Chief General Manager's Report, p.20.

13

The Changing Face of Banking
1971-1981

Because of the variety of developments and the major changes in banking philosophy and organization, the decade of the 1970s is dealt with in two chapters. The present chapter is largely concerned with the consequences of the computer, improved organization, and the changing philosophy of banking. Chapter 14 covers the same ten years but concentrates on the international business and the physical growth of the Bank.

The team that was to be responsible in the period of extraordinary change and burgeoning growth in the 1970s was already pretty much on the field. Nicks's death in early 1972, which was quite unexpected, did in fact occur at just about his normal retirement age. The Board elected Boyles in Nicks's place as Chairman and Chief Executive Officer and Crockett carried on as President. After the annual meeting in December 1972, Ritchie was elected President and Chief Executive Officer while Crockett became Deputy Chairman. Boyles continued as Chairman until 1974, when he retired, and Ritchie then became Chairman, President, and Chief Executive Officer.

THE NEW CHIEF GENERAL MANAGER

Meanwhile, when Ritchie was appointed President, Bell had become Chief General Manager, the operating head of the Bank. An intense and determined worker, he had joined the Bank almost by accident. Having decided not to attend university but to look for a job, he met, quite by chance in Toronto, an old family friend from the days when he lived in St. John's, Newfoundland. To use Bell's own words:

> It was the Hon. J.S. Curry, publisher of the *Daily News* in St. John's. When I was a youngster I knew this man and I thought he was quite a great man. So here I am standing on the corner of King and Bay and

J.A.G. Bell,
Chief General Manager,
1972 to Present;
Executive Vice-President,
1972-1979;
President,
1979 to Present;
Deputy Chairman,
1982.

I see this man coming down the street. I go up to him and tell him who I am and recall the fact that he had been very kind to me as a boy in my stamp-collection activities. And by gosh he wanted to talk to me. He said, "Look, I've got to go to the bank and get some money. Will you wait for me? We'll have a coffee or something and we'll talk." I thought this was quite marvellous. So he went into the manager's office, and I was standing outside waiting, and a chap by the name of Cal Hutchinson [at that time accountant, Toronto branch; later, AGM in charge of British Columbia] came up to me and asked me if there was anything he could do for me. And I said "Not unless you can give me a job." So by the time Mr. Curry got out of the manager's office, having gotten a cheque cashed, I had a job working for The Bank of Nova Scotia.

In short order Bell found himself at Queen & Church branch in Toronto, where, in due course, he received intensive and very useful training in credit analysis and business repair from the manager, J.S. Clinch (later AGM in charge of British Columbia, preceding Hutchinson), largely because he had the same habit as Clinch of getting into the office at 7 a.m. After some time spent as General Manager's clerk and then as a member of the inspection staff, Bell was transferred to London, England, as a business-development man under Crockett. Crockett, who desperately needed support in this area, was not impressed with Bell's qualifications, which for the job were very limited, and he made this clear. Bell responded to Crockett's concern by announcing that he would leave if there were any complaints at the end of three months.

"Well!" recalls Crockett, "It didn't take me long to realize I had a tiger by the tail." From then on, Bell moved quickly – assistant manager, Toronto, and manager at Halifax and Ottawa – and his last job before returning to Toronto was Managing Director of The Bank of Nova Scotia Jamaica Ltd. Alert, perceptive, courageous, and a bit impatient, he tended to complement Ritchie.

THE REST OF THE MANAGEMENT TEAM

Boyles, with his encyclopedic knowledge of every nook and cranny of the Bank and his incredible memory for customers and their successes and problems, continued to be an important member of the management team. Though he lessened his pace when Ritchie took over as President, he still did a good deal of travelling internationally. The remainder of the team at this time consisted of Crockett on business development and management, Hitchman mainly on credit, MacIntosh immersed in computers, investments, and education, and McDonald steering the great ship "International."

COMPUTERIZED BANKING

Probably the most important and urgent job facing the Bank at this time was the completion of its mastery of the computer – a revolutionary development in banking which has been compared to the replacement of the telephone operator by the automatic exchange. In some fundamental respects it was an even more far-reaching revolution, since, as well as making possible the handling of a rapidly growing volume of business, it opened the door to the introduction of new and more complicated services, which were out of the question earlier.

As noted in the previous chapter, the Bank got off to a rather uncertain start in the computer world, but finally made good progress when a major effort was mounted under the leadership of MacIntosh. As he puts it:

> In a few years we went from the rear of the pack to leadership in some parts of the business. The first big thing to happen was to move the Systems Department out of downtown Toronto where it was completely constrained. The next thing was to hire first-class consultants. We created a systems planning steering committee in which a number of senior officers, including the Chief General

Manager, participated and which gave guidance to the whole program and linkage between the Systems Department and the users.

The other two big decisions involved centralized processing, mentioned earlier, and the purchase of equipment from *one* supplier, as far as practicable.

THE BANK JOINS CHARGEX

Well before the computer plans had been fully implemented, the Bank decided to join Chargex, the consumer credit-card organization now known as VISA. "This decision," Ritchie reported in 1972, "was made after an extensive period of fact-finding and analysis, and also with a view to participating in the future development of cashless payment techniques. We concluded that the rapid advance of technological change required a co-operative effort, and that this could only be made feasible by joining those banks with a proven success in the field."[1]

Neither The Bank of Nova Scotia nor the Bank of Montreal had joined with the group of four banks which had started the Chargex system in 1966. When the Nova Scotia decided to become a member of the group in 1973, it had to pay a sizeable entrance fee. But, as it turned out, there were some advantages. "Because we joined the Chargex group relatively late," Bell remarked in 1974, "we were able to take advantage of the most recent technology and therefore to achieve a relatively efficient organization in a short time. We have already exceeded our expectations as to share of market."[2] The move into Chargex was a major undertaking. M.N. Logan, now General Manager, Personal Banking, who with W.E. Bailey, now director of administration, Toronto Regions, did most of the planning, had an eight-by-eight-foot chart identifying 280 separate procedures which in one way or another related to the introduction of Chargex. The Systems people in the midst of all their new activities had to add a major new system in very short order. Remarkably, the entire job from the point of non-existence to full operation was accomplished in six months!

By 1974, when J.F. Crean succeeded Meinig as head of the Systems Department, tremendous strides had been made. Some 600 branches had computerized their demand-deposit accounting and 150 branches had terminals for savings accounts. Scotia Plan was now on the computer, and commercial banking information was becoming increasingly available over a widening area. Moreover, the "BNS Systems Department had gained a reputation," in the words of MacIntosh, "which attracted good-quality computer people." "You had to learn another language," says Meinig, who, with a number of other Bank employees, met the qualifications to enter this new technical world. "Eventually, within a year or so, you are using the language in conversation. You had to do that because that was the normal language for those people to use, and many times using just one word would explain a process."

Scotiabank's VISA authorization system is one of the fastest in the country. The system handles both on-line verification of accounts and input of batch data. Operators may choose to work in either English or French or both.

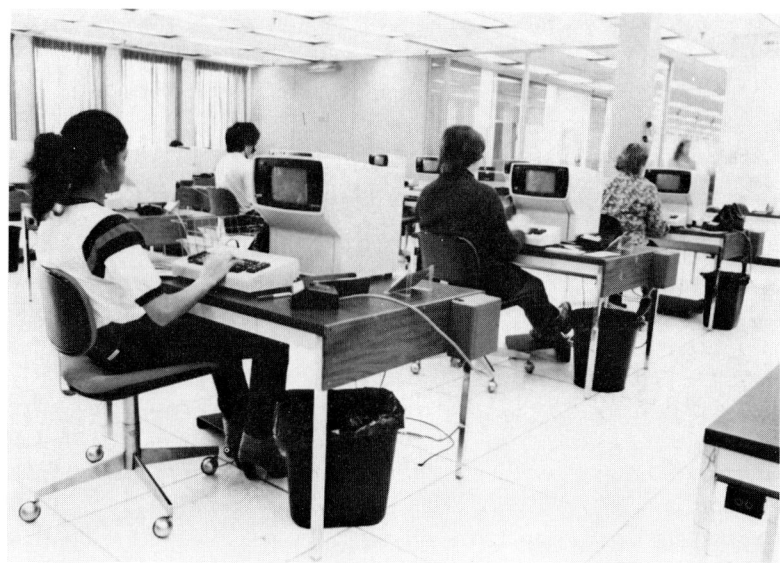

Computing Site 1.

Through these terminals, operators in the network control centre monitor the health of the central processing facilities of the on-line banking system.

CREDIT: HAROLD ARMITAGE

SYSTEMS – A MAJOR DEVELOPMENT

The workload of the Systems Department, which is now known as the Operations Department, was growing by 30 to 40 per cent per annum during the seventies and by the end of 1981 it had become extremely large, involving approximately 2,000 people. As of that date, the branch network had a total of nearly 6,000 on-line computer terminals. All the 1,027 Canadian branches (with the single exception of Churchill Falls in Labrador) were on line for savings accounts and demand-deposit accounting, and half the branches were capable of providing information on commercial loans with on-line equipment. As well, 99 per cent of all the Canadian branches had their Scotia Plan loans processed on a batch computer system.

At first, in the late sixties, the Department consisted of a relatively small group of creative people building a technological machine that was sorely needed. When Crean took over in 1974, the Department was already quite large and of necessity it was becoming more controlled. "Hopefully," says Crean, "you don't stifle creativity but you build your systems within very well-defined guidelines. So things become structured, more planned."

Systems are seldom perfect. In Crean's words, "You don't always have good internal disciplines. Sometimes when a system is installed, you find that the user has not been very good in specifying what he wants. The systems people may not have been able to get inside his mind, sometimes because his mind is fuzzy as to what he really wants." To overcome this persistent problem an effort is made to split it into two separate parts, involving the user on the one hand and the systems programmer on the other hand. "You have people who are very sound conceptually, and more and more that requires senior management in the actual operating department to be conceptually sound. And then they lay it out in a form of English which is clear and unambiguous. Once that's been done, it's a fairly easy step to translate it into clear specifications for programmers."

The development of Systems made possible a number of new services. One of these was Scotiafund Retirement Savings Plan, which, taking advantage of the income-tax provisions of the Registered Retirement Savings Plan (RRSP), offered customers an investment choice of a retirement deposit or a common stock fund. Another service, the Consolidated Cash Plan, combined cash balances for businesses operating in more than one centre, providing them with single nation-wide figures, thus saving them interest.

INSPECTION AFFECTED BY COMPUTER

One of the areas most affected by computer use has been the Inspection Department. The purpose of inspection is still the same – to see that the assets are there, properly accounted for, that systems are in order, that the policies of the Bank are carried out, and that staff members are performing satisfactorily. But, over time, the purpose has broadened. As D.R. McFarlane, the Chief Inspector, points out, more attention is now paid to improved methods and procedures, to good management, and to business development. The department has a more positive attitude. Inspection is still a surprise audit, and it still focusses on good housekeeping, but now there is more emphasis on performance and how to improve it. And this change is at least partly the result of the computer, which has shifted the accounting work from the branch to the computer centre and which can provide a full statement almost immediately.

Of course, the computer programming must be checked and there are standard procedures which can be built upon, but these procedures cannot be changed without major adjustments. A good deal of lead time is needed to install new systems. However, the operation has much improved. There is more time for thoughtful assessment of the branch's position. Another by-product of computerization is that the Inspection Department is an even better training ground than it used to be, and it will be remembered that many senior officers, including Nicks and Ritchie, acquired useful experience on the inspection staff. In addition, the Department can now be used to give a new senior employee a picture of how branch banking works, as was the case with the present Comptroller and Chief Accountant, J.K. Mitchell, who came to the Bank from the outside business world. It is also becoming a useful avenue for introducing employees with Master of Business Administration degrees to banking.

OBTAINING THE RESULTS PROMPTLY

Needless to say, the Comptroller and Chief Accountant's Department has also been much affected by the computer. It has still the same basic job of watching the progress and health of the body – the branches – and reporting on it to General Office and then back to the branches. The work now under way to automate the Canadian branch general ledger and to extract financial information centrally will be finished by 1983, and then for the first time it will be possible to follow the progress of the branches steadily and to avoid that vacuum which is faced now in the latter part of each quarter. In the words of Mitchell, "We are striving for a better information set-up for General Office and for the people who are running the regions so they can be up-to-date with what's going on."

TECHNOLOGY FOR INTERNATIONAL

Computerized services were of interest, of course, in every part of the Bank and in many cases were almost essential. A major example of a division requiring these necessary services was International; here the computer provided the technological base needed by its widespread operation. At times, convincing was necessary – Meinig remembers some vivid arguments on the subject between Godsoe and MacIntosh. Nevertheless, systems were set up to keep track of funds gathering so that the Bank's representatives could know where they stood at the present time rather than relying on notes on the backs of envelopes or cigarette packages. International's loan funding was brought into the system as well. Finally, foreign exchange was also included, enabling the chief trader to ascertain his position at any given moment, a capability which turned out to be of great value in some of the widely fluctuating markets in the years that followed.

GROWING INSTABILITY AND GATHERING INFLATION

Though the Bank grew rapidly in the seventies, the basic economic environment in which it operated was highly unstable and strongly inflationary. By enormously increasing the supply of Eurodollars, OPEC created a great deal more international banking business. The huge balance-of-payment surpluses of the Arab countries and their associates were there to be financed and they were needed by many countries of varying credit qualifications. But from every other point of view, OPEC's policies spelled trouble, except to its members. Suddenly, oil cost a great deal more, and every importing country was faced with two problems: one, how was the necessary extra foreign exchange to be found to pay for oil? and two, how was the extra burden to be shared within the importing country?

The way in which these problems were handled had a great deal to do with the state of the world economy for years to come. West Germany and Japan bit the bullet relatively quickly and followed strict policies of retrenchment to make the adjustment. The United States hesitated for quite a while and then through 1979 and 1980 adjusted to the realities of the high world price of oil. Canada has only recently decided on a policy of price adjustment which could drag out the price increases for some years to come, though much of the catch-up is likely to occur by 1983 with material inflationary consequences up to that time.

"ARE CANADIANS REALLY FACING THEIR PROBLEMS?"

Canada had done reasonably well, economically speaking, in the early seventies and it was in 1974 that, after pointing to the major world problems of recession, and oil and food shortages, Ritchie went on to say, "Canada is perhaps the most fortunate of all the major countries of the world in the two key problem areas of food and energy....this should continue to cushion the severity of the country's own adjustments, but what is perhaps more important is the opportunity it gives us to exert some constructive influences on the mutual problems that are now confronting the whole world."[3] But later in the same speech he questioned whether Canadians were really facing their problems: "...can one really take much gratification from our pattern of labour-management relations, of federal-provincial give-and-take, or of wage and price performance?...Are we yet awake to the common problems with which we are confronted in the energy sphere in particular?"[4] Sad to relate, the same questions can be raised with as much or more urgency eight years later.

FORCES BEHIND ONGOING INFLATION
LARGELY OF OUR OWN DOING

In 1975, Ritchie went on to point out that "the forces now contributing to the *ongoing* inflation in Canada are largely of our own doing....it should now be apparent that it is just not possible to achieve any meaningful moderation in the rate of Canada's price advance without a roughly equivalent moderation in the average percentage increase in wages and salaries."[5] It was at this time that the government introduced wage and price guidelines, the essential rationale for which in Ritchie's view was that they should facilitate "a *side-by-side* moderation without the necessity for a wrenching period of unemployment and of idle capacity." He went on to add, however, that the guidelines program "would appear more compelling with a greater display of moderation and restraint in basic aspects of the Government's own operations."[6]

INFLATIONARY INFLUENCE IN BANKING

As is evident from the record, the banks still did reasonably well in this disturbed and inflationary environment. There was some pressure on margins domestically, and higher interest rates were having restraining effects on some types of projects. However, spending remained high. The country was living beyond its means by borrowing heavily abroad, and government and consumer spending continued to increase, as did certain types of investment, such as that in electric power capacity and other energy resources. In addition, the inflationary sentiment continued to show itself in growing real-estate borrowing, in a greater tendency to speculate on inventories, and in decisions to go ahead with capital projects on the grounds that they would be sure to cost more later.

These tendencies became more evident as the decade progressed, and towards the end of the seventies additional and more disturbing consequences, including a rash of takeovers, became apparent. However, there was no lessening in the demand for credit – in fact, quite the reverse. It was becoming more and more difficult to raise money in the capital markets and more expensive inventories and larger receivables had to be financed. As a result, the demands on the banks mounted.

LOANS GREW SUBSTANTIALLY

In the Nova Scotia, loans of most kinds grew substantially in the first half of the decade. Scotia Plan as usual led the parade and increasing emphasis was placed on family banking – basically on personal loans and mortgages. There was a heavy demand for most kinds of business loans, big and small, and the Bank made a continuing effort to see that the needs of smaller customers were reasonably met. This involved, on several occasions, steering larger customers into the money market to borrow via commercial paper or through bankers' acceptances. In some cases, it led the Bank to obtain additional Canadian funds by borrowing from its foreign currency division on a fully hedged basis or, if more suitable to the borrower, by having him borrow U.S. funds. Tight money, or as it was now called, "restraint of the money supply," made money more expensive if not harder to obtain. But the system was flexible and, at a price or an additional risk, such as borrowing in U.S. funds, money was quite readily available.

ALL THE BANKS DEVISING NEW APPROACHES TO CUSTOMERS

Actually, the banking system remained highly competitive. All the banks were looking for good lending opportunities, and were devising new approaches to their customers. In the Nova Scotia's case, several new plans and organizations were set up. The BNS Mortgage Corporation was established as a new vehicle to gather funds for mortgage financing, and Scotia Covenants, in which at this time (1975) the Bank had a 49 per cent interest (later to become 100 per cent), also increased its mortgage financing considerably. Scotia Factors Limited was set up to assume credit risks on receivables and to administer credit and collections. Scotiafund Financial Services was expanded to include Registered Home Ownership Savings Plans (RHOSPs) as well as RRSPs, and the retirement savings arrangement provided an additional fixed-income investment fund. Scotia Club was set up as a new service, offering customers an all-inclusive personal banking package for a flat monthly fee. A new company, Scotia-Toronto Dominion Leasing, was established and became an active participant in leasing on behalf of the two banks. An income-tax advisory service that was offered on an experimental basis turned out to be unprofitable and was dropped.

Another interesting development was the Professional Business Loans Program. Originally conceived as a special term-financing plan for lawyers and chartered accountants, a group who might be expected to refer new customers to the Bank, the program was expanded to include doctors, dentists, and other professional self-employed people. In some respects the program worked well – a real effort was made with regard to chartered accountants by W.F. Ellis, Assistant General Manager of the Corporate Accounts Department – but as interest rates rose in the late seventies, fixed-rate term loans became increasingly unattractive to the Bank. At the time of its introduction, however, it must have looked very exciting, since one of the other Canadian banks copied the Nova Scotia's brochure word for word, changing only the name of the bank, and had it out on the street three weeks after the announcement of the Nova Scotia's program.

Of major importance, increasing attention was given to automobile financing through developing and marketing formal package-financing plans for dealers across the country and in 1980 a special automotive financing office was established in Toronto. Also important was the

The Scotia Farm Services program was launched to provide comprehensive financial services for farmers.

Bank's lending program for mobile homes – thus providing improved services to meet a considerable market need in the less developed parts of the country.

THE BANK'S FARM PROGRAM

One of the most interesting credit developments in the early seventies was the Bank's farm program. It was started in 1973 after a thorough study of possible approaches over a period of six months by the special projects desk in the Credit Department and an able agricultural specialist from Winnipeg. They explored the area, examined alternative approaches, and set out objectives. They concluded that the Bank's program would have to review the farmer's total needs for credit, not just a part of them, as, for example, was the case with Farm Improvement Loans, which the Bank had been making periodically for a good many years. They also concluded that the Bank should hire agrologists – not to go out and make loans themselves but to help to train managers in farm areas to do so. In this way, a greater volume of business better integrated into the organization could be achieved, in contrast to some banks that left the whole farm loans business to specialists. The Bank now has nine trained farm representatives.

"We try to staff farm branches with managers who are knowledgeable in agriculture," says G. E. Chamberlain, Director, Agricultural Services. "One way of assisting the manager to gain the experience he needs is to have him accompany the regional agricultural specialist on farm calls. By doing so, the manager can learn the right questions to ask in assessing the viability of a farming operation and thereby build up his confidence and his ability to make farm calls on his own.... As part of his job, the agricultural specialist also provides input into the credit function. He does so by evaluating the management ability of the farm customer. For example, if the farmer is a dairyman, the agricultural specialist can advise the credit officer whether the herd can generate the income necessary to carry the loan, on the basis of the calibre of the cows and how they are being fed and maintained."

"TO FACILITATE THE WHOLE OPERATION"

The idea was to facilitate the farmer's whole operation. In conjunction with its loans, the Bank offers a quarterly newsletter prepared jointly by Agricultural Services and the Economics Department, which discusses trends in farming and useful financial ideas. The continuing revolution in agriculture, which has increasingly made farming a commercial business, has attracted more young people and has developed larger and larger units, an indication of which is the fact that the Bank now has around seventy farm-loan accounts of over a million dollars each.

INFLATION – CHECKED A LITTLE, THEN FULL SPEED AHEAD

It is true that in the mid-seventies the recession in the United States and the imposition of wage and price controls at home checked the momentum of inflation in Canada – but not very much and not for very long. Whatever was gained during that period was lost by the end of the decade. Aware of the underlying power of inflationary forces, Ritchie commented in 1976 that "it would be wise... to be a little on the slow side this time, rather than too quick, in modifying the basic thrust of our... fiscal and monetary policy. Time and time again in the modern era, our biggest policy mistakes have been in moving too quickly into measures that turn out to be overly-expansive; and our biggest current need still is to solidify the progress thus far made not only in lowering the rate of wage and price advance but also in toughening up on government spending habits and business management practices." And going on to discuss the government paper *The Way Ahead* issued late in the same year, Ritchie added, "What is most disappointing about the Government's presentation... is its reluctance to face up to the way in which past broad financial policies in combination with those of other major countries have contributed to the continuous escalation of inflation."[7]

INFLATION LIFTS BUSINESS LOANS

For two or three years, the increase in domestic lending which took place was not unusual for a recovery period, though the rise was substantial. But as inflation regained momentum in 1979, business loans surged upward to meet requirements for higher-priced inventories, bigger dollar receivables, and more real estate lending. Takeovers were now also entering the scene.

In contrast to business lending, personal loans did not rise sharply and mortgage lending began to slacken in the face of soaring interest rates. Though it was still a "people" bank, the proportion of business lending rose significantly for the Nova Scotia. Businesses that could not raise funds in the bond market had to go somewhere, and there were few alternatives to the banks, who naturally wanted the protection of a variable interest rate, usually varying in relation to the prime lending rate.

COMPETITION FOR DEPOSITS

In the face of strong lending demands, the competition for deposits was very keen. Even in the early seventies, it became so severe, and interest rates rose to such an extent, that the banks at the suggestion of the Bank of Canada agreed to restrain their bidding for deposits, an arrangement known as the Winnipeg Agreement. Rates then levelled out and later, with recession in the United States, the pressure declined. Deposit banking had indeed become a rather different operation from what it had been ten years earlier. At that time deposits could be, and were in fact, attracted by means of better service and good salesmanship, with few changes in the rates paid. The Bank had had good success in building up personal deposits in this way, and a series of campaigns for the President's or the Chairman's Award, with prizes in the form of trips to the Caribbean, continued to produce useful results in terms of new accounts and positive staff morale.

What was different in the late seventies was the emphasis on rates. Depositors, like everyone else, were trying to protect themselves against inflation by obtaining the highest rates they could. Thus, a variety of new savings instruments, such as daily interest accounts, were developed; and some of the older instruments, particularly certificates of deposit and non-chequing savings accounts, became widely used. Customers' habits were gradually shifting to the practice of keeping small balances in current accounts and regular savings accounts and of putting as much as practicable into high-interest obligations. Such sales tools as "Hockey College" and "Scotia 59ers" were still effective in attracting customers in the young and the retired age groups, but the packages, including the rates, had to be competitive.

"Scotia Fifty-Niners" was introduced in 1976 to provide services to senior citizens at special rates.

CORPORATE TREASURERS LEAVE FEW BALANCES IDLE

The tendency to keep as small balances as possible had been long established in the business world. Corporation treasurers were in the habit of leaving few balances idle, unless the maintenance of a balance

Scotiabank Hockey College Team, Gander, Newfoundland, 1973.

Scotiabank Hockey College was started in 1971 and is designed to teach young customers two important habits – regular savings and good sportsmanship.

was part of a borrowing arrangement which, though common enough in the United States, was unusual in Canada. At the first hint of an inflow of funds, treasurers would look for the best deal they could find in the money market or from the banks or other financial institutions. Thus, when interest rates rose substantially and the effective use of funds became even more vital, a much larger and more sensitive market developed, which would determine what the banks would offer for short- and medium-term money.

The fuller development of the money markets, which could be either a source of funds or a destination for them, combined with the prevailing competitive atmosphere, brought about a profound change in the approach to banking. It opened the way to *liability* management in contrast to *asset* management. Now the approach was to borrow the funds required for the available lending opportunities – to take on the necessary additional liabilities – rather than to ration available funds among the varying lending demands. It was no longer the banks' practice to hold large portfolios of government securities as a tertiary reserve, as they had always done in the past. The banks came to rely increasingly on the market to supply funds for lending needs when these needs were profitable and to provide cash for unexpected demands as they occurred. A liquid reserve of cash and money market assets of about 15 per cent was considered to be adequate in the circumstances. And the fact that holdings of government bonds had been much reduced saved the banks heavy losses in the late seventies.

LIABILITY MANAGEMENT

The changeover to thinking in terms of liability management has not occurred overnight. As far back as 1958 the Bank had moved to take on a new form of liability – the term note, with a maturity of up to six years – in an effort to finance the growing volume of Scotia Plan loans. Faced with the choice, on the one hand, of cutting back on the new and profitable Scotia Plan or on other lending and, on the other, of finding additional funds, the Bank decided on the latter option. This emphasis on the liability side entailed making the effort and paying the cost of attracting more deposits – in short, increasing the Bank's liabilities.

The biggest push towards liability management, however, came in the international business. Here the Bank's efforts to obtain deposits were directly related to the lending opportunities available at the time and to the prospective spread between money costs and rates of return. Actually, almost half the assets of the Bank – the foreign currency assets – were already being handled on a liability-management basis when it was decided, in 1979, to adopt this policy for domestic purposes. It had been studied before. In 1972, R.M. Taylor, assisted by R.L. Brooks, had investigated the possibility, and the conclusion appeared to be that the time was not yet ripe, though the recommendations were in line with what was in fact carried out in 1979.

The Investment Department is now the liability-management department. It is no longer investing in government securities, certainly not in long-term ones, though it trades in them. It is now designated as the Bank's Canadian dollar treasury department. At any given time it tries to regulate the flow of money in relation to the Bank's needs. Every Thursday night, after the bank rate is set by the Bank of Canada, R.R. Holmes, General Manager in charge of the department, meets with Bell, Brooks, and others to set the rates on certificates of deposit and bearer deposit notes. On Monday, there is a meeting of the Policy Committee, consisting of those mentioned above, and, in addition, Ritchie, McDonald, Godsoe, and T.A. Healy, General Manager, Treasury Division. In addition to balancing the Bank's position, they decide whether the Bank should be moving shorter or longer, and they also are on the lookout for market opportunities.

IMPROVING ORGANIZATION

The pressure of rising costs, and the need to be an effective competitor, brought about considerable change in the organization of General Office. Apart from credit, which is discussed in more detail later, the changes affected three major areas: Finance and Administration, Marketing, and Operations. It may be remembered that the General Office Methods Group (GOMG) had come up with a number of proposals for improving organization in the late sixties, some of which had been adopted and some of which had been deferred. In the early seventies, a

Scotia Plan Loans launched a "We Approve" campaign in 1978 which was popular with both staff and customers.

group consisting of R.M. Taylor, Shaw, and Logan, together with outside consultants, made another study of organization. Though not much was done at the time, the theme of the study was that since the Bank could not change its customers, it had better organize itself around them: the personal or individual group of customers, the commercial group, and the big corporate group. In 1977, the validity of this approach was recognized in the development of a Personal Banking Department and in the separation from the main credit department of a special group known as Corporate Banking, to deal with big companies – Canadian multinationals, or American multinationals with operations in Canada.

The Personal Banking Department under Logan and the Marketing Department under L.R. Woolsey are, of course, closely related and together they might be more accurately construed as a marketing group. Operations, a new department started in 1980 under G.E. Hare, represents a major reorganization in the headquarters staff. Absorbing much of the work done by the Administration group, which included methods and procedures in the branches, regional offices, and General Office, taking over Purchasing and merging with Systems, the new Department is, in effect, responsible for the state of communications, systems, and work organization throughout the Bank. Hare, who is an expert in business organization, was for several years a part-time consultant to the Bank before joining the staff in 1977. He believed there were important savings to be made in the organization of work from the time the customer comes in until the time the work enters the computer system, and also from the time the work leaves the computer until it is returned to the customer. These are known as the front and back ends of the system. In our enthusiasm for technology, Hare says, the Bank has tended to forget the old methods and procedures which can still provide some important savings. There were also gains to be made in systematizing the older methods to take advantage of the technology available.

RESPONSIBILITIES OF THE OPERATIONS GROUP

To quote Hare on his job, "My operating group's responsibilities are from the time that the customer comes in with the transaction. It is up to us to process it in the most effective and efficient manner. The Marketing Department and the General Office departments in charge of product definition can say whether it's blue, or green, or yellow, and if they want to offer it in a special way, and how they want to price it. But once they have done that, then we will look at it and say if that's what you want, here is the most efficient way of processing it, here is the most effective way to meet the delivery schedules you want, the turnarounds you want. And then we try to drive the operating cost down on that."

Operations has its own five-year budget, set up as though "Operations" were a separate company; thus an accurate assessment can be made of its progress. What it is currently planning to do will save money by saving staff. Thus, the numbers of the Bank's staff should level out in the reasonably near future rather than continue the steady expansion of recent years. The biggest problem, in Hare's view, is not technology or return on investment. It is people, whose work will change, and particularly older people, who will often be uncomfortable or even embarrassed in changing to new and unfamiliar work.

Meanwhile, in the financial area, the continuing problem between the Chief Accountant's Department and the Comptroller's Department was cleared up, though not without some headaches caused by a decision to make the Comptroller responsible to the Chief Accountant when the two Departments thought they were of equal status or each superior to the other. In 1977, the two Departments were merged under one head, Brooks, with one deputy Chief Accountant and two deputy Comptrollers reporting to him, and this arrangement appears to have worked well.

CREDIT SUPERVISION – COST AND EFFECTIVENESS

There was not much change in the basic structure of credit supervision. Rising costs had become a major problem because decentralization had created new levels of supervision, which could be offset only very gradually by reduced supervision at General Office, or by greater efficiency in the whole operation. Though decentralization remained the accepted norm, the development of new lending and lending-related services, aided by the computer, sustained and increased the headquarters establishment. This latter trend was further strengthened by concern over the quality of credit and by the strength of the central credit machine in preserving itself.

Guided first by Hitchman and Younker and then by R.G. Gage, the commercial banking group coped not only with a rapidly growing volume of business, but also with the added credit demands generated by the developing, and now deeply ingrained, inflation, with its mounting effects on property values of all kinds. Credit was a much more complicated business than it used to be and standards and attitudes tended to change in a highly competitive environment. It was not surprising that quality control of loans through the whole system, initiated by Younker in the mid-sixties, was established in 1977 as a separate division of Canadian Commercial Banking known as "Loan Administration" under Gage. "The function of the loan auditor," says W.P. Penney (no relation to the earlier Guy Penney), who headed the department a year later, "is to be the eyes, and ears really, of the executive officers as to the adherence to Bank policies and the quality of the portfolio at the regional level....They look at all accounts over $50,000, every one of them."

In 1977, Canadian Commercial Banking, headed by C.F. Gill, a second-generation Scotiabanker, underwent a substantial reorganization and in 1979 credit arrangements were again changed. From then on, credit meetings were held, consisting of the head of the Department and the three newly appointed Senior Vice-Presidents, Meinig, J.F. McRae, and R.J. Kavanagh, who covered Ontario, the East, and the West, respectively.

In the same year, Ritchie commissioned L.A. Shaw to review the whole commercial credit organization. This was the third or fourth time that Shaw had been asked to do a study for Ritchie and the second for which he was later asked to carry out his own recommendations. In 1980, Shaw became head of Canadian Commercial Banking and began to put his ideas into practice. Increased emphasis was laid on the prompt turnaround of credit applications. In effect, applications that came in one day were replied to the next, and if that did not always happen, it certainly did the day after. In the early part of the morning, Shaw would peruse, with Meinig, Kavanagh, and Gill (who was now Senior Vice-President, Eastern Canada) the credits coming up under each of their jurisdictions; this review would be carried out on an individual basis since in the interest of saving time there was no longer a general meeting. These discussions would be completed by 11 a.m. when the Executive Committee met and could discuss any very large or unusual credits.

A FRESH LOOK AT CREDIT MANAGEMENT

Shaw was approaching the problem of credit management from a number of directions. One was that too many people were involved; in his words, "Here is a regional application coming to me with four signatures on it – there's an assistant administrator, an administrator, an Assistant General Manager, and there's the regional head. And I say that if you have one guy in this region to do the legwork – I don't care whether he is an assistant administrator, an administrator, or an Assistant General Manager – he and the regional head can sign, and that's enough." Shaw also believed there were significant economies in better communication. "I think as the computer system develops further, we can find better ways to communicate credit information from branches to regional offices and headquarters. You may well do it through a computer rather than type it out on paper and send it. The branch can put a balance sheet into a terminal – we can press a button here and have it printed out without moving any paper across the country. We are starting to do this." Another way of keeping costs in hand was by "having a better concentration of credit in commercial branches, where there are more people competent to deal with credit applications, so we shall get better input than we are getting now."

Shaw summed up by saying, "You have got to tackle your systems, you have got to tackle the quality and skills of the people concerned with credit, you have got to tackle the ways by which information is moved, and you have got to deal with some organizational issues such as handling the people who handle the paper.... If you do these kinds of things, then we should also be able to give higher credit limits and that again is another saving in overhead costs because fewer decisions come all the way to the top." It might also have been added, as did I.M. MacGregor, General Manager, Canadian Commercial Banking, in discussing how the writing of communications could be improved, "We are still a bank that deals in the written word and there could be some improvement in the way it is written. If you get a credit application and it makes sense, then it's a question of checking some of the figures and making a decision. But if you have to read a four-to-six-page communication which is not concise and clear, and perhaps confused, it slows up the process."

Shaw died at the age of forty-four in the summer of 1981. He came from Freeport, Nova Scotia, and was one of the promising members of the Bank's staff. In his energetic approach, he was reminiscent of an earlier staff member, Donald Gordon. Almost self-educated – he went to university at nights when working in MacIntosh's department – curious about everything, willing and able to complete new and difficult assignments, possessed of a capacity to see things in perspective, a forceful leader, and a likeable person, he is sorely missed.

SPECIAL ARRANGEMENTS FOR CORPORATE CREDIT

Another important credit development was the establishment of a new Department, Corporate Banking, under B.R. Birmingham in 1977. This Department was formed with the idea of providing headquarters service to larger corporations, generally companies which operated across the country and often internationally, whose needs were complicated, involving such matters as foreign exchange commitments, trading arrangements, and international credits. Some problems were experienced in fitting such corporate arrangements into the existing domestic credit structure and there were some management difficulties as well. Finally, however, the problems were solved by placing Birmingham in charge of the North American International Region, as well as of Corporate Banking, so that he would be in a position to deal with large American corporations as well as their Canadian subsidiaries. The arrangements appear to be working well, even though they involve a bridge from one major part of the Bank to another below the top level. Perhaps this is another indication supporting Shaw's view that procedures in the domestic and international areas are moving closer together.

Another way in which international and domestic banking are moving together has been through the establishment of International Banking Centres across the country. The purpose of these centres is to provide better foreign exchange services to customers and to make

Scotia Business Plan was introduced in 1980 to facilitate financing of equipment and machinery for businesses large and small.

widely available all forms of trade financing, including letters of credit. Working with the bank managers concerned, the trade-centre representative helps to arrange export financing and other external deals, thus providing the expertise which only the largest branches had before. There are now six such centres, from Halifax to Vancouver.

SCOTIA BUSINESS PLAN

In the closing years of the decade and into 1981, a number of new commercial banking activities were developed. The first in importance, starting in 1980, was Scotia Business Plan. Reminiscent in some ways of the original Scotia Plan, the operation started working in 40 so-called "hub" branches and was then expanded by the hiring of a substantial group of professionals (well over 100) from sales finance companies. In order to make prompt decisions on equipment financing and leasing, these experienced people were given appropriate limits, which, in relation to branch limits, often appeared to be high. The program broadens the range of bank lending and often brings with it other banking business. While substantial new business has been forthcoming, the amount would have been larger had it been possible to offer fixed interest rates instead of flexible ones in the last year and a half.

CASH MANAGEMENT BY COMPUTER

These new lending arrangements formed part of Commercial Banking Services headed by J.F. O'Donnell, General Manager. In this major division automobile finance, agricultural services, and cash management services were also included. The last-named enables a corporate customer to obtain directly and immediately on a video screen all his balances in all the branches of the Bank. Before the end of 1982, it will be possible for the customer not only to see his position on his video screen but also to transfer balances directly from one account to another. Commercial Banking Services are now in a position to review all the banking requirements of a commercial customer and to provide an economical and efficient plan of operation.

The development of such new services and the growth of existing ones have now led to an important change in organization. Beginning very recently, sales managers of Commercial Banking Services were appointed in each region to promote the sale of banking services in a co-ordinated and effective way. The new sales managers report to the appropriate regional Vice-President and have become members of the regional team. They work closely with the district managers and managers and they receive guidance and help, of course, from the experts at headquarters.

TREND TOWARDS DECENTRALIZATION SLOWING

But despite these changes, the strong trend towards decentralization appears to be slowing. Of course, the regional offices grew because business was growing notably – in terms of senior staff they more than doubled in size during the decade. And there was a further enhancement of titles; the regional head was now a "Vice-President and General Manager," rather than an "Assistant General Manager."

However, the senior supervisory personnel in headquarters grew even more rapidly. In the corporate administration in Toronto there were four times as many officers in 1980 with the title of Assistant

General Manager or higher as there were in 1970. Even if allowance is made for some inflation of titles, the increase in supervisory personnel in General Office was substantially more than in the regions, reflecting the appearance of more specialized departments as well as more credit supervision.

After the vigorous and sustained push towards decentralization in the late fifties and early sixties, the momentum gradually decreased and was almost lost by the early seventies. As Brooks says, "The Bank was trying again in the late sixties and early seventies to become more effective in decentralizing....there were a lot of loose ends and we were trying to build the systems to cover them effectively." Hitchman reflects that "the Bank had been evolving from a branch system to a regional system, but specialization was now working the other way." All those new headquarters departments with their expensive expertise and computer systems were not going to be reproduced in the field and the regional offices would be more dependent on headquarters. Ritchie was not too impressed with regional performance, and Bell was against further decentralization for the time being, believing the present to be "an era where greater efficiency would be obtained by the development of informational, transactional, and control systems best implemented by and directed from headquarters."

Still, real progress had been made. The regions had substantial discretion in lending, and in other areas, such as personnel, a workable decentralized system had been developed. The head of personnel in the region was not a directing arm of headquarters, but rather the expert who advised and assisted the regional authorities to whom he reported. As A.E. Taylor, now General Manager, Canadian Personnel – a man with a good deal of regional experience – puts it, "We have decentralized pretty effectively. The controls that we have, possibly with the exception of credit, work well. And if we had better credit resources in the region, we would be able to decentralize more."

Most of the people in the field would like higher credit limits. R.L. Mason, Vice-President and General Manager in British Columbia, like E.D. MacNevin, Vice-President and General Manager of Toronto Central Region, are inclined in this direction though they realize there are some real problems in raising credit limits. Others, like Gage, think the present limits are high enough and Shaw agreed with him. They may not be as high as those of some of the other banks, but the quality and growth of the Nova Scotia's loans compare favourably.

Meanwhile, in most areas, the process of decentralization has involved the breakdown of each region into districts, each comprising twenty to twenty-five branches. Originally thought of as market areas, some districts now include branches in different parts of the region. For example, in British Columbia, one northern branch is included in each southern district where most of the branches are; this was done deliberately, so as to lessen the burden of travelling on the district managers. Similarly, Ottawa is divided into three districts, to each of which are joined eastern Ontario branches to the north, east, and west.

There is a growing tendency to think of the districts as the best avenues for business development. The district manager is expected to, and to a substantial degree does, encourage the business-development side of his responsibilities. As everywhere else, the regular routines – discussions of credit, consumer loans, branch locations, and personnel – take up too much time. But the theory (and, to a growing degree, the practice) is to find time for the district manager to get out into the community and call on potential customers. In Mason's words, "The district concept has only been in place for about three years, and I think it's starting to pay dividends, even though there can be some improvements in the organizational structures. We are making progress now because the district manager is close to his managers – his branch team."

DECENTRALIZATION AND LESSENED MOBILITY OF STAFF

In a sense, decentralization of the Bank was fortified by the decreasing mobility of the staff. Fewer people were prepared to move about the country, or indeed out of the country, in order to obtain the varied experience desirable for a top-level job. More than that, with the country divided into regions and the regions, in turn, into districts, the local district had a tendency to hoard its better people. As a director of administrative services said to one of the district managers in his region, "The rest of the districts can't afford to have you have all the best people."

Similar tendencies are to be found in regions. Many regions like to keep their best people and in some provinces, of which British Columbia and Alberta are the outstanding examples, it is hard to persuade anyone to leave at all. The three Senior Vice-Presidents and General Managers stationed in Toronto and responsible for the West, Ontario, and the East keep an eye on the up-and-coming people in their three parts of the country, with a view to moving them both within their own regions and from one major area to another. Working with the heads of Personnel and Personnel Planning, these three Senior Vice-Presidents keep a sharp eye open for officers who have the capabilities of moving upward, and to convince them it is in their interest to do so. But despite the efforts to improve it, mobility is limited and is not sufficient to achieve ideal results. Ironically, because of this bias against moving, ambitious people sometimes become stuck in a rut, like the young man who had worked in a couple of branches in a Toronto suburb for five years, and who finally in desperation phoned the head of Personnel and asked, "How do I get out of Scarborough?"

HIRING UNIVERSITY GRADUATES

The acute shortage of staff had been pretty well overcome by the mid-sixties. Fortunately, there were now few stories of complete misfits, such as the young hopeful pulled out of a village in the mid-fifties and put in charge of a new branch in a posh suburb of a big city, who blurted out to his most important customer that he did not like his new job and could not understand why he had been sent there. Most employees were now reasonably trained and prepared.

Interest now shifted towards university graduates as a source of management personnel. As W.H. Milne, who had much to do with these changes in his long experience in Personnel before he was appointed Secretary of the Bank, says, "We divided up the universities – Sandy McLean and I had Queen's – and we would visit and try to find promising people. We had some success. At one point, we had a scheme going whereby we brought in a limited number of undergraduates for special summer assignments, to get them interested in the Bank." Before long, emphasis was placed on finding graduates with Master of Business Administration degrees (MBAs) and efforts were made to provide them with an adequate background by sending them to large branches which had been designated as training centres. Godsoe, now a Vice-Chairman of the Board, and Brooks, now General Manager, Finance and Administration, both entered the Bank in this way.

The MBAs are believed to have adjusted a good deal better to International than to the regular branch system of the Bank. There is more "romance" about International and, with its flexibility and need for new ideas, it is less difficult for an MBA to fit into the Bank there. The branch system, in contrast, operates under well-established customs and rules. As Brooks says, "The MBA finds himself in a rigid, hard-to-change structure. He is going to have trouble with the people and the system all the way through." But despite these problems, there are sixty-two MBAs in Canadian operations, compared with eighty-two in International operations and seventy-four in General Office Departments. Moreover, a new commercial officer development program for MBAs has recently been put into effect, which provides for training in depth and augurs well for the future.

As a matter of interest, it might be added that the main branch in Toronto, Toronto branch, seems to be an exception to most of these problems. It is the best place to work in the Bank in the view of many who have done so. This is the testimony of one manager after another – Nicks, Touchie, Crockett, and MacNevin, the last two of whom could scarcely bear to leave – and also of Ritchie, who was there as accountant and assistant manager. "The work is demanding and interesting," as MacNevin says. "Toronto branch is harder to run than a region.... The customers are as nice as you could find anywhere.... Most of the people who are going to the top should go through Toronto branch." In

Ritchie's words, "They were a great bunch and they all knew their jobs"—referring to Hugh Washburn, Ivan Younker, Dolly O'Brien, Scotty Heenan, Jack Cantwell, Gene Baker, to name just a few of the old-timers.

PROGRESS OF WOMEN

As noted earlier, the proportion of women on the staff of The Bank of Nova Scotia in the mid-sixties was about 60 per cent; by the mid-seventies it had risen to 70 per cent, and in 1981 it was about 75 per cent. The increase in the number of women in senior posts was, however, gradual. At the end of 1981, there were 70 women who were branch managers, quite an accomplishment in view of the fact that the first woman branch manager was appointed barely twenty years ago. In the interval, women throughout the Bank have demonstrated that they can perform competently and can progress in line and staff roles.

There are a number of senior women in the Bank. One, Candace Craddock, is now Executive Assistant to the Chairman, having earlier been in charge of government relations; and another, Louise Cannon, an MBA, is a General Manager, Canadian Commercial Banking. With Doris Pretty having led the way some years ago in Personnel, Diane Caravan has the rank of Supervisor in that department. Also, Margaret Fisher has the title of Administrator in the Economics Department, and Louise Boyd is Assistant Secretary of the Bank. While substantial experience in banking has provided the base for advancement of many women, others have specific educational qualifications and/or expertise gained outside the Bank. None the less, the common denominator has been a desire and a capacity for hard work. As Cannon puts it, "I really think that if you have a good education, are reasonably bright, and are prepared to work, you are not going to have any troubles just because you are a woman. I think the last thing is probably the most important—you have got to be prepared to work. I find that the job takes long hours."

PERSONNEL REORGANIZATION AND TRAINING

In 1979 the personnel function was broken into two divisions, Personnel and Personnel Policy and Planning, recognizing formally a situation that had developed some time earlier. W.J. Lomax, General Manager of the policy division, describes his job as "problems of tomorrow" and works closely with the operating heads, A.E. Taylor for Canada and D.W. Whitaker for International. The kinds of problems that arise are as varied as having a fresh look at the training of tellers to developing salary policies and benefit plans suitable to International operations, such as the Bank's branch in Japan. The department also attempts to look ahead at the ever-changing environment and endeavours to have

The Changing Face of Banking, 1971-1981 303

in place career development plans for clerical, supervisory, and management employees. Continued forward planning of staffing requirements is necessary for the ongoing success of the Bank, and top management recognizes this.

Training programs for both staff and management, now in the Management Development and Training Department under A.C. Giles and E.F. Forcey, have been improved and extended. A comprehensive supervisory course for accountants is provided. A course on customer relations for tellers and other counter staff is given in the branches. There are also university courses on banking arranged through the Institute of Canadian Bankers. The number of courses taken by Bank employees came to about 7,300 in 1981 – a figure which does not include those enrolled in management programs at Spencer Hall.

SPENCER HALL

In 1978 the Bank moved towards a broader and higher level of staff training when, in conjunction with the University of Western Ontario, Spencer Hall was established on the campus of that university in London, Ontario. Planned and developed by P.T. Johnson (a prominent educator who joined the Bank for this purpose) and by Shaw, it started as a management training centre. As Ritchie saw it, it would gradually

Located on the campus of the University of Western Ontario, Spencer Hall was established in 1978 as the Bank's management training centre. Here Bank people from around the world share their knowledge and experience while strengthening the skills needed to serve our customers in increasingly competitive markets.

evolve into something broader – "an education centre which would develop a style and character for The Bank of Nova Scotia."

There was no doubt about the need for management and credit training. The insufficient supply of good management and credit personnel has been the principal factor limiting decentralization; thus, a rather expensive and unwieldy system of supervision by the regional offices and General Office has had to be continued. Bell, as Chief Operating Officer, wanted Spencer Hall to emphasize "analysis and hard banking subjects." Hitchman wanted the emphasis put on case studies. As time went on, it became clear that Spencer Hall was improving the quality of credit work in the Bank and, as Cannon puts it, "This was essential, since credit applications were becoming more complicated year by year."

The courses, which were mainly concerned with management, credit, and corporate finance, were generally well regarded by the students, who up to 1981 totalled 2,200. In each session, Spencer Hall brought together Bank people from all over the world. Many found that their problems were quite similar, whether in British Columbia, Newfoundland, General Office, or Puerto Rico, and they developed a sense of the Bank as a group. Spencer Hall has certainly been good for morale.

In 1982 a new course was introduced on selling in the broadest sense – a program designed to put the banker in a position of really helping the customer solve his problems rather than just pushing the sale of services. Another advantage of the Spencer Hall meetings is the opportunity it gives senior officers to meet promising young men and women and to form impressions of their abilities.

NOTES

1. BNS Annual Report, 1972, Chief General Manager's Report, p.12.
2. BNS Annual Report, 1974, Executive Vice-President and Chief General Manager's Report, p.19.
3. BNS Annual Report, 1974, Chairman of the Board and President's Report, p.3.
4. *Ibid.*, p.14.
5. BNS Annual Report, 1975, Chairman's Report, pp.4-5.
6. *Ibid.*, p.5.
7. BNS Annual Report, 1976, Chairman's Report, p.4.

14

Just Around the Corner, Right Around the World 1971-1981

From its original base in Nova Scotia, the Bank reached outward to the Maritime provinces and then westward across Canada. At the same time, it was developing its international connections along the United States' eastern seaboard, across to Europe, and south to the Caribbean.

But it is in more recent years that the Bank's balanced diversification – into markets around the world, and into an ever-increasing variety of services to customers – has been such a pronounced feature.[1]

BALANCED DIVERSIFICATION AND REMARKABLE GROWTH

Balanced diversification and remarkable growth in the international business of the Bank are the main subjects of this chapter, the last in the chronology of the Bank's 150-year history. Greater diversification was achieved through extension of international business to new countries, particularly in the Pacific Rim, and through the development of new services in Canada, as described in the preceding chapter. And this increase in diversification was accompanied by a concentration on more profitable activities in more promising parts of the world.

The remarkable further surge of growth in international business brought international assets to a level where they were almost as large as domestic assets. Indeed, international earnings exceeded domestic earnings in both 1980 and 1981. The Bank could now properly be described as a Canadian-based international bank – a far cry from the small local bank started in 1832 in Halifax.

ASSETS REACH $50 BILLION

By the end of 1981, the Bank's assets had reached $50 billion. The overall rate of growth in dollar terms in the ten years ending in 1980 was 21 per cent per annum – the greatest percentage increase in any decade of the Bank's history. Even when the high rate of inflation is

In the early 1970s, the Bank's international representation continued to be emphasized in advertisements.

allowed for, the increase – the real growth rate – was 11½ per cent per annum. This is higher than the real rate of growth of the 1960s and probably also higher than that of the 1890s when the Bank was first moving beyond the Maritimes.

In the seventies, as in the sixties, growth in the international part of the Bank's business was greater than in its domestic business. The growth was roughly 25 per cent per annum in dollars and, after allowing for inflation, it was 15 per cent per annum, continuing the extraordinary rate of advance achieved in the preceding decade and expanding twice as fast as the Bank's business in Canada.

OPEC SURPLUS EXPANDS INTERNATIONAL BANKING

As noted in the preceding chapter, the huge balance-of-payments surplus of the OPEC group created a great deal more international banking business, though it was accompanied by serious strain in the worldwide flow of funds and much-intensified balance-of-payment difficulties for the poor countries. The recycling of OPEC surpluses and the creation of new international credit through the Eurodollar banking system kept the wheels of multilateral trade turning, though less efficiently than before and at the cost of more inflation, slower growth, and lessened productivity.

In a sense, it is a miracle that the OPEC policies did not result in a complete breakdown of the international economic system. It is certainly a tribute to the ingenuity of commercial bankers and to the patience and co-operation of central bankers that the system continued to function as well as it did. But it is not a tribute to the policies of the governments of the industrial countries; as Ritchie put it in 1975, "...there still appears to be an inadequate appreciation of how much [the industrial countries] will continue to depend on OPEC supplies unless there are greater strides in conservation and/or a more effective development of alternative energy sources...."[2] It is quite evident that there is a long way to go before a healthy international system is restored and the sort of international stagflation from which so many countries are now suffering can be overcome. It is also evident that Canada has a long way to go in restoring her own economic health and efficiency before she can play the constructive role in international policies and arrangements in which she had been so successful in the decade following the Second World War.

BANK'S ACHIEVEMENT IN SEVENTIES EXTRAORDINARY

But in spite of the problems, and partly because of them, the growth of international banking in the seventies was enormous. The growth in Canadian international banking was particularly striking and no Canadian bank had a better growth record in this sphere than The Bank of Nova Scotia. Indeed, the share of the Nova Scotia in the total international assets of all the Canadian banks rose from 17 per cent in 1960 and 18 per cent in 1970 to 24 per cent of a much-increased total by 1980. At that point, the Nova Scotia was second only to the Royal Bank, whose estimated international assets were slightly higher than the Nova Scotia's, but whose domestic assets were twice as large.

The Bank's global progress in the seventies was all the more impressive in the light of its remarkable international growth rate in the sixties and of the disturbed conditions of the seventies. In modern times there has been no decade in which interest rates rose so much and fluctuated so much and few decades in which the Canadian exchange rate fell so much. The Bank's success in these erratic circumstances reflects the firm foundations of its earlier growth, most of all in the United States, but also in London and other parts of Europe. It reflects Ritchie's push into the huge Pacific area and the development of an around-the-world twenty-four-hour-a-day foreign exchange and banking system. It also reflects the Bank's determination to maintain a major position in the West Indies. And most of all, it reflects the drive of a group of people led by Ritchie, Bell, and McDonald and including Godsoe, Marsman, Kent, and R.G. Taylor.

TOP PERSONNEL, LEADING EDGE OF INTERNATIONAL BUSINESS

There can be little doubt that top personnel are the leading edge of the international business. Where the credit volumes are large, the possibilities great, and the arrangements complicated, trust and understanding between top officers are essential. As in Nicks's day it is one-to-one communication at the senior level that counts. Crockett refers to a tour in Europe with Marsman which he took shortly after Nicks's death as a "killer trip," going all the time, seeing top people, and looking for new opportunities. As time went on, Ritchie embarked on his program of regular tours, which, in addition to his very frequent visits to the United States, usually have included a major trip to Europe as well as one to the Far East every year.

Ritchie's first tour to the Far East in 1973 with Marsman and Peel led to the opening of a branch in Kuala Lumpur and a little later to offices in Singapore, Jakarta, and Hong Kong. This was an area which Marsman had known as a young man, when he worked for a Dutch bank. It was now blossoming into great activity with Singapore developing into a huge entrepôt centre like Hong Kong. As Marsman says, "We were looking for places that had been through the turmoil of colonialism to independence and now once again welcomed the skill and help of the former colonial powers, as in Indonesia and Malaysia."

MANILA – NEW REGIONAL CENTRE

The next year, 1974, found Ritchie in Manila, clearly taken with its possibilities and thinking in terms of making it the Bank's regional centre for the Pacific area. And in 1975 this step was taken, and Lindsay with his long experience in the Spanish-speaking countries of the Caribbean was placed in charge. At the same time, a 30 per cent share in the Security Bank and Trust Company of the Philippines was acquired; and to mark the founding of the new Pacific base, a Board meeting was held there early in 1978.

RITCHIE GETS TO THE POINT

Though it may be hard to believe, particularly for anyone who knew Nicks well and saw the preparation and concern with which he approached his tours, Ritchie accomplishes more in a day than Nicks in the way of calls and time spent in conversation with customers and prospective customers.

He has the ability of not pushing and yet getting to the point, of finding common interests without bringing out differences. And the truth is that he has been travelling considerably more than Nicks, and accomplishing that in addition to a heavy workload at home. As he did with Nicks, Peel almost always accompanies Ritchie on his tours, making sure that the detailed arrangements work out the way they are supposed to.

CALLS BY OTHER SENIOR OFFICERS

McDonald, the head of International since 1970, also spends a great deal of his time abroad – probably more today than eight or nine years ago. As the head man, he had, and still has, the job of putting out fires and of dealing with emergencies and problems that could not be solved at a lower level. For example, he visited Manila four times in the early part of 1980 in connection with the sale of the Bank's shares in the Security Bank and Trust Company of the Philippines, which, though now completed, indicates no diminution in the Bank's interest in that area. And because his responsibilities cover a good deal of the world, McDonald travels great distances to attend area planning meetings and, like the Chairman, to make a growing number of customer calls.

Business does not all come from calls by the top men, though they are important and can sometimes be decisive in developing a fruitful relationship. New business also results from continuous hard work and good ideas. It means keeping in touch with possible customers and finding approaches that meet their needs as nearly as practicable. Good locations and facilities are another factor in acquiring business. As Healy, General Manager of the Treasury Division in Toronto, says with regard to deposits, the Nova Scotia is "a convenient place to park short-term money – it is competitive, it provides a good service, and it is represented in most places."

In the United States, the team that arranges the loans and obtains the money works out of New York and through nine other branches,

Just Around the Corner, Right Around the World, 1971–1981 309

agencies, and representative offices across the continent. As noted in Chapter 11, the United States provides the biggest part of the Bank's international business because of its proximity, enormous size, and familiar ways of doing business. Also, the United States market is of particular importance to Canadian banks because the Canadian branch-banking system has enabled Canadian banks to grow large and internationally competitive relative to the majority of their U.S. counterparts, which in many cases are restricted as to branch banking, particularly outside their home states. As a place to lend money and as a place to arrange deposits, whether domestically, or abroad through multinationals, the United States is of central importance to Canadian banking.

BROADENING U.S. ACTIVITIES

In the late sixties, under Randall, McPhedran, Webster, and Kurt Helstern (who had served in New York since the twenties and who was especially well-informed on foreign exchange and call loans), the Bank was broadening its U.S. activities. It was moving from its long-established grain, sugar, foreign exchange, and call-loan business to a wider field, including shipping and many other multinational industries, and to a more active posture in the Eurodollar market. It was at this juncture, actually in 1969, that Godsoe was transferred to New York, on

LEFT

Opened in 1907, the New York Agency is located in the heart of the city's financial district at the corner of Wall, Pearl, and Beaver streets.

CREDIT: MARC NEUHOF

RIGHT

P.C. Godsoe, Executive Vice-President, International, 1980-1982; Vice-Chairman, 1982.

CREDIT: V. TONY HAUSER

his own initiative. At the time he was an assistant manager in Montreal and Nicks had asked him to go to Nassau as manager. But Godsoe felt that he could serve the Bank better by gaining experience in New York. After a three-month interval during which he brooded on his future in the Bank, he was in fact appointed as one of the general agents in New York. There he learned a great deal about the international business and, as he puts it, "about how very much I didn't know."

He was moved from New York to Toronto in 1971, where he continued to be involved in the U.S. business, and where he helped set up the Western Hemisphere International Regional Office which brought the United States and Latin American divisions under organized control from Toronto. "This was a big operation," says Godsoe (who is now a Vice-Chairman of the Bank). "The game is positioning with regard to interest rates and to a lesser degree foreign exchange. International banking is essentially asset banking – you get the loans and fund the money on a basis you can live with."

This is really another way of describing liability management. The Bank has to find liabilities that provide some reasonable margin of return over what it receives on the loans. And there must be protection provided against rising interest rates on those liabilities – either by matching the term with that of the asset or, what is more usually the case, by relating the interest rate on the asset to the quarterly or monthly change in the interest-rate structure. Forty per cent or more of foreign currency assets are kept in the form of deposits with other banks, for reasons of both liquidity and balance-sheet appearance. And there is no hesitation about moving money from one bank to another. As Healy observes, "The deposit market is impersonal and strongly rate-conscious."

POISED FOR FURTHER GROWTH IN THE U.S.

Acquiring international business is a skilled job. According to McGinn (who in Chapter 11 described the development of international business in the United States), "The deposit side is pretty cut and dried because you cannot be undercutting your other customers, though you may have some special instrument or exchange arrangement that meets the need.... But the loan side is full of negotiations, exchange, and also tax angles.... You have to send good men and we have them."

Nevertheless, it is difficult to staff the new international branches and offices, five of which have been opened in the United States since 1977. The new people are given a year's training before they are sent out. The Boston area, where an earlier branch had been closed during the Second World War, is once again the scene of a thriving operation, which marks a welcome return of The Bank of Nova Scotia to New England. Agencies in Atlanta and Miami extend the Bank's interests in the prosperous South. There is a new representative office in Cleveland and a branch in Portland, Oregon. With 10 offices, well-spaced geo-

The Boston, Massachusetts, Branch was opened on Federal Street in 1978. The Bank had its first office in Boston in 1899, but this early operation was closed in 1942.

graphically to serve U.S. industry and finance, the Bank is poised for further growth in this wealthy and competitive economy.

USUALLY LATE FOR PLANES

Nicks was usually late for planes – so late he almost missed them. Boyles was always ahead of time and sometimes wore his rubbers when he didn't need them. Ritchie was on time, but he tried to smoke even when there were "No Smoking" signs in the aircraft. Marsman and others had many opportunities to observe the idiosyncrasies of the visiting brass from General Office. They were normally well behaved, but always in a hurry, always anxious to make another call. Marsman, who organized the London Regional Office in 1967 and who headed it up for most of the period until his retirement in 1980, believed that his area – the United Kingdom, continental Europe, and the Middle East (and now Africa) – was the best-diversified in the Bank. He liked London, partly because it was well away from the Bank's headquarters.

London, England, 1979.

The Bank of Nova Scotia moved into this London, England, office on Threadneedle Street, just across from the Bank of England (at centre), in 1972.

CREDIT: MICHEL PROULX

A STRONG LONDON OFFICE

More than any other place in the Bank, London is a centre in its own right, not only because it is a fair distance from headquarters, but also because it is the world centre of the Eurodollar market as well as of the market for syndicated loans. Much has happened since the days before the war when the Nova Scotia's representation in London was largely concerned with the movement of funds to and from the West Indies and with the efforts to pick up accounts of British firms setting up branches or subsidiaries in Canada. In 1980, looking over his network of branches and offices (more than twice the size of the establishment of 1967), his wholesale banking figures in the billions, and his group of bright young men, Marsman had every right to be proud of the fine operation which he was handing over to his successor, L.L. Fox, the new Vice-President and General Manager of the Region.

RIGHT ACROSS FROM THE BANK OF ENGLAND

Heralding the bright future of the London Regional Office, the Bank moved into a fine new building on Threadneedle Street in 1972, right across from the Bank of England. The new building houses the Bank's main London branch and the treasury, special loans, and foreign exchange facilities of the regional organization. As in New York and Toronto, wholesale lending had become more complicated. There were multi-currency options. Instruments could even be drawn in terms of SDRs (Special Drawing Rights of the International Monetary Fund). Business went to those who were intelligent and perceptive about interest rates and foreign exchange trends. According to C.A. Barnes, who with R.N. Brandman now runs the Treasury and the London portion of the Special Loans Department, the London Office is trying to develop specialized spheres of interest for its branches. Frankfurt, for example, works on Euromark loans, while London, of course, is the unquestioned centre for Eurodollars.

Barnes and Brandman are university graduates from Britain and both worked in Toronto, Barnes in the Economics Department and Brandman in the Investment Department. Both returned to London, Barnes to a special economics post established to assist regional management as well as to provide a European input in the Bank's general monitoring of international developments. The present London economist – Geoffrey Holt – also worked in the Economics Department in General Office for several years before going back to London, where he keeps a keen eye on developments in the money and exchange markets and on international trade and payments.

THE NEW SPECIAL LOANS DEPARTMENT

The new Special Loans Department run by S.D.N. Belcher in Toronto includes the London portion under Barnes and Brandman; this department puts together loan syndicates for substantial financing – $500 million or $1 billion are not out of the ordinary. Suppose a company or a province in Canada wants a large Eurodollar loan, or suppose the Bank suggests it as an alternative to other means of financing. Then the Special Loans Department would investigate through London whether it might get together a group of multinational banks to finance a Eurodollar loan. From the Bank's point of view there is extra remuneration for running the syndicate, and from the customer's standpoint there is the tailored effort to meet his needs. The Bank has been successful in this area of special loans in the last few years and its close contacts in London indicate a promising future. Indeed, one of this department's more recent efforts was a billion-dollar loan in Eurodollars for the province of Quebec.

CHINA AND JAPAN

Ritchie took his first trip to China in 1974 and has followed that with three others. The Bank wanted to have a representative office in China, and approval for such an office has recently been granted. Meanwhile, in Japan, the Bank achieved another long-cherished goal when it was permitted to open a branch there in 1981 – the first such authority granted to any Canadian bank. This was the culmination of the Nova Scotia's presence in the form of a representative office in Japan for almost twenty years, and it no doubt also reflects the Bank's support of the recent change in the Canadian Bank Act permitting foreign banks to operate branches in Canada.

REGIONAL OFFICE IN MANILA

The new Pacific Regional Office in Manila has generated some encouraging business. Both the Philippines and South Korea have become very substantial borrowers. After many years of effort the Bank succeeded in setting up a representative office in Sydney and in developing some business in Australia, a country whose financial industry has long been sheltered by government protection. Indonesia, Malaysia, Hong Kong, and Singapore all offer promise, as does Thailand. Thus far, outstanding loans and deposits with banks in the Pacific Rim amount to about $2\frac{1}{2}$ billion.

The story in Latin America is perhaps not as dramatic as that of the Pacific Rim, partly because it started earlier and partly because balance-of-payments problems have bedevilled the position of some of the countries concerned. For example, Venezuela, with its oil, looks stronger than Brazil, though the long-term outlook for Brazil with its vast storehouse of natural resources is encouraging. When the Caribbean is included, outstanding loans and deposits with banks are large, totalling about $4\frac{1}{2}$ billion.

ASSESSING "COUNTRY" RISKS

Loans in international banking are usually large and of relatively high quality. Where loans are to countries or government agencies, the risks pertain entirely to the country – to its ability and willingness to meet interest and repayment commitments. Where loans are to corporations (and the majority of corporate borrowers in the international market are large and strong), the risks may still be largely "country": assuming that the borrower in question is able to repay domestically, the risk involved will depend on economic and political conditions in the country concerned. Even in the case of the subsidiary of a strong multinational corporation, the risk is still "country" unless repayment is guaranteed by the parent, a practice which most parents endeavour to avoid.

So "country" risks are important, and are under continuous assessment by senior officers in the field and in Toronto. To help in their judgment, a formal structure of credit guidelines is worked out annually, and reviewed as the occasion warrants. Points are assigned for the political and economic attributes that have a bearing on a country's creditworthiness. These are: foreign-exchange earning capacity, fiscal

Santo Domingo, Dominican Republic.

The Bank of Nova Scotia opened in the Dominican Republic in 1920. This building was erected in 1974.

responsibility, burden of debt, education of the people, political balance, degree of order, and major resources. Using a points system built on these considerations and relating it to what would be reasonable limits for some test countries, the Bank finally produces limits for each country, varying from low-figure limits for small, insecure countries to very substantial limits for Britain, West Germany, France, Japan, and Switzerland, and no limit at all for the United States. Many of the larger international banks have broadly similar, though by no means identical, approaches.

Of the Bank's total foreign currency assets, those which are heavily concentrated in North America and western Europe account for over two-thirds. Latin America, the Caribbean, and Asia account for the rest. From the standpoint of stage of development, industrial countries represent 70 per cent of the borrowers, developing countries represent 18 per cent, with oil-producing countries accounting for much of the rest. Another indication of the Bank's responsible approach towards foreign lending is that it keeps a fairly high proportion of its foreign currency assets in the form of deposits with other banks – in recent years the ratio has been well over 40 per cent (see chart 31).

SEVENTEEN BANKS AND FOURTEEN CURRENCIES

The Caribbean Region is an extensive one: from the Bahamas off the tip of Florida in the north, to Guyana in South America in the south, and to Belize in Central America in the west. It is a diverse area in terms of people and economies; indeed, as R.G. Taylor, Vice-President in charge of the region, likes to say, "The Bank of Nova Scotia operates seventeen

One of eleven branches of Scotiabank in Nassau, Bahamas, the Paradise Island Branch is located in a key tourist area.

banks using fourteen different currencies." And it is also diverse in the forms of organization that have been developed to suit the varying needs and circumstances for banking. The Bank itself has about 50 branches, and its subsidiaries and affiliates have about 75. The branches vary all the way from small tourist-oriented branches to large commercial branches in such cities as San Juan, Santo Domingo, Kingston, and Port-of-Spain. To lessen the problem of distance, and distances are great, managers of key branches in each area or country act as area managers and supervise the credit applications of the smaller branches in the region up to the key branch's limit, thereby giving more efficient service and eliminating a lot of correspondence to and from Toronto, where the headquarters for the whole Caribbean Region is located.

Most, though not all, of the seventeen banks grew substantially in the seventies and a few, of which Puerto Rico is the main example, grew notably. Some of the seventeen banks made their first appearance in this decade as members of the Nova Scotia group, including Maduro & Curiel's Bank in the Netherlands Antilles, with which the Nova Scotia has a developing connection, and also the new branches in Haiti and St. Vincent.

BAHAMAS: GOOD EXAMPLE OF NEW ARRANGEMENTS

The Bahamas provide a good example of the new arrangements – there are eleven branches and they all apply to the main branch at Nassau for approval for loans above their individual limits of credit. While a significant amount of wholesale business is also conducted at the main branch in Nassau, the major portion of this business is processed through The Bank of Nova Scotia International Limited, a wholly-owned subsidiary. The hotel and tourist business was good during much of the decade. After an active career in Canada in credit, personnel, and administration, K.W. London took over from Donald Fleming as Managing Director of The Bank of Nova Scotia Trust Company (Bahamas) Ltd. in 1980.

The branches in Barbados and the islands of the eastern Caribbean – Antigua, St. Lucia, Grenada, and St. Vincent – are all heavily involved in the tourist industry, and business grew further in the seventies, except in Grenada, where political developments produced a sense of insecurity. In the Dominican Republic, with an improved, though still highly restrictive, political environment, the branch system was expanded in the city of Santo Domingo and into some smaller towns. With five new branches, there are now twelve in this potentially rich land. Having opened in Haiti in 1972, the Bank added a second branch there in 1976.

MAJOR GROWTH IN PUERTO RICO

One of the most encouraging developments in the Caribbean area in the seventies was the improvement of the Bank's position in Puerto Rico. From its situation as a respected but rather small bank on the island, the Nova Scotia developed into a sizeable operation. It was now permitted, as it had not been before, to engage in the incentive programs which were part of "Operation Bootstrap" and which had much to do with the growth of modern Puerto Rico. In July 1975, the Bank bought control of Banco Mercantil de Puerto Rico, which provided the Bank with a broader base, though admittedly at a substantial cost. In the years that followed, the Bank took a leading part in financing the Puerto Rican sugar industry and became an active participant in the government-sponsored money market for financing of business. This program, known as "936 financing," had its genesis in profits from "Operation Bootstrap" left in Puerto Rico. If profits of U.S. subsidiaries earned in Puerto Rico were taken out of the country they were subject to a 10 per cent tax, but if left in it, they were tax-free and this created a market for the use of such money.

In 1979, the Bank merged the business of Banco Mercantil de Puerto Rico with most of the business of The Bank of Nova Scotia branch system in Puerto Rico into a new subsidiary, Scotiabank de Puerto Rico. One branch of The Bank of Nova Scotia was maintained and in total there were now seven branches of a strong bank with a future. K.S. Rowe (until he left in 1977 to become head man in Manila), and his successor, C.F. Henriques, formerly General Manager of The Bank of Nova Scotia Jamaica Limited, were the men on the spot, and with strong head office support they shook an old-fashioned business out of the doldrums and made it an important contributor to Puerto

Rico and to the Bank's earnings. The new Bank incorporated in Puerto Rico with its own directors is chaired by Rafael J. Martinez, who is a Director of The Bank of Nova Scotia.

Like Puerto Rico, the U.S. Virgin Islands provide a direct connection with American financial markets, though the Bank's operations in the Virgin Islands are much smaller than in Puerto Rico. The manager of the main branch at Charlotte Amalie, St. Thomas, provides credit supervision up to his limit over the other three branches in the U.S. islands, as well as over the branch at Road Town in the British Virgin Islands.

ASSOCIATION WITH MADURO & CURIEL'S BANK

One of the most interesting developments of the seventies was the growth of the Nova Scotia's connection with Maduro & Curiel's Bank, which has already been referred to. This connection began in 1970 and has now developed to the point where the Nova Scotia owns 49 per cent of the stock and has appointed a number of its own employees to the Board of Maduro & Curiel's Bank, which operates branches in Curaçao, Aruba, Bonaire, and St. Maarten in the Netherlands Antilles. This efficient institution has access to the advice and counsel of the Nova Scotia, as well as to the services of several of its employees. It provides the Nova Scotia with full information about its activities and it uses the methods, techniques, and staff-training facilities of its larger associate. It has turned out to be a happy association in which mutual respect and trust transcend formal relationships. It should be noted that The Bank of Nova Scotia, the year before its association with Maduro & Curiel's Bank, had incorporated a branch in Philipsburg, St. Maarten. Hence, in a dignified sense, the two banks are competitors in St. Maarten.

STRATEGIC RETREAT IN BERMUDA

Another arrangement having to do with a local bank did not turn out as well, though its ultimate result was satisfactory. The Bermuda National Bank was established in 1967 by The Bank of Nova Scotia, in conjunction with a group of Bermudian citizens, with 40 per cent of the stock owned by the Nova Scotia. The venture turned out to be a continuing uphill battle, even though the Bank saw fit to put its then senior New York agent, McPhedran, into the job of Managing Director for six years. The Bermuda National Bank did become a profitable operation in a modest way, but the Nova Scotia finally decided to accept an offer by the Bank of N. T. Butterfield and Son and to sell the Nova Scotia's 40 per cent interest to Butterfield's in exchange for 10 per cent of Butterfield's stock; subsequent purchases of Butterfield's stock increased the Nova Scotia's interest to nearly 14 per cent. The result is a close association between the Nova Scotia and Butterfield's in Bermuda, extending to methods and organization and including the use of Spencer Hall.

Just Around the Corner, Right Around the World, 1971-1981 319

Belize City,
Belize,
opened in 1968.

Just as in Canada, the branches of the Bank abroad vary in size and style. In Belize, the formality of the Belize City main branch contrasts with the more casual, almost residential style of the branch at Orange Walk Town.

Orange Walk Town,
Belize,
opened in 1976.

REPRESENTATION AT THE FAR EDGES

Way off, on the fringes of the Caribbean area, two other branches had been started in the late sixties – one at Georgetown in Guyana, and one at Belize City in Belize (formerly British Honduras). Guyana, in particular, has intriguing resource possibilities – one of them being bauxite, originally developed by Canadian interests but now nationalized by the Guyanese government. However, Canadian interests are still active in the country – in oil exploration at the present time. Belize, on the western edge of the Caribbean, is part of Central America, and there are now 3 branches of the Bank located there. The main branch in Belize City boasts one of the most impressive banking rooms in the Americas, popularly known as the Taj Mahal.

JAMAICA – LOOKING FORWARD TO BETTER TIMES

In Jamaica, the decade was a tough one, though The Bank of Nova Scotia Jamaica Ltd. grew substantially. At the end of 1980, it had almost 40 branches compared with 30 ten years earlier. Assets had grown markedly in dollars, but only moderately in real terms because the rate of inflation was high. Ownership of The Bank of Nova Scotia Jamaica Ltd. remained at 70 per cent by the parent bank; unlike the situation in Trinidad the environment was decidedly unfavourable to the local sale of stock. But the development of Jamaican management was encouraging; the process of Jamaicanization reached the point where only three or four northerners remained on a staff of 1,400, though one of them, Jack Keith, is the head man.

Times are changing again in Jamaica – for the better. The new government has gone a long way towards restoring order and a sense of confidence in the society. The tourist trade is gradually picking up in response to better management and a more stable environment. There will be more courses at the Bank's education centre – the old Acadia Club – and Bank people will attend them from all over the island and other nearby countries. In its ninety-third year in Kingston, the Bank looks forward to better times.

GROWTH IN TRINIDAD AND TOBAGO

In 1973 in Trinidad, The Bank of Nova Scotia Trinidad and Tobago Ltd. sold 17,000 shares in its operation to local shareholders, who thus acquired about 23 per cent of the capital funds. Again in 1979, additional shares were sold, bringing the local holding to slightly over 50 per cent. The local bank's growth in assets and profits has been encouraging and it now has 16 branches. The Managing Director of The Bank of Nova Scotia Trinidad and Tobago Ltd. is R.A. Chan, a Trinidadian.

CARIBBEAN NOT LIKE REST OF INTERNATIONAL

Banking in the Caribbean is not like banking in the rest of International. In many ways it is quite similar to banking in Canada because it is largely retail and involves many of the same kinds of transactions. Indeed, innovations introduced in Canada usually work well in the Caribbean, for example, Scotia Plan loans, and more recently, VISA. But in other ways banking in the Caribbean presents special problems, because laws and customs are different. A big branch in the Caribbean,

Acadia Training Centre, Kingston, Jamaica, 1979.

The staff of the Bank in Jamaica is now, with few exceptions, drawn from the local population. The old Acadia Club, which once housed Canadian staff posted to Jamaica, has been transformed into a modern staff-training centre.

CREDIT: MICHEL PROULX

similar in size to a big branch in Canada, is likely to have to deal with foreign exchange and government policy and regulation, and probably unions, in addition to the regular routine of a Canadian branch. As R.G. Taylor says, "Running a big branch in this area is very different from running a sizeable branch at home. It is broader and it can be more rewarding."

CHANGES IN ORGANIZATION OF INTERNATIONAL

The organization of International changed considerably during the seventies. As noted earlier, a major office in Toronto – Western Hemisphere International Regional Office – was founded early in the decade. Godsoe became head of the region in 1974, and in 1979, when he was promoted to second-in-command of International, the Region was split in two – the North American Region under Birmingham and the Latin American Region under R. Cooke. Meanwhile, a new region, the Pacific Region under Lindsay, was started in 1974. Then there was the Caribbean Region under Taylor; and of course London under Fox. In structure, all regions were equal, but the North American International Office was handling a very large and growing volume of business, as was the London Office with its responsibility for sterling-area transactions and special loan services, and its central position in the Eurodollar market. Two of the headquarters departments had responsibilities which sometimes conflicted with regional responsibilities and this eventually led to a system of joint responsibility. One case was that of the Treasury Department under Healy, who, because of the problem of co-ordinating the activities of the regional offices on the movement of money, foreign exchange, and gold, was given authority to overrule a regional office. Similarly, P.S. Dodd, as the officer who determines the degree of exposure in companies and countries, is in a position to enforce his broad policy. At times, this means that people in the field may have two bosses, but thus far, according to McDonald, "Things have worked out fairly well."

FURTHER GROWTH IN GOLD OPERATIONS

The Bank's activities in gold showed a further expansion, including a spell of very rapid growth in the latter part of the seventies. The Nova Scotia had been an active participant in the precious-metals markets since 1958, and during twenty-four years, largely under the direction of E.E. Keith, had developed considerable experience and expertise as an intermediary among the three market sectors: the producer, the investor, and the end-user of precious metals. In addition to dealing in actual gold and silver, the Bank issues bullion certificates, which are evidence of the Bank's liability to deliver bullion to the registered owner upon notice. The certificate business has grown substantially and provides a

London,
Trading Desk

CREDIT: MICHEL PROULX

convenient method for the customer to invest in precious metals without involving physical delivery and storage problems.

The Bank of Nova Scotia currently purchases about 65 per cent of the total Canadian gold-mining production and a significant amount of this bullion is sold by the mines to the Bank on a forward basis. For example, if bullion delivery is six months from now, the Bank will quote a price for payment in six months, based upon the prevailing spot price at the time of the transaction plus a forward premium. More recently, the Bank has developed extensive bullion dealings with central banks by offering a variety of deposit- and refining-related facilities. The Bank also provides a variety of bullion services to the industrial users of gold and silver, particularly spot-and-forward purchase and sales contracts and bullion loan financing.

The Bank originally started in the gold business in 1958 in partnership with Samuel Montagu and Company of London (as was recounted in Chapter 10). The joint arrangements were amicably terminated in 1975 in light of the Bank's developed expertise and market connections. Today, with trading operations in Hong Kong and London, England, to support the existing Toronto operation, The Bank of Nova Scotia has become an internationally recognized leader in this unique business.

INTERNATIONAL IN FULLEST SENSE

With such a variety of external interests, it is quite evident that the Nova Scotia has become international in the fullest sense and nobody realizes this more than Ritchie. He knows how to use his advisers – whether directly or through his executive assistants – advisers such as the Chief Accountant, the tax people, the Economics Department, and his senior colleagues. As well, Ritchie makes it his business to be well informed. One of the activities which he finds useful and enjoys is his participation in the annual three-day meetings of the International Monetary Conference, arranged under the auspices of the American Bankers Association for top officers of some of the large international banks. The presence of central bankers and ministers of finance usually makes the off-the-record exchange of views extremely interesting.

IMPRESSIVE TOTAL EARNINGS

Largely on account of the substantial increase in profits from international business, the Bank's total earnings after taxes and appropriations rose impressively in the seventies. Profits represented the best rate of return on record on shareholders' equity, and of course the highest rate of return on earnings per share. As has already been noted, profits had risen considerably in the sixties, and by 1971 the return on average shareholders' equity had increased to just over 12 per cent, where, with the exception of one upward jump in 1975 to 14.7 per cent, it remained throughout the decade. In 1981, profits levelled out and the rate of return on shareholders' equity dropped to 11½ per cent, as compared with 12½ per cent in 1980. The pause was mainly the result of sharply rising interest costs from the funding of Scotia Plan and mortgages.

CHANGED CALCULATION OF EARNINGS

Following the 1967 Bank Act Revision, transfers to the Accumulated Appropriations for Losses Account (the reserve for unforeseen contingencies) became public knowledge. This led to some debate on the question of the best measure of bank operating earnings and at the time of this writing it had become widely acknowledged that "Balance of Revenue after Taxes" (that is, *before* Appropriation for Losses) might be a more appropriate measure of annual results than "Balance of Profits."

If one adopts this view, it is logical to agree also that the balance in the Accumulated Appropriations for Losses Account is (at least for the measurement of rate of return) an allocation of shareholders' funds. On this basis then, the return on equity (including Accumulated Appropriations) was almost 15½ per cent in 1981 compared with 17 per cent in 1980. And the trend was quite similar to the figures calculated without transfers from Accumulated Appropriations, rising sharply in the late sixties and levelling out between 16 per cent and 17 per cent during most of the seventies.

For a number of years, the Bank's policy of balanced diversification had helped to smooth out the growth of earnings and to reduce the likelihood of sudden decline. Actually, from 1975 onward, the trend in the return on domestic assets had been generally downward, the consequence of narrowing interest margins resulting from the higher costs of funding the Bank's fixed-rate Scotia Plan and mortgage portfolios. However, this downward tendency had been more than offset by increased volume in Canada, while the international business had been blessed with mounting volume and more or less level rates of return. It was only after two years of unparalleled advances in interest rates that the squeeze showed up and checked the growth in total earnings.

HIGH EARNINGS NEEDED

These are times when banks need high earnings. Twelve per cent on shareholders' equity or even 15 per cent on the balance-of-revenue basis – high as these figures would have seemed a decade or so ago – does not make much impression on investors when high quality bonds yield 15 per cent. To raise the additional capital that a bank needs to support the rising structure of liabilities brought about by inflation, higher earnings are essential – higher earnings to plough back into capital and to provide the financial record without which additional stock and debenture issues could not be floated. And new issues, whether of stock or debentures, have to be competitive with the high returns offered in the market.

The fact of the matter is that capital ratios have been declining. Shareholders' equity has not been maintained in line with deposit liabilities. The ratio of shareholders' equity to deposits has declined from 3.9 per cent in 1971 to 2.8 per cent in 1980.* With a lower ratio, the rate of return on shareholders' equity is, of course, higher than if equity had been maintained in line with deposits. Thus, in assessing profits, the decrease in capital ratios should also be borne in mind.

DECLINE IN CAPITAL AND LIQUIDITY RATIOS

The decline in capital ratios has been a common phenomenon in Canadian banking and indeed in banking worldwide. Compared with past standards, capital ratios have declined to low levels in the leading countries. The Canadian figure, excluding debentures, of around 3 per cent compares with about $3\frac{1}{2}$ per cent in the United States, is about the same as in Japan, and is a bit lower than in West Germany.

* When these ratios are regarded as a measure of adequacy of capital rather than as a guide to profitability, some think it appropriate to include debentures as another form of capital. On this basis the ratio of shareholders' equity plus debentures to deposits was 4.5 per cent in 1971 and 3.5 per cent in 1980.

Liquidity ratios have also gone down – the 14 per cent figure for The Bank of Nova Scotia in 1980, which is the same as the average for all the Canadian banks, compares with 26 per cent in 1970. Banks are bigger and in many cases, like the Nova Scotia's, are better-balanced and more diversified. In any case, federal government securities, whose proportionate reduction as a source of liquidity accounts for most of the difference in liquidity ratios between 1970 and 1980, have turned out to be a very unsatisfactory and expensive source of liquidity. Moreover, with the development of the Eurodollar market and of what amounts to a world banking system, cash is available at a price, usually a not unreasonable one, to any well-run bank. Thus, the readier availability of cash provides substantial added flexibility to the banking world.

AUTOMATION AND PRODUCTIVITY

The growth of assets in real terms, that is, after correction for inflation, is probably the best measure of growth in the banking industry. Real growth for The Bank of Nova Scotia during the seventies occurred at the rate of 11½ per cent per annum, as has already been pointed out. During the same period the number of staff grew at the rate of 5 per cent per annum. At first sight, since this figure is almost half as much as that for the growth in assets, it might be assumed that the productivity of workers in the Bank increased by approximately 5 per cent per annum. However, such an inference would probably be an exaggeration because the character of the staff in the Bank is changing, changing towards more "knowledge" workers and fewer routine workers. And the balancing factor is an increase in capital investment, particularly in the form of computer arrangements.

The rapid development of automation which has come about as a result of the introduction of the computer means that the same number of people can do more work. Furthermore, they can do more interesting and demanding work. In the case of the teller, the most visible bank employee, the laborious entries by hand in a passbook or ledger are pretty well gone. But more is expected of tellers. They are selling new services, such as special accounts, with different interest rates and terms, and making transfers, buying and selling foreign exchange, and paying bills. There is less drudgery and more thinking and salesmanship. As one can see, their output is increasing. In the international sphere a high proportion of the staff are "knowledge" workers and fewer are clerks. The people that handle the business and complete the deals are knowledgeable about interest rates, foreign exchange, and often taxes. The rewards of success are large and productivity can be high.

A NEW TURN IN BRANCH DEVELOPMENT

Another traditional measure of the growth of the Bank has been the number of branches, and here again there has been a shift of emphasis. As recently as the late sixties, Crockett stressed the importance of opening new branches. This was seen as the key to success. The number of new branches opened was an index of the Bank's increasing ability to secure new business. To some degree this is still the case, but as the seventies wore on, opening branches became relatively more expensive. Salaries were rising sharply and rentals and real estate costs were going through the roof. Branches could no longer be opened in shopping centres and other locations on the once-reasonable assumption that they would become profitable in three to five years. Competition for personal loans and mortgages was increasing dramatically, and towards the end of the decade interest rates were rising to unheard-of levels, and margins on personal loans were being squeezed. Thus, more emphasis was placed on the larger commercial branches, on improving existing branches in this category, as well as on opening new ones to some extent. In the domestic market, where the Bank now had excellent branch representation and where further progress had been made in Quebec, the increase in new branches was relatively smaller than in the past. From 1970 to 1980 the rate of growth was about $2^{1}/_{2}$ per cent per annum, compared with 4 per cent the decade before and with 5 per cent in the fifties. As would be expected, advances were above average in some parts of the West and there was a considerable increase in the number of offices outside of Canada.

THE REAL ESTATE DEPARTMENT

The change in emphasis in branch expansion is not to say that the Bank is spending relatively less on premises and real estate but rather that it is spending in somewhat different ways. Even if fewer new small branches are required, the right kinds of offices in the best locations are still essential, and if more big commercial offices are needed, there will be no lessening in the importance of real estate. This has been recognized in the reorganization of the old Premises Department as the Real Estate Department. It still does the same job of branch network expansion and renovation but, in addition, it has a development group concerned with acquiring income-producing properties, with bank premises and probably also offices in them.

Such developments may be large or medium-sized, and often include a partner or sometimes more than one partner. The fine buildings in which the Bank is housed in Vancouver, Calgary, and Saint John are examples of such developments and a new one, somewhat differently organized, is in progress in Edmonton. Understandably, there are pressures from the regions to enter such development projects, but because of the large sums involved and the significant risks in

BILINGUAL CAPACITY IN QUEBEC

One of the recent notable changes in The Bank of Nova Scotia has been the drive towards bilingualism in Quebec. In ten years, the Bank has fully adjusted to the linguistic pattern of the province under the leadership of André Bisson, Vice-President and General Manager. Ninety-one per cent of the staff have a good working knowledge of the French language. Of approximately one hundred and twenty-five managers and assistant managers, only about 5 per cent do not have a good knowledge of French, compared with about 40 per cent in 1970. All communications, except those going to headquarters, are in French and the language of business in most branches is French.

The change was expensive in terms of both money and personal adjustment. It did not occur easily, since it involved a major shift in management staff, with English-speaking employees moving out of Quebec and with an even larger number of only partially prepared but well-educated French Canadians moving into the organization. Fortunately, the Bank's growth in Ontario and the West was sufficient to provide enough new openings for staff at the management level to make the adjustment without extreme difficulty – an adjustment which in some cases was no longer unwelcome because of the changed social environment in Quebec. As Bisson says, "The English-speaking who were moving represented a high proportion of the senior credit and management people." Many of the new people coming in were university graduates and some were MBAs. Bisson, with his former university associations, employed a bright group. But when they first came in they were not adequately trained and they were replacing the older, experienced English-speaking employees too quickly. As Bisson realizes, "People made mistakes. Some could not say no to the customer." As time went on, some problems diminished, but staff turnover was high and, while the organization was changing, the development of a really efficient operation was turning out to be a slow process.

A DIFFERENT BANK IN QUEBEC

There was no doubt that the Bank in Quebec was different. In the first place it was French-Canadian – run by a French Canadian and staffed almost entirely by French Canadians. It was developing roots in the community and was procuring some French-Canadian business. Of course, even ten years ago the Bank in Quebec was largely staffed by French Canadians, but many of the senior jobs were still held by English-speaking personnel and there were relatively fewer up-and-coming French Canadians in the organization. Today, most of the top jobs are held by quite young French Canadians. English Canadians and

New York, Trading Desk

CREDIT: MICHEL PROULX

French Canadians have learned to work together and they have a good morale, partly the result of Bisson's conferences, three-day get-togethers at which to look ahead and plan.

Three important facets of the new approach were a French-language approach to publicity, more branch openings in predominantly French-speaking areas, and the hiring and training of able university graduates. Real progress has been made in all directions. Advertising is French in every sense – not translated from English. For a good many years, the Bank had used the French translation of its name, "La Banque de Nouvelle Ecosse," in advertisements, signs, letterheads, etc., in Quebec and still does to a degree. But almost by accident the abbreviation "BNE" took hold, just as "Scotiabank" had taken hold in English in the sixties. Thus, the Bank is becoming known as "BNE" and the signs are being lettered and letterheads are being printed that way. When it comes to branches, more have been opened, about thirty in the ten years, almost all in French-speaking areas. Finally, the third facet of the approach – hiring and training university graduates – has been carried a long way, though Bisson thinks the whole process might have been handled better and been more successful. Competition to hire university graduates was very keen and to attract the best-quality people and keep them was difficult. For example, the success of Scotia Plan in Quebec made its officers a frequent target of other banks.

TO BE PERCEIVED AS A LARGE INTERNATIONAL BANK

The Bank's capacity in the international sphere, combined with persistent efforts by Ritchie and Bisson, finally earned it some significant Quebec government business – first as agent and lead manager of a debt issue in 1979; then, in 1980, as the agent and one of three lead managers in a one-billion U.S.-dollar and Canadian-dollar issue. These events were especially important because Bisson wanted the "BNE to be perceived as a large international bank, serving Quebec with its international expertise." The emphasis was on international rather than Canadian because the international side appeared to be of more interest to the young French-Canadian bankers, just as it was to some of the rising English-speaking bankers in Ontario and the West. And there have already been examples of French Canadians who have done well in the international area. But the prospect of some reasonable mobility among the bright young French and English Scotiabankers and of their developing a distinctive "Nova Scotia" style or way of seeing things is still well in the future. Bell keeps asking Bisson when he is going to send him a few promising people for Toronto branch, but Bisson has few to spare and fewer yet who are ready to come to Toronto. The educational facilities at Spencer Hall will no doubt help, but it may be some time yet before a young French Canadian presents himself at Toronto or Vancouver as an assistant manager. And as for International, English is the language of business and finance in the great majority of countries and there simply is not the business to develop what might be called a French Division.

A DELAYED AND RATHER DISAPPOINTING BANK ACT

Another part which The Bank of Nova Scotia played in Canadian banking in the seventies was its pressure for revisions in the Bank Act aimed at producing a more competitive banking environment. The previous revision, of 1967, had moved strongly in this direction; and the Nova Scotia and a number, but not all, of the other banks held quite similar views. Scotiabank's position was very clearly set forth in a statement by Ritchie and Bell in the annual report for 1978 in which they commented on the government's proposals for changing the Act: "We have found much to commend in the proposals for change, such as the stated objective of increased competition, on a more equal footing, between financial institutions in Canada. At the same time we are disturbed that the proposed changes do not move far enough toward that objective. In particular, we have argued that the Federal Government has failed to recognize the importance of bringing the 'near banks' – many of which are provincially incorporated institutions – under adequate federal control. In fact, there seems a real danger that without these changes, Canada will be moving increasingly toward

Just Around the Corner, Right Around the World, 1971-1981   331

a dual or even multiple banking system, partly under and partly free of control by federal monetary and regulatory authorities."³

However, in the finally revised Bank Act, which became law in November 1980, after three years of on-and-off discussion, the hopes of Ritchie and Bell were dashed. Because of strong opposition from the trust, mortgage, and finance companies, indeed from most of the "near banks," little was done to move further towards an open and uniformly controlled domestic financial system. Moreover, to quote the annual report for 1980, the result of a number of last-minute amendments "will be more to protect other financial companies from vigorous competition, than to serve the interests of customers, whether individuals or businesses."⁴

TREATMENT OF FOREIGN BANKS

The changes in the Bank Act concerning foreign banks were more to the Nova Scotia's liking, though they did not fit into an overall plan for regulating all banking institutions and appeared to be more restrictive than necessary. As Ritchie and Bell said in the 1978 annual report, "At the heart of our concern is the basic belief that open competition on an equitable basis ultimately is good for banking, and therefore good for our customers. As well, we are mindful of the fair and reasonable treatment our bank has been accorded in so many other nations. We contend that the services we can provide to customers in other countries do benefit those countries, and have argued that Canada itself could benefit from the experience and knowledge of other, non-resident bankers. More important, we foresee considerable opportunities to develop major international financial centres in Canada."⁵

As an international bank, Scotiabank supported legislation to allow foreign banks to operate in Canada. When the first foreign banks got their charters under the Bank Act passed in late 1980, the Bank extended this welcome in several Canadian publications.

The Bank had devoted a great deal of effort and research to its proposals for the revision of the Bank Act. The Government Relations Department, under MacIntosh's direction and run by Craddock, who later became executive assistant to the Chairman, worked for years on the revision, with particular emphasis on foreign banking aspects. Earlier, Crean (before moving to Systems) had done a major, related study of the Canadian clearing system. In terms of results, it might be questioned whether all this effort was worthwhile. Scotiabank's influence in Ottawa, judged by the lack of attention paid to practicable workable suggestions, seemed to be at a low ebb – though not lower than that of other banks. MacIntosh was chairman of the Bank Act Revision Committee representing all the banks and Craddock was secretary. It is no coincidence that MacIntosh retired from The Bank of Nova Scotia in April 1980 to become President of the Canadian Bankers' Association. Difficult jobs often attract able men and there is no doubt that MacIntosh, with more support and discretionary power than the Association had given any employee before, intends to be an effective voice for the Canadian banking industry.

ECONOMICS DEPARTMENT NOT FADING AWAY

MacIntosh came originally from the Economics Department and it is quite apparent that, because of his initiative and energy, some research which would normally have been done in that Department was carried out under his direct jurisdiction. The work on the recent Bank Act revision was a case in point. In earlier times it might have been done in Economics. Yet this is not to suggest that the Economics Department was fading away. As already noted, its functions had broadened notably with the growth of the Bank's international business. It is used regularly by Ritchie in checking out new economic developments, in preparing background for meetings with the Bank of Canada, in briefing him on the economic side of his overseas trips, and so on. Rogers prepares reports for the Board of Directors on key developments or policy issues and the Economics Department works with the Public and Corporate Affairs Department in the preparation of the annual report. As well, there is the work in connection with operational and profit planning, including national and regional forecasts and assessment of interest and exchange rates, and the monitoring and analysing of the flow of assets and liabilities of the Bank in relation to the system. Last, but not least, is the Bank's *Monthly Review*, which has been published now for fifty-five years and which promotes the Bank's good name for Canadian and foreign economic studies. There are 55,000 copies of every issue printed in English and 11,000 in French. Rogers has had his hands full and he is now nearing retirement. He has recently been appointed Chairman of the Steering Committee of the International Conference of Commercial Bank Economists.

EXECUTIVE CHANGES

There were no top executive changes after the readjustment of the early seventies until 1979. At that time, Bell became President and Chief Operating Officer, a function which he was already performing, while Ritchie continued as Chairman and Chief Executive Officer. They remained the top two leaders. Godsoe was also promoted in 1979 to be Senior Vice-President and the second man in International, his title being changed to Executive Vice-President the following year, while McDonald became Senior Executive Vice-President at that time.

With the loss of MacIntosh in 1980 and the retirement of Hitchman and Crockett early in 1981 and 1982, respectively, there was a fairly large gap at the top, further accentuated by the fact that Younker had passed retirement age and by the death of Shaw in 1981. While Shaw's job had been taken by L.A. Thurston, formerly in charge of Western and Northern Ontario, and while Hitchman and Younker are filling in temporarily, there is a sizeable added workload, which inevitably falls on Bell and Ritchie. The first step in strengthening the top executive occurred in January 1982, when McDonald and Godsoe were appointed Vice-Chairmen, next in line to Ritchie and Bell.

Just Around the Corner, Right Around the World, 1971-1981

Bell keeps watching the bottom line and is quick to sense potential weakness or opportunity. Once a quarter he invites all the senior people in General Office to hear his analysis of the Bank's profit and loss and of its balance sheet. From all accounts it is a clear and thorough presentation not only of the facts but also of what needs to be done in the light of those facts. There is, of course, discussion, but Bell is not a man with whom to cross swords lightly, and his figures, fresh from Brooks and Mitchell, are impeccable.

A LIVELY, RESPONSIBLE BOARD

There was some further change in the composition of the Board of Directors in the seventies. On the average, the Director was younger – 59 as opposed to 63 – partly because of the maximum age of 70 established under the Bank bylaws. The average Director was also a bit more western-Canadian and non-Canadian-oriented, reflecting the nature of the growth of the Bank. There were also two women on the Board, Helen Parker and Marie Wilson. The old-timers – those with 15 or more years of service – were Lewis H. M. Ayre, Frank H. Sherman, D.G. Willmot, E. Jacques Courtois, John J. Jodrey, and the Rt. Hon. Earl of Iveagh. One of the old-timers, the Hon. John Aird, resigned to serve as Lieutenant-Governor of Ontario, following in the steps of the Hon. W.D. Ross, who retired from the Bank in 1927 to do the same job. Another able director, René Amyot, Q.C., resigned to become Chairman of Air Canada. Their counsel is already missed.

While it is difficult for an outside observer to judge the quality of a Board, the people on the Nova Scotia's, and their backgrounds, are enough to indicate strength, knowledgeability, business skill, and broad interest. Ritchie, who, as Chief Executive Officer for almost a decade, has had to cope with more surprises and sudden changes in economics and banking conditions than in any previous ten years of peacetime, speaks very highly of the Board's value to management. "We have a good Board and it is a great help to be able to review major policy matters with them. The Board and the Executive Committee bring together a variety of points of view which are useful and constructive when difficult issues are at stake."

In the opinion of many of those who are around to make the comparison, the Board has improved in the last ten years. Boyles made a real effort to bring more information to the Board not just from Economics and International but also from other officers who had a story to tell. And Ritchie has carried on with the principle of providing information and opinions relevant to the problems facing the Board. Some of the Directors speak highly of the presentations which they have received, referring particularly to Bell and Hitchman on credit matters, to McDonald and Godsoe on International, to Brooks on finance, and to Rogers and MacIntosh on more general subjects.

NOTES

1. BNS Annual Report, 1979, A Report to the Shareholders by the Chairman and the President, p.5.
2. BNS Annual Report, 1975, Chairman's Report, pp.9-10.
3. BNS Annual Report, 1978, A Joint Report by the Chairman and by the Chief General Manager, p.9.
4. BNS Annual Report, 1980, A Report to the Shareholders by the Chairman and the President, p.11.
5. BNS Annual Report, 1978, A Joint Report by the Chairman and by the Chief General Manager, p.10.

15

A Story of Adaptability and Strength

In 1982, The Bank of Nova Scotia looks back on 150 years; it is the second-oldest Canadian bank, with a more than usually interesting past, with more than its share of great bankers, with unbroken dividend payments from the beginning, and with a record of solid achievement – $50 billion worth. It is a history in which a host of Scotiabankers may take pride.

Perhaps the most striking characteristic of the Bank's story as recounted in the past fourteen chapters is its ability to adapt itself to changing circumstances. Somehow the Bank managed to do the right thing when it was needed and the right person always seemed to be there to do it.

Forman's systematic theft of $315,000 over 25 years, which came to light in 1870, might have destroyed another institution. The Bank's paid-up capital was only $560,000, and its assets were $2 million. Sorting out the books, which had been "cooked" for twenty-five years, was beyond the capacity of the committee of the Board of Directors. Thus, they hired a new Cashier, W.C. Menzies, from the Bank of British North America to do the job.

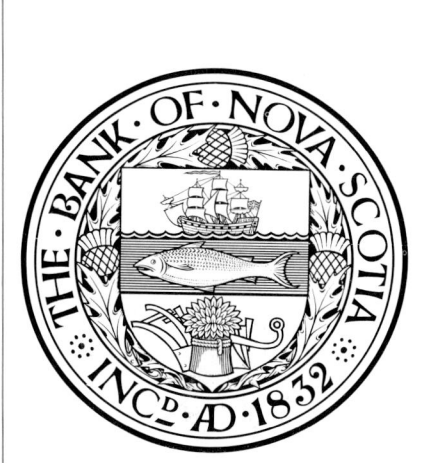

The Bank of Nova Scotia Seal, designed in 1921 to replace several different seals which had been used up to that time.

MENZIES DID TWO GREAT THINGS

Menzies did two great things for the Bank. He got it back on track quite rapidly and he obtained a top-notch successor. By March of 1872, he was able to report that the Bank had recovered from the machinations of its late Cashier, and by 1875, when Menzies was forced to retire because of poor health, the Bank's assets had risen to $3.6 million and its total capital to $1.2 million. He had opened two new branches, bringing the total to five, and he had set up the first set of rules and regulations for the Bank's operations. Before retiring, he was able to hire a former colleague from the Bank of British North America,

Thomas Fyshe, to take his place. Like a number of other banks on this continent, the Nova Scotia was indebted to this British colonial bank for a number of its senior officers – the elder Forgan, as well as Fyshe and Menzies. As Fyshe said, it was a bank "which seems to have sown its men all over the continent."[1]

FYSHE, AN OUTSTANDING CANADIAN BANKER

Fyshe was one of Canada's outstanding bankers, running The Bank of Nova Scotia for twenty-one years. He gives the impression that he could have coped with any situation, and he had both good times and bad with which to deal. He established the Nova Scotia in a leading position in the Maritimes. When he first took over the Bank in the mid-1870s, the Maritime provinces were struggling with the demise of the wooden-shipbuilding industry, poor world markets for both lumber and codfish, and the readjustments involved in Confederation. But in the face of these difficulties the Bank continued to grow. In the early 1880s, the Union Bank of Prince Edward Island was taken over and a sizeable number of branches were opened in New Brunswick as well as in Nova Scotia. At the end of 1883, there were 23 branches of The Bank of Nova Scotia throughout the Maritimes, an increase of 15 in ten years. Assets had grown only moderately but the base was there for a larger bank when the economic conditions were more favourable. For the time being, they were not. Apart from 1870, the year of the discovery of the defalcation, 1884 produced the worst financial results in the Bank's history.

That did not deter Fyshe from looking for new opportunities. There were few in the Maritimes and indeed it was difficult to make use of all the Bank's resources. Looking outward, therefore, the Bank opened in Winnipeg, then at the height of a land boom. Though this venture turned out to be quite costly, it paved the way to a profitable interlude in Minneapolis and then Chicago. Following that came the first move into the rest of Canada – to Montreal in 1888. The next step was expansion south to Kingston, Jamaica, in 1889; thus, The Bank of Nova Scotia was the first Canadian bank in the Caribbean. And, finally, there was the race to reach Newfoundland at the time of the local financial crisis of 1894 – a race won by The Bank of Nova Scotia.

McLEOD GOES TO TORONTO

Fyshe was succeeded by another able man with a very different personality – the extraordinary H.C. McLeod. McLeod's first major decision was probably the most courageous act in the Bank's history – to move the General Manager's office (what is now called General Office) to Toronto. McLeod was convinced that the Bank's centre of gravity had to shift westward – he saw that the building of railways and the opening of the West heralded a great period of Canadian development

LEFT:

Coat of Arms in Banking Hall, Rotterdam, The Netherlands. Designed in 1921 by A. Scott Carter and approved by the College of Heralds in 1951.

RIGHT:

Stylized Version of The Bank of Nova Scotia Coat of Arms

which could be shared fully only by a bank operated from Toronto or Montreal. The first branch in Toronto had been opened as recently as two years earlier and the Bank was represented in few places outside of the Maritime provinces. Yet, the Board in Halifax, who were all Maritimers, approved the decision unanimously.

McLeod saw what was becoming increasingly clear – that any bank in the developing Canadian environment would sooner or later have to struggle to either become a big national bank or else be taken over by another bank. In line with his ambition to make the Nova Scotia a national bank, McLeod reopened the branch in Winnipeg. In short order, branches were opened in Edmonton, Vancouver, Calgary, and a bit later in Regina and Saskatoon, though the going was tough in the West since other banks had arrived there earlier. Of at least equal significance to the development of the Bank was the opening of 16 branches in Ontario and 19 in Nova Scotia and New Brunswick, all between 1897 and 1909. And then there was a further push in the Caribbean, including expansion in Jamaica and opening in Cuba. The Bank of Nova Scotia was on its way to becoming a national bank with some international flavour.

A STRONG SENSE OF PUBLIC RESPONSIBILITY

McLeod, together with all his push, brought another dimension to The Bank of Nova Scotia. He had a strong sense of public responsibility which, partly because he was right and partly because he was a difficult man, did nothing to enhance his popularity among his banking confreres or even with the Department of Finance in Ottawa. He was obsessed with the need for external inspection of the chartered banks, but no one paid any attention. He went so far as to have The Bank of Nova Scotia's books certified by outside auditors – a revolutionary step in 1907. His views were finally vindicated in 1923 when the Home Bank failed, and, as a consequence, government inspection was at last introduced the following year.

RICHARDSON RANKS VERY HIGH

If the builders of The Bank of Nova Scotia were to be ranked according to their accomplishments against the background of the times, H.A. Richardson would be at or close to the top of the list. He was responsible for three amalgamations during the years 1913 to 1919; thus, the Bank was enabled to move from the position of accounting for $4^1/_2$ per cent of the assets of the Canadian banking system to 8 per cent of the total. It had become the fourth bank in size in Canada, a rank which it enjoys today.

By means of amalgamation, Richardson was simply carrying out more effectively what McLeod had been trying to do by adding new branches. Both realized that the Bank was sooner or later going to reach the point where it would have to either grow in order to provide something approaching national service and national opportunity, or sell out, or, what would have been even worse, struggle along with diminishing prospects. The Nova Scotia chose the national approach, and was able to achieve a better balance by taking over two banks in the centre of Canada.

THE THREE AMALGAMATIONS

But first came the takeover of the Bank of New Brunswick in 1913, an old friend and neighbour which had chosen the path of comfortable stagnation and which, if it had to be taken over, preferred to amalgamate with someone it knew. Next to be taken over was the Metropolitan, also a good friend through its General Manager, W.D. Ross; this amalgamation in 1914 helped to strengthen The Bank of Nova Scotia where strength was most needed – in Toronto and southern Ontario. And finally there was the amalgamation with the Bank of Ottawa in 1919, the largest of the three, which made The Bank of Nova Scotia a major partner in the Ottawa Valley and also added to its representation in the West. The motivations of the shareholders of these three banks in joining a larger partner were fairly similar. For all, the outlook on the present basis seemed mediocre; it suggested problems rather than opportunities and held no great promise for the performance of their stock, which carried double liability. In contrast, amalgamation appeared to assure these shareholders a bright future and a good investment.

J.A. McLEOD, PATTERSON, AND BURNS

Whether J.A. McLeod, who followed Richardson, would be considered to be a builder of The Bank of Nova Scotia, or for that matter whether either Patterson or Burns would be, is an interesting question. With the possible exception of Patterson, who never had a chance to show what he could do since his regime covered only depression and war years, these men were conservative in their approaches and decisions. But perhaps they also were the men for their times.

Perhaps it was best for the Bank to slow up after the aggressive Richardson era. Perhaps there were no other reasonable deals to be made – certainly there were not very many in the time between 1923 and the depression. A period of consolidation was needed, but for how long? When the depression came, the Bank was lucky to have the strength which was a result of the conservative policies of the late 1920s; unlike some other banks, the Nova Scotia did not have to draw on its published reserves or unduly press its customers. This was the period in which Enman picked up a number of important accounts from other banks in the Maritimes, while Frost was able to work out a number of sensible accommodations with farm customers in the West.

After the opening of the new General Office building in Toronto in 1951, a sketch of the building appeared on the letterhead and on Bank publications.

GROWTH RESUMES WITH ENMAN

There is no doubt that the right man, Enman, was at the helm when the war came to an end. While the Enman approach was traditional, it was vigorous and it produced results. Much progress was made in filling in the gaps in western Canada and in growing with the big cities. Then there was the revolution in attitude, from that of a conservative bank – almost as conservative as the Bank of Montreal – to that of an aggressive bank trying to find new ways of making loans and obtaining business. As evidence of the effectiveness of the change in attitude, the Bank's share of the total assets of the system rose from $8\frac{1}{2}$ per cent to $9\frac{1}{2}$ per cent in the ten years after the war. Frost, who was also traditionalist but a little less aggressive in style, made his mark at this time by improving both staff and customer relations.

NICKS ENTERS NEW LENDING AREAS

With Nicks came the breakthrough into a broad new field of lending – that of the consumer. Scotia Plan certainly increased the Bank's share of domestic lending, and an active new deposit approach, which was also revolutionary, helped support new lending activities. Banking had become more consumer-oriented. It had also become more sales-oriented with regard both to lending and to obtaining deposits.

Even more striking was the expansion of international operations, again under Nicks's leadership. By being early, active, and aggressive, the Nova Scotia gained an important position in the international sphere just as it did in consumer lending. Nicks believed the Bank could much more readily develop profitable business by going into new, uncultivated areas rather than by ploughing the same fields with increasing intensity. By 1970, the Bank's share of the total assets of the Canadian banking system was up to $13^1/_2$ per cent from 12 per cent in 1960 and $9^1/_2$ per cent in 1955.

As time went on, rising costs became a growing problem for the Nova Scotia as well as for the other banks. Better management techniques, improved methods, and later, more effective use of computers became increasingly important. Gibson's resignation in the mid-sixties was, in part, a protest against the slowness in improving management methods. New services might attract business but they were of little interest if they could not carry their costs and one way or another bring in some profit. Ritchie turned increasing attention to these matters and much progress was made. Staff training, staff hiring, as well as more credit training and broader preparation at Spencer Hall, all received new emphasis.

RITCHIE COMPLETES WORLD BANKING CHAIN

Ritchie completed Scotiabank's wholesale banking chain around the world, so that foreign exchange business and gold business, for example, could be conducted twenty-four hours a day, and so that the Bank could participate in the burgeoning growth of the Pacific countries. A notable degree of diversification, geographically and in terms of products, had been achieved and this promised to smooth fluctuations in earnings. Assets reached $50 billion in 1981 – $14^1/_2$ per cent of all the assets of the Canadian banks. Unfortunately, this great growth was accompanied by continuing inflation, which increasingly threatened the efficient operation of the domestic and indeed the whole global economic system.

IMPORTANCE OF ENVIRONMENT

It is quite evident that the Bank's record reflects the environment within which it has evolved and grown. No one could change the economic conditions. All the banks, except perhaps the French-Canadian banks with their strong local support and flavour, had to go west, and all had to adapt to the competitive environment or lose out. In the development of Canadian branch banking, there was little room for specialized banks. (However, it may be that this situation is now changing with the recent appearance of some specialized Canadian institutions and even more with the opening of branches of international banks in Canada.) The environment was highly competitive and

Globe & Arrow Letterhead.

The use of "Scotia" in script with "Bank" in printed typestyle was introduced in 1961.

the tendency was to follow the leader if he had something better, and sometimes even if he had not.

PEOPLE MAKE A DIFFERENCE

But having said this, there is no doubt that the Nova Scotia's history would have been very different, and indeed much shorter, if Menzies and Fyshe had not steered the Bank on a sound course. This chronicle would probably have been part of the history of another bank if McLeod had not moved the headquarters to Toronto and if Richardson had not taken over three fair-sized banks. Certainly, the Bank would have been a less interesting and a less important institution if Enman had not given it the drive he did after the war. And the Bank would be much smaller if Nicks had not been early in introducing Scotia Plan and entering the international wholesale business. By the mid-sixties, everyone had to go international and Ritchie was the man to maintain the Nova Scotia's leading position. Without him, growth would have been less marked and less diversified. The Bank's image might well have been less open and less public-spirited.

People do make a difference – a big difference. And so does tradition. The tradition of The Bank of Nova Scotia is non-conformist and non-establishment. The number of Scots in the Bank, particularly in its early days, may have had something to do with this. From the beginning, the Bank had to fight the colonial establishment in the shape of the Halifax Banking Company, just to obtain a charter and then to stay alive. Fyshe carried on the non-establishment tradition with his dogged pursuit of "the Liverpool boodlers" – important citizens who were trying to avoid their double-liability obligations when the Bank of Liverpool failed. And H.C. McLeod took on the Canadian banking establishment in his campaign for outside inspection of the banks.

NOT AN ESTABLISHMENT BANK

The same thread is apparent in the Bank's entry into Scotia Plan, which cut the cost of borrowing for individual consumers considerably but which was regarded as an inappropriate, or indeed an improper, kind of business for a bank by some bankers. Even the Bank's entry into an insured savings program, which was somewhat unconventional, led to raised eyebrows – was the Bank getting involved in the insurance business? As a non-member of the establishment, with only a limited number of big accounts, The Bank of Nova Scotia has had to scurry for a living. Since it was difficult to obtain more big accounts in Canada, the Bank pursued big accounts abroad. If life had been comfortable, the Nova Scotia might not have been a leader in consumer credit or international wholesale banking. Nor would Ritchie have been referred to by some of his friends as the "Harry Truman of Canadian banking."

All the men who led this non-establishment bank were professionals. While none of them was poor, none was really rich. From the early days, it was understood that bankers should not take advantage of inside information for their own benefit; in other words, they should not seek personal gain from opportunities about which they had privileged information. As time went on, this rule or tradition became even more entrenched.

BANK IS STRONGLY INTERNATIONAL

The Bank's strengths today are manifold. It is innovative. It is strongly international, more so than any other Canadian bank; it can properly be regarded as an international bank based in Canada. It has wide diversification abroad, where its business is placed only after a careful weighing of the "country" risks. Its external business is conservatively funded and a relatively high ratio of deposits with other banks to international loans is maintained. And though the Bank engages in many syndicated loans, it is also true that a high proportion of its lending is direct to the borrower, which means a thorough knowledge of the account involved.

The Bank has intensified its efforts to co-ordinate its domestic and international business. The Corporate Banking Department and the North American International Region, working under the same head, are designed to accomplish this for larger-scale business, to which can be added Special Loan Services making available Eurodollar loans to either domestic or international customers. And now the International Banking Centres – six of them, spread across the country – are providing foreign exchange, letter-of-credit and informational services to Canadian customers from coast to coast.

A GOOD MORALE

It is probably true to say that the morale of Scotiabankers has been good for a long time. It certainly improved markedly when growth was resumed after the long period of stagnation during the depression and the war. The change from a very conservative to a very active and aggressive stance in a few years under Enman was a tonic that did wonders for the staff. Then the development of International, with its need for trained and ambitious people, provided new opportunities, as did the opening of new and larger branches across the country. While there were problems in mixing university graduates (particularly MBAs) with those advancing through the ranks, the great solvent of growth produced better results than might have been expected. Now at the higher levels there is an effective blending of people who joined after high school with those who came from university backgrounds.

The young people in International are sure they are employed in the best part of the Bank; they think of themselves as members of a team who work closely together. And in the domestic branch system, there is a healthy competitive atmosphere and far more interesting jobs than a generation ago – both in the branches themselves and in General Office. Some areas are more popular than others and Toronto branch is still regarded as a very special place to work. In many, many cases, there is loyalty and interest which is nothing short of inspiring.

It might be noted for those who were not around before the war that the Bank has become quite cosmopolitan. In big centres like Toronto, Montreal, and Vancouver there are people of every racial origin, reflecting the influx of new Canadians, not just from Europe, from which many came earlier, but from the Far East and the South. The Bank certainly reflects the Canadian mosaic and benefits accordingly.

INTEREST IN BANKING NEEDS OF INDIVIDUALS

Another strong point about Scotiabank is its demonstrated interest in the banking needs of individuals. Its pioneering record in consumer credit, its active mortgage department, and its strongly competitive attitude have helped to bring in new business in a form which provides a steady flow of repayments and a continuing and reliable source of liquidity. It is true that the high levels of interest rates prevailing since 1980, together with their extreme variability, have made the whole area of consumer and household financing difficult and unsatisfactory for both customer and Bank. It is to be hoped that the rate structure settles at a considerably lower level or, to put it another way, that inflation is materially lessened. If not, the prospect for customer and banker will become increasingly less satisfactory.

In 1974, the new visual-image program introduced the flying "S" symbol and the "Scotiabank" wordmark. Use of the word "Scotiabank" was not new, however, since the Bank had arranged to use this term as its cable address as early as 1906.

Some of the senior officers of the Bank believe that one of its strengths is that the top executives know what is happening down the line and are therefore sensitive to emerging problems. But others are not so sure, and think that there is so much administration – so many layers of it – between the branch manager and the Chief Operating Officer that what information does sift through becomes muted.

DECENTRALIZATION GONE FAR ENOUGH

There are other officers, a considerable number of them, who are relieved that decentralization has gone no further than it has, and not as far as in some of the other banks. As Bell puts it, "We have had three or four years of an environment that has seen increasing risks – a decline in the quality of credit. The result is that the audit and monitoring side of credit has been intensified." Thus, from at least a short-term point of view, a lesser degree of decentralization could turn out to be an element of strength.

As the reader will undoubtedly have observed, credit supervision is the most difficult and expensive element in banking. Regionalization of

credit, in which all the Canadian banks have been engaged for many years, made sense from many points of view. But it has been slowed – in some cases perhaps even halted – by three factors. The first is the growing number of specialized services provided or planned by headquarters, including corporate banking services and international trade centres. The second is the capability of the regional officers to deal with more and larger credits. Many of the credit officers are, of course, highly competent, but there is a question about whether there are enough experienced people in the regions to back increased lending limits. The result has been that discretionary limits have not been changed much in the last few years. The third factor is the view expressed by Bell, that "this is no time to be increasing limits – risks are increasing as it is. It is rather a time when even the most seasoned of lenders should value additional analysis and judgment."

THE NEW BANKING SYSTEM

The Canadian banking system is much more competitive than it used to be, and in a considerable number of areas the Nova Scotia has led the way. Indeed, the system has changed so much that it almost seems like a new one. Lending has been extended in all directions, first towards the consumer and, as the bond market dried up, towards meeting more business needs. The fear that there might not be enough demand for loans, which prevailed for so many years before the war, is hard to imagine in an environment where there has been a continuous effort to raise more deposits to finance loans. Indeed, the old philosophy of banking has been shaken to its foundations. Instead of limiting lending to the new deposits that come in, as was once the case, banks use their liquidity to the fullest extent and keep looking for lending opportunities which they will in turn finance by bidding for additional deposits. Banks no longer limit their loans to the funds already on hand. Wholesale certificate-of-deposit rates for corporations are changed minute by minute and individual rates change daily at least. The whole structure of interest rates is now watched somewhat in the way people used to watch stock quotations in brokers' boardrooms.

In addition to bidding for additional deposits, banks have also changed the way in which they regard liquidity. Liquid assets which traditionally consisted of cash, money-market instruments, and federal government securities now amount to only 14 or 15 per cent of major Canadian dollar assets compared with 29 or 30 per cent in the mid-sixties. In reality, however, this comparison is highly misleading since the largest element in the so-called liquid assets of the sixties and earlier was government securities, which, except for the short-term maturities, turned out to be poor investments and at times far from liquid as well. Thus, while liquidity ratios appear low by past standards, there is an active and effective money market, through which liabilities are managed, and there is a continuous flow of repayments on consumer loans and mortgages, which can be used to strengthen the liquid position. Behind all this, there is the relatively new and very large and important source of liquidity – the Eurodollar market. In contrast to the situation of thirty years ago when the procedure for obtaining funds from abroad was rather formal, money now flows back and forth continuously in response to interest and exchange rate changes.

BANK IS SIGNIFICANT PART OF EURODOLLAR MARKET

The Bank of Nova Scotia is indeed a significant part of the Eurodollar market, and the International division, which is run from Toronto, handles about as many Eurodollars as the Bank handles Canadian dollars. In the Eurodollar market, there are no restraints in the form of cash reserves, though there are a number of other restraining influences. For example, there are only a limited number of first-class risks and they do not always wish to borrow. At the other end of the scale, there are many potential borrowers who are not regarded as adequate risks. This is particularly true of governments and businesses in countries whose balance-of-payments positions are weak.

Another restraint is the practice among the larger banks of keeping 40 per cent or more of their foreign assets in the form of deposits with other banks. A bank needs to be strong enough and competitive enough to attract large deposits from international banks if it is to do a big international business. In this context, because of the disturbed international environment since the early seventies and declining ratios of capital to deposit liabilities in many countries, regulation has become a matter of more concern to bank supervisory authorities. In most countries, there has been increased emphasis on detailed reporting and, in some, on capital-asset ratios of one sort or another.

Whatever else may be said of the new Canadian banking system, it is obviously highly competitive and it will become even more so now that foreign banks are establishing themselves in this country under the provisions of the new Bank Act. Increased competition for business and indeed for trained bankers is already being felt; a number of promising people have been enticed away from the Canadian banks. Banking may be more impersonal, and the old branch banker, that symbol of sympathetic help in the small town, may be less evident. After all, deposit-taking is largely automatic and the simpler forms of lending are automated to a degree. Business has become bigger and a bank manager often finds himself dealing with the assistant treasurer of a corporate customer rather than with the boss. Hence, there may be fewer personal contacts at the higher level and perhaps less loyalty and friendship. Department-store banking has its defects.

Yet this highly competitive system is something that The Bank of Nova Scotia helped to build. In building it, the Bank found many opportunities and there will undoubtedly be more. Automation need not destroy personal contact and service. By eliminating routine, it should give time for more purposeful service and improved relationships. The computer should give branch managers and district managers more of the time they need to get out and see their customers.

LEARNING TO MANAGE BIGNESS

The Bank of Nova Scotia is learning to manage bigness. A bank has to be big to be international. The loans are big and the deposits are big. If a bank is not big and strong it cannot play in the game at all. Even a domestic bank needs to be big, as the record in Canada around the turn of the century showed. Bigness makes much possible but it also creates massive problems. Some of these problems have been partly overcome by the effective use of the computer and the improvement in the job content which the computer has made possible. Other problems still await detailed redefinition of the work to be done and computer programming to carry it through. And yet other problems seem to be buried in the remnants of old ways of doing things, in functions and jobs which are not required in the same way that they originally were. And then there is always the normal tendency of individuals and groups to protect their jobs and to find new reasons why they are still needed.

STRUGGLE TO IMPROVE EFFICIENCY

In the Bank there is an almost continuous struggle going on to get rid of the non-essentials, to get right down to basics – What are the functions of a department? To what extent are its activities still required? How far can they be pared down? Can they be carried out by another department in a more efficient manner?

And there is another problem about bigness which never entered the heads of bankers in pre-computer days. Today, if a service is to be automated, particularly if it fits in with or is closely related to other services, the Bank can be looking at a very costly investment over a period of as much as three years. The lead time for major programs is even longer and once they are fully embarked upon, it is difficult and expensive to change course. The result is that, if one bank figures out and carries out a better program than another, it may gain a competitive advantage which extends over a considerable time. Thus, the groups of bright young people who are trying to figure out the best courses of expansion for each bank – best in relation to both costs and services – have a major responsibility. They are becoming more like the people who must plan the research and capital investment required for a new automotive or electronic line.

BANKS DO NOT BENEFIT FROM INFLATION

Automation involves important changes but it is scarcely a matter of major concern. It is part of the process of rising productivity which will improve living standards by enabling routine work to be done more efficiently. What *is* of major concern in assessing the economic and banking outlook is the persistence of inflation. Canada's inflation rate is now up to a 12 per cent level with little sign of decline yet, despite the weakness in business. Contrary to some popular views, banks do not benefit from inflation, or at least not for long. Of course, the dollar amounts – the assets and deposits – go way up and profits go up too. But eventually, margins are squeezed as they have been in the last few years, the quality of credit deteriorates, and losses start to mount up. And banks simply cannot benefit from a situation which weakens and makes poorer so many of their customers.

In an inflationary environment, too, banks find it more and more difficult to maintain the proportion of capital (or shareholders' equity) to their deposit liabilities. During the period 1971 to 1980, the big international banks in the United States saw their capital ratios decline from approximately 5 per cent to 3½ per cent. In Japan, the ratios were almost the same and moved in the same way, and in Canada the decline in shareholders' equity was from just under 4 per cent in 1971 to about 3 per cent in 1980. Interestingly enough, in Switzerland, where there has been less inflation than anywhere else, the capital ratios of the big banks have risen – from an average of 4½ per cent in 1971 to over 6 per cent in 1980.[2] Yet, if Canadian, American, and Japanese banks had kept their capital ratios where they were a decade earlier, it would have been at the expense of their dividends and probably also at the expense of their stock prices and earnings per share.

Again, contrary to some popular opinions, bank profits are not helped by high and variable interest rates, which, of course, are a major symptom of inflation. High and variable rates check loan demand and this does not help the banking business. If market rates are also rising rapidly, as they were last year, bank profits tend to be squeezed, as the rates fixed on personal loans and mortgages for terms ranging from one to five years are all too quickly outrun by the rising rates that banks have to pay on certificates of deposit and other savings instruments. The Nova Scotia has certainly had this experience. For this reason, banks have been backing away from fixed-interest loans of substantial duration and of course borrowers also are frequently unhappy about taking on the unknown commitment of a flexible interest rate. The result, for a time at least, is a considerable reduction in fixed-rate lending business.

Canadian banks have already reached the point where the business community is dependent upon them to an exaggerated degree. The long-term bond market has become more difficult and much less attractive. Financing today has to be fairly short and has often to be

For the 150th Anniversary, the numbers 150 were superimposed on the "S" and the years 1832-1982 added underneath.

supported by such special extra features as extendability, retractability, and convertibility. The foreign banks will provide more competition but mainly for good-sized businesses. With all the new banks looking for connections, the effect will certainly be to make the Eurodollar market even more accessible to sizeable Canadian businesses than it has been, although the increased accessibility will no doubt be tempered by the hesitation of most banks to make fixed-term commitments of any considerable length.

INFLATION HAS SERIOUS EFFECTS ON BUSINESS LIQUIDITY

Meanwhile, many businesses which are unable to raise long-term capital have run down their liquidity simply to keep going. A small number of very large businesses have also run down their liquidity to finance takeovers which were believed to be a cheap way of buying assets. Most businesses are borrowing more from the banks and in many cases the banks' funds are locked in until inflation lessens and the bond market recovers at least to some degree. The effect of inflation at a rate of 12 per cent per annum on business liquidity can be quite serious even if volume is increasing and margins are maintained. If volume is not increasing and margins are being squeezed, 12 per cent inflation can be a critical problem. The customer needs more money and sales are not increasing. This is not a good proposition to set before a bank, yet bankers have to look at more and more like it.

It might also be added that banks usually have a considerable number of customers who are not adequately capitalized and who in fact depend on their bankers for part of their capital. These are the kind of accounts on which money is often lost and which led Fyshe long ago to remark that "the main condition of success in banking is not large profits but small losses."[3] In any case these accounts, which are highly vulnerable to inflation, are surfacing in increasing numbers.

What does a bank do when it is faced with a wide variety of deteriorating accounts, or a real decline in the quality of credit? On the one hand, if standards are lowered to accommodate many of the weaker accounts – and there is bound to be some movement in this direction – the problems will return in aggravated form unless inflation declines and business improves. On the other hand, if standards are maintained, there will undoubtedly be more failures and increasing pressure on the government to intervene.

There are those who, considering these possibilities, say that the obvious solution is to make credit easier and, thus, it is hoped, to reduce interest rates, even if that means a cheaper dollar, as it most certainly would. But a cheaper dollar means higher Canadian prices, even higher than those in prospect. And such a confirmation of inflation could not fail to make inflation worse.

NOT THE BEST OCCASION FOR A 150TH ANNIVERSARY

This is certainly not the environment The Bank of Nova Scotia would have chosen for its 150th anniversary. It would have been pleasant not only to report a fine past record but to reflect on a cheerful future. Instead, while pride can be taken in the record – and it certainly is a fine one – the future prospect is uncertain. Our own country, Canada, presents a disturbed and unbalanced economy caught in both inflation and recession. And the world around us abounds in problems, though there are some rays of light: the much more widespread price and policy adjustments to world oil-supply realities and the appreciable lessening of upward price pressures, particularly in the United States. The world economic system, though showing signs of wear and tear, has survived the oil crises, and the world's principal currency – the U.S. dollar – has become stronger.

Fortunately, the Bank has shown itself to be adaptable, strong, and competitive and it has been a leader in developing new types of business at home and abroad. With its experience and know-how, it should continue to grow in the international sphere, and with its adaptability, it will make the best of the problems in Canada. Wealth in every real sense – from skilled and educated people, to natural resources, to plant and equipment – abounds in this rich land. All that is needed are the will and the co-operation to use this wealth effectively.

NOTES

1. BNS Archives, Fyshe to Thomas Paton, dated Halifax, Sept. 2, 1887; also quoted in BNS *Monthly Review*, Aug.-Sept. 1952.
2. The foreign capital-ratio figures are derived from data in David Fairlamb, "Capital Ratios Come Under Scrutiny," *The Banker* (London), September 1981, pp.103-9.
3. BNS Archives, Circular No. 483, Jan. 15, 1892.

THE BANK OF NOVA SCOTIA

A
History in Charts

LONG-TERM TRENDS

1. Significant Stages of Development, 1832-1981
2. Assets in Constant Dollars compared to All Canadian Banks
3. Assets in Current Dollars
4. Deposits and Notes in Circulation in Current Dollars
5. Growth in Assets and Canada's Gross National Product in Constant Dollars
6. Staff and Branches
7. Number of Shareholders

FINANCIAL RESULTS OVER THE DECADES

8. Earnings and Dividends From 1873
9. Return on Capital From 1873
10. Stock Price and Earnings per Share From 1897
11. Price/Earnings Ratio From 1897
12. Stock Price in relation to Book Value From 1897
13. Capital Ratios From 1961
14. Interest Profit Margin From 1961
15. Return on Assets From 1961
16. Interest Rates From 1871
17. The Course of Prices From 1871
18. The Rate of Inflation From 1871
19. Five Canadian Banks: Earnings
20. Five Canadian Banks: Return on Capital

ASSETS AND LIABILITIES

21. Total Assets From 1946
22. Canadian and Foreign Currency Assets as a Percentage of Total Assets From 1946
23. Canadian Dollar Assets From 1946
24. Foreign Currency Assets From 1946
25. Five Canadian Banks: Assets as a Percentage of the Five-Bank Total, 1950 to 1980

Canadian Dollar Assets and Deposits From 1946

26. Loans and Securities
27. Business and Personal Loans
28. Deposits

Foreign Currency Assets and Deposits From 1946

29. Loans and Deposits with Banks
30. Deposits
31. Deposits with Banks as a Percentage of Foreign Currency Assets

1. THE BANK OF NOVA SCOTIA: SIGNIFICANT STAGES OF DEVELOPMENT

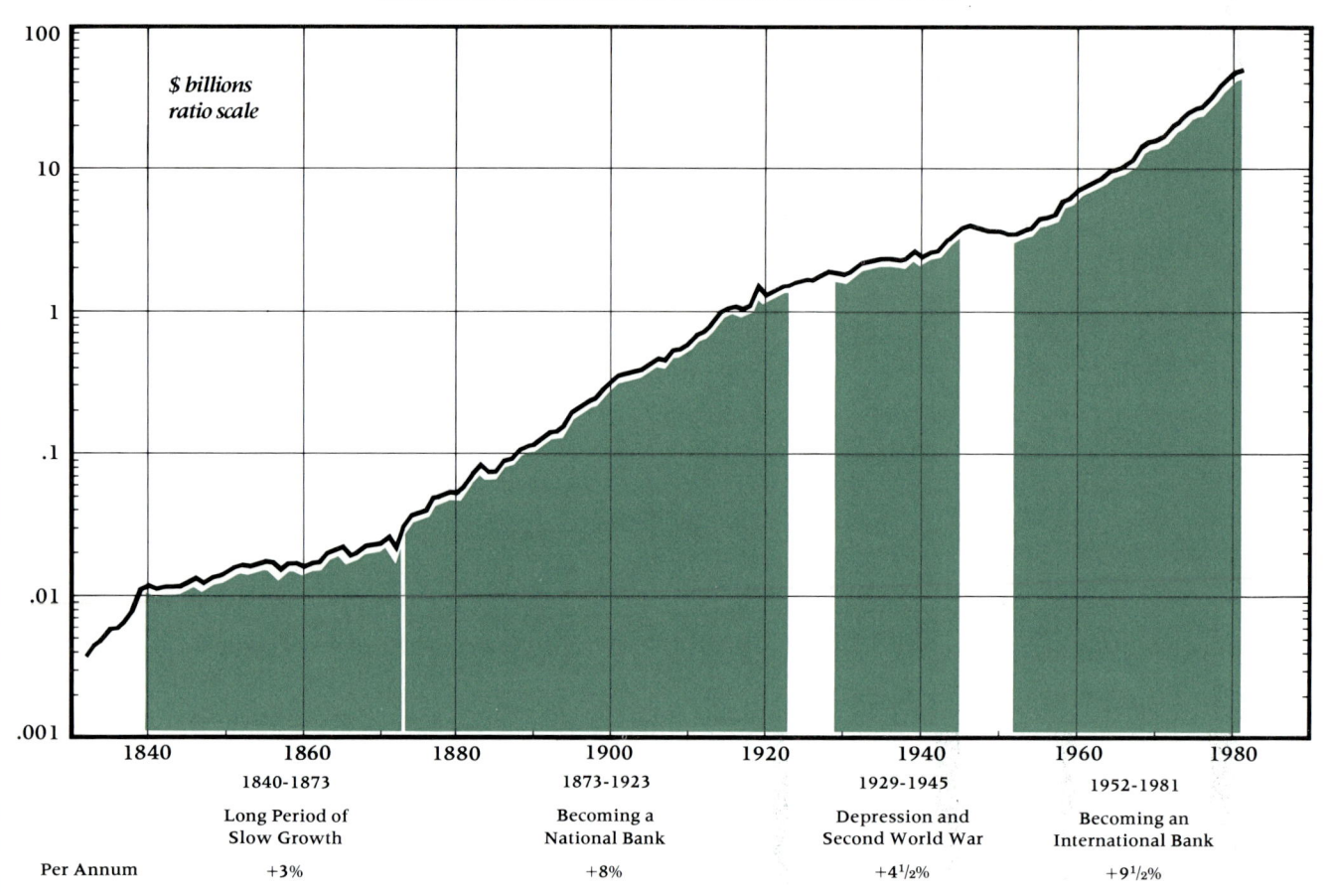

LONG-TERM GROWTH – THE BANK OF NOVA SCOTIA

Chart 1 gives a vivid picture of the real growth of The Bank of Nova Scotia over its full history from 1832 to 1981. The Bank's total assets are expressed in terms of constant dollars. In other words, they are corrected for the changing value of money and thus show the real trend without inflation or deflation.

One of the most interesting features of the chart is the almost continuous growth of the Bank during its 150 years. The upward trend has never been more than briefly interrupted, and even then, only on a few occasions for more than a year, notably at the end of each of the two world wars.

The two periods of most rapid growth have been from the early eighteen-seventies until the First World War, and during the last twenty-five to thirty years. The earlier period is the time of the great development of western Canada. The rapid growth of 8 per cent a year shown on the chart indicates the success of Thomas Fyshe, H.C. McLeod, and H.A. Richardson in taking advantage of their opportunities by participating in the stream of Canadian growth. The second period, from the early 1950s up to the present, shows an impressive rate of increase – almost 10 per cent a year. It reflects not only growth in Canada but also the remarkable international expansion of the Bank under Nicks's and Ritchie's direction.

Another interesting aspect of this chart is the slow growth of the Bank in its earlier years when it was weakened by the rather indifferent business conditions in the Maritimes and the long-continued Forman defalcation. The restrictive effects of the Great Depression, the Second World War, and immediate postwar adjustments are also evident. The way in which the Bank weathered these difficult periods is remarkable.

In Chart 2, the real growth of the Bank's total assets is compared with that of the whole Canadian banking system. It is clear that The Bank of Nova Scotia has been growing at a consistently faster rate than the system as a whole – from 1870 to 1920 averaging 8 per cent a year compared with 5 per cent for all the banks, and from 1952 to 1981 averaging $9^{1}/_{2}$ per cent a year compared with 8 per cent for all the banks.

Charts 3 and 4 show the total assets of the Bank, as well as its total deposits and note circulation, in current dollar figures rather than constant dollars. The increases, of course, are much larger but the patterns are very similar. It should be observed that the right of note circulation, formerly an important source of profit, was restricted from 1935 and came to an end in 1950.

LONG-
TERM
TRENDS

2. THE BANK OF NOVA SCOTIA AND ALL CANADIAN BANKS
TOTAL ASSETS EXPRESSED IN CONSTANT DOLLARS OF 1981

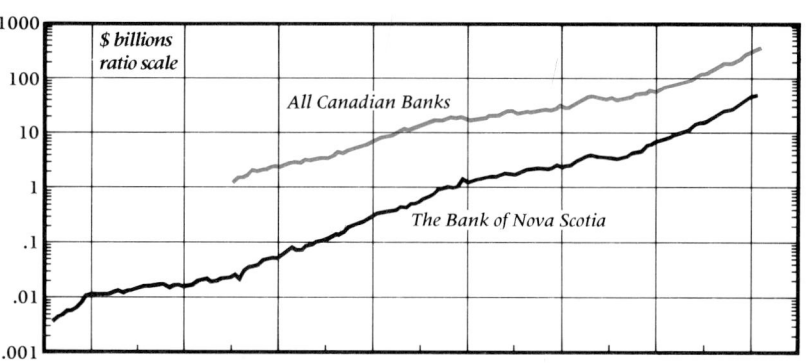

3. THE BANK OF NOVA SCOTIA
TOTAL ASSETS IN CURRENT DOLLARS

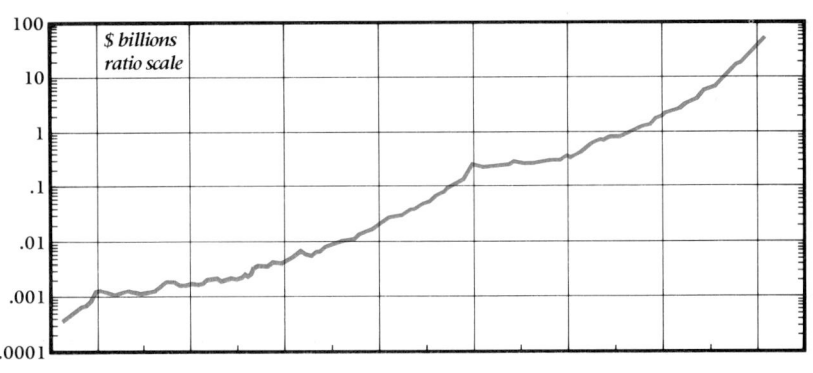

4. THE BANK OF NOVA SCOTIA
DEPOSITS AND NOTES IN CIRCULATION IN CURRENT DOLLARS

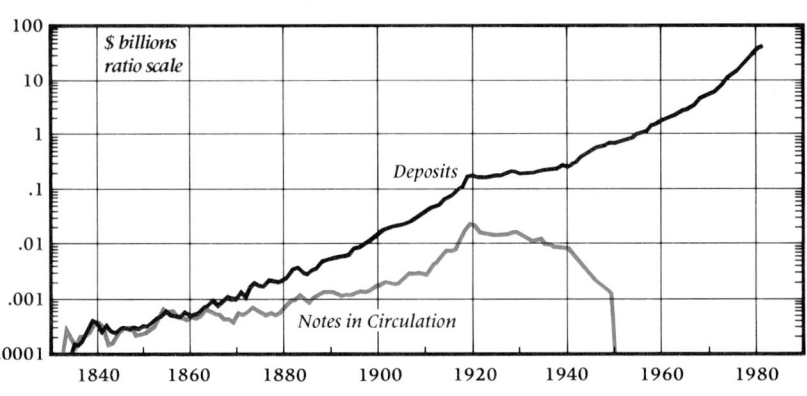

FURTHER MEASURES
OF REAL GROWTH

A number of other measures of real growth (as opposed to money growth) are shown in Charts 5 to 7.

Chart 5 shows how much faster the Bank has grown than the country's total output. This reflects increasing use of all banking services as well as the unusually rapid growth of Scotiabank. On a constant-dollar basis, the rate of growth of the Bank's assets from 1870 to 1980 was 7 per cent a year, while that of the national economy was 4 per cent.

Charts 6 and 7 show other physical measures of the Bank's growth. The increase in the number of branches and staff has not been as rapid as the increase in the volume of the Bank's business – a clear demonstration of the improvement in efficiency which has taken place. Nevertheless, the growth has been substantial, a 5 per cent a year increase in number of branches from 1870 to 1981 and a 6 per cent increase in staff from 1890 to 1981. The number of shareholders, as shown in Chart 7, is now over 22,000. It has grown at an annual rate of 4 per cent since 1870.

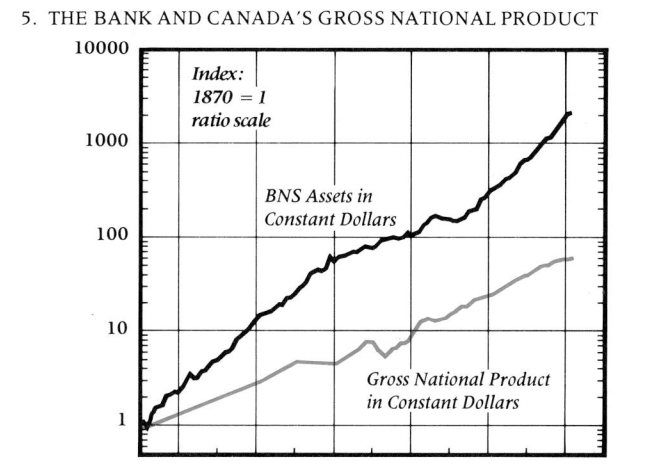

5. THE BANK AND CANADA'S GROSS NATIONAL PRODUCT

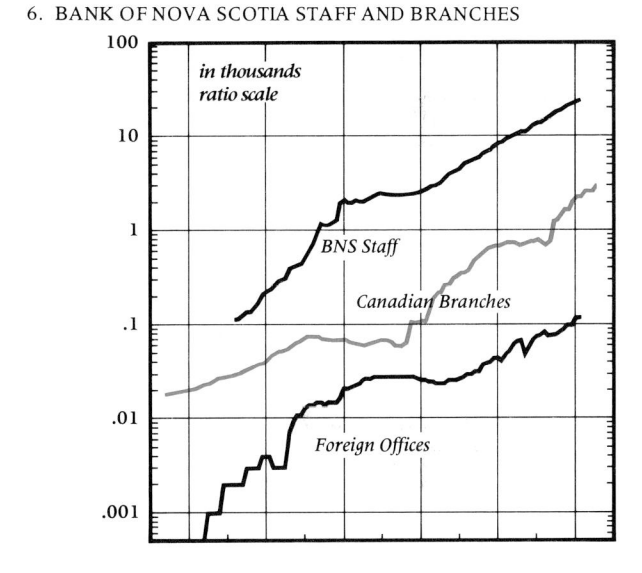

6. BANK OF NOVA SCOTIA STAFF AND BRANCHES

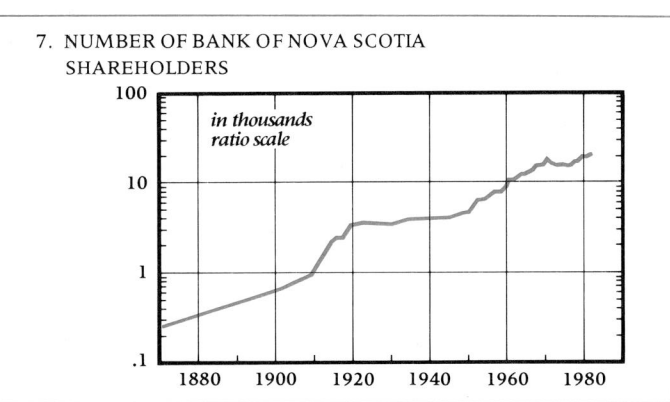

7. NUMBER OF BANK OF NOVA SCOTIA SHAREHOLDERS

THE SCOTIABANK STORY

FINANCIAL RESULTS OVER THE DECADES

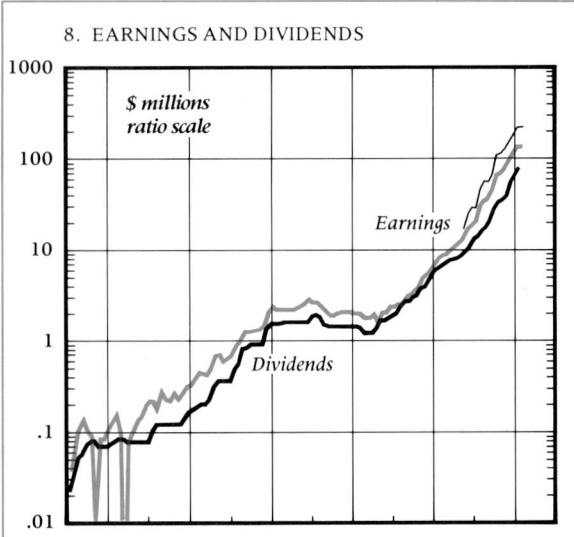

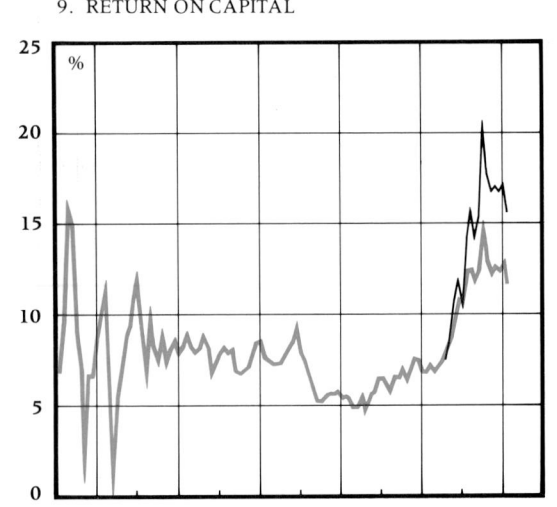

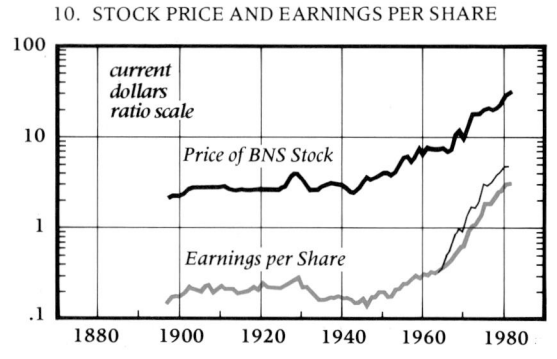

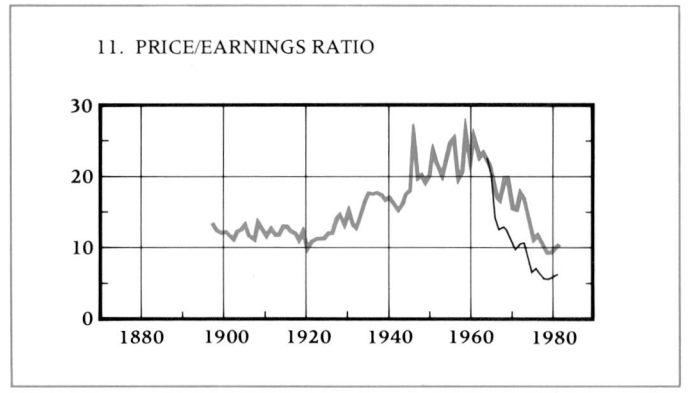

Chart 8 shows the movement of the Bank's earnings and dividends in current dollars for over one hundred years. Earnings have varied from year to year, particularly in the early period, but dividend payments have never been missed. The period of rapid growth from the eighteen-nineties to the First World War and the even more striking increases (accompanied by inflation in the last decade) during the last thirty years stand out in earnings and dividends as they do in assets.

As shown in Chart 9, the rate of return on capital – defined as balance of profits as a percentage of shareholders' equity – remained fairly steady at around 8 per cent during the period from approximately 1890 to 1930. There was a notable decline during the Great Depression and the Second World War to about 5 per cent. A gradual rise in the fifties back to 8 per cent followed, and then, with mounting inflation, there was a marked upturn to around the 13 per cent level. When the rate of return on capital is calculated using an alternative measure available since the Bank Act of 1967 – balance of revenue after taxes as a percentage of shareholders' equity plus accumulated appropriations for losses – recent rates of return run between 15 per cent and 20 per cent. This is shown as a second line on the chart. (See the Notes at the end of the charts.)

The price of the Bank's stock (Chart 10), which was more or less static during the long period from 1900 to 1940, rose substantially during the next forty years. Earnings per share rose even more rapidly, with the result that the price/earnings ratio (Chart 11) declined to its lowest level in recent years. Similarly, in Chart 12, the ratio of the market price of the Bank's stock to its book value, which rose between 1940 and 1961 to over 2.0 times, declined in the seventies to almost the 1:1 ratio that had prevailed in the first four decades of this century.

Chart 13 shows the decline in capital ratios over the last twenty years. Shareholders' equity as a proportion of deposit liabilities has decreased substantially, as indicated by line (1). However, when other near-equity items are included, the proportion is of course higher. This is shown by line (2), which includes accumulated appropriations for losses with equity in the calculation of the ratio, and by line (3), which includes, in addition, subordinated debentures. Capital ratios for the other large banks in Canada have been reduced in much the same way, as have those for the larger banks in the United States and other countries.

Charts 14 and 15 show how inflation and high interest rates have curtailed the rate of profit, particularly in domestic business. For six years the overall interest profit margin has declined. The return on domestic assets has declined over the six-year period, but the return on international assets has been more stable.

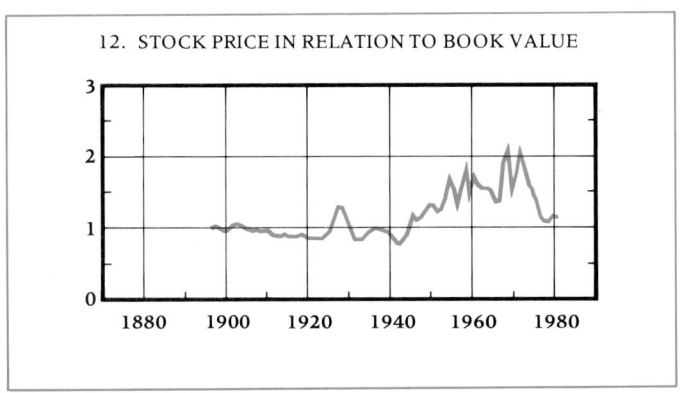

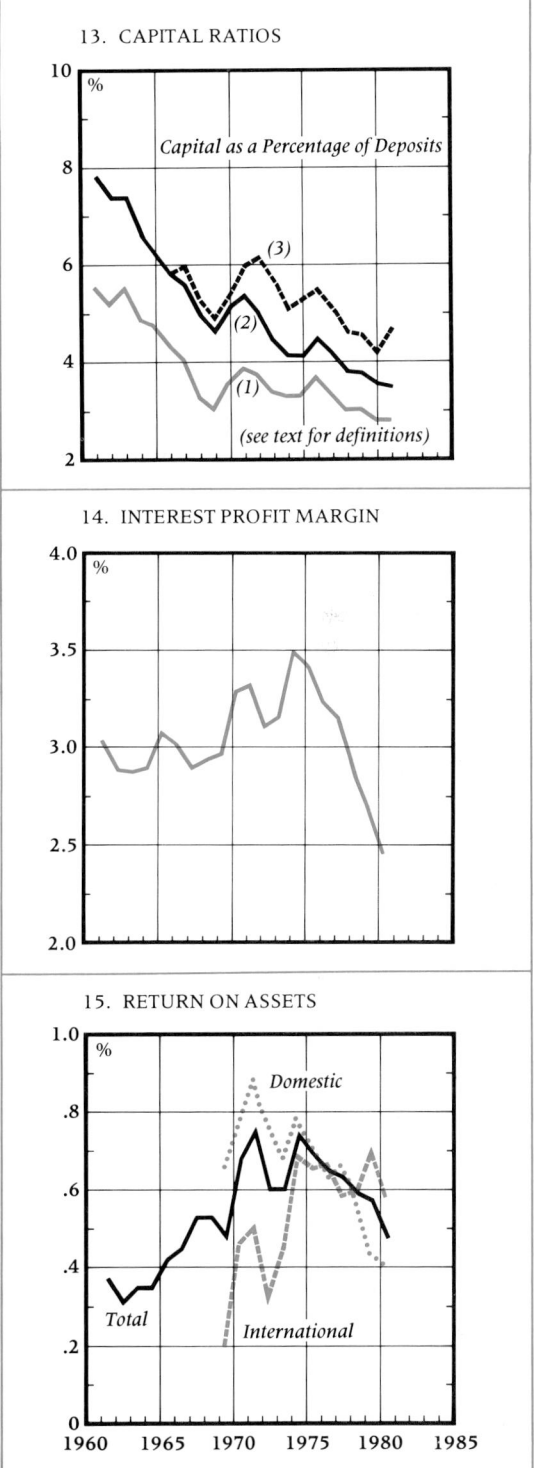

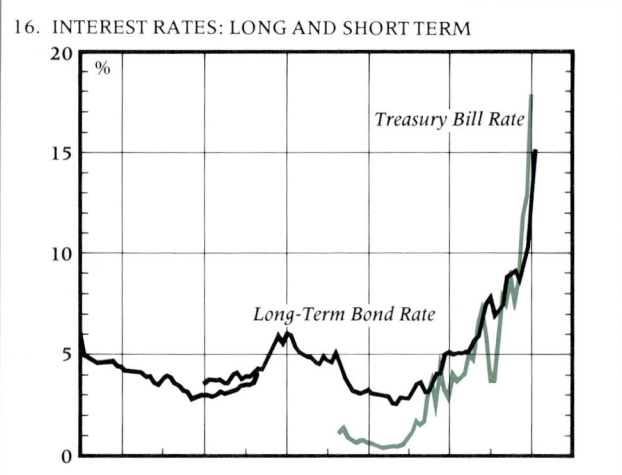

16. INTEREST RATES: LONG AND SHORT TERM

17. THE COURSE OF PRICES

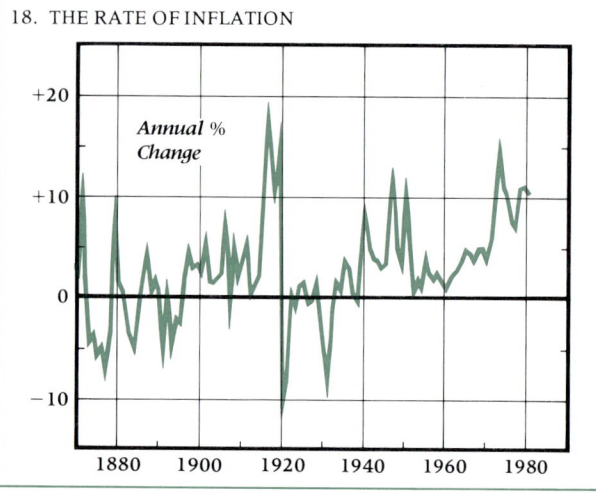

18. THE RATE OF INFLATION

INTEREST RATES AND INFLATION

The high rates of interest and rapid price increases of the last few years are evidence of the most prolonged inflation this country has ever known (see charts 16 and 17).

Chart 18 shows the annual rate of increase (or decrease) in the price level – the annual rate of inflation. Over the past one hundred and ten years, the annual rates of change, while sometimes fluctuating sharply, have shown no long-sustained trend until the past twenty years. The only other periods of substantial inflation were a five-year period during and just after the First World War, and another in the late 1940s.

The relationship between the rate of inflation and interest rates is fairly clear. If 3 per cent or 4 per cent is regarded as a reasonable real return on low-risk assets such as Canada bonds, then an approximate long-term interest rate on Canada bonds should be 3 per cent or 4 per cent plus the expected rate of inflation. If that rate of inflation is 10 per cent, then the interest rate would be 13 per cent or 14 per cent, and if it is 5 per cent the interest rate would be 8 per cent or 9 per cent. Recent high rates of interest are consistent with the inflation rates of 10 per cent to 12 per cent which have been prevailing.

Charts 19 and 20 show changes in balance of revenue after taxes, and balance of revenue after taxes as a percentage of capital (including accumulated appropriations), for the five largest Canadian banks from 1967 to date. (The 1967 Bank Act revision required banks to disclose figures of their annual appropriations to contingency reserves as well as the accumulation of such reserves; and many analysts believe that earnings figures should be shown before appropriations and that capital should be defined to include accumulated appropriations with equity.)

One of the most striking aspects of the two sets of charts is the similarity of the profit record of the individual banks over the fourteen-year period. Taking 1967 as 100, the Nova Scotia ranks high through most of the period, as do the Royal and Toronto-Dominion. Looking at the percentage return on equity, in 1981 four of the five banks were fairly close to each other, with the Royal considerably higher.

THE FIVE LARGEST CANADIAN BANKS

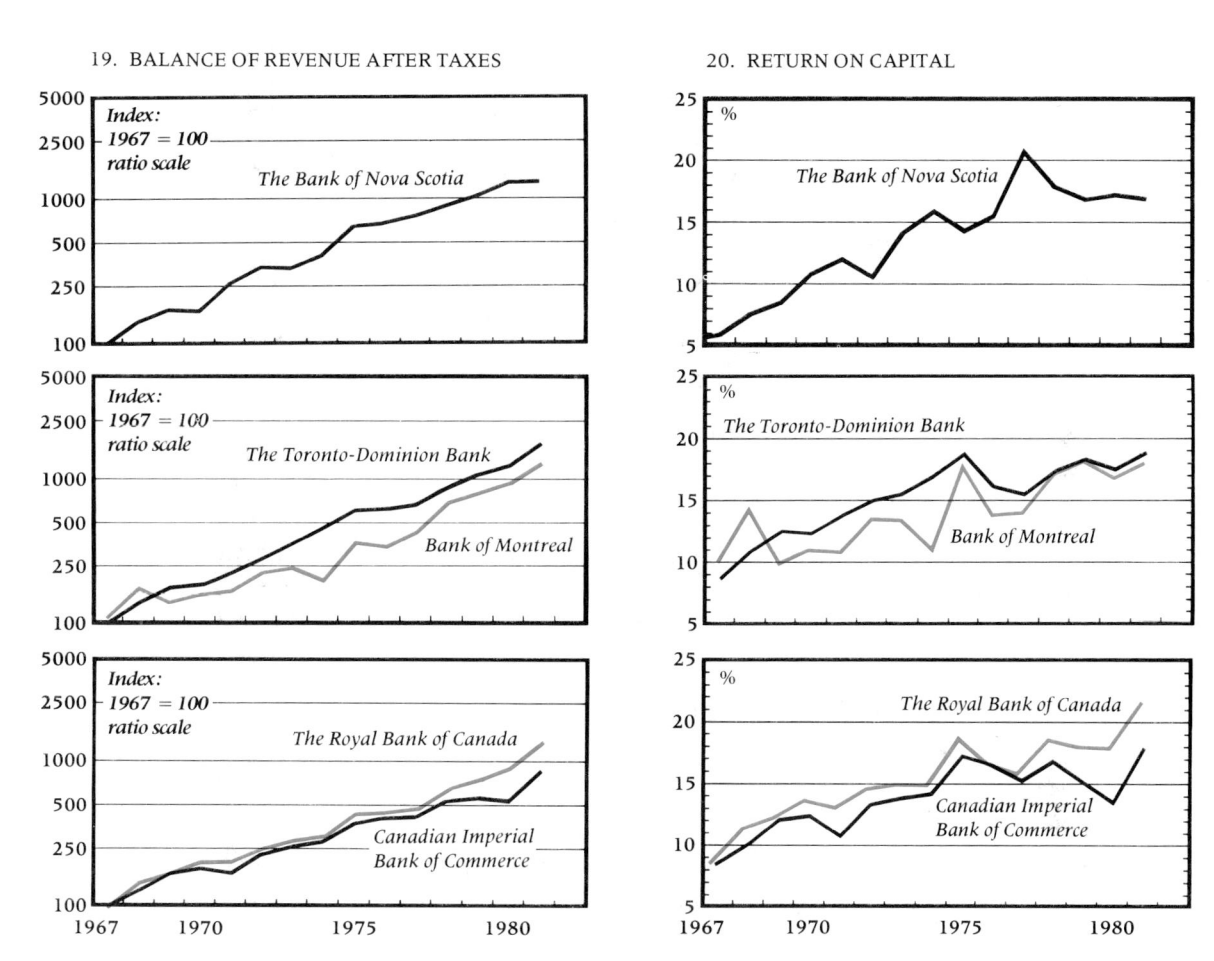

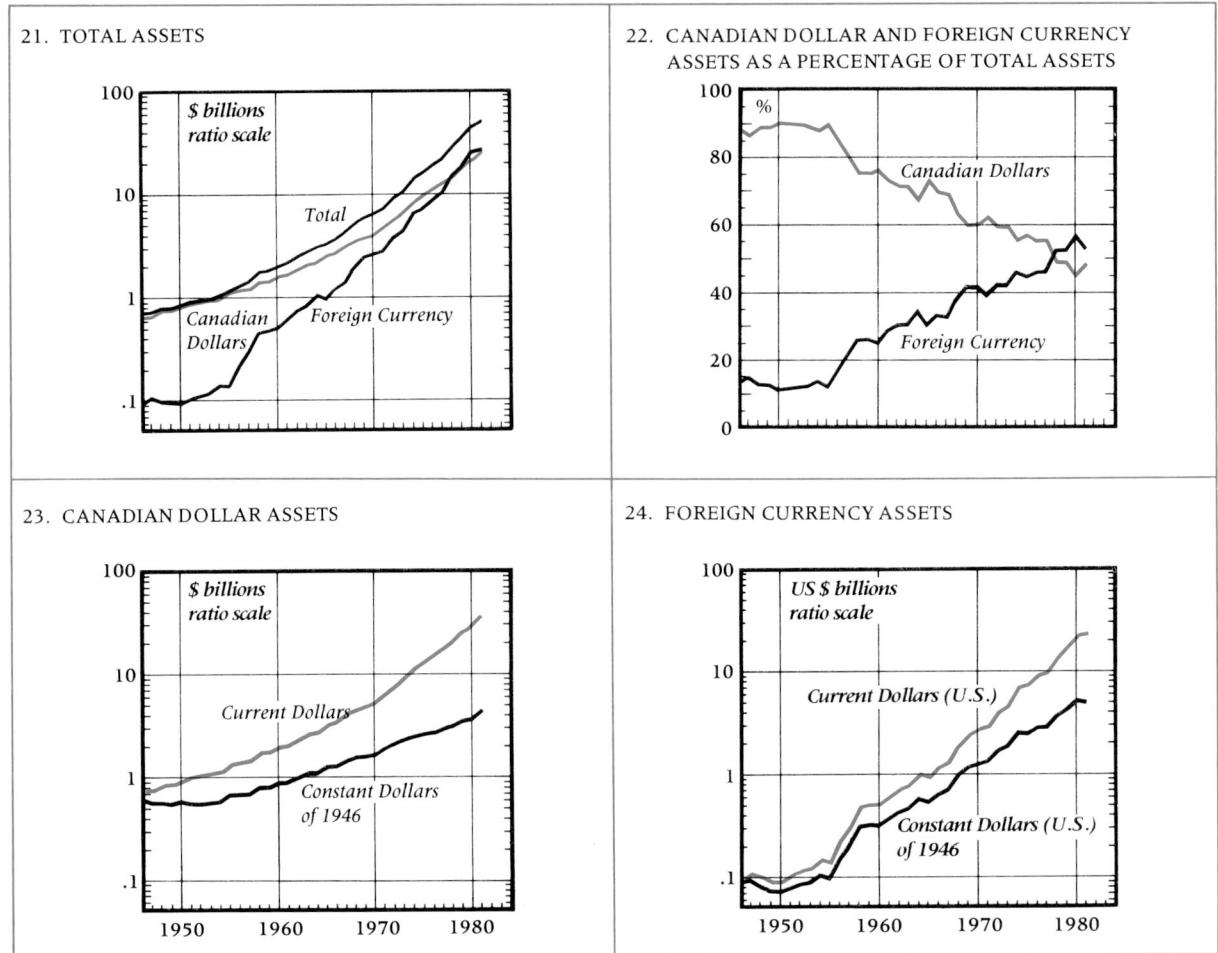

ASSET GROWTH SINCE THE SECOND WORLD WAR

Charts 21 and 22 bring out the marked increase in the Bank's foreign currency business, which by the end of 1981 resulted in assets exceeding $26 billion – 53 per cent of the total assets of the Bank.

For the past three decades Canadian dollar assets have grown at an average annual rate of 12 per cent. In real terms (i.e., after allowing for inflation) the rate has been 7 per cent (see Chart 23). This is considerably more than the growth of the economy, which averaged less than 5 per cent over the period.

The real rate of increase in foreign currency business dwarfs the domestic advance and works out to around 15 per cent a year over the period since the early 1950s (see Chart 24).

THE FIVE LARGEST CANADIAN BANKS

25. ASSETS OF EACH BANK AS A PERCENTAGE OF THE FIVE-BANK TOTAL

CANADIAN DOLLAR ASSETS

Year	BNS	TD	B of M	CIBC	Royal
1950	9.5	11.5	26.2	26.9	25.9
1960	11.5	11.9	23.8	27.4	25.4
1970	12.9	13.2	22.2	26.2	25.5
1980	13.5	14.1	21.1	25.1	26.2

FOREIGN CURRENCY ASSETS

Year	BNS	TD	B of M	CIBC	Royal
1950	11.6	4.2	18.5	17.3	48.5
1960	18.7	9.6	14.4	20.5	36.7
1970	19.7	12.5	17.8	20.8	29.2
1980	24.6	13.9	16.7	19.1	25.7

The growth of the Bank in Canadian dollar assets has been well above that of the average for Canadian banks during the post-war period. Of the other large banks, only the Toronto-Dominion shows a significant increase in its proportion of the total. The Nova Scotia's domestic growth was particularly rapid in the sixties, when it had the advantage of a head start in consumer lending.

It is in foreign currency business that the Bank's proportionate growth is most impressive – The Bank of Nova Scotia had 25 per cent of the five-bank total for foreign currency assets in 1980, only a little less than the Royal with 26 per cent. Again an early start was of considerable advantage, but even when other banks became involved in foreign currency dealings, the Bank of Nova Scotia still gained in its relative position.

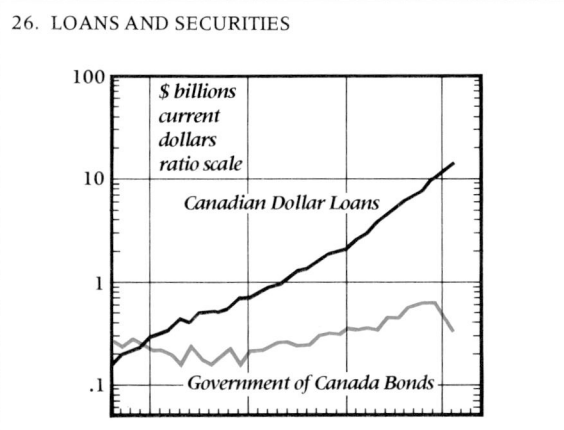

26. LOANS AND SECURITIES

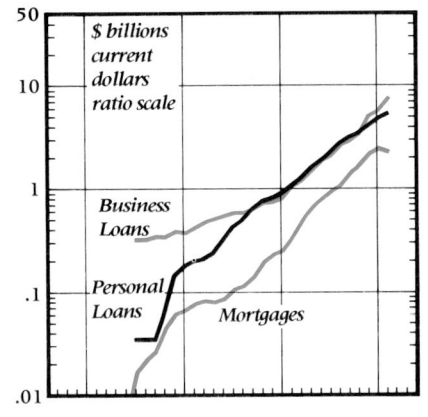

27. BUSINESS AND PERSONAL LOANS

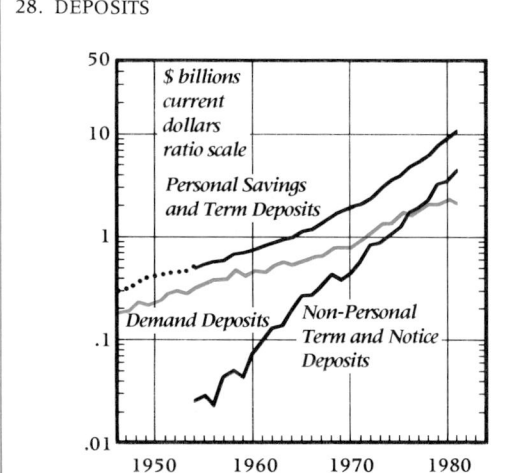

28. DEPOSITS

CANADIAN DOLLAR ASSETS AND DEPOSITS

The upward trend of The Bank of Nova Scotia's Canadian dollar loans has continued steady and almost uninterrupted throughout the postwar period, and has gained momentum recently as inflation took hold (see Chart 26). As shown in Chart 27, business loans were increasing slowly until the end of the sixties and then pushed rapidly upward with the rising rate of inflation. The sharp upsurge of personal loans dates from the introduction of Scotia Plan in 1958; by 1967 personal loans had reached a level equal to Canadian dollar business loans.

The increase in mortgage lending has also been striking (see Chart 27); this, along with the rise in personal loans, reflects Scotiabank's attention to meeting the financial needs of individuals and families.

Chart 28 shows where the money came from to finance this notable growth in lending. Demand deposits have increased moderately but have become a smaller and smaller fraction of the total. Few companies leave money on deposit at low or zero interest rates without reason, keeping their operating balances as low as possible. Personal savings and term deposits have increased considerably. The biggest percentage rise has been in corporate and other non-personal term deposits.

FOREIGN CURRENCY ASSETS
AND DEPOSITS

Foreign currency assets consist mainly of loans and deposits with banks. Until the early seventies, The Bank of Nova Scotia's foreign currency loans exceeded its foreign currency deposits with banks, but in recent years, deposits with banks have been almost as large as loans.

The ratio of foreign currency deposits with banks to foreign currency assets is shown in Chart 31 for The Bank of Nova Scotia and for all Canadian banks. It will be observed that the ratios for this Bank and all banks have remained between 40 per cent and 60 per cent for a number of years, though prior to 1970 they were much lower.

On the liability side of the foreign currency business, deposits by banks account for close to 50 per cent of the total in recent times, as will be seen in Chart 30.

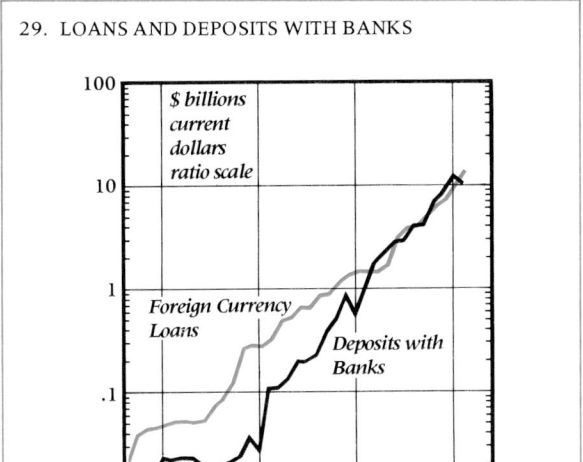

29. LOANS AND DEPOSITS WITH BANKS

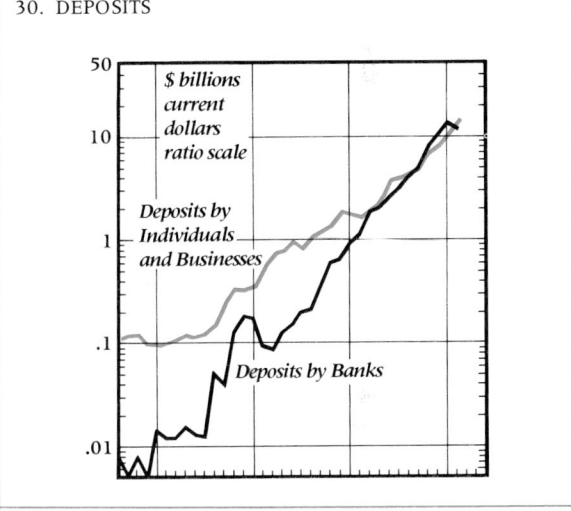

30. DEPOSITS

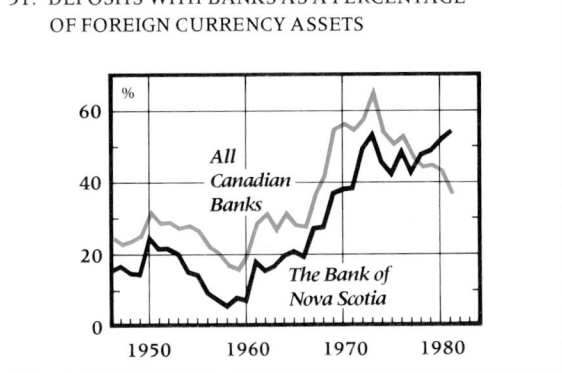

31. DEPOSITS WITH BANKS AS A PERCENTAGE OF FOREIGN CURRENCY ASSETS

GENERAL NOTES ON DATA USED IN THE CHARTS

1. Long-term series use The Bank of Nova Scotia's fiscal year-end for assets and liabilities (January 31 from 1833 to 1871, December 31 from 1871 to 1943, and October 31 from 1944). Earnings figures for 1944 have been converted to a twelve-month basis. Asset and deposit series for the 1946-1981 charts are December 31, since greater detail exists for loans for December than for October. Figures for 1981 are for October 31, because December figures incorporate the changes in reporting required by the new Bank Act and are not comparable with earlier series. Calendar-year averages have been used for interest rates and for the five-bank comparison of assets. Shareholders' Equity is expressed as an average of year-ends when used with earnings data.

2. Assets have been deflated using the GNP deflator since 1926, linked backwards to the Cost of Living Index for the 1913-1925 period, the Wholesale Price Index for the 1870-1912 period, and the U.K. Rousseaux Index for the period to 1869. For Chart 24, in order to derive a series illustrating real growth in foreign business, foreign currency assets were first converted back into U.S. dollars and then adjusted using the U.S. GNP deflator.

3. A distinction must be made between the "foreign currency – Canadian dollar" split in assets and deposits, and the "international-domestic" split in assets, deposits and earnings, because of important foreign currency business in Canada. Since 1954, published balance sheet figures for The Bank of Nova Scotia (and comparable figures for All Banks) have been on a currency basis. Figures for Balance of Revenue for recent years are published on an international-domestic basis. For The Bank of Nova Scotia, estimates for the international-domestic split in assets are used in the text, but charts give the published currency split. In Chart 25, which compares Canadian dollar and foreign currency assets of five chartered banks, an adjustment has been made to the 1980 figures to include with foreign currency assets holdings of foreign currency securities of Canadian issuers. These are classified as Canadian dollar assets in the published sources.

4. Earnings and Capital: Earnings for the long-term period are Balance of Profits figures; that is, Balance of Revenue after taxes and after transfers to appropriations for losses. Capital is taken to be paid up capital, rest account, and undivided profits. From the mid-1960s an alternative series is used which shows earnings as Balance of Revenue after Taxes but before transfers to appropriations for losses. When this measure is used for earnings, capital is taken to include the Accumulated Appropriations for Losses account. The capital ratio chart has an additional line where capital is defined to include debentures.

5. Discontinuities in data: Real GNP: 10-year intervals to 1920, then continuous from 1926. Number of Shareholders: before 1920, figures are available for only a few years. These have been plotted and joined by a straight line.

NOTES TO SPECIFIC CHARTS

6. Canadian branches include Newfoundland branches for the whole period. For foreign offices the three decreases in the 1960s and 1970s relate to the sale of the Bank's branches in Cuba in 1961 and the sale of part ownership to local residents in Jamaica and Trinidad and Tobago in 1967 and 1973 respectively.

8. Earnings shown in Chart 8 and used in calculating figures plotted in Charts 9, 10, and 11 are Balance of Profits (Balance of Revenue after both taxes and transfers to appropriations for losses). The second line shown from the mid-1960s is Balance of Revenue after Taxes (before transfers to appropriations).

9. Return on Capital is Balance of Profits as a percentage of average Shareholders' Equity and for the more recent period the second line is Balance of Revenue after Taxes as a percentage of average Shareholders' Equity plus Accumulated Appropriations for Losses.

12. Book Value is Shareholders' Equity at year-end divided by the number of shares outstanding.

13. Capital Ratios are Capital as a percentage of Deposits at year-end with Capital defined in three ways: (1) Shareholders' Equity; (2) Shareholders' Equity plus Accumulated Appropriations for Losses; (3) Shareholders' Equity plus Accumulated Appropriations for Losses plus Debentures.

14. Interest Profit Margin is interest earned on assets minus interest paid on deposits as a percentage of average earning assets (taxable equivalent from 1972).

15. Return on Assets is Balance of Revenue after Taxes as a percentage of average total assets.

16. The long-term bond rate combines three series: a Canada bond from 1870 to 1913; an Ontario bond from 1900 to 1940; and the average rate on Government of Canada bonds ten years and over since 1940.

20. Return on Capital is Balance of Revenue after Taxes as a percentage of average Shareholders' Equity and Accumulated Appropriations for Losses.

Statements of Assets and Liabilities of The Bank of Nova Scotia 1833-1981

GENERAL STATEMENT OF AFFAIRS ON THE 28TH FEBRUARY, 1833.

Liabilities

Capital Stock paid in	£50,000.00.00
Notes in Circulation	16,613.10.00
Amount of Deposits in the Bank	18,943.13.10
Net Profits in hand	310.17.09
	£85,868.01.07

Resources

Amount of Gold and Silver in the Vaults	£27,716.14.04
Amount of Copper Coin	93.10.00
Amount of Provincial Treasury Notes	1,592.00.00
Amount of Notes of other Banks	283.09.00
Balance in the hands of the Agents of the Bank at New York and London	153.08.03
Debts due to the Bank on Discounted Notes	56,029.00.00
	£85,868.01.07

The Directors do not consider any of the debts to be bad or doubtful.

GENERAL STATEMENT OF AFFAIRS ON THE 31ST JANUARY, 1843.

Liabilities

Capital Stock	£140,000.00.00
Notes in Circulation	45,858.10.00
Deposits	64,341.18.07
Due to Agents abroad	6,673.12.10
Agency drafts on the Bank in transitu	553.17.00
Due to other Banks	922.05.05
Unclaimed dividends	1,378.06.09
Dividend of 3½% on £140,000; payable 6th March, 1843	4,900.00.00
Rest	2,568.18.03
	£267,197.08.10

Resources

Debts due to the Bank	£227,726.00.06
Securities in the hands of and balances due by Agents abroad	7,316.10.00
Agency Remittances in transitu	1,525.13.09
Real Estate	3,878.19.09
Bank Furniture and Bank Plates	161.00.00
Bills of Exchange on hand	5,866.17.09
Gold and Silver in the vaults	17,038.17.05
Provincial Treasury Notes	1,438.00.00
Notes of other Banks	2,245.09.08
	£267,197.08.10

GENERAL STATEMENT OF AFFAIRS ON THE 31ST JANUARY, 1853.

Liabilities

Capital Stock	£140,000.00.00
Bills in Circulation	76,648.05.00
Amount of Guarantee Fund	5,355.07.05
Balances due to other Banks	nil
Cash deposited, including all sums whatever due from the Bank not bearing interest, its Bills in circulation, profits, and balances due to other banks excepted	20,864.16.06
Cash deposited bearing interest	77,199.18.04
	£320,068.07.03

Resources

Gold, Silver, and other coined metals on hand	£ 47,273.12.10
Real Estate	2,846.02.06
Bills of other Banks	5,952.05.00
Balances due from other Banks	2,138.15.10
Amount of all debts due including notes, Bills of Exchange, and all Stocks and Funded Debts of every description, excepting balances due from other Banks	261,857.11.01
	£320,068.07.03
Amount of Debts due and unpaid, and considered doubtful	£338.06.08

GENERAL STATEMENT OF AFFAIRS ON THE 31ST JANUARY, 1863.

Liabilities

Capital Stock	$ 560,000.00
Bills in Circulation	480,771.00
Balances due to other Banks	21,675.87
Cash deposited, including all sums whatever due from the Bank, its Bills in Circulation, profits, and balances due to other Banks excepted	569,697.26
Guarantee Fund	80,000.00
Balance in favour of the Bank to Profit and Loss Account	1,061.30
	$1,713,205.43

Resources

Gold, Silver, and other coined metals on hand	$ 217,645.59
Bills of other Banks	13,523.94
Real Estate	20,000.00
Amount of all debts due, including Notes, Bills of Exchange, and all Stock and Funded Debts of every description	1,462,035.90
	$1,713,205.43

Amount of Debts due and unpaid, and considered doubtful $3,710.69

GENERAL STATEMENT OF AFFAIRS ON THE 31ST DECEMBER, 1872.

Liabilities

Capital	$ 490,000.00
Reserve Fund	55,066.67
Dividends unpaid	24,790.73
Notes in Circulation	574,057.55
Due to other Banks	10,539.15
Current Accounts	332,659.05
Deposit Receipts	728,928.22
Profit and Loss	2,622.23
	$2,218,663.60

Assets

Specie	$ 126,290.98
Dominion Notes	67,851.50
Notes and Cheques of other Banks	81,560.73
Due by other Banks	89,061.28
Investments	251,345.33
Mortgages over Real Estate sold	52,500.00
Forman property not yet realized	38,711.97
Bank Building	20,000.00
Bills of Exchange, Notes Discounted, and other Assets not included above	1,491,341.81
	$2,218,663.60

GENERAL STATEMENT OF AFFAIRS ON THE 31ST DECEMBER, 1882.

Liabilities

To the Public:

Deposits at Call		$1,020,956.57
Deposits subject to notice	$2,058,664.02	
Interest reserved on Deposits	48,879.30	
		2,107,543.32
Due to other Banks in Canada	44,152.96	
Due to other Banks not in Canada	31,928.91	
Due to other Banks in the United Kingdom £3,024.04.02	14,701.00	
		90,782.87
Notes in Circulation	936,929.40	
Drafts drawn between Head Office and Agencies outstanding	44,883.60	
		981,813.00
Drafts drawn on London Agents not yet matured, £60,288.04.11		289,951.58
		4,491,047.34

To the Shareholders:

Capital paid up	1,000,000.00	
Reserve Fund	400,000.00	
Profit and Loss	3,261.77	
Dividends unpaid	428.00	
Dividend No. 24, payable 1st February, 1883	40,000.00	
		1,443,689.77
		$5,934,737.11

Assets

Specie		$ 122,587.35
Dominion Notes		359,557.25
Due from other Banks		158,998.34
Notes and Cheques of other Banks		243,065.57
Immediately Available		884,208.51
Sterling Bills of Exchange on hand and remitted to London, not matured, £128,841.12.01		619,861.79
Investments (6 p. c. Bonds, Municipal and School, &c.)	$ 24,298.73	
Loans to Provincial Governments	37,728.22	
Loans secured by Bonds, Debentures, and Stocks	226,520.55	
Loans to Corporations	132,114.29	
Cash Credit Accounts and Secured Overdrafts	292,112.28	
Authorized Overdrafts not specially secured	59,545.69	
Notes and Bills, discounted and current	3,516,243.44	
Notes and Bills overdue and not specially secured	25,611.91	
Overdue debts secured	18,025.97	
Real Estate sold (secured by Mortgage) and property not realized	9,561.07	
Bank Premises, Safes, and Office Furniture	88,127.26	
		4,429,889.41
Stationery and Stamps		777.40
		$5,934,737.11

GENERAL STATEMENT OF AFFAIRS ON THE 31ST DECEMBER, 1892.

Liabilities

Deposits at call		$ 1,690,283.23
Deposits subject to notice	$4,212,116.88	
Interest reserved on Deposits	94,277.33	
		4,306,394.21
Due to other Banks in Canada	19,850.31	
Due to other Banks in Foreign Countries	51,939.61	
Due to other Banks in United Kingdom	105,301.28	
		177,091.20
Notes in Circulation	1,128,060.08	
Drafts drawn between Head Office and Agencies outstanding	142,814.17	
		1,270,874.25
Capital paid up	1,500,000.00	
Reserve Fund	1,050,000.00	
Profit and Loss	3,639.45	
Dividends unpaid	419.00	
Dividend No. 118, payable 1st February, 1893	60,000.00	
		2,614,058.45
		$10,058,701.34

Statements of Assets and Liabilities

Assets

Specie		$	378,816.37
Dominion Notes			492,358.99
Deposits with Dominion Government for Security of Note Circulation	$ 61,379.55		
Due from other Banks	311,797.06		
Notes and Cheques of other Banks	347,780.18		
			720,956.79
Investments (Provincial, Municipal, and other Bonds)			1,683,736.79
Loans to Provincial Governments	30,376.86		
Call Loans, secured by Bonds, Debentures, Stocks, &c.	442,291.31		
Time Loans, secured by Bonds, Debentures, Stocks, &c.	100,000.00		
Cash Credit Accounts and Secured Overdrafts	110,820.56		
Authorized Overdrafts not specially secured	32,117.50		
Notes and Bills, discounted and current	5,938,474.45		
Notes and Bills overdue and not specially secured	9,054.68		
Notes and Bills overdue and other overdue debts secured	4,717.46		
Real Estate, Mortgages on Real Estate sold, and other property not realized	30,714.92		
Bank Premises, Safes, and Office Furniture	83,694.24		
			6,782,261.98
Stationery			570.42
			$10,058,701.34

GENERAL STATEMENT OF AFFAIRS AS AT DECEMBER 31ST, 1902.

Liabilities

Deposits at Call	$ 7,317,933.96	
Deposits subject to notice	11,984,050.64	
Interest accrued on deposits	230,296.22	
		$19,532,280.82
Deposits by other Banks in Canada	355,849.35	
Deposits by other Banks in Foreign Countries	250,039.66	
		605,889.01
Notes in Circulation	1,903,834.08	
Drafts drawn between Branches, outstanding	418,798.17	
		2,322,632.25
Capital paid up	2,000,000.00	
Reserve Fund	3,000,000.00	
Profit and Loss	12,025.33	
Rebate of Interest @ 6% on Time Loans	85,730.59	
Dividend No. 138, payable 2nd February, 1903	100,000.00	
		5,197,755.92
		$27,658,558.00

Statements of Assets and Liabilities

Assets

Specie	$1,340,521.98	
Dominion Notes – Legal Tenders	1,944,709.25	
	3,285,231.23	
Notes of and Cheques on other Banks	1,310,773.06	
Due from other Banks in Canada	519.79	
Due from other Banks in Foreign Countries	903,393.02	
Sterling Exchange	281,615.89	
Investments (Provincial, Municipal, and other Bonds)	3,856,385.77	
Call and Demand Loans, secured	5,348,280.01	
		$14,986,198.77
Loans to Provinces and Municipalities	338,392.31	
Current Loans, secured by Bonds, Debentures, and Stocks	1,132,500.33	
Current Loans, secured by Grain and other Staple Commodities	1,343,698.60	
Overdrafts, secured	253,424.96	
Overdrafts, authorized but not specially secured	90,622.89	
Notes and Bills discounted and current	9,224,623.25	
Notes and Bills overdue	1,593.84	
Bank Premises	189,320.22	
Deposits with Dominion Gov't for security of Note Circulation	98,182.83	
		12,672,359.23
		$27,658,558.00

GENERAL STATEMENT OF AFFAIRS AS AT DECEMBER 31ST, 1912.

Liabilities

Deposits not bearing Interest	$12,786,308.59	
Deposits bearing Interest	38,159,369.95	
Interest accrued on Deposits	93,789.75	
		$51,039,468.29
Deposits by other Banks		896,058.00
Notes in Circulation	4,256,738.94	
Drafts drawn between Branches outstanding	1,218,340.64	
		5,475,079.58
		57,410,605.87
Capital paid up	4,734,390.00	
Reserve Fund	8,728,146.00	
Profit and Loss, balance carried to 1913	54,854.48	
Rebate of Interest @ 6% on Time Loans	190,908.43	
Dividend Warrants outstanding	689.99	
Dividend No. 172, payable 2nd January, 1913	159,704.18	
		13,868,693.08
		$71,279,298.95

Contingent Liability:
Sterling Letters of Credit Current,
£139,182.7.7.

NOTE: When the unmatured calls on subscribed capital are paid, the Paid up Capital will be $5,000,000 and the Reserve Fund $9,100,000. The average Paid up Capital for 1912 is $4,168,126.

Assets

Specie	$ 3,491,558.27	
Dominion Notes – Legal Tenders	5,100,972.50	
Notes of and Cheques on other Banks	5,031,233.30	
Due from other Banks	1,482,317.80	
Sterling Exchange	1,861,845.72	
Investments (Provincial, Municipal, and other Bonds)	4,947,246.47	
Call and Demand Loans, secured	11,092,499.50	
		$33,007,673.56
Deposit with Dominion Government for security of Note Circulation	190,520.78	
Loans to Governments and Municipalities	1,952,887.00	
Current Loans, secured by Bonds, Debentures, and Stocks	947,995.35	
Current Loans, secured by Grain and other Staple Commodities	2,226,203.66	
Overdrafts, secured	376,518.53	
Overdrafts, authorized but not specially secured	538,867.22	
Notes and Bills discounted and current	30,580,077.17	
Notes and Bills overdue (estimated loss provided for)	65,555.65	
Bank Premises	1,377,020.23	
Stationery Department	15,979.80	
		38,271,625.39
		$71,279,298.95

GENERAL STATEMENT OF AFFAIRS AS AT DECEMBER 30TH, 1922.

Liabilities

Capital Stock paid in	$ 10,000,000.00	
Reserve Fund	19,500,000.00	
Balance of Profits, as per Profit and Loss Account	173,162.96	
Dividends declared and unpaid	394,403.84	
		$ 30,067,566.80
Notes of the Bank in circulation	15,399,640.40	
Deposits not bearing interest $ 35,172,569.82		
Deposits bearing interest, including interest accrued to date 137,252,032.01		
	172,424,601.83	
	187,824,242.23	
Balances due to other Banks in Canada	1,835,627.46	
Balances due to Banks and Banking Correspondents in the United Kingdom	88,108.32	
Balances due to Banks and Banking Correspondents elsewhere than in Canada and the United Kingdom	774,452.18	
Bills Payable	576,560.04	
		191,098,990.23
Acceptances under Letters of Credit		480,767.29
		$221,647,324.32

Statements of Assets and Liabilities

Assets

Current Coin	$11,419,548.84	
Dominion Notes	25,115,653.50	
United States Currency and British Treasury Demand Notes	1,243,264.18	
Notes of other Banks	1,300,491.12	
Cheques on other Banks	10,286,771.81	
Balances due by Banks and Banking Correspondents	2,258,433.31	
	51,624,162.76	
Deposit in the Central Gold Reserves	6,000,000.00	
Dominion and Provincial Government securities, not exceeding market value	25,719,088.83	
Canadian municipal securities and British, Foreign and Colonial public securities other than Canadian, not exceeding market value	10,373,948.51	
Railway and other bonds, debentures, and stocks, not exceeding market value	5,105,286.28	
Call and demand loans, secured	28,163,606.22	
		$126,986,092.60
Deposit with the Minister of Finance for the purposes of the circulation fund	474,491.01	
Loans to governments and municipalities	2,471,343.12	
Other loans and discounts (less rebate of interest)	83,601,045.40	
Liabilities of Customers under Letters of Credit, as per contra	480,767.29	
Bank Premises, at not more than cost, less amounts written off	7,221,656.47	
Real Estate other than Bank Premises	87,907.42	
Other assets not included in the foregoing	324,021.01	
		94,661,231.72
		$221,647,324.32

GENERAL STATEMENT OF AFFAIRS AS AT DECEMBER 31ST, 1932.

Liabilities

Capital Stock paid in	$ 12,000,000.00	
Reserve Fund	24,000,000.00	
Balance of Profits, as per Profit and Loss Account	578,224.74	
Dividends declared and unpaid	424,738.00	
		$ 37,002,962.74
Notes of the Bank in circulation	11,079,008.08	
Deposits not bearing interest $ 27,969,913.69		
Deposits bearing interest, including interest accrued to date 175,159,661.35		
	203,129,575.04	
Advances under the Finance Act	3,214,000.00	
	217,422,583.12	
Balances due to other Banks in Canada	2,539,257.76	
Balances due to Banks and Banking Correspondents in the United Kingdom and foreign countries	2,609,795.76	
Bills Payable	230,170.91	
		222,801,807.55
Letters of Credit outstanding		4,834,757.42
Other Liabilities not included in the foregoing		274,589.77
		$264,914,117.48

Assets

Current Coin	$ 9,829,480.10	
Dominion Notes	19,656,293.50	
United States and other foreign currencies	1,382,316.75	
Notes of other Banks	1,013,389.05	
Cheques on other Banks	6,770,172.08	
Balances due by Banks and Banking Correspondents	7,440,109.26	
	46,091,760.74	
Deposit in the Central Gold Reserves	1,250,000.00	
Dominion and Provincial Government securities, not exceeding market value	46,808,773.34	
Canadian municipal securities and British, Foreign, and Colonial public securities other than Canadian, not exceeding market value	20,355,282.75	
Railway and other bonds, debentures, and stocks, not exceeding market value	8,024,924.90	
Call and short (not exceeding thirty days) loans on stocks, debentures, and bonds and other securities, of a sufficient marketable value to cover	15,245,051.80	
		$137,775,793.53
Other loans and discounts (less rebate of interest) after making full provision for all bad and doubtful debts	110,848,829.05	
Liabilities of Customers under Letters of Credit, as per contra	4,834,757.42	
Bank Premises, at not more than cost, less amounts written off	7,983,801.79	
Shares of and Loans to Controlled Companies	2,689,032.03	
Deposit with the Minister of Finance for the purposes of the circulation fund	568,910.34	
Other assets not included in the foregoing	212,993.32	
		127,138,323.95
		$264,914,117.48

GENERAL STATEMENT OF AFFAIRS AS AT DECEMBER 31ST, 1942.

Liabilities

Capital paid up	$12,000,000.00	
Reserve fund	24,000,000.00	
Dividends declared and unpaid	302,106.45	
Balance of profits, as per profit and loss account	1,286,755.62	
		$ 37,588,862.07
Notes in circulation	5,033,216.45	
Deposits by and balances due to Dominion Government $ 25,522,326.01		
Deposits by and balances due to provincial governments 1,068,520.61		
Deposits by the public not bearing interest 130,587,563.90		
Deposits by the public bearing interest, including interest accrued to date of statement 180,413,570.06		
	337,591,980.58	
	342,625,197.03	
Deposits by and balances due to banks	8,009,571.75	
		350,634,768.78
Acceptances and letters of credit outstanding		21,244,614.62
Liabilities not included in the foregoing		998,809.53
		$410,467,055.00

Assets

Gold and coin	$ 1,165,257.61	
Notes of Bank of Canada	10,399,029.25	
Deposits with Bank of Canada	22,160,494.04	
Notes and cheques of other banks	26,534,060.46	
	60,258,841.36	
Due by banks and banking correspondents elsewhere than in Canada	28,843,881.66	
	89,102,723.02	
Dominion and provincial government direct and guaranteed securities, not exceeding market value	137,251,856.73	
Canadian municipal securities, not exceeding market value	9,095,690.60	
Public securities other than Canadian, not exceeding market value	3,691,794.40	
Other bonds, debentures, and stocks, not exceeding market value	10,482,058.64	
Call and short (not exceeding thirty days) loans on stocks, debentures, bonds and other securities, of a sufficient marketable value to cover	4,538,836.37	
		$254,162,959.76
Current loans and discounts not otherwise included, estimated loss provided for	124,859,259.66	
Loans to governments and municipalities	1,584,886.52	
Non-current loans, estimated loss provided for	333,301.21	
	126,777,447.39	
Liabilities of customers under acceptances and letters of credit, as per contra	21,244,614.62	
Bank premises, at not more than cost, less amounts written off	5,607,060.44	
Deposit with the Minister of Finance for the security of note circulation	343,414.61	
Shares of and loans to controlled companies	2,050,000.00	
Other assets not included in the foregoing	281,558.18	
		156,304,095.24
		$410,467,055.00

GENERAL STATEMENT OF AFFAIRS AS AT DECEMBER 31ST, 1952.

Liabilities

Capital paid up	$ 15,000,000.00
Rest or reserve fund	30,000,000.00
Dividends declared and unpaid	604,867.95
Balance of profits, as per profit and loss account	3,751,909.26
	49,356,777.21
Notes in circulation	41,917.26
Deposits by and balances due to Dominion government	10,398,450.84
Deposits by and balances due to provincial governments	6,921,198.47
Deposits by the public not bearing interest	314,086,828.39
Deposits by the public bearing interest, including interest accrued to date of statement	487,857,559.56
	868,662,731.73
Deposits by and balances due to other chartered banks in Canada	12,336,050.25
Deposits by and balances due to banks and banking correspondents elsewhere than in Canada	9,683,115.56
	890,681,897.54
Acceptances and letters of credit outstanding	22,533,514.10
Liabilities to the public not included under the foregoing heads	1,164,563.40
	$914,379,975.04

Assets

Gold and subsidiary coin	$ 2,117,431.47
Notes of Bank of Canada	24,225,745.50
Deposits with Bank of Canada	52,898,388.69
Notes of and cheques on other banks	66,277,736.25
Government and bank notes other than Canadian	5,104,920.38
Due by banks and banking correspondents elsewhere than in Canada	19,554,595.98
	170,178,818.27
Dominion government direct and guaranteed securities maturing within two years, not exceeding market value	71,605,043.92
Other Dominion government direct and guaranteed securities, not exceeding market value	128,586,076.30
Provincial government direct and guaranteed securities maturing within two years, not exceeding market value	7,216,960.85
Other provincial government direct and guaranteed securities, not exceeding market value	6,360,620.43
Canadian municipal securities, not exceeding market value	9,708,293.55
Public securities other than Canadian, not exceeding market value	7,831,044.61
Other bonds, debentures, and stocks, not exceeding market value	22,699,750.39
Call and short (not exceeding thirty days) loans on stocks, debentures, bonds, and other securities, of a sufficient marketable value to cover	35,052,313.29
	459,238,921.61
Current loans and discounts, not otherwise included, estimated loss provided for	401,642,220.99
Loans to provincial governments	21,510.95
Loans to cities, towns, municipalities, and school districts	7,599,282.39
Non-current loans, estimated loss provided for	107,282.74
	868,609,218.68
Liabilities of customers under acceptances and letters of credit, as per contra	22,533,514.10
Bank premises at not more than cost, less amounts written off	22,610,325.01
Shares of and loans to controlled companies	600.00
Other assets not included under the foregoing heads	626,317.25
	$914,379,975.04

STATEMENT OF ASSETS AND LIABILITIES, AS AT OCTOBER 31, 1962.

Assets

Cash Resources

Gold and coin	$ 9,519,030
Notes of and deposits with Bank of Canada	123,922,915
Government and bank notes other than Canadian	6,601,215
Deposits with other banks	84,011,720
Cheques and other items in transit, net	78,906,764
	302,961,644

Securities

Government of Canada direct and guaranteed securities, at amortized value	284,982,771
Canadian provincial government direct and guaranteed securities, at amortized value	22,672,086
Other securities, not exceeding market value	131,651,862
	439,306,719

Loans

Day-to-day, call, and short loans to investment dealers and brokers, secured	235,320,589
Other current loans, less provision for estimated loss	1,326,700,400
Mortgages and hypothecs insured under the National Housing Act, 1954	65,734,424
Non-current loans, less provision for estimated loss	1,000
	1,627,756,413

Customers' liability under acceptances, guarantees, and letters of credit, as per contra	31,676,480
Bank premises at cost, less amounts written off	35,426,368
Shares of and loans to corporations controlled by the bank	10,235,205
Other assets	686,784
	$2,448,049,613

Liabilities

Deposits

Deposits by Government of Canada	$ 2,680,063
Deposits by Canadian provincial governments	21,913,045
Deposits by other banks	135,016,536
Personal savings deposits payable after notice, in Canada, in Canadian currency	888,666,048
Other deposits	1,236,457,240
	2,284,732,932
Acceptances, guarantees, and letters of credit	31,676,480
Other liabilities	12,094,098
	43,770,578

Shareholders' Equity

Capital paid up	27,000,000
Rest account	92,000,000
Undivided profits	546,103
	119,546,103
	$2,448,049,613

STATEMENT OF ASSETS AND LIABILITIES, AS AT OCTOBER 31, 1972.

Assets

Cash and due from banks	$1,816,737,080
Cheques and other items in transit, net	69,917,243
TOTAL CASH RESOURCES	1,886,654,323
Securities issued or guaranteed by Canada, at amortized value	675,870,859
Securities issued or guaranteed by provinces, at amortized value	56,907,652
Other securities, not exceeding market value	344,516,140
TOTAL SECURITIES	1,077,294,651
Day, call, and short loans to investment dealers and brokers, secured	389,484,459
Other loans, including mortgages, less provision for losses	4,732,425,006
TOTAL LOANS	5,121,909,465
Bank premises at cost, less amounts written off	64,609,685
Securities of and loans to corporations controlled by the bank	45,055,082
Customers' liability under acceptances, guarantees, and letters of credit, as per contra	326,291,385
Other assets	20,005,671
	$8,541,820,262

Liabilities

Deposits by Canada	$ 58,198,541
Deposits by provinces	212,558,088
Deposits by banks	1,597,622,612
Personal savings deposits payable after notice, in Canada, in Canadian currency	2,417,102,222
Other deposits	3,433,114,147
TOTAL DEPOSITS	7,718,595,610
Acceptances, guarantees, and letters of credit	326,291,385
Other liabilities	22,654,418
Accumulated appropriations for losses	94,615,321

Capital Funds

Debentures issued and outstanding	89,350,000

Shareholders' Equity

Capital paid up	33,750,000
Rest account	255,000,000
Undivided profits	1,563,528
TOTAL SHAREHOLDERS' EQUITY	290,313,528
TOTAL CAPITAL FUNDS	379,663,528
	$8,541,820,262

STATEMENT OF ASSETS AND LIABILITIES, AS AT OCTOBER 31, 1977.

Assets

Cash and due from banks	$ 5,394,459,410
Cheques and other items in transit, net	140,428,453
TOTAL CASH RESOURCES	5,534,887,863
Securities issued or guaranteed by Canada, at amortized value	1,030,931,207
Securities issued or guaranteed by provinces, at amortized value	69,061,199
Other securities, not exceeding market value	844,848,829
TOTAL SECURITIES	1,944,841,235
Day, call, and short loans to investment dealers and brokers, secured	553,673,095
Other loans, including mortgages, less provision for losses	13,000,789,283
TOTAL LOANS	13,554,462,378
Bank premises at cost, less amounts written off	132,879,144
Securities of and loans to corporations controlled by the bank	111,424,600
Customers' liability under acceptances, guarantees, and letters of credit, as per contra	1,060,204,129
Other assets	20,547,899
	$22,359,247,248

Liabilities

Deposits by Canada	$ 323,160,587
Deposits by provinces	389,802,138
Deposits by banks	5,461,075,460
Personal savings deposits payable after notice, in Canada, in Canadian currency	5,505,546,364
Other deposits	8,540,026,428
TOTAL DEPOSITS	20,219,610,977
Acceptances, guarantees, and letters of credit	1,060,204,129
Other liabilities	46,776,104
Accumulated appropriations for losses	159,801,439

Capital Funds

Debentures issued and outstanding	191,730,000

Shareholders' Equity

Capital paid up	41,250,000
Rest account	639,000,000
Undivided profits	874,599
TOTAL SHAREHOLDERS' EQUITY	681,124,599
TOTAL CAPITAL FUNDS	872,854,599
	$22,359,247,248

STATEMENT OF ASSETS AND LIABILITIES, AS AT OCTOBER 31, 1978.

Assets

Cash and due from banks	$ 7,607,239,708
Cheques and other items in transit, net	323,138,119
TOTAL CASH RESOURCES	7,930,377,827
Securities issued or guaranteed by Canada, at amortized value	1,223,613,543
Securities issued or guaranteed by provinces, at amortized value	62,618,893
Other securities, not exceeding market value	1,308,076,853
TOTAL SECURITIES	2,594,309,289
Day, call, and short loans to investment dealers and brokers, secured	608,667,240
Other loans, including mortgages, less provision for losses	15,039,810,274
TOTAL LOANS	15,648,477,514
Bank premises at cost, less amounts written off	188,743,588
Securities of and loans to corporations controlled by the bank	177,976,312
Customers' liability under acceptances, guarantees, and letters of credit, as per contra	1,130,828,731
Other assets	16,000,700
	$27,686,713,961

Liabilities

Deposits by Canada	$ 542,086,221
Deposits by provinces	546,122,664
Deposits by banks	7,277,389,130
Personal savings deposits payable after notice, in Canada, in Canadian currency	6,197,118,519
Other deposits	10,769,894,299
TOTAL DEPOSITS	25,332,610,833
Acceptances, guarantees, and letters of credit	1,130,828,731
Other liabilities	55,401,301
Accumulated appropriations for losses	191,824,069

Capital Funds

Debentures issued and outstanding	204,641,000

Shareholders' Equity

Capital paid up	41,250,000
Rest account	729,000,000
Undivided profits	1,158,027
TOTAL SHAREHOLDERS' EQUITY	771,408,027
TOTAL CAPITAL FUNDS	976,049,027
	$27,686,713,961

STATEMENT OF ASSETS AND LIABILITIES, AS AT OCTOBER 31, 1979.

Assets

Cash and due from banks	$10,140,819,387
Cheques and other items in transit, net	251,476,747
TOTAL CASH RESOURCES	10,392,296,134
Securities issued or guaranteed by Canada, at amortized value	1,249,767,424
Securities issued or guaranteed by provinces, at amortized value	66,253,349
Other securities, not exceeding market value	1,711,968,721
TOTAL SECURITIES	3,027,989,494
Day, call, and short loans to investment dealers and brokers, secured	802,353,469
Other loans, including mortgages, less provision for losses	18,856,442,893
TOTAL LOANS	19,658,796,362
Bank premises at cost, less amounts written off	222,403,070
Securities of and loans to corporations controlled by the bank	73,805,188
Customers' liability under acceptances, guarantees, and letters of credit, as per contra	1,451,694,262
Other assets	41,884,155
	$34,868,868,665

Liabilities

Deposits by Canada	$ 309,518,857
Deposits by provinces	201,883,874
Deposits by banks	10,764,299,933
Personal savings deposits payable after notice, in Canada, in Canadian currency	7,409,178,536
Other deposits	13,190,532,473
TOTAL DEPOSITS	31,875,413,673
Acceptances, guarantees, and letters of credit	1,451,694,262
Other liabilities	91,573,209
Accumulated appropriations for losses	224,198,353

Capital Funds

Debentures issued and outstanding	248,630,000

Shareholders' Equity

Capital paid up	46,096,597
Rest account	930,267,508
Undivided profits	995,063
TOTAL SHAREHOLDERS' EQUITY	977,359,168
TOTAL CAPITAL FUNDS	1,225,989,168
	$34,868,868,665

STATEMENT OF ASSETS AND LIABILITIES, AS AT OCTOBER 31, 1980.

Assets

Cash and due from banks	$12,707,831,569
Cheques and other items in transit, net	129,889,409
TOTAL CASH RESOURCES	12,837,720,978
Securities issued or guaranteed by Canada, at amortized value	1,092,294,359
Securities issued or guaranteed by provinces, at amortized value	58,864,096
Other securities, not exceeding market value	1,682,007,725
TOTAL SECURITIES	2,833,166,180
Day, call, and short loans to investment dealers and brokers, secured	731,654,825
Other loans, including mortgages, less provision for losses	23,424,407,565
TOTAL LOANS	24,156,062,390
Bank premises at cost, less amounts written off	300,942,870
Securities of and loans to corporations controlled by the bank	110,917,998
Customers' liability under acceptances, guarantees, and letters of credit, as per contra	2,827,745,694
Other assets	110,235,298
	$43,176,791,408

Liabilities

Deposits by Canada	$ 391,623,472
Deposits by provinces	374,968,017
Deposits by banks	11,962,654,556
Personal savings deposits payable after notice, in Canada, in Canadian currency	8,941,093,483
Other deposits	16,933,115,341
TOTAL DEPOSITS	38,603,454,869
Acceptances, guarantees, and letters of credit	2,827,745,694
Other liabilities	126,899,286
Accumulated appropriations for losses	272,424,723

Capital Funds

Debentures issued and outstanding	248,073,000

Shareholders' Equity

Capital paid up	46,406,250
Rest account	1,050,992,188
Undivided profits	795,398
TOTAL SHAREHOLDERS' EQUITY	1,098,193,836
TOTAL CAPITAL FUNDS	1,346,266,836
	$43,176,791,408

STATEMENT OF ASSETS AND LIABILITIES, AS AT OCTOBER 31, 1981.

Assets

Cash and due from banks	$11,801,541,026
Cheques and other items in transit, net	55,759,525
TOTAL CASH RESOURCES	11,857,300,551
Securities issued or guaranteed by Canada, at amortized value	1,106,560,066
Securities issued or guaranteed by provinces, at amortized value	49,672,007
Other securities, not exceeding market value	1,831,241,727
TOTAL SECURITIES	2,987,473,800
Day, call, and short loans to investment dealers and brokers, secured	610,580,538
Other loans, including mortgages, less provision for losses	29,574,010,888
TOTAL LOANS	30,184,591,426
Bank premises at cost, less amounts written off	355,383,847
Securities of and loans to corporations controlled by the bank	288,380,090
Customers' liability under acceptances, guarantees, and letters of credit, as per contra	4,329,716,226
Other assets	135,207,282
	$50,138,053,222

Liabilities

Deposits by Canada	$ 439,339,833
Deposits by provinces	111,950,441
Deposits by banks	12,391,218,193
Personal savings deposits payable after notice, in Canada, in Canadian currency	10,649,601,204
Other deposits	19,400,348,904
TOTAL DEPOSITS	42,992,458,575
Acceptances, guarantees, and letters of credit	4,329,716,226
Other liabilities	798,968,854
Accumulated appropriations for losses	286,376,497

Capital Funds

Debentures issued and outstanding	517,171,000

Shareholders' Equity

Capital paid up	46,406,250
Rest account	1,166,000,000
Undivided profits	955,820
TOTAL SHAREHOLDERS' EQUITY	1,213,362,070
TOTAL CAPITAL FUNDS	1,730,533,070
	$50,138,053,222

THE SCOTIABANK STORY

Directors
1832–1982

1832-1870	Almon, The Honourable M.B.	1837-1872	Keith, The Honourable Alexander
1832-1837	Binney, Stephen N.	1837-1840	Roche, Charles
1832-1833 1836-1837 1838-1840	Black, William F.	1837-1870	Tremain, James
		1840-1871	Anderson, The Honourable John H.
		1840-1845	Starr, Joseph
1832-1845	Bliss, Lewis	1842-1848	Brown, Robert M.
1832-1835	Bliss, The Honourable W.B.	1842-1846	Sawyer, John J.
1832-1834	Brown, John	1842-1852 1856-1876	Uniacke, Andrew M.
1832-1875	Donaldson, James		
1832-1834 1835-1836	Johnston, James W.	1844-1852	Maynard, Captain Thomas
		1845-1852	Snelling, Foster H.
1832-1837	Lawson, William	1845-1858	Starr, David
1832-1842	Leishman, James	1847-1856	Billing, Edward
1832-1833 1834-1849	Murdoch, William	1848-1856	Robinson, John
		1849-1853	Hume, Robert
1832-1844	Murison, Alexander	1853-1863	Esson, John
1832-1842 1847-1852	Uniacke, James B.	1856-1860	Boggs, Henry
		1858-1865	Merkel, James W.
1833-1834	Morris, John S.	1860-1865	Cunard, William
1833-1838	Snelling, William H.	1863-1865	Hume, Dr. James C.
1834-1842	Bazalgette, Major John	1864-1892	Cronan, Daniel
1834-1846	Wallace, Dr. Alexander	1864-1867	MacKinlay, Andrew
1836-1837	Black, William A.	1865-1871	Hare, William

400

Directors, 1832-1982

1867-1899	Doull, John	1923-1951	Starr, F.P.
1870-1889	Maclean, John S.	1924-1934	Smith, O.E.
1871-1884	Bremner, James J.	1927-1946	McLeod, J.A.
1871	Hart, Jairus	1927-1947	Smith, Sydney T.
1884-1899		1927-1941	Tory, The Honourable James C.
1871-1886	White, S.A.	1928-1950	Birks, W.M.
1883-1897	Burns, Adam	1928-1942	Fraser, The Honourable J. Fred
1889-1918	Payzant, John Y.	1928-1950	McCarthy, Leighton
1892-1900	Seeton, R.B.	1929-1950	Ellsworth, A.L.
1897-1928	Archibald, Charles	1929-1952	McCurdy, The Honourable F.B.
1899-1927	Allison, J. Walter	1934-1969	Fraser, Col. J.D.
1899-1911	Borden, The Right Honourable Sir Robert L.	1934-1962	Murdoch, James Y.
		1935-1945	Patterson, H.F.
1899-1927	Campbell, George S.	1937-1947	Lovett, L.A.
1900-1937	McInnes, Hector	1937-1951	Spencer, Christopher
1904-1910	McLeod, H.C.	1939-1940	MacLaren, Albert
1910-1931	Curry, The Honourable N.	1940-1958	Maclaren, Brig. Gen. C.H.
1910-1915	Plummber, J.H.	1941-1950	MacDougall, Dr. J.G.
1912-1915	Harris, Robert E.	1943-1948	Kilpatrick, J.A.
1913-1950	White, Dr. W.W.	1943-1952	Winfield, W.A.
1914-1923	Manchester, James	1944-1959	Burns, H.D.
1915-1928	Grant, The Honourable MacCallum	1945-1974	Harris, William C.
1915-1947	Moore, S.J.	1945-1947	Crockett, Edwin
1915-1947	Ross, The Honourable W.D.	1946-1949	Hastie, W.J.
1919-1955	Blackburn, Russell	1946-1957	Mackay, Hugh
1919-1937	Bryson, The Honourable George	1947-1954	Murphy, W.A.
1919-1920	Burn, Sir George	1947-1965	Gardiner, Percy R.
1919-1923	Egan, Sir Henry K.	1947-1959	Enman, Horace L.
1919-1934	Fraser, John B.	1947-1964	McLeod, W. Norman
1919-1942	Gordon, The Honourable George	1947-1959	Manning, Fred C.
1919-1939	Maclaren, Alexander	1948-1965	Whiteford, William K.
1919-1923	O'Brien, The Honourable M.J.	1949-1962	Sherman, Frank A.
1919-1920	Perley, The Honourable Sir George H.	1950-1959	Graham, F. Ronald
1919-1924	Whitney, Edwin C.	1950-1963	Macklaier, William F.
1920-1924	MacGregor, The Honourable R.M.	1950-1976	McCarthy, John L.

401

1950-1964	Jodrey, Roy A.	1963-	Courtois, E. Jacques
1950-1971	Wilson, Charles N.	1963-1971	O'Brien, The Honourable J. Leonard
1950-1969	Frost, C. Sydney		
1951-1962	Asselin, The Honourable Edouard	1964-1972	Bell, G. Maxwell
1951-1955	Berg, Ole, Jr.	1964-1966	Kramer, Robert A.
1951-1959	Spencer, Col. J.V.N.	1964-1974	Browne, W. Herman
1952-1968	Rahilly, Thomas F.	1964-	Jodrey, John J.
1952-1961	Fraser, Albert S.	1965-1969	Hay, Charles
1952-1961	Bell, Ralph P.	1965-1972	Brockett, E. Delwin
1952-1954	Porter, Marshall M.	1966-	The Right Honourable Earl of Iveagh
1954-1975	Smith, C. Gordon		
1954-1970	Dales, Robert L.	1966-1977	Boyles, Thomas A.
1955-1973	Bradfield, John R.	1968-1972	Todd, F. Foster
1955-1970	Brown, Fred B.	1969-1977	McAfee, Jerry
1955-1960	Beringer, Milton S.	1970-	Crockett, Arthur H.
1955-1977	Baker, Albert T.	1971-1979	MacCulloch, Charles E.
1955-1977	Rea, W. Harold	1971-	McCain, H. Harrison
1956-1972	Hayden, The Honourable Salter A.	1971-	Pierce, Robert L.
1957-1972	Nicks, F. William	1971-	Hobbs, Gerald H.D.
1958-1973	Maclaren, A. Barnet	1972-1982	McGavin, Allan M.
1958-	Ayre, Lewis H.M.	1972-1981	Amyot, René
1959-1973	McLean, Cyrus H.	1972-	Cox, Kenneth V.
1960-	Sherman, Frank H.	1972-	McGregor, William S.
1960-1973	Mountain, Sir Brian (Bt.)	1972-	Mitchell, David E.
1960-1965	Loughney, Edward D.	1972-	Ritchie, Cedric E.
1960-1969	MacKenzie, The Honourable Norman A.M.	1973-	McAlpine, Malcolm H.D.
		1973-	Cork, E. Kendall
1960-1976	McInnes, Donald	1973-	Maclaren, Donald
1961-1974	Jackman, Henry R.	1973-1976	Smith, Dr. Arthur J.R.
1961-1980	Aird, The Honourable John B.	1974-1977	Purves, Robert P.
1961-	Willmot, Donald G.	1974-	Wolfe, Ray D.
1961-1972	Schwartz, William H.C.	1974-	Rust, Thomas G.
1962-1974	Lowson, Sir Denys (Bt.)	1974-1981	Barr, David W.
1962-1965	Gibson, J. Douglas	1974-	Bell, J.A. Gordon
1962-1976	Proctor, John S.	1974-	Hitchman, George C.

Directors, 1832 - 1982

1976-	Stewart, William A.	1979-	Johnson, F. Ross
1976-	Barber, Dr. Lloyd I.	1980-	Macdonald, The Honourable Donald S.
1976-	Wilson, Miss Marie		
1976-	Parker, Mrs. Helen A.	1980-	Phillips, J.C.
1977-	Martinez, Rafael J.	1981-	McDougall, Ian
1978-	Mountain, Sir Denis (Bt.)	1982-	MacFarlane, Gordon F.
1978-	The Right Honourable Lord Keith of Castleacre	1982-	McDonald, W. Scott
		1982-	Godsoe, Peter C.

THE BANK OF NOVA SCOTIA:

LEFT TO RIGHT, STANDING: *Ray D. Wolfe, Frank H. Sherman*
SEATED: *Peter C. Godsoe, The Honourable Donald S. Macdonald, George C. Hitchman*

CREDIT: V. TONY HAUSER

BOARD OF DIRECTORS, 1982

STANDING: *Rafael J. Martinez*
LEFT TO RIGHT, SEATED: *Ian McDougall, W. Scott McDonald*

CREDIT: V. TONY HAUSER

Malcolm H. D. McAlpine
CREDIT: BARON STUDIOS

The Right Honourable Earl of Iveagh

F. Ross Johnson

LEFT TO RIGHT, SEATED: *The Right Honourable Lord Keith of Castleacre, J. A. Gordon Bell, Lloyd I. Barber, Cedric E. Ritchie*

CREDIT: DENIS GARON

William S. McGregor   *David E. Mitchell*   *Sir Denis Mountain, Bt.*

LEFT TO RIGHT, STANDING: *E. Kendall Cork, Robert L. Pierce*
SEATED: *Donald G. Willmot, E. Jacques Courtois*
CREDIT: DENIS GARON

LEFT:
Thomas G. Rust

RIGHT:
Donald Maclaren

STANDING:
J. C. Phillips
LEFT TO RIGHT, SEATED:
Lewis H. M. Ayre,
Helen A. Parker

CREDIT: DENIS GARON

LEFT TO RIGHT:
*John J. Jodrey,
Arthur H. Crockett*

CREDIT: DENIS GARON

LEFT TO RIGHT, STANDING: *William A. Stewart, Kenneth V. Cox, Gordon F. MacFarlane*
SEATED: *Gerald H. D. Hobbs, Marie Wilson, H. Harrison McCain*

THE BANK OF NOVA SCOTIA

Executive Officers 1832–1982

(ARRANGED CHRONOLOGICALLY BEGINNING WITH THE FIRST PRESIDENT)

NOTE: *A hyphen after a single year means the officer is still incumbent.*
A single year without a hyphen indicates the officer held the post during that year only.

NAME	GENERAL MANAGER*	EXECUTIVE VICE-PRESIDENT	PRESIDENT	DEPUTY CHAIRMAN	C.E.O.	CHAIRMAN
Lawson, William			1832-1837			
Forman, James	1832-1870					
Almon, Hon. M.B.			1837-1870			
Donaldson, James			1870-1871			
Menzies, William C.	1870-1876					
Doull, John			1871-1872; 1889-1899			
Uniacke, Andrew M.			1872-1874			
Maclean, John S.			1874-1889			
Fyshe, Thomas	1876-1897					
Hart, Jairus			Sept. 1899-Dec. 1899			
Payzant, John Y.			1899-1918			
McLeod, H.C.	1897-1910					
Archibald, Charles			1918-1923			
Richardson, H.A.	1910-1923					
Campbell, G.S.			1923-1927			

*The General Manager was known as Cashier until 1898 when the title was changed. The title General Manager changed in 1963 to Chief General Manager and in 1979 to Chief Operating Officer.

Executive Officers, 1832–1982

NOTE: *A hyphen after a single year means the officer is still incumbent.*
A single year without a hyphen indicates the officer held the post during that year only.

NAME	GENERAL MANAGER*	EXECUTIVE VICE-PRESIDENT	PRESIDENT	DEPUTY CHAIRMAN	C.E.O.	CHAIRMAN
Moore, S.J.			1927-1934			1933-1945
McLeod, J.A.	1923-1933		1934-1945			1945-1946
Patterson, H.F.	1933-1941	1941-1943				
Burns, Herbert D.	1941-1945		1945-1949			1949-1955
Crockett, E.		1945-1947				
Enman, Horace L.	1945-1949	1947-1949	1949-1956			1955-1959
Frost, C. Sydney	1949-1954	1955-1956	1956-1958			
Nicks, F. William	1954-1958		1958-1970		1960-1972	1962-1972
Dales, Robert L.		1958-1964		1962-1964		
Gibson, J. Douglas	1958-1964	1964-1965		1964-1965		
Boyles, Thomas A.	1964-1966	1966-1972		1969-1972	1972	1972-1974
Proctor, John S.		1962-1971		1962-1971		
Touchie, Gordon J.	1966-1968					
Hitchman, G.C.		1972-1974		1974-1981		
MacIntosh, R.M.		1972-1980				
Crockett, A.H.	1968-1970		1970-1972	1972-1982		
Ritchie, C.E.	1968-1972		1972-1979		1972-	1974-
Bell, J.A.G.	1972-	1972-1979	1979-	1982-		
McDonald, W. Scott		1972-† ‡				
Godsoe, P.C.		1980-‡				

*The General Manager was known as Cashier until 1898 when the title was changed. The title General Manager changed in 1963 to Chief General Manager and in 1979 to Chief Operating Officer.

† in 1980 named the first Sr. Executive Vice-President.
‡ in 1982 named Vice-Chairman.

THE SCOTIABANK STORY

Index

Aberhart, William, 165, 167
Acadia Club, 93-4, 320
Acadian Recorder, 81
Adams, T. G., 206
Addis, Sir Charles, 158
agencies. *See* branches
Aird, The Honourable John, 333
Alberta: Social Credit government's effect on banking, 167-8; growth of branches in, 189-90; regional office, 198
Alley, B. P., 88
Allison, J. Walter, 80, 88
Almon, Mather Byles: background, 8, 35-6; subscription list, 10; Director, 18; President, 33, 35-6, 47; loan to Cunard, 44
amalgamations: Union Bank of Prince Edward Island, 58; Bank of New Brunswick, 105-11; Metropolitan Bank, 111, 115-18; Bank of Ottawa, 121, 125-9; summary, 338
Ames, Alfred Ernest, 111
Amyot, René, 333
Antigua, 242, 317
Archibald, C. I., 228, 236, 238, 275
Archibald, Charles: background, 80, 143; directors' trip to western Canada, 88; President, 121, 127, 138; travelling, 133
Armstrong, W. D., 277
Ash, C.J., 163, 221, 235
Atlanta, 310
Australia, 314
automation and productivity, 326. *Also see* mechanization of Bank's procedures
automobile loans, 202
automotive financing office, 287
Avison, T. L., 151
Ayre, Lewis H. M., 333; photograph in Board of Directors album

Bahamas, 216, 242, 263, 316-17
Bailey, W. E., 281
Baker, Gene, 302
Banco Mercantil de Puerto Rico, 317
Bank Act: limit on bank's note issue, 94-6; bank inspection, 96; establishment of central bank, 155, 157-60; right to issue bank notes terminated, 181; reduction of interest rates, 181; changes in 1954 legislation, 202; new legislation in 1967, 231-2; changed calculation of earnings, 324; failed to bring "near banks" under control, 330; treatment of foreign banks, 331
Bank Inspection: The Necessity for External Examination, 98
bank notes: purchase of, 19, 24; Halifax Banking Company controversy, 25, 27-8; issuance of, 39; legal limit on issue, 94-6, 103-4; became legal tender, 119; Bank of Canada, 159; right to issue terminated, 181
Bank of America, 203
Bank of British North America: founding, 31; competition from, 40; loan to Cunard, 44
Bank of Canada: creation, 159-60; developing operations, 168; exchange rate, 201; restraint on consumer credit, 206; competition for deposits, 290; bank rate, 292
Bank of Liverpool, 55-8
Bank of N. T. Butterfield and Son, 318
Bank of New Brunswick: founding, 6, 7; cashier trained at, 20; reduced capital, 66; situation in 1910, 105-6; amalgamation, 106-11, 338
Bank of Nova Scotia: bill of incorporation, 12-16; supplies for, 19-20; hiring staff, 20; John Romans's building, 23-4; opening, 24-5, 27; foreign agencies, 29-30; new building, 31-2; proper conduct of employees, 39-40, 82; charter extended, 41; difficulties during early 1880s, 66-7; unit system of work, 84; argument about limit on note issue, 94-6, 103-4; first audited statement, 97; changes in administration, 134; conservative posture during twenties, 137; reduction of outside reserves, 154-5;

413

problems of recovery, 1933-35, 161; post-war assets and profits, 179-80; increase in loans, 189; growth in fifties, 201; foreign wholesale banking, 201; solid growth, 1945-60, 221; major reorganization, 234-5; growth in foreign business, 242; foundations laid for expansion in late sixties, 250; continued solid growth in domestic business, 268; lending to individuals, 269; organization of credit function on regional basis, 271-2; new services, 287; increase in demand for business loans, 290; liability management, 291-2, 310; reorganization, 292-3; domestic and international banking move closer together, 296; changed calculation of earnings, 324-5; growth during seventies, 326-7; 150th anniversary, 349
Bank of Nova Scotia International Limited, 317
Bank of Nova Scotia Jamaica Limited, 263, 320
Bank of Nova Scotia Trinidad and Tobago Limited, 320
Bank of Nova Scotia Trust Company (Bahamas), 216
Bank of Nova Scotia Trust Company of New York, 216
Bank of Ottawa, 121-9, 338
Bank of the United States, 29, 35
Baptie, Muriel, 209
Barbados, 215, 263, 317
Barber, Lloyd I., photograph in Board of Directors Album
Baring Brothers & Co., 29-30
Barnes, C. A., 313
Bartlett, Harry, 161
Beirut, 246
Belcher, Andrew, 10
Belcher, S. D. N., 313
Belfast, 255
Belize, 263, 319
Bell, J. A. G.: background, 199; Jamaican operation, 263; President, 332; General Manager, 267; Chief General Manager, 278-9; Liability Committee, 292; decentralization, 299, 313; Spencer Hall, 304; Bank's achievement in seventies, 307; on revised Bank Act, 330, 331; photograph in Board of Directors album
Bell, Max, 222
Bell, Ralph P., 222, 223
Bennett, R. B., 153
Beresford, D. A., 176
Berkinshaw, N. W., 149
Bermuda National Bank, 264, 318
Betancourt, M. J., 210
Binney, Stephen N., 19, 44
Birmingham, B. R., 296, 322
Bisson, André, 275, 328, 329, 330
Black, William F., 18
Blackburn, Russell, 129
Blanchard, Jotham, 13
Bliss, Henry, 8, 12, 29
Bliss, Lewis: Halifax Banking Company, 8, 10, 14; Director, 19; London agent, 30; loan to Cunard, 44
Bliss, William Blowers, 8, 13, 14, 19
Bluethner, P. D., 176

Bond, Walter S., 163, 174, 221
Book of Remembrance, 176
Borden, Robert L., 80
Boston, 30, 310
Boville, Thomas, 103
Bowlby, C. L., 220, 221
Boyd, H. G., 175
Boyd, Louise, 302
Boyles, Thomas A.: amalgamation with Bank of Ottawa, 123; bank hockey, 163; government and business working together, 182; background, 220; General Manager, 235; Chief General Manager, 235, 249; credit applications in International, 261; Executive Vice-President, 265; management team, 280; travelling habits, 311
Bradshaw, Thomas, 111
branches: New York, 19, 29, 218; London, 29-30, 217, 245; Boston, 30; Saint John, N.B., 37; status of agent, 37; local agencies, 37-8, 40; eastern Canada, 58-60, 72, 90; Winnipeg, 62-6, 79; Minneapolis, 67-9; Chicago, 70; Montreal, 70, 223; Jamaica, 71-2, 213-14, 263, 320; growth between 1876 and 1897, 73; Toronto, 79; western Canada, 87-9, 189-90; Cuba, 90, 210-13; Caribbean expansion, 90-3, 263-4, 318; Puerto Rico, 104, 216, 264, 317-18; growth during 1910-23, 130; at centenary, 144; in Sask. during the depression, 164; licensing of, in Alta., 167; restrictive measures during wartime, 173; in fifties, 190, 201; Dominican Republic, 215-16, 264; Bahamas, 216, 316-17; in 1960, 221; growth of suburban, 226; profit planning, 235-7; women managers, 241; Scotland, 245, 255; Greece, 246, 257; reporting to London, 255; U.S. Virgin Islands, 264, 318; expansion in Canada, 1969-70, 270; Quebec, 275; computerized banking, 281, 282-3; breakdown of regions into districts, 299; Far East, 307; Japan, 314; Caribbean Region, 315-16; St. Maarten, 318; Guyana, 319; Belize, 319-20; Trinidad and Tobago, 320; development in seventies, 327
Brandman, R. N., 313
British Columbia, 190
British Virgin Islands, 263, 318
Brooks, R.L., 292, 299, 301
Brown, A. G., 176
Brown, John, 10, 19
Brown, R. M., 238
Brown, Thomas, 229
Brownlee, J. E., 158
Brussels, 255
Bryson, George, 123-5, 127, 129
Buller, Charles, 36
bullion certificates, 322
Burchell, J. S., 189
Burke, Marguerite, 209
Burn, George, 123
Burns, H. D.: background, 76, 134, 160; General Manager, 172-3; nationalization of banks, 180-1; President, 184; new General Office building, 195; credit meetings, 198; Honorary President, 206; death, 218; contribution of, 339

Calder, B. R., 206, 221
Caldwell, H. W., 175, 220, 228, 229, 237
Campbell, G. S.: Director, 80; directors' trip to western Canada, 88; amalgamation with Bank of Ottawa, 127; enjoyed travelling, 133; President, 138, 139; background, 142
Canadian Bankers' Association: H. C. McLeod withdraws from, 84-6; McLeod's unpopularity, 97-8; social credit theory, 167
Canadian Commercial Banking, 294
Cann, H. V., 108-9, 123-7, 129
Cannon, Louise, 302, 304
Cantwell, Jack, 302
Caravan, Diane, 302
Caribbean: branch opened in Kingston, Jamaica, 71-2; problems accompanying growth in, 90-3; expansion in, 190, 215, 216, 242, 263-4; banking similar to Canada, 320-1; 17 banks and 14 currencies, 315-16
Carlile, Benjamin, 20, 39
Carmichael, J. W., 46
Carter, A. Scott, 176
Carter, John R., 113
cash credit, 38
cash reserves, 97, 202, 230-1
Castleacre, The Right Honourable Lord Keith of, photograph in Board of Directors album
Cawthra, William, 191
Cayman Islands, 263
centenary, 144
central bank, 155, 157-60
Central Covenants Ltd., 233
certificates of deposit, 226, 290
Chalklin, Betty, 209
Chalklin, George W., 209
Chamberlain, G. E., 288-9
Chan, R.A., 320
Chapman, Olive, 209
Chargex, 281
Charlottetown, 58-9
chattel mortgages, 202, 206
Chicago, 70
Chief Accountant's Department, 148, 241
China, 313
Chisholm, J. W., 276
Clark, E. R., 151
Clarkson, E. R. C., 118
Cleveland, 310
Clinch, J. S., 220, 279
Cobb, Andrew R., 141
Cochran, Rupert, 12, 19, 24, 29
Cogswell, Hezekiah; Halifax Banking Company, 6, 7; Board of Health, 22; bank-note controversy, 25-6, 27
Collins, Enos, 5, 6, 7
Commercial Bank of Windsor, 40
Commercial Banking Services, 298
computer operations, 273-4, 280-4, 298
Confederation, adjustment in Maritimes, 53
Consolidated Cash Plan, 283
consumer credit, 170, 200, 206-8, 233, 269, 281
contingency reserves, 181, 324
Cooke, R., 322
Coombs, P. B., 176

Coon, H. J., 149, 158
Cork, E. Kendall, photograph in Board of Directors album
Cornwallis, Edward, 1
Corporate Banking, 296
Council of Twelve, 4, 14
coupon-banking system, 175
Courtois, E. Jacques, 333; photograph in Board of Directors album
Cox, Kenneth V., photograph in Board of Directors album
Cox, Victor, 210, 212-13
Craddock, Candace U., 302, 331
Cranstoun, J. A., 163
Crawford, E. S., 188, 206, 210, 216
Crean, J. F., 281, 283, 331
credit meetings, 198-9, 276
Crockett, A. H., 176, 199; international banking, 218; expansion in Montreal, 223; credit applications in International, 261; Chief General Manager, 267; President, 267; lending services, 269; branch expansion in Canada, 270, 327; business-development and management, 280; Toronto branch, 301; retirement, 332; photograph in Board of Directors album
Crockett, Edwin: Assistant Manager, 148; background, 160; Vice-President, 184
Cuba, 90, 210-13
Cunard, Joseph, 43
Cunard, Samuel, 30, 31, 41-4
Cunard, William, 45
Cunard loan, 43-4
currency, defective state of, 5, 6
Custodian of Enemy Property, 175

daily interest accounts, 290
Dales, Robert L.: background, 186, 198; training for managers, 199; Vice-President, 206; Executive Vice-President, 218; helped train Gibson, 220
Dalhousie College, 3, 22-4
Daly, Donald, 230
Davies, W. H., 107
decentralization: in western Canada, 197-8; profit planning, 237; in regions, 241-2; trend slowed in seventies, 298-9; decreasing mobility of staff, 300; current position on, 343-4
Dennis, P. W., 176
deposit campaigns, 203, 209, 226-9, 290
Deposit Development Department, 209
Depression, the Great. See Great Depression
directors: first Board of, 18-19; first meeting in Bank's own building, 26; in 1870, 44-5; General Office move to Toronto, 79; trip to western Canada, 88-9; Metropolitan Bank, 118; Bank of Ottawa, 123, 126-8; composition of Board in 1960, 222; lively, responsible Board, 333
districts, breakdown of regions into, 299
dividends, 28, 154, 180, 221-2
Dixon, W. J., 207, 232, 238
Dodd, P. S., 322
Dominican Republic, 215-16, 264, 317
Donaldson, James, 19, 26, 45, 47
Douglas, C. H., 165
Doull, John, 45, 46, 47, 73

Dublin, 255
Dudley, E. J. S., 175
Duffus, John, 43, 44

Easson, C. H., 106-8
Economics Department, 149-51, 276, 331-2
Edinburgh, 255
Edmonton, 88
Ellis, H. R. S., 175
Ellis, W. F., 287
employees: for new Bank, 20; oath, 22; proper conduct of, 39-40, 82; Fyshe's personnel policies, 53, 75; emphasis on efficiency, 82, 84; unit system of work, 84; H. C. McLeod's attitude toward, 84; in Jamaica, 92, 93-4, 214, 320; during World War I, 119-20; during the depression, 144; junior's duties, 145-6; licensing of, in Alta., 167; during World War II, 173-4; war record, 175-6; fitting in veterans, 179; post-war period, 191; Frost's attitude toward, 197; staff training, 199-200, 239-40; staff magazine, 203; consumer credit introduced, 208; in Cuba, 212; in 1960, 221; deposit campaigns, 228; outside professionals develop Scotia Plan, 232-3; job evaluation, 237-9; salary administration, 239; manpower planning, 240; Touchie's attitude toward, 249; branch performance, 274; in Quebec, 275, 328-9; personnel function a double-headed arrangement, 276; lessened mobility of, 300; hiring university graduates, 301; progress of women, 302; personnel reorganization and training, 302-3; top personnel in international business, 307; automation and productivity, 326
Enman, Horace L.: bank hockey, 161; J. A. McLeod brought in, 173; General Manager, 184, 186-8; encouraged growth of branches, 190; new General Office building, 193; President, 196; inflation in early fifties, 200; Chairman, 206; delay in posting, 210; death, 218; opposed Gibson's appointment, 220; contribution of, 339
Eurodollar market, 249, 253-5, 345
Evans, Thomas, 214-15
Exchange Bank of Yarmouth, 40
Export Credit Insurance Corporation, 182
Export Development Corporation, 182

Farm Improvement Loans, 182, 189, 288
farm program, 288-9
Federal Business Development Bank, 182
federal government: failure of Bank of Liverpool, 55-7; banks agents of, 119; valuation of securities and bonds of banks, 153; securities during World War II, 180; working together with business, 182; Conversion Loan of 1958, 209; securities a source of liquidity, 326
Federation of the British West Indies, 215
Felsenstein, Edgar, 243, 255
fiftieth anniversary, 60
Finance Act (1914), 119
Finlay, Fred J., 163, 205, 210
Finnie, D. M., 123

Fiott, James, 197, 206
Fisher, Margaret, 302
Fleming, Donald, 263
floating exchange rate, 201
Forcey, E. F., 303
foreign banks, 331
foreign currency assets, 242, 252, 259, 292, 315
foreign exchange: New York, 29; London and Boston, 29-30; Minneapolis, 67-8; Chicago, 70; control, 174; floating rate, 201
Forgan, David R., 52, 54, 63-4, 68
Forgan, James R., 54, 55-7, 65-6, 67-8, 77
Forman, James: Cashier, 20-1; bank-note controversy, 25-6; defalcation, 41, 45-6, 335
Forman, Jerome F., 217
Fox, L. L., 312
Frankfurt, 256
Fraser, C. M., 175
Fraser, James D., 37, 38
Fraser, John B., 129
Freestone, Harry, 145, 147-8
Froats, Mae, 209
Frost, C. Sydney: war record, 120; manager at Saskatoon, 164; General Manager, 176, 195; background, 196-7; President, 206; retirement, 218
Frost, Leslie, 195
Fyshe, Thomas: Cashier, 48, 50, 52-3; background, 51-2; personnel policies, 53, 75; Forgan brothers join Bank, 54; Bank of Liverpool, 55; Bank's fiftieth anniversary, 60; Winnipeg experiment, 64-5; difficulties in early 1880s, 66-7; Bank's move to Chicago, 70; opening in Montreal, 70; branch in Kingston, Jamaica, 71-2; resigns, 73-5; external bank inspection, 96; contribution of, 336

Gage, R. G., 294, 299
Gardiner, Percy, 222
General Mining Association, 30, 40
General Office: moved to Toronto, 79-83; new building, 191-5; decentralization, 198; Methods Group, 271-2, 292; union of eastern and western credits in, 275; increase in supervisory personnel, 299
German, D. R., 277
Germany, 246, 257
Gibson, J. Douglas: Economics Department, 151; bank hockey, 163; loaned to Prices Board, 183; Assistant General Manager, 206; General Manager, 218, 219-20, 235; member of Royal Commission, 230; Director, 234; job evaluation, 238; Executive Vice-President and Deputy Chairman, 249; resigns, 250
Giles, A. C., 303
Gill, C. F., 295
Glasgow, 245
Godsoe, Peter C.: built up U.S. business, 261; Liability Committee, 292; entry into Bank, 301; Western Hemisphere International Regional Office, 309-10, 322; Vice-Chairman, 332; photograph in Board of Directors album
gold trading, 217, 244, 322
Gordon, Donald, 149, 160, 183, 195

Gordon, George, 126, 129
Graham, F. L., 210
Graham, J. Maxtone, 97
Great Depression: severity of, 140; Investment Department formed, 149; financial markets, 152; Wheat Pool collapsed, 152; economic situation in 1935, 160-1; bank hockey during, 161-3; drought, 163; heavy government borrowing, 169; partial recovery by 1939, 168
Greece, 246, 256, 257
Grenada, 242, 317
Griffiths, G.A., 213, 216
Guyana, 263, 319

Haiti, 316, 317
Haldenby, E. W., 192
Halifax: in 1830s, 1; development of, 2-4; explosion, 131-3; new Head Office, 141-2; Bank's attachment to, 142
Halifax Banking Company: founding, 6, 7; opposition to, 7-8; bank-note controversy, 25, 27-8; competition from, 40
Halifax Morning Herald, 70
Hamilton, Alexander, 29
Hammett, E. T., 88, 90
Hampson, H. A., 230
Hare, G. E., 293-4
Harris, W. C., 222
Harrold, Gordon, 230
Hay Associates, 237, 239
Hayman, J. M., 228
Head Office, 141-3
Healy, T. A., 292, 308, 322
Heenan, Scotty, 302
Heeney, E. H., 151
Hellingrath, Baron Karl Max von, 218
Helstern, Kurt, 309
Henriques, C. F., 317
Hinchcliffe, G. F., 206, 216
Hitchman, George C.: junior's duties during the depression, 145-6; background, 163, 199; war record, 176; international banking, 218; Assistant General Manager, 221; expansion in Montreal, 223; Deputy General Manager, 235; job evaluation, 238; credit applications in International, 261; Joint General Manager, 265; senior credit man, 276, 280; decentralization, 299; Spencer Hall, 304; retires, 332; photograph in Board of Directors album
Hobbs, Gerald H. D., photograph in Board of Directors album
hockey, 161-3, 277
"Hockey College," 290
Holmes, R. R., 292
Holt, Geoffrey, 313
Holtrop, Marius, 230
Home Improvement Plan, 182
Hong Kong, 307
Hood, W. C., 230
household loans, 202
Houston, 248
Howard, Basil, 149
Howe, Joseph, 8, 10, 33
Howe, Sydenham, 57
Hubbert, J. D., 218
Huie, D. H., 97
Hunter, E. D., 215, 216

Hutchinson, C. V., 220, 275
Hway, G. N., 277

Ilsley, J. L., 181
incorporation, 15-16
Industrial Development Bank, 182
inflation: post-war, 179, 185; during World War II, 183; in fifties, 200; growth without, 225; mounting in late sixties, 268; response to rising costs, 270; in seventies, 285-6, 289-90; effect on banks, 347-8
inspection, by government, 96-7, 98-9
Inspection Department, 283
Institute of Canadian Bankers, 274
insured savings plan, 203
interest rates: on cash deposits, 40; under Bank Act, 158, 159; reduction of maximum charged on loans, 181; in 1950, 200; consumer credit, 207; Royal Commission recommendations, 230-1; competition for deposits, 268, 290
International Division: Ritchie heads, 259-61; formalization of credit procedures, 261; McDonald takes over, 263; technology for, 284; MBAS join, 301; changes in organization of, 322
international banking: gold business, 217, 322-3; London and New York, 218; growth during 1960-65, 226; expansion, 245-6; growth in Latin America, 255; Nicks's contribution, 264-5; liability management, 292; in seventies, 305-7; broadening U.S. activities, 309-10; assessing "country" risks, 314; Ritchie's contribution, 324; current position, 342
International Banking Centres, 296
Investment Department, 148-9, 209, 234, 292
Ironside, Isobel, 209
Irvine, Frank, 202
Iveagh, The Right Honourable Earl of, 333; photograph in Board of Directors album

Jackson, Gilbert, 149
Jakarta, 307
Jamaica: Kingston branch, 71-2; earthquake, 92; Acadia Club, 93-4, 320; branches, 213-14, 320; operation gained autonomy, 242; separate bank, 263, 320
Jameson, C. W., 205, 221, 265, 272
Japan, 313-14
Jarvis, Aemilius, 98-9
job evaluation, 237-9
Jodrey, John J., 333; photograph in Board of Directors album
Jodrey, Roy, 187, 222
Johnson, F. Ross, photograph in Board of Directors album
Johnson, Harry, 230
Johnson, P. T., 303
Johnston, J. D., 176
Johnston, James W., 8, 10, 19, 26
Johnstone, Robert, 230
Jones, Jacobine, 194

Keith, E. E., 322
Keith, Jack, 320
Kennedy, C. A., 85-6
Kent, W. H., 238, 259, 261, 307

Kessen, Robert B., 106-7
King, Harry, 37, 38
Kingston, Jamaica, 71-2, 92, 93-4
Kinnear, Morris, 88
Kinsman, Hugh, 208, 232
Korenaga, George, 246
Kuala Lumpur, 307

Latin America, 255, 314
Lawson, John, 9
Lawson, William: Halifax Banking Company, 9, 10, 12; President, 18; hiring staff, 20; suitable building, 22; banknote controversy, 26-7; retires, 31-3
Lawson, William, consumer credit, 207
Leishman, James, 19
Leman, Beaudry, 158
Leman, Paul, 229
Lennon, M., 261
Leonowens, Anna, 52, 143
Leslie, John A., 55, 57
liability management, 291-2, 310
Lindsay, D. L.: in Cuba, 210, 216; Caribbean regional office, 259; General Manager, 261; regional centre in Manila, 308
liquidity ratio, 269-70
"Liverpool boodlers," 57, 58
loans: two forms of, 38; to Cunard, 43-4; instalment payments for Victory Bonds, 119; reduction of maximum interest rate on, 181; upturn during post-war period, 189; in fifties, 201; mortgage, 202, 231, 233, 243, 269; automobile and household, 202; government's Conversion, 209; in Dominican Republic, 215; in early sixties, 233; emphasis on lending to people, 269; quality control of, 275, 294; in seventies, 286; inflation lifts demand for business, 290; Special Loans Department, 313; assessing "country" risks, 314
Logan, M. N., 281, 293
Lomax, W. J., 302
London, K. W., 317
London, 29-30, 217, 245, 312-13
Los Angeles, 248
Lyle, John M., 141, 192

MBAS, 301
MacDonald, A. L., 148
Macdonald, Angus L., 195
Macdonald, Arthur, 110-11
Macdonald, The Honourable Donald S., photograph in Board of Directors album
MacDonald, Thomas V., 70
MacDonell, George, 191, 271
MacFarlane, Gordon F., photograph in Board of Directors album
MacGregor, D. C., 151
MacGregor, I. M., 296
MacIntosh, G. F. H., 175
MacIntosh, Robert M.: Investment Department, 209; sale of long-term bonds at loss, 234; job evaluation, 238; Joint General Manager, 265; systems planning, 273, 280; Institute of Canadian Bankers, 274; foreign banking aspects of revised Bank Act, 331
Macintyre, Grant, 153
MacKeen, Jack, 230

Mackenzie, Norman, 222
Mackintosh, James C., 45-6
Mackintosh, Dr. W. A., 229
Macklaier, William, 222
Maclaren, Alexander, 129
Maclaren, Donald, photograph in Board of Directors album
Maclean, John S., 46, 55-7
Macmillan, The Right Honourable Lord Hugh Pattison, 158
MacNevin, E. D., 299, 301
Maduro & Curiel's Bank, 316, 318
Manchester, James, 106, 111
Manila, 307-8, 314
Manning, Fred, 187
manpower planning, 240
Maritime Bank, 66
Markborough Properties, 232, 233
Marketing Department, 293
Marsman, R.: London regional office, 255, 259, 311; General Manager, 261; background, 307
Martinez, Rafael J., 318; photograph in Board of Directors album
Mason, R. L., 299, 300
Massey, Chester D., 111
Mathers, A. S., 192
Maxwell, James, 20
McAlpine, Malcolm H.D., photograph in Board of Directors album
McCain, H. Harrison, photograph in Board of Directors album
McCracken, G. E., 175
McDonald, W. H., 202
McDonald, W. Scott: Nicks's team, 205; built up U.S. business, 261; takes over International, 263, 267, 280; Liability Committee, 292; Bank's achievement in seventies, 307; world travels, 308; Vice-Chairman, 332; photograph in Board of Directors album
McDougall, Ian, photograph in Board of Directors album
McFarlane, D. R., 283
McGinn, Hugh, 249, 310
McGregor, I. M., 176
McGregor, William S., photograph in Board of Directors album
McInnes, Donald, 222
McInnes, Hector, 80, 138
McKie, A. B., 241, 248
McKinnon, Neil, 202
McKinnon, W. C., 205
McLeod, E. C., 217
McLeod, H. C.: agent in P.E.I., 58; manager in Winnipeg, 66; sent to Minneapolis, 67-8; moved to Chicago, 70; General Manager, 76, 79; General Office moved to Toronto, 81-2; attitude toward employees, 84; unit system of work, 84; withdraws from Canadian Bankers' Association, 84-6; tour of the West, 88-9; Acadia Club, 93-4; limit on Bank's note issue, 94-6; bank inspection, 96-7, 98-9; contribution of, 100, 336-8
McLeod, J. A.: opening in Nfld., 72; background, 76, 130, 134, 184; anecdotes about Richardson and, 131; General Manager, 137-9; dangers of speculation, 138-9; severity of the depression, 140;

establishment of central bank, 157-9; President, 160; contribution of, 172, 339; post-war inflation, 179; controls, 182-3; post-war employment, 183; disappointment in Cuba, 210
McLeod, Norman, 222
McPhedran, A.: wartime service, 176; regional supervisor, 220; deposit campaigns, 228; profit planning, 236; Assistant General Manager, 259; Bermuda National Bank, 318
mechanization of Bank's procedures, 145, 191, 210. *Also see* automation and productivity
Meek, W. C., 210, 238
Meinig, W. P., 271, 273-4, 295
Menzies, W. C., 47, 48, 335
Merchants Bank of Halifax, 40
Merchants Exchange Coffee House, 10-11, 18, 27
Mercure, Gilles, 230
Merrick, D. A. Y., 176, 206, 228, 236
Metropolitan Bank, 111-18, 338
Miami, 310
Milne, W. H., 176, 301
Minneapolis, 67-9
Minneapolis Tribune, 67
Mitchell, Alice, 209
Mitchell, David E., photograph in Board of Directors album
Mitchell, J. K., 284
mobile homes lending program, 288
Monetary Times, 60, 62, 66, 82, 96
Monnot, Sally, 208
Monthly Review, 149-51, 165-7, 201, 332
Montreal, 70-1, 223
Moore, S. J.: Metropolitan Bank, 111-14; Director, 118; President, 138; dangers of speculation, 138; Chairman of the Board, 160
Morgan, Dr. Lucy, 201, 276
Mortgage Insurance Company of Canada, 232, 233
mortgage loans, 202, 231, 233, 243, 269
Moseley-Williams, W. R., 176
Mountain, Sir Denis, Bt., photograph in Board of Directors album
Mowatt, E. A., 176, 213
Mullan, Helen, 209
Mundell, Henry, 39
Munn, Rita, 209
Murcell, H. A., 259
Murdoch, J. Y., 222, 223
Murdoch, William, 19, 26
Murison, Alexander, 10, 18, 19
Murray, L. D., 96, 104

National Housing Act, 202
nationalization of banks: advocates of, 180-1; in Cuba, 210-13
Netherlands, 246
Netherlands Antilles, 264, 316, 318
New Brunswick, 37, 60
New York, 19, 29, 218
New Yorker, The, 195
Newfoundland, 72
Nicks, F. W.: background, 149, 203-5; bank hockey, 163; Personal Security Program, 203; General Manager, 205-6; consumer credit, 207; trading in gold, 217; international banking, 218, 246, 255; President, 218, 220; on inflation, 225, 268; Chairman of the Board, 234; major reorganization, 235; manpower planning, 240; foreign business contacts, 246, 255; Eurodollar market, 253; Greek shipping magnates, 257; world travels, 257, 311; credit applications in International, 261; contribution of, 264-5, 339-40; death, 268; Bank's interest in Quebec, 275; Toronto branch, 301
non-chequing savings accounts, 290
Northern Crown, 121
Nova Scotia: government of, 4-5; branches of Bank in, 37-8, 60, 90
Nova Scotia Royal Gazette, 24

O'Brien, Dolly, 302
O'Donnell, J. F., 298
Oliver, Robert E., 203
OPEC, 306
Operations, 282, 293-4
Osborne, J. A. C., 160
outside reserves, reduction of, 154-6

Pacific Regional Office, 307-8, 314
Parizeau, Jacques, 230
Parker, Helen A., photograph in Board of Directors album
Parkinson, J. F., 151
patriot doubloons, 24
Patterson, H. F.: background, 76, 130, 134; General Manager, 160; bank hockey, 161; heavy government borrowing, 169; contribution of, 172, 339
Paul, Alexander, 20
Payzant, John Y., 80, 82, 96, 127
Peel, R. E., 221, 257, 259, 261, 308
Penney, Guy, 198, 206
Penney, W. P., 294
pensions, for employees, 53, 241
People's Bank of Halifax, 40
Perez, Gloria, 209
Personal Banking Department, 293
personal savings deposits, 226-8
Personal Security Program, 203, 257
personnel management, 237-40, 302-3
Phillips, J. C., photograph in Board of Directors album
Pictou Bank, 66
Pierce, Robert L., photograph in Board of Directors album
Pitblado, John, 85
Plumptre, A. F. W., 158
Porter, Dana, 230
Portland, Oregon, 311
posting operation, delay in, 210
Pretty, Doris, 302
price controls, during World War II, 182-3
Primrose, James, 38-9
Prince Edward Island, 58, 60
Proctor, John S., 234
Professional Business Loans Program, 287
profit planning, 235-7
provincial treasury notes, 5, 28
Puerto Rico, 104, 216, 264, 317-18

Quebec: branches in 1950, 190; Bank's bilingual capacity in, 275, 328-9

Randall, Harry: on Nicks, 204-5; loans in Dominican Republic, 215; trading in gold, 217, 244; Deputy General Manager, 235; representative in Latin America, 243; International, 259, 261
Rasminsky, Louis, 230
Ratz, Betty, 149
Rea, Harold, 222
Real Estate Department, 327
regional offices: functions of, 198, 234-5; profit planning, 235-7; job evaluation of second man in, 238; decentralization, 241-2; London, 255, 312-13; credit functions, 271-2; quality control of loans, 275; growth of, 298; Manila, 307, 308, 314; organization of International, 322
Reid, Morgan, 151
resort and hotel financing, 243
Reuber, Grant, 230
Rhodes, T. A. T., 176
Richardson, H. A.: background, 76, 103; limit on note issue, 96; General Manager, 100; Bank of New Brunswick, 106-10; Metropolitan Bank, 111, 115-18; staff relations after World War I, 120; Bank of Ottawa, 121, 124-8; reflects on past, 130-1; anecdotes about J. A. McLeod and, 131; strain of continuous travel, 133; contribution of, 338
Ritchie, Cedric E.: Chief Accountant, 205, 221; profit planning, 241; international operations, 259; heads International, 260-1; Joint General Manager, 265; Chief General Manager, 267; General Office Methods Group, 271; Bank's position in Quebec, 275; President, 278; on inflation, 286, 289; Liability Committee, 292; decentralization, 299; Spencer Hall, 303; OPEC policies, 306; interest in Pacific area, 307; Bank's achievement in seventies, 307; method of doing business, 308, 324; travelling habits, 311; trip to China and Japan, 313; on revised Bank Act, 330, 331; Chairman, 332; contribution of, 340; photograph in Board of Directors album
Robertson, Sir Denis, 230
Robinson, W. L., 176
Rogers, F. L., 276, 332
Rogers, William A., 114
Rogerson, J. G., 148
Ross, F. W., 88-9, 90, 163-4
Ross, The Honourable William Donald, 114, 115-18, 333
Rowe, A. G., 176
Rowe, K. S., 317
Royal Commission on Banking and Currency, 154, 158-9
Royal Commission on Banking and Finance, 229-31
Royal Commission on Dominion-Provincial Relations, 168
Rust, Thomas G., photograph in Board of Directors album

Saint John, N.B., 37
St. John's, Nfld., 72
St. Lucia, 242, 263, 317
St. Maarten, 318
St. Thomas, 318
St. Vincent 316, 317
Samuel Montagu and Company, 217, 323
Samuelson, Paul, 230
San Juan, 104
Saskatchewan: description of branch during the depression, 164; regional office, 198
Scotia Business Plan, 297
Scotia Club, 287
Scotia Covenants, 287
Scotia Factors Limited, 287
"Scotia 59ers," 290
Scotia Plan, 200, 202, 207-8, 232, 268-9
Scotia-Toronto Dominion Leasing, 287
Scotiabank de Puerto Rico, 317
Scotiafund Financial Services, 287
Scotiafund Retirement Savings Plan, 283
Scotland, 245, 255
Security Bank and Trust Company of the Philippines, 308
Seeton, R. B., 80
shareholders: obligations of, 13-14; double liability of, 16; first meeting to select Board of Directors, 18; dividend paid to, 28, 154; Forman defalcation, 47; audit compulsory for all banks, 97; "Bank Inspection" pamphlet, 98; Bank of New Brunswick, 110; Metropolitan Bank, 118; Bank of Ottawa, 124; changes introduced in post-war Bank Act, 181; during 1945-60, 221-2; record returns to, 253; ratio of equity to deposits, 325
Sharp, Mitchell, 231
Shaw, L. A.: General Office Methods Group, 271; study of organization, 293; review commercial credit organization, 295-6; decentralization, 299; Spencer Hall, 303; death, 332
Sherman, Frank H., 333; photograph in Board of Directors album
Singapore, 307
six-year savings certificates, 226
Slocombe, G., 176
Smith, Reid J., 206, 223
Smith, Sidney T., 138
Social Credit Party, 165
Soviet Union, 246
Special Loans Department, 313
specie: use of, 5; held by Bank, 24; hoarding of, 27; redemption of notes, 35
speculation, dangers of, in twenties, 138
Speicher, Neil, 209, 228, 238
Spencer Hall, 303-4
Staff Department, 240-1
Starr, F. P., 106-9
Stavert, Sir William E., 72, 106
Stewart, Alexander, 8, 12, 14, 31
Stewart, William A., photograph in Board of Directors album
subscription list, 10-12, 14
Systems Department, 273-4, 282-3

Tanner, C. E., 210
Tapley, Blanche, 209
Taylor, A. E., 299, 302
Taylor, E. H., 62, 64
Taylor, R. G., 307, 315, 322
Taylor, R. M.: disappointment in Cuba, 212; profit planning, 236, 240; job eval-

uation, 238; study of organization, 292
term notes, 209, 226, 293
Thurston, L. A., 332
Time, 195
Tokyo, 246
Toronto: General Office moved to, 79-83; Metropolitan Bank, 111, 115-18; building project postponed, 140; new General Office building, 191-5; gold market centre, 217
Touchie, Gordon J.: Assistant General Manager, 221; Deputy General Manager, 235; job evaluation, 238; General Manager, 249-50; Chief General Manager, 265; retires, 267; lending services, 269; Toronto branch, 301
Towers, Graham, 160
training, staff, 199-200, 239-40, 302-3
Trinidad and Tobago, 215, 263, 320
trust companies, Bank's relationship with, 232

Uniacke, Andrew M., 45, 47
Uniacke, James Boyle, 8, 14, 19, 26
Union Bank of Halifax, 40
Union Bank of Prince Edward Island, 58
unit system of work, 84
United States: financial upheavals in banking, 29; banking during the depression, 153; building base in, 246-8; Eurodollars, 253-4; growth of wholesale banking business in, 258; importance of market to Canadian banks, 309; broadening activities in, 309-11
U.S. Virgin Islands, 242, 264, 318

veterans, 175-9. *Also see* world wars
Victory Bonds, 119, 174
VISA, 281

Wainwright, Gilbert, 214
Walker, H. A., 176
Walsh, J. O., 220
War Savings Certificates, 174
Warden, R. H., 111
Washburn, Hugh, 302
Waters, Daniel, 68, 72, 100
Waters, W. Keith, 149, 209
Webster, C. G., 199, 218, 221, 259
Western Hemisphere International Regional Office, 310, 322
Wheat Pool, collapse of, 152
Whipple, A. W., 37
Whitaker, D. W., 302
White, Sir Thomas, 119, 125, 126, 158
Willmot, D. G., 222, 333; photograph in Board of Directors album
Wilson, Marie, photograph in Board of Directors album
Winnipeg Agreement, 290
Winnipeg branch, 62-6, 79; charges against manager, 85-6
Witt, Beatrice, 209
Wolfe, Ray D., photograph in Board of Directors album
women: employees during World War I, 119-20; employees during World War II, 174; status as "emergency" employees, 179; employees from 1945 to 1960, 221; branch managers, 241; progress of, 302
world wars, 119, 173-80, 182-3
Wong, H. R., 261
Woolsey, L. R., 293
Worters, Joe, 163

Young, John, debate about the bill, 13, 14
Young, John, fitting in veterans, 179
Young, John H., 230
Young, T., 176
Younker, H. R., 146, 265, 275, 294, 332
Younker, Ivan, 302